## In Praise of *High-Performance Embedded Computing: Architectures, Applications, and Methodologies*

*High-Performance Embedded Computing* is a timely addition to the literature of system design. The number of designs, as well as the number of installed embedded systems, vastly surpasses those of general purpose computing, yet there are very few books on embedded design. This book introduces a comprehensive set of topics ranging from design methodologies to metrics to optimization techniques for the critical embedded system resources of space, time, and energy. There is substantial coverage of the increasingly important design issues associated with multiprocessor systems. Wayne Wolf is a leading expert in embedded design. He has personally conducted research on many of the topics presented in the book, as well as practiced the design methodologies on the numerous embedded systems he has built. This book contains information valuable to the embedded system veteran as well as the novice designer.

**—Daniel P. Siewiorek, Carnegie Mellon University**

*High-Performance Embedded Computing* addresses high-end embedded computers—certainly an area where a skilled balance between hardware and software competencies is particularly important for practitioners, and arguably a research domain which will be at the heart of the most interesting methodological evolutions in the coming years. Focusing on best industrial practices and real-world examples and applications, Wayne Wolf presents in an organized and integrated way an impressive amount of leading-edge research approaches, many of which will most likely become key differentiators for winning designs in the coming decade. This is a timely book ideally suited both for practitioners and students in advanced embedded computer engineering courses, as well as researchers and scientists who want to get a snapshot of the important research taking place at the confluence of computer architecture and electronic design automation.

**—Paolo Ienne, Ecole Polytechnique Fédérale de Lausanne (EPFL), Lausanne, Switzerland**

As processors continue to leap off our desks and embed themselves into our appliances, our cars, our phones, and perhaps soon our clothing and our wallets, it's become clear that embedded computing is no longer a slow, boring sideshow in the architecture circus. It's moved to the center ring. Wayne Wolf's book pulls all the diverse hardware and software threads together into one solid text for the aspiring embedded systems builder.

**—Rob A. Rutenbar, Carnegie Mellon University**

Educators in all areas of computer systems and engineering should take a look at this book. Its contrasting perspective on performance, architecture, and design offer an enhanced comprehension of underlying concepts to students at all levels. In my opinion, it represents the shape of things to come for anyone seeking a career in "systems."

**—Steven Johnson, Indiana University**

More and more embedded devices are available, as people now walk around with cell phones, PDAs, and MP3 players at their side. The design and constraints of these devices are much different than those of a generic computing system, such as a laptop or desktop PC. *High-Performance Embedded Computing* provides an abundance of information on these basic design topics while also covering newer areas of research, such as sensor networks and multiprocessors.

**—Mitchell D. Theys, University of Illinois at Chicago**

*High-Performance Embedded Computing* not only presents the state of the art in embedded computing augmented with a discussion of relevant example systems, it also features topics such as software/hardware co-design and multiprocessor architectures for embedded computing. This outstanding book is valuable reading for researchers, practitioners, and students.

**—Andreas Polze, Hasso-Plattner-Institute, Universität Potsdam**

Embedded computer systems are everywhere. This state-of-the-art book brings together industry practices and the latest research in this arena. It provides an in-depth and comprehensive treatment of the fundamentals, advanced topics, contemporary issues, and real-world challenges in the design of high-performance embedded systems. *High-Performance Embedded Computing* will be extremely valuable to graduate students, researchers, and practicing professionals.

**—Jie Hu, New Jersey Institute of Technology**

# High-Performance Embedded Computing

# About the Author

Wayne Wolf is a professor of electrical engineering and associated faculty in computer science at Princeton University. Before joining Princeton, he was with AT&T Bell Laboratories in Murray Hill, New Jersey. He received his B.S., M.S., and Ph.D. in electrical engineering from Stanford University. He is well known for his research in the areas of hardware/software co-design, embedded computing, VLSI, and multimedia computing systems. He is a fellow of the IEEE and ACM and a member of the SPIE. He won the ASEE Frederick E. Terman Award in 2003. He was program chair of the First International Workshop on Hardware/Software Co-Design. Wayne was also program chair of the 1996 IEEE International Conference on Computer Design, the 2002 IEEE International Conference on Compilers, Architecture, and Synthesis for Embedded Systems, and the 2005 ACM EMSOFT Conference. He was on the first executive committee of the ACM Special Interest Group on Embedded Computing (SIGBED). He is the founding editor-in-chief of *ACM Transactions on Embedded Computing Systems*. He was editor-in-chief of *IEEE Transactions on VLSI Systems* (1999–2000) and was founding co-editor of the Kluwer journal *Design Automation for Embedded Systems*. He is also series editor of the Morgan Kaufmann Series in Systems on Silicon.

# High-Performance Embedded Computing

## Architectures, Applications, and Methodologies

Wayne Wolf
*Princeton University*

ELSEVIER

AMSTERDAM • BOSTON • HEIDELBERG • LONDON
NEW YORK • OXFORD • PARIS • SAN DIEGO
SAN FRANCISCO • SINGAPORE • SYDNEY • TOKYO
MORGAN KAUFMANN PUBLISHERS IS AN IMPRINT OF ELSEVIER

MORGAN KAUFMANN PUBLISHERS

| | |
|---|---|
| *Publisher* | Denise E. M. Penrose |
| *Publishing Services Mgr.* | George Morrison |
| *Developmental Editor* | Nate McFadden |
| *Editorial Assistant* | Kimberlee Honjo |
| *Cover Design* | Dick Hanus |
| *Cover Image* | Corbus Design |
| *Text Design* | Rebecca Evans & Associates |
| *Composition* | Multiscience Press, Inc. |
| *Technical Illustration* | diacriTech |
| *Proofreader* | Jodie Allen |
| *Indexer* | Steve Rath |
| *Printer* | Maple-Vail Book Manufacturing Group |

Morgan Kaufmann Publishers is an imprint of Elsevier.
500 Sansome Street, Suite 400, San Francisco, CA 94111

 This book is printed on acid-free paper.

**Library of Congress Cataloging-in-Publication Data**

Application submitted.

ISBN 13: 978-0-12-369485-0
ISBN 10: 0-12-369485-X

For information on all Morgan Kaufmann publications,
visit our Web site at *www.mkp.com* or *www.books.elsevier.com*

Printed in the United States of America
06  07  08  09  10      5  4  3  2  1

*To Nancy and Alec*

## Supplemental Materials

Resources for this book are available at *textbooks.elsevier.com/012369485X*. The instructor site, which is accessible to adopters who register at *textbooks.elsevier.com*, includes:

- Instructor slides (in .ppt format)
- Figures from the text (in .jpg and .ppt formats)
- Solutions to exercises (in .pdf format)

The companion site (accessible to all readers) features:

- Links to related resources on the Web
- A list of errata

Various additonal materials are also available at http://www.princeton.edu/~wolf/hiperf-book.

# Contents

# Preface

This book's goal is to provide a frame of reference for the burgeoning field of high-performance embedded computing. Computers have moved well beyond the early days of 8-bit microcontrollers. Today, embedded computers are organized into multiprocessors that can run millions of lines of code. They do so in real time and at very low power levels. To properly design such systems, a large and growing body of research has developed to answer questions about the characteristics of embedded hardware and software. These are real systems—aircraft, cell phones, and digital television—that all rely on high-performance embedded systems. We understand quite a bit about how to design such systems, but we also have a great deal more to learn.

Real-time control was actually one of the first uses of computers—Chapter 1 mentions the MIT Whirlwind computer, which was developed during the 1950s for weapons control. But the microprocessor moved embedded computing to the front burner as an application area for computers. Although sophisticated embedded systems were in use by 1980, embedded computing as an academic field did not emerge until the 1990s. Even today, many traditional computer science and engineering disciplines study embedded computing topics without being fully aware of related work being done in other disciplines.

Embedded computers are very widely used, with billions sold every year. A huge number of practitioners design embedded systems, and at least a half million programmers work on designs for embedded software. Although embedded systems vary widely in their details, there are common principles that apply to the field of embedded computing. Some principles were discovered decades ago while others are just being developed today. The development of embedded computing as a research field has helped to move embedded system design from a craft to a discipline, a move that is entirely appropriate given the important, sometimes safety-critical, tasks entrusted to embedded computers.

One reasonable question to ask about this field is how it differs from traditional computer systems topics, such as client-server systems or scientific computing. Are we just applying the same principles to smaller systems, or do we need to do something new? I believe that embedded computing, though it makes use of many techniques from computer science and engineering, poses some unique challenges.

First, most if not all embedded systems must perform tasks in real time. This requires a major shift in thinking for both software and hardware designers. Second, embedded computing puts a great deal of emphasis on power and energy consumption. While power is important in all aspects of computer systems, embedded applications tend to be closer to the edge of the energy-operation envelope than many general-purpose systems. All this leads to embedded systems being more heavily engineered to meet a particular set of requirements than those systems that are designed for general use.

This book assumes that you, the reader, are familiar with the basics of embedded hardware and software, such as might be found in *Computers as Components*. This book builds on those foundations to study a range of advanced topics. In selecting topics to cover, I tried to identify topics and results that are unique to embedded computing. I did include some background material from other disciplines to help set the stage for a discussion of embedded systems problems.

Here is a brief tour through the book:

- Chapter 1 provides some important background for the rest of the chapters. It tries to define the set of topics that are at the center of embedded computing. It looks at methodologies and design goals. We survey models of computation, which serve as a frame of reference for the characteristics of applications. The chapter also surveys several important applications that rely on embedded computing to provide background for some terminology that is used throughout the book.

- Chapter 2 looks at several different styles of processors that are used in embedded systems. We consider techniques for tuning the performance of a processor, such as voltage scaling, and the role of the processor memory hierarchy in embedded CPUs. We look at techniques used to optimize embedded CPUs, such as code compression and bus encoding, and techniques for simulating processors.

- Chapter 3 studies programs. The back end of the compilation process, which helps determine the quality of the code, is the first topic. We spend a great deal of time on memory system optimizations, since memory behavior is a prime determinant of both performance and energy consumption. We consider performance analysis, including both simulation and worst-case execution time analysis. We also discuss how models of computing are reflected in programming models and languages.

■ Chapter 4 moves up to multiple-process systems. We study and compare scheduling algorithms, including the interaction between language design and scheduling mechanisms. We evaluate operating system architectures and the overhead incurred by the operating system. We also consider methods for verifying the behavior of multiple process systems.

■ Chapter 5 concentrates on multiprocessor architectures. We consider both tightly coupled multiprocessors and the physically distributed systems used in vehicles. We describe architectures and their components: processors, memory, and networks. We also look at methodologies for multiprocessor design.

■ Chapter 6 looks at software for multiprocessors and considers scheduling algorithms for them. We also study middleware architectures for dynamic resource allocation in multiprocessors.

■ Chapter 7 concentrates on hardware and software co-design. We study different models that have been used to characterize embedded applications and target architectures. We cover a wide range of algorithms for co-synthesis and compare the models and assumptions used by these algorithms.

Hopefully this book covers at least most of the topics of interest to a practitioner and student of advanced embedded computing systems. There were some topics for which I could find surprisingly little work in the literature: software testing for embedded systems is a prime example. I tried to find representative articles about the major approaches to each problem. I am sure that I have failed in many cases to adequately represent a particular problem, for which I apologize.

This book is about embedded computing; it touches on, but does not exhaustively cover, several related fields:

■ Applications—Embedded systems are designed to support applications such as multimedia, communications, and so on. Chapter 1 introduces some basic concepts about a few applications, because knowing something about the application domain is important. An in-depth look at these fields is best left to others.

■ VLSI—Although systems-on-chips are an important medium for embedded systems, they are not the only medium. Automobiles, airplanes, and many other important systems are controlled by distributed embedded networks.

■ Hybrid systems—The field of hybrid systems studies the interactions between continuous and discrete systems. This is an important and interesting area, and many embedded systems can make use of hybrid system techniques, but hybrid systems deserve their own book.

- Software engineering—Software design is a rich field that provides critical foundations, but it leaves many questions specific to embedded computing unanswered.

I would like to thank a number of people who have helped me with this book: Brian Butler (Qualcomm), Robert P. Adler (Intel), Alain Darte (CNRS), Babak Falsafi (CMU), Ran Ginosar (Technion), John Glossner (Sandbridge), Graham Hellestrand (VaSTSystems), Paolo Ienne (EPFL), Masaharu Imai (Osaka University), Irwin Jacobs (Qualcomm), Axel Jantsch (KTH), Ahmed Jerraya (TIMA), Lizy Kurian John (UT Austin), Christoph Kirsch (University of Salzburg), Phil Koopman (CMU), Haris Lekatsas (NEC), Pierre Paulin (ST Microelectronics), Laura Pozzi (University of Lugano), Chris Rowen (Tensilica), Rob Rutenbar (CMU), Deepu Talla (TI), Jiang Xu (Sandbridge), and Shengqi Yang (Princeton).

I greatly appreciate the support, guidance, and encouragement given by my editor Nate McFadden, as well as the reviewers he worked with. The review process has helped identify the proper role of this book, and Nate provided a steady stream of insightful thoughts and comments. I'd also like to thank my long-standing editor at Morgan Kaufmann, Denise Penrose, who shepherded this book from the beginning.

I'd also like to express my appreciation to digital libraries, particularly those of the IEEE and ACM. I am not sure that this book would have been possible without them. If I had to find all the papers that I have studied in a bricks-and-mortar library, I would have rubbery legs from walking through the stacks, tired eyes, and thousands of paper cuts. With the help of digital libraries, I only have the tired eyes.

And for the patience of Nancy and Alec, my love.

Wayne Wolf
Princeton, New Jersey

*Chapter*

# 1

# Embedded Computing

- Fundamental problems in embedded computing
- Applications that make use of embedded computing
- Design methodologies and system modeling for embedded systems
- Models of computation
- Reliability and security
- Consumer electronics

## 1.1 The Landscape of High-Performance Embedded Computing

The overarching theme of this book is that many embedded computing systems are high-performance computing systems that must be carefully designed so that they meet stringent requirements. Not only do they require lots of computation, but they also must meet quantifiable goals: real-time performance, not just average performance; power/energy consumption; and cost. The fact that it has quantifiable goals makes the design of embedded computing systems a very different experience than the design of general-purpose computing systems for which their users are unpredictable.

When trying to design computer systems to meet various sorts of quantifiable goals, we quickly come to the conclusion that no one system is best for all applications. Different requirements lead to making different trade-offs between performance and power, hardware and software, and so on. We must create different implementations to meet the needs of a family of applications. Solutions should be programmable enough to make the design flexible and long-lived, but

1

need not provide unnecessary flexibility that would detract from meeting system requirements.

General-purpose computing systems separate the design of hardware and software, but in embedded computing systems we can simultaneously design the hardware and software. Often, a problem can be solved by hardware means, software means, or a combination of the two. Various solutions can have different trade-offs; the larger design space afforded by joint hardware/software design allows us to find better solutions to design problems.

*architectures, applications, methodologies*

As illustrated in Figure 1-1 the study of embedded system design properly takes into account three aspects of the field: **architectures**, **applications**, and **methodologies**. Compared to the design of general-purpose computers, embedded computer designers rely much more heavily on both methodologies and basic knowledge of applications. Let us consider these aspects one at a time.

*architectures*

Because embedded system designers work with both hardware and software, they must study architectures broadly speaking, including hardware, software, and the relationships between the two. Hardware architecture problems can range from special-purpose hardware units as created by hardware/software co-design, microarchitectures for processors, multiprocessors, or networks of distributed processors. Software architectures determine how we can take advantage of parallelism and nondeterminism to improve performance and lower cost.

*applications*

Understanding your application is key to getting the most out of an embedded computing system. We can use the characteristics of the application to optimize the design. This can be an advantage that enables us to perform many powerful optimizations that would not be possible in a general-purpose system. But it also means that we must have enough understanding of the application to take advantage of its characteristics and avoid creating problems for system implementers.

*methodologies*

Methodologies play an especially important role in embedded computing. Not only must we design many different types of embedded systems, but we

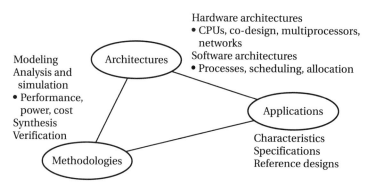

**Figure 1-1** *Aspects of embedded system design.*

also must do so reliably and predictably. The cost of the design process itself is often a significant component of the total system cost. Methodologies, which may combine tools and manual steps, codify our knowledge of how to design systems. Methodologies help us make large and small design decisions.

The designers of general-purpose computers stick to a more narrowly defined hardware design methodology that uses standard benchmarks as inputs to tracing and simulation. The changes to the processor are generally made by hand and may be the result of invention. Embedded computing system designers need more complex methodologies because their system design encompasses both hardware and software. The varying characteristics of embedded systems—system-on-chip for communications, automotive network, and so on—also push designers to tweak methodologies for their own purposes.

Steps in a methodology may be implemented as tools. Analysis and simulation tools are widely used to evaluate cost, performance, and power consumption. Synthesis tools create optimized implementations based on specifications. Tools are particularly important in embedded computer design for two reasons. First, we are designing an application-specific system, and we can use tools to help us understand the characteristics of the application. Second, we are often pressed for time when designing an embedded system, and tools help us work faster and produce more predictable tools.

*modeling*
The design of embedded computing systems increasingly relies on a hierarchy of models. Models have been used for many years in computer science to provide abstractions. Abstractions for performance, energy consumption, and functionality are important. Because embedded computing systems have complex functionality built on top of sophisticated platforms, designers must use a series of models to have some chance of successfully completing their system design. Early stages of the design process need reasonably accurate simple models; later design stages need more sophisticated and accurate models.

*embedded computing is multidisciplinary*
Embedded computing makes use of several related disciplines; the two core ones are real-time computing and hardware/software co-design. The study of real-time systems predates the emergence of embedded computing as a discipline. Real-time systems take a software-oriented view of how to design computers that complete computations in a timely fashion. The scheduling techniques developed by the real-time systems community stand at the core of the body of techniques used to design embedded systems. Hardware/software co-design emerged as a field at the dawn of the modern era of embedded computing. Co-design takes a holistic view of the hardware and software used to perform deadline-oriented computations.

*history of embedded computing*
Figure 1-2[*] shows highlights in the development of embedded computing. We can see that computers were embedded early in the history of computing:

---

* Many of the dates in this figure were found in Wikipedia; others are from *http://www.motofuture.motorola.com* and *http://www.mvista.com*.

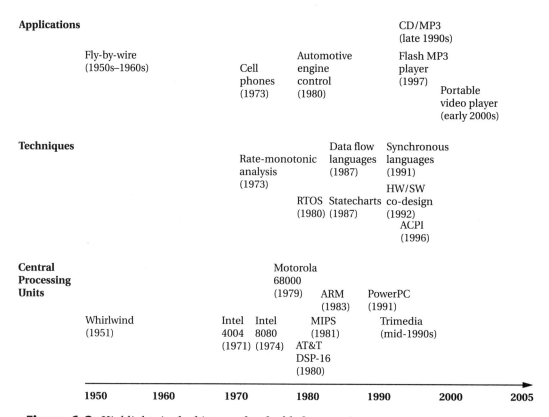

**Figure 1-2** *Highlights in the history of embedded computing.*

one of the earliest computers, the MIT Whirlwind, was designed for artillery control. As computer science and engineering solidified into a field, early research established basic techniques for real-time computing. Some techniques used today in embedded computing were developed specifically for the problems of embedded systems while others, such as those in the following list, were adapted from general-purpose computing techniques.

- Low-power design began as primarily hardware-oriented but now encompasses both software and hardware techniques.

- Programming languages and compilers have provided tools, such as Java and highly optimized code generators, for embedded system designers.

- Operating systems provide not only schedulers but also file systems and other facilities that are now commonplace in high-performance embedded systems.

■ Networks are used to create distributed real-time control systems for vehicles and many other applications, as well as to create Internet-enabled appliances.

■ Security and reliability are an increasingly important aspect of embedded system design. VLSI components are becoming less reliable at extremely fine geometries while reliability requirements become more stringent. Security threats once restricted to general-purpose systems now loom over embedded systems as well.

## 1.2  Example Applications

Some knowledge of the applications that will run on an embedded system is of great help to system designers. This section looks at several basic concepts in three common applications: communications/networking, multimedia, and vehicles.

### 1.2.1  Radio and Networking

*combined wireless/network communications*

Modern communications systems combine wireless and networking. As illustrated in Figure 1-3 radios carry digital information and are used to connect to networks. Those networks may be specialized, as in traditional cell phones, but increasingly radios are used as the physical layer in Internet protocol systems.

*networking*

The Open Systems Interconnection (OSI) model [Sta97a] of the International Standards Organization (ISO) defines the following model for network services.

1. **Physical layer**—The electrical and physical connection

2. **Data link layer**—Access and error control across a single link

3. **Network layer**—Basic end-to-end service

4. **Transport layer**—Connection-oriented services

5. **Session layer**—Control activities such as checkpointing

6. **Presentation layer**—Data exchange formats

7. **Application layer**—The interface between the application and the network

Although it may seem that embedded systems are too simple to require use of the OSI model, it is in fact quite useful. Even relatively simple embedded networks provide physical, data link, and network services. An increasing number

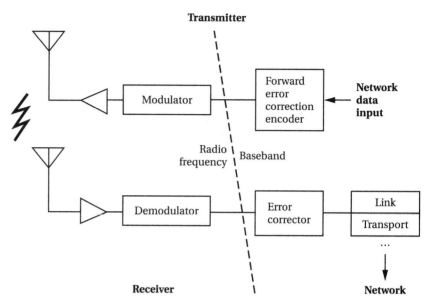

**Figure 1-3** *A radio and network connection.*

of embedded systems provide Internet service that requires implementing the full range of functions in the OSI model.

The **Internet** is one example of a network that follows the OSI model. The **Internet Protocol (IP)** [Los97; Sta97a] is the fundamental protocol of the Internet. An IP is used to **internetwork** between different types of networks—the **internetworking** standard. The IP sits at the network layer in the OSI model. It does not provide guaranteed end-to-end service; instead, it provides **best-effort routing** of packets. Higher-level protocols must be used to manage the stream of packets between source and destination.

*wireless*     Wireless data communication is widely used. On the receiver side, digital communication must perform the following tasks.

- *Demodulate* the signal down to the baseband

- *Detect* the baseband signal to identify bits

- *Correct errors* in the raw bit stream

*software radio*     Wireless data transmitters may be built from combinations of analog, hardwired digital, configurable, and programmable components. A **software radio** is, broadly speaking, a radio that can be programmed; the term **software-defined radio (SDR)** is often used to mean either a purely or partly programmable radio. Given the clock rates at which today's digital processors operate, they are used primarily for baseband operations. Several processors can run fast enough to be used for some radio-frequency processing.

*software radio tiers*

The SDR Forum, a technical group for software radio, defines the following five tiers of SDR [SDR05].

- Tier 0—A **hardware radio** cannot be programmed.

- Tier 1—A **software-controlled radio** has some functions implemented in software, but operations like modulation and filtering cannot be altered without changing hardware.

- Tier 2—A **software-defined radio** may use multiple antennas for different bands, but the radio can cover a wide range of frequencies and use multiple modulation techniques.

- Tier 3—An **ideal software-defined radio** does not use analog amplification or heterodyne mixing before A/D conversion.

- Tier 4—An **ultimate software radio** is lightweight, consumes very little power, and requires no external antenna.

*digital demodulation*

Demodulation requires multiplying the received signal by a signal from an oscillator and filtering the result to select the signal's lower-frequency version. The bit-detection process depends somewhat on the modulation scheme, but digital communication mechanisms often rely on phase. High-data rate systems often use multiple frequencies arranged in a **constellation**. The phases of the component frequencies of the signal can be modulated to create different symbols.

*error correction*

Traditional error-correction codes can be checked using combinational logic. For example, a convolutional coder can be used as an error-correction coder. The convolutional coder convolves the input with itself according to a chosen polynomial. Figure 1-4 shows a fragment of a trellis that represents possible states of a decoder; the label on an edge shows the input bit and the produced output bits. Any bits in the transmission may have been corrupted; the decoder must determine the most likely sequence of data bits that could have produced the received sequence.

Several more powerful codes that require iterative decoding have recently become popular. **Turbo codes** use multiple encoders. The input data is encoded by two convolutional encoders, each of which uses a different but generally simple code. One of the coders is fed the input data directly; the other is fed a permuted version of the input stream. Both coded versions of the data are sent across the channel. The decoder uses two decoding units, one for each code. The two decoders are operated iteratively. At each iteration, the two decoders swap likelihood estimates of the decoded bits; each decoder uses the other's likelihoods as a priori estimates for its own next iteration.

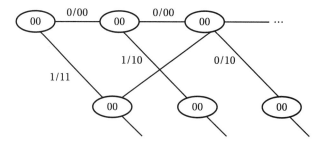

**Figure 1-4** *A trellis representation for a convolutional code.*

**Low-density parity check** (**LDPC**) codes also require multiple iterations to determine errors and corrections. An LDPC code can be defined using a bipartite graph like the one shown in Figure 1-5; the codes are called "low density" because their graphs are sparse. The nodes on the left are called **message nodes**, and the ones on the right are **check nodes**. Each check node defines a sum of message node values. The message nodes define the coordinates for codewords; a legal codeword is a set of message node values that sets all the check nodes to 1. During decoding, an LDPC decoding algorithm passes messages between the message nodes and check nodes. One approach is to pass probabilities for the data bit values as messages. Multiple iterations should cause the algorithm to settle onto a good estimate of the data bit values.

*networking*      A radio may simply act as the physical layer of a standard network stack, but many new networks are being designed that take advantage of the inherent characteristics of wireless networks. For example, traditional wired networks have only a limited number of nodes connected to a link, but radios inherently broadcast; broadcasts can be used to improve network control, error correction, and security. Wireless networks are generally ad hoc in that the members of the

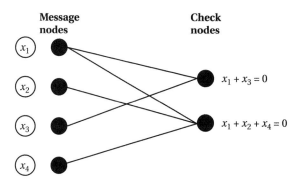

**Figure 1-5** *A bipartite graph that defines an LDPC code.*

network are not predetermined, and nodes may enter or leave during network operation. **Ad hoc networks** require somewhat different network control than is used in fixed, wired networks.

Example 1-1 looks at a cell phone communication standard.

## Example 1-1

*cdma2000*

cdma2000 [Van04] is a widely used standard for spread spectrum-based cellular telephony. It uses direct sequence spread spectrum transmission. The data appears as noise unless the receiver knows the pseudorandom sequence. Several radios can use the same frequency band without interference because the pseudorandom codes allow their signals to be separated. A simplified diagram of the system follows.

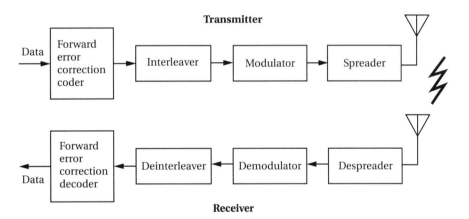

The spreader modulates the data with the pseudorandom code. The interleaver transposes coded data blocks to make the code more resistant to burst errors. The transmitter's power is controlled so that all signals have the same strength at the receiver.

The physical layer protocol defines a set of channels that can carry data or control. A **forward channel** goes from a base station to a mobile station, while a **reverse channel** goes from a mobile station to a base station. Pilot channels are used to acquire the CDMA signal, provide phase information, and enable the mobile station to estimate the channel's characteristics. A number of different types of channels are defined for data, control, power control, and so on.

The link layer defines **medium access control** (**MAC**) and **signaling link access control** (**LAC**). The MAC layer multiplexes logical channels onto the physical medium, provides reliable transport of user traffic, and manages quality-of-service. The LAC layer provides a variety of services: authentication, integrity, segmentation, reassembly, and so on.

Example 1-2 describes a major effort to develop software radios for data communication.

## Example 1-2

*Joint Tactical Radio System*

The Joint Tactical Radio System (JTRS) [Joi05; Ree02] is an initiative of the U.S. Department of Defense to develop next-generation communication systems based on radios that perform many functions in software. JTRS radios are designed to provide secure communication. They are also designed to be compatible with a wide range of existing radios as well as to be upgradeable through software.

The reference model for the hardware architecture has two major components. The front-end subsystem performs low-level radio operations while the back-end subsystem performs higher-level network functions. The information security enforcement module that connects the front and back ends helps protect the radio and the network from each other.

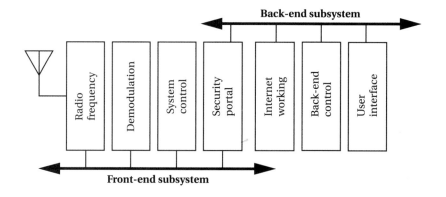

### 1.2.2  Multimedia

Today's dominant multimedia applications are based on compression: digital television and radio broadcast, portable music, and digital cameras all rely on compression algorithms. This section reviews some of the algorithms developed for multimedia compression.

*lossy compression and perceptual coding*

It is important to remember that multimedia compression methods are lossy—the decompressed signal is different from the original signal before compression. Compression algorithms make use of **perceptual coding** techniques that try to throw away data that is less perceptible to the human eye and ear. These algorithms also combine lossless compression with perceptual coding to efficiently code the signal.

*JPEG-style image compression*

The **JPEG** standard [ITU92] is widely used for image compression. The two major techniques used by JPEG are the **discrete cosine transform** (**DCT**) plus quantization, which performs perceptual coding, plus **Huffman coding** as a form of entropy coding for lossless encoding. Figure 1-6 shows a simplified view of DCT-based image compression: blocks in the image are transformed using the DCT; the transformed data is quantized and the result is entropy coded.

The DCT is a frequency transform whose coefficients describe the spatial frequency content of an image. Because it is designed to transform images, the DCT operates on a two-dimensional set of pixels, in contrast to the Fourier transform, which operates on a one-dimensional signal. However, the advantage of the DCT over other two-dimensional transforms is that it can be decomposed into two one-dimensional transforms, making it much easier to compute. The form of the DCT of a set of values $u(i)$ is

$$(v)(k) = \sqrt{\frac{2}{N}} C(k) \sum_{1 \le t \le N} u(t) \cos\left[\pi(2t+1)\frac{k}{2N}\right],$$    (EQ 1-1)

where

$$C(k) = 2^{-1/2} \text{ for } k = 0, 1 \text{ otherwise.}$$    (EQ 1-2)

Many efficient algorithms have been developed to compute the DCT.

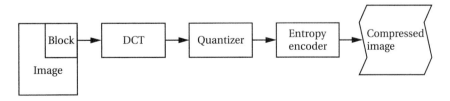

**Figure 1-6** *Simplified view of a DCT-based image-compression system.*

JPEG performs the DCT on $8 \times 8$ **blocks** of pixels. The discrete cosine transform itself does not compress the image. The DCT coefficients are quantized to add loss and change the signal in such a way that lossless compression can more efficiently compress them. Low-order coefficients of the DCT correspond to large features in the $8 \times 8$ block, and high-order coefficients correspond to fine features. Quantization concentrates on changing the higher-order coefficients to zero. This removes some fine features but provides long strings of zeros that can be efficiently encoded to lossless compression.

Huffman coding, which is sometimes called *variable-length coding*, forms the basis for the lossless compression stage. As shown in Figure 1-7, a specialized technique is used to order the quantized DCT coefficients in a way that can be easily Huffman encoded. The DCT coefficients can be arranged in an $8 \times 8$ matrix. The 0,0 entry at the top left is known as the **DC coefficient** since it describes the lowest-resolution or DC component of the image. The 7,7 entry is the highest-order AC coefficient. Quantization has changed the higher-order AC coefficients to zero. If we were to traverse the matrix in row or column order, we would intersperse nonzero lower-order coefficients with higher-order coefficients that have been zeroed. By traversing the matrix in a zigzag pattern, we move from low-order to high-order coefficients more uniformly. This creates longer strings of zeroes that can be efficiently encoded.

*JPEG 2000*

The JPEG 2000 standard is compatible with JPEG but adds wavelet compression. *Wavelets* are a hierarchical waveform representation of the image that do not rely on blocks. Wavelets can be more computationally expensive but provide higher-quality compressed images.

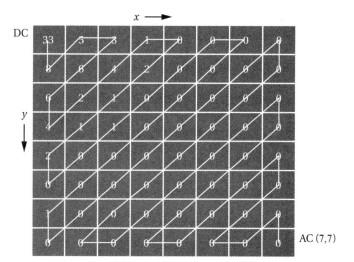

**Figure 1-7** *The zigzag pattern used to transmit DCT coefficients.*

*video*
*compression*
*standards*

There are two major families of video compression standards. The **MPEG** series of standards was developed primarily for broadcast applications. Broadcast systems are asymmetric—more powerful and more expensive transmitters allows receivers to be simpler and cheaper. The **H.26x** series is designed for symmetric applications, such as videoconferencing, in which both sides must encode and decode. The two groups have recently completed a joint standard known as **Advanced Video Codec** (**AVC**), or **H.264**, designed to cover both types of applications. An issue of the *Proceedings of the IEEE* [Wu06] is devoted to digital television.

*multiple streams*

Video encoding standards are typically defined as being composed of several streams. A useful video system must include audio data; users may want to send text or other data as well. A compressed video stream is often represented as a **system stream,** which is made up of a sequence of system packets. Each system packet may include any of the following types of data.

- Video data

- Audio data

- Nonaudiovisual data

- Synchronization information

Because several streams are combined into one system stream, synchronizing the streams for decoding can be a challenge. Audio and video data must be closely synchronized to avoid annoying the viewer/listener. Text data, such as closed captioning, may also need to be synchronized with the program.

Figure 1-8 shows the block diagram of an MPEG-1 or MPEG-2 style encoder. (The MPEG-2 standard is the basis for digital television broadcasting in the United States.) The encoder makes use of the DCT and variable-length coding. It adds **motion estimation** and **motion compensation** to encode the relationships between frames.

*motion*
*estimation*

Motion estimation allows one frame to be encoded as translational motion from another frame. Motion estimation is performed on $16 \times 16$ **macroblocks**. A macroblock from one frame is selected and a search area in the **reference frame** is searched to find an identical or closely matching macroblock. At each search point, a sum-of-absolute-differences (SAD) computation is used to measure the difference between the search macroblock $S$ and the macroblock $R$ at the selected point in the reference frame:

$$SAD = \sum_{0 \leq x \leq 15} \left[ \sum_{0 \leq y \leq 15} |S(x, y) - R(x, y)| \right] \qquad \text{(EQ 1-3)}$$

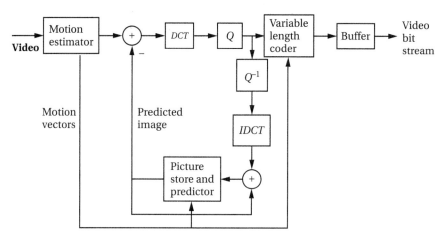

**Figure 1-8** *Structure of an MPEG-1 and MPEG-2 style video encoder.*

The search point with the smallest SAD is chosen as the point to which $S$ has moved in the reference frame. That position describes a **motion vector** for the macroblock (see Figure 1-9). During decompression, motion compensation copies the block to the position specified by the motion vector, thus saving the system from transmitting the entire image.

*error signal*     Motion estimation does not perfectly predict a frame because elements of the block may move, the search may not provide the exact match, and so on. An

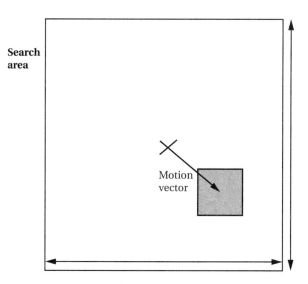

**Figure 1-9** *Motion estimation results in a motion vector.*

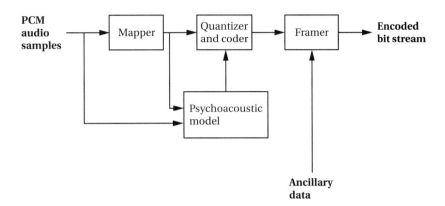

**Figure 1-10** *Structure of an MPEG-1 audio encoder.*

*error* signal is also transmitted to correct for small imperfections in the signal. The inverse DCT and picture/store predictor in the feedback are used to generate the uncompressed version of the lossily compressed signal that would be seen by the receiver; that reconstruction is used to generate the error signal.

*audio compression*
Digital audio compression also uses combinations of lossy and lossless coding. However, the auditory centers of the brain are somewhat better understood than the visual center, allowing for more sophisticated perceptual encoding approaches.

Many audio-encoding standards have been developed. The best known name in audio compression is **MP3**. This is a nickname for *MPEG-1 Audio Layer 3*, the most sophisticated of the three levels of audio compression developed for MPEG-1. However, U.S. HDTV broadcasting, although it uses the MPEG-2 system and video streams, is based on Dolby Digital. Many open-source audio codecs have been developed, with Ogg Vorbis being one popular example.

*audio encoder*
As shown in Figure 1-10, an MPEG-1 audio encoder has four major components [ISO93]. The mapper filters and subsamples the input audio samples. The quantizer codes subbands, allocating bits to the various subbands. Its parameters are adjusted by a psychoacoustic model, which looks for phenomena that will not be heard well and so can be eliminated. The framer generates the final bit stream.

## 1.2.3  Vehicle Control and Operation

Real-time vehicle control is one of the major applications of embedded computing. Machines like automobiles and airplanes require control systems that are physically distributed around the vehicle. Networks have been designed specifically to meet the needs of real-time distributed control for automotive electronics and avionics.

*safety-critical systems*

The basic fact that drives the design of control systems for vehicles is that they are safety-critical systems. Errors of any kind—component failure, design flaws, and so on—can injure or kill people. Not only must these systems be carefully verified, but they also must be architected to guarantee certain properties.

*microprocessors and automobiles*

As shown in Figure 1-11, modern automobiles use a number of electronic devices [Lee02b]. Today's low-end cars often include 40 microprocessors while high-end cars can contain 100 microprocessors. These devices are generally organized into several networks. The critical control systems, such as engine and brake control, may be on one network while noncritical functions, such as entertainment devices, may be on a separate network.

*harnesses versus networks*

Until the advent of digital electronics, cars generally used point-to-point wiring organized into **harnesses**, which are bundles of wires. Connecting devices into a shared network saves a great deal of weight—15 kilograms or more [Lee02b]. Networks require somewhat more complicated devices that include network access hardware and software, but that overhead is relatively small and is shrinking over time thanks to Moore's Law.

*specialized automotive networks*

But why not use general-purpose networks for real-time control? We can find reasons to build specialized automotive networks at several levels of

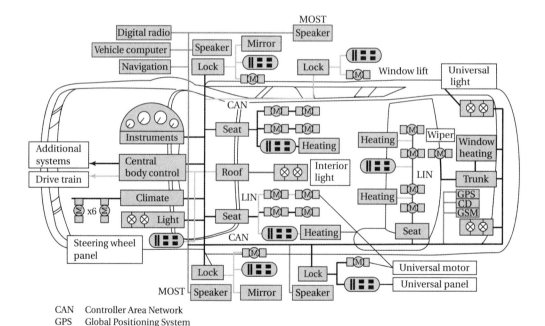

CAN   Controller Area Network
GPS   Global Positioning System
GSM   Global System for Mobile Communications
LIN   Local Interconnect Network
MOST  Media-Oriented Systems Transport

**Figure 1-11** *Electronic devices in modern automobiles. From Lee [Lee02b] © 2002 IEEE*

abstraction in the network stack. One reason is electrical—automotive networks require reliable signaling under vary harsh environments. The ignition systems of automobile engines generate huge amounts of electromagnetic interference that can render many networks useless. Automobiles must also operate under wide temperature ranges and survive large doses of moisture.

Most important, real-time control requires guaranteed behavior from the network. Many communications networks do not provide hard real-time requirements. Communications systems are also more tolerant of latency than are control systems. While data or voice communications may be useful when the network introduces transmission delays of hundreds of milliseconds or even seconds, long latencies can easily cause disastrous oscillations in real-time control systems. Automotive networks must also operate within limited power budgets that may not apply to communications networks.

*avionics*      Aviation electronics systems developed in parallel to automotive electronics are now starting to converge. Avionics must be certified for use in aircraft by governmental authorities (in the U.S., aircraft are certified by the Federal Aviation Administration—FAA), which means that devices for aircraft are often designed specifically for aviation use. The fact that aviation systems are certified has made it easier to use electronics for critical operations such as the operation of flight control surfaces (e.g., ailerons, rudders, elevators). Airplane cockpits are also highly automated. Some commercial airplanes already provide Internet access to passengers; we expect to see such services become common in cars over the next decade.

*X-by-wire*      Control systems have traditionally relied on mechanics or hydraulics to implement feedback and reaction. Microprocessors allow us to use hardware and software not just to sense and actuate but to implement the control laws. In general, the controller may not be physically close to the device being controlled: the controller may operate several different devices, or it may be physically shielded from dangerous operating areas. Electronic control of critical functions was first performed in aircraft where the technique was known as **fly-by-wire**. Control operations performed over the network are called **X-by-wire** where X may be brake, steer, and so on.

*noncontrol uses*      Powerful embedded devices—television systems, navigation systems, Internet access, and so on—are being introduced into cars. These devices do not perform real-time control, but they can eat up large amounts of bandwidth and require real-time service for streaming data. Since we can only expect the amount of data being transmitted within a car to increase, automotive networks must be designed to be future-proof and handle workloads that are even more challenging than what we see today.

In general, we can divide the uses of a network in a vehicle into several categories along the following axes.

■  **Operator versus passenger**—This is the most basic distinction in vehicle networks. The passenger may want to use the network for a variety of purposes: entertainment, information, and so on. But the passenger's network must never interfere with the basic control functions required to drive or fly the vehicle.

■ **Control versus instrumentation**—The operation of the vehicle relies on a wide range of devices. The basic control functions—steering, brakes, throttle, and so on in a car or the control surfaces and throttle in an airplane—must operate with very low latencies and be completely reliable. Other functions used by the operator may be less important. At least some of the instrumentation in an airplane is extremely important for monitoring in-flight meteorological conditions, but pilots generally identify a minimal set of instruments required to control the airplane. Cars are usually driven with relatively little attention paid to the instruments. While instrumentation is very important, we may separate it from fundamental controls in order to protect the operation of the control systems.

### 1.2.4  Sensor Networks

Sensor networks are distributed systems designed to capture and process data. They typically use radio links to transmit data between themselves and to servers. Sensor networks can be used to monitor buildings, equipment, and people.

*ad hoc computing*

A key aspect of the design of sensor networks is the use of ad hoc networks. Sensor networks can be deployed in a variety of configurations and nodes can be added or removed at any time. As a result, both the network and the applications running on the sensor nodes must be designed to dynamically determine their configuration and take the necessary steps to operate under that network configuration.

For example, when data is transmitted to a server, the nodes do not know in advance the path that data should take to arrive at the server. The nodes must provide **multihop routing** services to transmit data from node to node in order to arrive at the network. This problem is challenging because not all nodes are within radio range, and it may take network effort and computation to determine the topology of the network.

Examples 1-3 and 1-4 describe a sensor network node and its operating system, and Example 1-5 describes an application of sensor networks.

---

### Example 1-3

*The Intel mote² Sensor Node*

The Intel mote², which uses a 802.15.4 radio (the ChipCon 2420 radio) as its communication link, is a third-generation sensor network node.

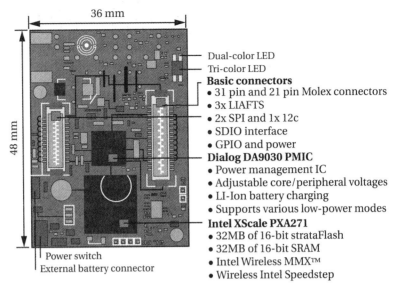

Source: Courtesy Intel.

An antenna is built into the board. Each side of the board has a pair of connectors for sensor devices, one side for basic devices and another for advanced devices. Several boards can be stacked using these connectors to build a complete system.

The on-board processor is an Intel XScale. The processor can be operated at low voltages and frequencies (0.85V and 15 MHz, respectively) and can be run up to 416 MHz at the highest operating voltage. The board includes 265 MBytes of SRAM organized into four banks.

## Example 1-4

*TinyOS and nesC*

TinyOS (*http://www.tinyos.net*) is an operating system for sensor networks. It is designed to support networks and devices on a small platform using only about 200 bytes of memory.

TinyOS code is written in a new language known as nesC. This language supports the TinyOS concurrency model based on tasks and hardware event handlers. The nesC compiler detects data races at compile time. An nesC program includes one set of functions known as **events**. The program may also include functions called **commands** to help implement the program, but another component uses the events to call the program. A set of components can be assembled into a system using interface connections known as **wiring**.

TinyOS executes only one program using two threads: one containing tasks and another containing **hardware event handlers**. The tasks are scheduled by TinyOS; tasks are run to completion and do not preempt each other. Hardware event handlers are initiated by hardware interrupts. They may preempt tasks or other handlers and run to completion.

The sensor node radio is one of the devices in the system. TinyOS provides code for packet-based communication, including multihop communication.

## Example 1-5

*ZebraNet*

ZebraNet [Jua02] is designed to record the movements of zebras in the wild. Each zebra wears a collar that includes a GPS positioning system, a network radio, a processor, and a solar cell for power. The processors periodically read the GPS position and store it in on-board memory. The collar reads positions every three minutes, along with information indicating whether the zebra is in sun or shade. For three minutes every hour, the collar takes detailed readings to determine the zebra's speed. This generates about 6 kilo (k) of data per zebra per day.

Experiments show that computation is much less expensive than radio transmissions:

| Operation | Current @ 3.6V |
| --- | --- |
| Idle | <1 mA |
| GPS position sampling and CPU/storage | 177 mA |
| Base discovery only | 432 mA |
| Transmit data to base | 1622 mA |

Thus conservation of radio energy is critical. The data from the zebras is read only intermittently when biologists travel to the field. They do not want to leave behind a permanent base station, which would be difficult to maintain. Instead, they bring with them a node that reads data from the network.

Because the zebras move over a wide area, not all of them are within range of the base station, and it is impossible to predict which (if any) of the zebras will be. As a result, the ZebraNet nodes must replicate data across the network. The nodes transmit copies of their position data to each other as zebras come within range of each other. When a zebra comes within range of a base station, the base station reads all of that zebra's data, including data it has gathered from other zebras.

The ZebraNet group experimented with two data-transfer protocols. One protocol—flooding—sent all data to every other available node. The other, history-based protocol chose one peer to send data to based on which peer had the best past history of delivering data to the base. Simulations showed that flooding delivered the most data for short-range radios, but the history-based protocol delivered the most data for long-range radio. However, flooding consumed much more energy than history-based routing.

---

## 1.3 Design Goals

Given an application area for which we want to design an embedded system, we must determine specific goals for the project and estimate their feasibility. The application determines the basic **functional requirements**. We must also determine the **nonfunctional requirements**, some of which are derived directly from the application and some from other factors, such as marketing. An embedded system design project may have many goals. Some of these are measurable, and others are less so.

*varieties of performance*

Several key metrics of a digital system design can be accurately measured and predicted. The first is **performance**, by which we mean some aspect of speed. (Every field seems to use performance as the name for its preferred metric—image quality, packet loss, and so on.) Performance, however, can be measured in many different ways, including:

- Average performance versus worst-case or best-case
- Throughput versus latency
- Peak versus sustained

*energy/power*

**Energy** and/or **power consumption** are critical metrics for many embedded systems. Energy consumption is particularly important for battery life. Power consumption affects heat generation.

*cost*

The monetary cost of a system is clearly of interest to many people. Cost can be measured in several ways. **Manufacturing cost** is determined by the cost of components and the manufacturing processes used. **Design cost** is determined both by labor and by the equipment used to support the designers. (The server farm and CAD tools required to design a large chip cost several million dollars.) **Lifetime cost** takes into account software and hardware maintenance and upgrades.

*design time*

The time required to design a system may be important. If the design program takes too long to finish, the product may miss its intended market. Calculators, for example, must be ready for the back-to-school market each fall.

*reliability*

Different markets place different values on reliability. In some consumer markets, customers do not expect to keep the product for a long period. Automobiles, in contrast, must be designed to be safe.

*quality*

Quality is important but may be difficult to define and measure. It may be related to reliability in some markets. In other markets—for instance, consumer devices—factors such as user interface design may be associated with quality.

## 1.4 Design Methodologies

*design repeatability*

Design methodology has traditionally been important to VLSI design but not to general-purpose computer architecture. Many different chips are designed; methodologies codify design practices. However, computer architecture has traditionally been treated as a field of invention for which methodologies are irrelevant.

However, the situation is different in embedded computing. While invention is useful and important when designing novel embedded systems, so are repeatability and design time. Although high-end embedded platforms are heterogeneous multiprocessors, many more of them are designed per year than are general-purpose processors. As a result, we need to understand and document design practices. Not only does this save time in the long run, but it also makes system design more repeatable. When embarking on a new project, we need to be able to predict the time and resources required to complete the project. The better we understand our methodology, the better able we are to predict design costs.

*synthesis and simulation*

A design methodology is not simply an abstraction—it must be defined in terms of available tools and resources. The designers of high-performance embedded systems face many challenges, some of which include the following.

- The design space is large and irregular. We do not have adequate synthesis tools for many important steps in the design process. As a result, designers must rely on analysis and simulation for many design phases.

- We cannot afford to simulate everything in extreme detail. Not only do simulations take time, but also the cost of the server farm required to run large simulations is a significant element of overall design cost. In particular, we cannot perform a cycle-accurate simultion of the entire design for the large data sets required to validate large applications.

■ We need to be able to develop simulators quickly. Simulators must reflect the structure of application-specific designs. System architects need tools to help them construct application-specific simulators.

■ Software developers for systems-on-chips need to be able to write and evaluate software before the hardware is completed. They need to be able to evaluate not just functionality but performance and power as well.

System designers need tools to help them quickly and reliably build heterogeneous architectures. They need tools to help them integrate several different types of processors, and they need tools to help them build multiprocessors from networks, memories, and processing elements.

*the design productivity gap*    Figure 1-12 shows the growth of design complexity and designer productivity over time, as estimated by the Sematech in the mid-1990s. Design complexity is fundamentally estimated by Moore's Law, which predicts a 58% annual increase in the number of transistors per chip. Sematech estimates that designer productivity has grown and will continue to grow by only 21% per year. The result is a wide and growing gap between the chips we can manufacture and the chips we can design. Embedded computing is one partial answer to the designer productivity problem, since we move some of the design tasks to software. But we also need improved methodologies for embedded computing systems to ensure we can continue to design platforms and load them with useful software.

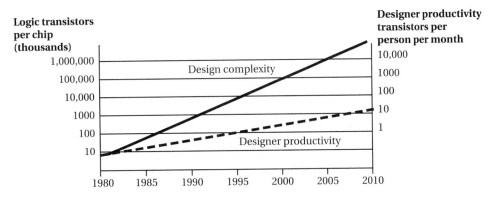

**Figure 1-12** *Design complexity and designer productivity trends.*

### 1.4.1 Basic Design Methodologies

Much of the early writings on design methodologies for computer systems cover software, but the methodologies for hardware tend to use a wider variety of tools since hardware design makes more use of synthesis and simulation tools. An ideal embedded systems methodology makes use of the best of both hardware and software traditions.

*waterfall software development*

One of the earliest models for software development was the **waterfall model** illustrated in Figure 1-13. The waterfall model is divided into five major stages: requirements, specification, architecture, coding, and maintenance. The software is successively refined through these stages, with maintenance including software delivery and follow-on updates and fixes. Most of the information in this methodology flows from the top down—that is, from more abstract stages to more concrete stages—although some information could flow back from one stage to the preceding stage to improve the design. The general flow of design information down the levels of abstraction gives the waterfall model its name. The waterfall model was important for codifying the basic steps of software development, but researchers soon realized that the limited flow of information from detailed design back to improve the more abstract phases was both an unrealistic picture of software design practices and an undesirable feature of an ideal methodology. In practice, designers can and should use experience from design steps to go back, rethink earlier decisions, and redo some work.

*spiral software development*

The **spiral model**, also shown in Figure 1-13, was a reaction to and a refinement of the waterfall model. This model envisions software design as an iterative process in which several versions of the system, each better than the last, are created. At each phase, designers go through a requirements/architecture/coding

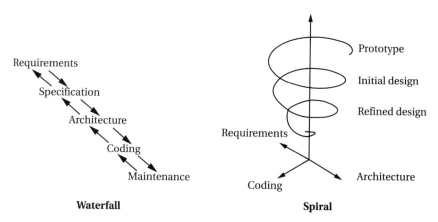

**Figure 1-13** *Two early models of software development.*

cycle. The results of one cycle are used to guide the decisions in the next round of development. Experience from one stage should both help produce a better design at the next stage and allow the design team to create that improved design more quickly.

*hardware design*
*methodologies*

Figure 1-14 shows a simplified version of the hardware design flows used in many VLSI designs. Modern hardware design makes extensive use of several techniques not as frequently seen in software design: search-based synthesis algorithms and models and estimation algorithms. Hardware designs also have more quantifiable design metrics than traditional software designs. Hardware designs must meet strict cycle-time requirements, power budgets, and area budgets. Although we have not shown backward design flow from lower to higher levels of abstraction, most design flows allow such iterative design.

Modern hardware synthesis uses many types of models. In Figure 1-14, the cell library describes the cells used for logic gates and registers, both concretely in terms of layout primitives and more abstractly in terms of delay, area, and so on. The technology database captures data not directly associated with cells, such as wire characteristics. These databases generally carry static data in the form of tables. Algorithms are also used to evaluate models. For example,

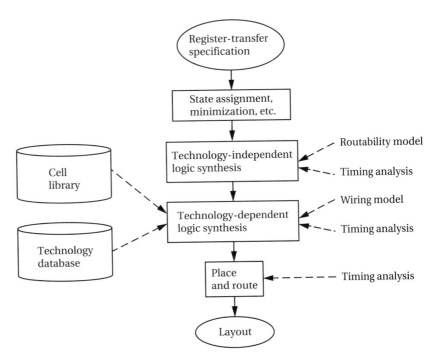

**Figure 1-14** *A digital synthesis design flow.*

several types of wirability models are used to estimate the properties of the wiring in the layout before that wiring is complete. Timing and power models evaluate the performance and power consumption of designs before all details of the design are known; for example, although both timing and power depend on the exact wiring, wire length estimates can be used to help estimate timing and power before the delay is complete. Good estimators help keep design iterations local. The tools can search the design space to find a good design, but within a given level of abstraction and based on models at that level. Good models combined with effective heuristic search can minimize the need for backtracking and throwing out design results.

## 1.4.2 Embedded Systems Design Flows

Embedded computing systems combine hardware and software components that must work closely together. Embedded system designers have evolved design methodologies that play into our ability to embody part of the functionality of the system in software.

*co-design flows*     Early researchers in hardware/software co-design emphasized the importance of concurrent design. Once the system architecture has been defined, the hardware and software components can be designed relatively separately. The goal of co-design is to make appropriate architectural decisions that allow later implementation phases to be carried out separately. Good architectural decisions, because they must satisfy hard metrics such as real-time performance and power consumption, require appropriate analysis methods.

Figure 1-15 shows a generic co-design methodology. Given an executable specification, most methodologies perform some initial system analysis to determine parallelism opportunities and perhaps break the specification into processes. Hardware/software partitioning chooses an architecture in which some operations are performed directly by hardware and others are performed by software running on programmable platforms. Hardware/software partitioning produces module designs that can be implemented separately. Those modules are then combined, tested for performance or power consumption, and debugged to create the final system.

*platform-based*     Platform-based design is a common approach to using systems-on-chips.
*design*     Platforms allow several customers to customize the same basic platform into different products. Platforms are particularly useful in standards-based markets where some basic features must be supported but other features must be customized to differentiate products.

*two-stage*     As shown in Figure 1-16, platform-based design is a two-stage process.
*process*     First, the platform must be designed based on the overall system requirements (the standard, for example) and how the platform should be customizable. Once the platform has been designed, it can be used to design a product. The product makes use of the platform features and adds its own features.

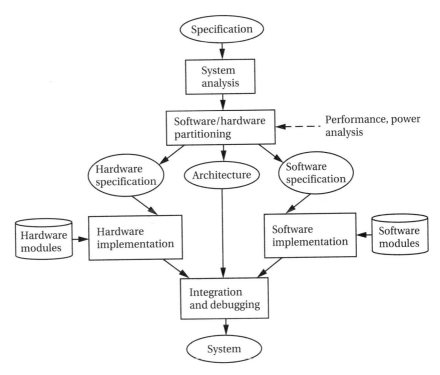

**Figure 1-15**  *A design flow for hardware/software co-design*

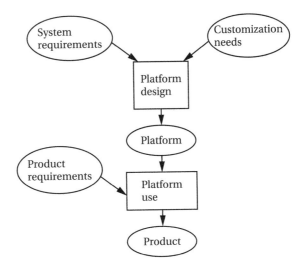

**Figure 1-16**  *Platform-based design.*

*platform design phases*

Platform design requires several design phases:

- Profiling and analysis turn system requirements and software models into more specific requirements on the platform hardware architecture.

- Design space exploration evaluates hardware alternatives.

- Architectural simulation helps evaluate and optimize the details of the architecture.

- Base software—hardware abstraction layers, operating system ports, communication, application libraries, debugging—must be developed for the platform.

*programming platforms*

Platform use is challenging in part because the platform requires a custom programming environment. Programmers are accustomed to rich development environments for standard platforms. Those environments provide a number of tools—compilers, editors, debuggers, simulators—in a single graphical user interface. However, rich programming environments are typically available for uniprocessors. Multiprocessors are more difficult to program, and heterogeneous multiprocessors are even more difficult than homogeneous multiprocessors. The platform developers must provide tools that allow software developers to use the platform. Some of these tools come from the component CPUs, but other tools must be developed from scratch. Debugging is particularly important and difficult, since debugging access is hardware-dependent. Interprocess communication is also challenging but is a critical tool for application developers.

## 1.4.3 Standards-Based Design Methodologies

Many high-performance embedded computing systems implement standards. Multimedia, communications, and networking all provide standards for various capabilities. One product may even implement several different standards. This section considers the effects of the standards on embedded systems design methodologies [Wol04].

*pros and cons of standards*

On the one hand, standards enable products and in particular systems-on-chips. Standards create large markets for particular types of functions: they allow devices to interoperate, and they reassure customers that the devices provide the required functions. Large markets help justify any system design project, but they are particularly important in system-on-chip (SoC) design. To cover the costs of SoC design and manufacturing, several million of the chips must be sold in many cases. Such large markets are generally created by standards.

On the other hand, the fact that the standard exists means that the chip designers have much less control over the specification of what they need to design. Standards define complex behavior that must be adhered to. As a result, some features of the architecture will be dictated by the standard.

Most standards do provide for improvements. Many standards define that certain operations must be performed, but they do not specify how they are to be performed. The implementer can choose a method based on performance, power, cost, quality, or ease of implementation. For example, video compression standards define basic parameters of motion estimation but not which motion estimation algorithm should be performed.

The intellectual property and effort required to implement a standard goes into different parts of the system than would be the case for a blank-sheet design. Algorithm design effort goes into unspecified parts of the standard and parts of the system that lie beyond the standard. For example, cell phones must adhere to communication standards but are free to be designed for many aspects of their user interfaces.

Standards are often complex, and standards in a given field tend to become more complex over time. As a field evolves, practitioners learn more about how to do a better job and strive to build that knowledge into the standard. While these improvements may lead to higher-quality systems, they also make system implementation more extensive.

*reference implementations*   Standards bodies typically provide a **reference implementation**. This is an executable program that conforms to the standard. It is often written in C, but may be written in Java or some other language. The reference implementation is first used to aid standard developers. It is then distributed to implementers of the specification. (The reference implementation may be available free of charge, but in many cases, an implementer must pay a license fee to the standards body to build a system that conforms to the specification. The license fee goes primarily to patent holders whose inventions are used within the standard.) There may be several reference implementations if multiple groups experiment with the standard and each releases results.

The reference implementation is something of a mixed blessing for system designers. On the one hand, the reference implementation saves designers a great deal of time; on the other hand, it comes with some liabilities. Of course, learning someone else's code is always time-consuming. Furthermore, the code generally cannot be used as-is. Reference implementations are typically written to run on large workstations with infinite memory; they are generally not designed to operate in real time. The code must often be restructured in many ways: eliminating features that will not be implemented; replacing heap allocation with custom memory management; and improving cache utilization, function, inlining, and many other tasks.

*design tasks*   The implementer of a standard must perform several design tasks:

■  The unspecified parts of the implementation must be designed.

■  Parts of the system not specified by the standard (user interface, for example) must be designed.

- An initial round of platform-independent optimization must be used to improve the chosen reference implementation.

- The reference implementation and other code must be profiled and analyzed.

- The hardware platform must be designed based on initial characterization.

- The system software must be further optimized to better match the platform.

- The platform itself must be further optimized based on additional profiling.

- The platform and software must be verified for conformance to the standard as well as nonfunctional parameters such as performance and energy consumption.

The next example introduces the Advanced Video Coding standard.

## Example 1-6

*AVC/H.264*

The latest generation of video compression standards is known by several names. It is officially part 10 of the MPEG-4 standard, known as Advanced Video Coding (AVC). However, the MPEG group joined forces with the H.26x group, so it is also known as H.264.

The MPEG family of standards is primarily oriented toward broadcast, in which the transmitter is more complex in favor of cheaper receivers. The H.26x family of standards, in contrast, has traditionally targeted videoconferencing, in which systems must both transmit and receive, giving little incentive to trade transmitter complexity for receiver complexity.

The H.264 standard provides many features that give improved picture quality and compression ratio. H.264 codecs typically generate encoded streams that are half the size of MPEG-2 encodings. For example, the H.264 standard allows multiple reference frames so that motion estimation can use pixels from several frames to handle occlusion. This is an example of a feature that improves quality at the cost of increased receiver complexity.

The reference implementation for H.264 is more than 120,000 lines of C code; it uses a fairly simple algorithm for some unspecified parts of the standard, such as motion estimation. However, it implements both video coding and decoding, and reference implementation does so for the full range of display sizes supported by the standard, ranging from $176 \times 120$ resolution of NTSC quarter CIF (QCIF) to high-definition resolutions of $1280 \times 720$ or more.

### 1.4.4  Design Verification and Validation

Making sure that the implementation is correct is a critical part of any design. A variety of techniques are used in practice to ensure that the final system operates correctly.

*testing, validation, verification*

We can distinguish between several types of activities:

- **Testing** exercises an implementation by providing stimuli and evaluating the implementation's outputs.

- **Validation** generally refers to comparing the implementation to the initial requirements or specification.

- **Verification** may be performed at any stage of the design process and compares the design at one level of abstraction to another.

*techniques*

A number of different techniques are used to verify designs.

- Simulation accepts stimulus and computes the expected outputs. Simulation may directly interpret a design model, or the simulator may be compiled from the model.

- Formal methods perform some sort of proof; they require some sort of description of the property to be tested but not particular input stimuli. Formal methods may, for example, search the state space of the system to determine whether a property holds.

- Manual methods can catch many errors. Design walkthroughs, for example, are often used to identify problems during the implementation.

*verification and design*

Verification and validation should not be performed as a final step to check the complete implementation. The design should be repeatedly verified at each level of abstraction. Design errors become more expensive to fix as they propagate through the design—allowing a bug to be carried to a more detailed level of implementation requires more engineering effort to fix the bug.

### 1.4.5  A Methodology of Methodologies

The design of high-performance embedded systems is not described well by simple methodologies. Given that these systems implement specifications that are millions of lines long, it should not be surprising that we have to use many different types of design processes to build complex embedded systems.

We discuss throughout this book many tools and techniques that can be built into methodologies. Quite a few of these tools are complex and require specialized knowledge of how to use them. Methodologies that we use in embedded system design include:

- **Software performance analysis**—Executable specifications must be analyzed to determine how much computing horsepower is needed and which types of operations must be performed. We will discuss performance analysis in Section 3.4.

- **Architectural optimization**—Single processor architectures can be tuned and optimized for the application. We will discuss such methods in Chapter 3. We can also tune multiprocessor architectures, as will we discuss in Chapter 5.

- **Hardware/software co-design**—Co-design helps create efficient heterogeneous architectures. We will look at co-design algorithms and methodologies in detail in Chapter 7.

- **Network design**—Whether in distributed embedded systems or systems-on-chips, networks must provide the necessary bandwidth at reasonable energy levels. We will look at on-chip networks in Section 5.6 and multichip networks, such us those used in automobiles, in Section 5.8.

- **Software verification**—Software must be evaluated for functional correctness. We will look at software-verification techniques for concurrent systems in Section 4.5.

- **Software tool generation**—Tools to program the system must be generated from the hardware and software architectures. We will discuss compiler generation for configurable processors in Section 2.9. We will look at software generation for multiprocessors in Section 6.3.

## 1.4.6 Joint Algorithm and Architecture Development

*algorithms ≠*
*software*

It is important to keep in mind that algorithmic design occurs at least in part before embedded system design. Because algorithms are eventually implemented in software to be used, it is easy to confuse algorithmic design and software design. But, in fact, the design of algorithms for signal processing, networking, and so on is a very different skill than that of designing software. This book is primarily about embedded software and hardware, not algorithms. One of the goals here is to demonstrate the skills required to design efficient, compact software and to show that those skills are applicable to a broad range of algorithms.

However, it is also true that algorithm and embedded system designers need to talk more often. Algorithm designers need to understand the characteristics of their platforms in order to design implementable algorithms. Embedded system designers need to understand which types of features are needed for algorithms in different application spaces to ensure that the systems they design are optimized for the proper characteristics.

*joint algorithm and architecture development*

Embedded systems architectures may be designed along with the algorithms they will execute. This is true even in standards-based systems, since standards generally allow for algorithmic enhancements. Joint algorithm/architecture development creates some special challenges for system designers.

Algorithm designers need estimates and models to help them tailor the algorithm to the architecture. Even though the architecture is not complete, the hardware architects should be able to supply estimates of performance and power consumption. These should be useful for simulators that take models of the underlying architecture.

Algorithm designers also need to be able to develop software. This requires functional simulators that run as fast as possible. If hardware were available, algorithm designers could run code at native speeds. Functional simulators can provide adequate levels of performance for many applications even if they do not run at hardware speeds. Fast turnaround of compilation and simulation is very important to successful software development.

## 1.5    Models of Computation

A **model of computation** defines the basic capabilities of an abstract computer. In the early days of computer science, models of computation helped researchers understand the basic capabilities of computers. In embedded computing, models of computation help us understand how to correctly and easily program complex systems. This section considers several models of computation and the relationships between them. The study of models of computation have influenced the way real embedded systems are designed; we balance the theory in this section with mentions of how some of these theoretical techniques have influenced embedded software design.

### 1.5.1    Why Study Models of Computation?

*expressiveness*

Models of computation help us understand the expressiveness of various programming languages. Expressiveness has several different aspects. On the one hand, we can prove that some models are more expressive than others—that some styles of computing can do some things that other styles cannot. But expressiveness also has implications for programming style that are at least as important for embedded system designers. Two languages that are both equally expressive, formally, may be good at different types of applications. For example, control and data are often programmed in different ways; a language can express one only with difficulty but the other easily.

*language styles*

Experienced programmers can think of several types of expressiveness that can be useful when writing programs.

- **Finite versus infinite state**—Some models assume that an infinite number of states can exist; other models are finite-state.

- **Control versus data**—This is one of the most basic dichotomies in programming. Although control and data are equivalent formally, we tend to think about them very differently. Many programming languages have been developed for control-intense applications such as  protocol design. Similarly, many other programming languages have been designed for data-intense applications such as signal processing.

- **Sequential versus parallel**—This is another basic theme in computer programming. Many languages have been developed to make it easy to describe parallel programs in a way that is both intuitive and formally verifiable. However, programmers still feel comfortable with sequential programming when they can get away with it.

The astute reader will note that we are not concerned here with some traditional programming language issues such as modularity. While modularity and maintainability are important, they are not unique to embedded computing. Some of the other aspects of languages that we mention are more central to embedded systems that must implement several different styles of computation so that they can work together smoothly.

*heterogeneity and interoperability*

Expressiveness may lead to the use of more than one programming language to build a system—we call these systems **heterogeneously programmed**. When programming languages are mixed, we must satisfy the extra burden of correctly designing the communication between modules of different programming languages. Within a given language, the language system often helps verify certain basic operations, and it is much easier to think about how the program works. When we mix and match multiple languages, it is much more difficult for us to convince ourselves that the programs will work together properly. Understanding the model under which each programming language works, and the conditions under which they can reliably communicate, is a critical step in the design of heterogeneously programmed systems.

## 1.5.2   Finite versus Infinite State

*finite versus infinite state*

The amount of state that can be described by a model is one of the most fundamental aspects of any model of computation. Early work on computability emphasized the capabilities of finite-state versus infinite-state machines; infinite state was generally considered to be good because it showed that the machine was more capable. However, finite-state models are much easier to verify in

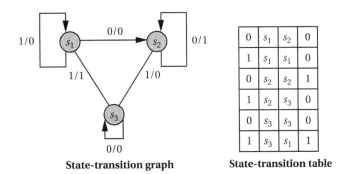

| 0 | $s_1$ | $s_2$ | 0 |
|---|---|---|---|
| 1 | $s_1$ | $s_1$ | 0 |
| 0 | $s_2$ | $s_2$ | 1 |
| 1 | $s_2$ | $s_3$ | 0 |
| 0 | $s_3$ | $s_3$ | 0 |
| 1 | $s_3$ | $s_1$ | 1 |

**State-transition graph**        **State-transition table**

**Figure 1-17** *A state-transition graph and table for a finite-state machine*

both theory and practice. As a result, finite-state programming models have an important place in embedded computing.

*finite-state machine*

Finite-state machines (FSMs) are well understood by both software and hardware designers. An example is shown in Figure 1-17. An FSM is typically defined as

$$M = \{I, O, S, \Delta, T\} \qquad \text{(EQ 1-4)}$$

where $I$ and $O$ are the inputs and outputs of the machine, $S$ is its current state, and $\Delta$ and $T$ are the states and transitions, respectively, of the state-transition graph. In a **Moore machine**, the output is a function only of $S$, while in a **Mealy machine** the output is a function of both the present state and the current input.

Although there are models for asynchronous FSMs, a key feature in the development of the finite-state machine model is the notion of synchronous operation: inputs are accepted only at certain moments. Finite-state machines view time as integer-valued, not real-valued. At each input, the FSM evaluates its state and determines its next state based on the input received as well as the present state.

*streams*

In addition to the machine itself, we need to model its inputs and outputs. A **stream** is widely used as a model of terminal behavior because it describes sequential behavior—time as ordinals, not in real values. The elements of a stream are symbols in an alphabet. The alphabet may be binary, may be in some other base, or may consist of other types of values, but the stream itself does not impose any semantics on the alphabet. A stream is a totally ordered set of symbols $<s_0, s_1, \ldots>$. A stream may be finite or infinite. Informally, the time at which a symbol appears in a stream is given by its ordinality in the stream. In this equation

$$S(t) = s_t \qquad \text{(EQ 1-5)}$$

the symbol $s_t$ is the $t^{\text{th}}$ element of the stream $S$.

We can use streams to describe the input/output or terminal behavior of a finite-state machine. If we view the FSM as having several binary-valued inputs, the alphabet for the input stream will be binary numbers; in some cases, it is useful to think of the inputs as forming a group whose values are determined by a single symbol that defines the states of all the inputs. Similar thinking can be applied to the outputs. The behavior of the inputs is then described as one or more streams, depending on the alphabet used. Similarly, the output behavior is described as one or more streams. At time $i$, the FSM consumes a symbol on each of its input streams and produces a symbol on each of its output streams. The mapping from inputs to outputs is determined by the state-transition graph and the machine's internal state. From the terminal view, the FSM is synchronous because the consumption of inputs and generation of outputs is coordinated.

*verification and finite state*

Although synchronous finite-state machines may be the most familiar to hardware designers, synchronous behavior is a growing trend in the design of languages for embedded computing. Finite-state machines make interesting models for software because they can be more easily verified than infinite-state machines. Because an FSM has a finite number of states, we can visit all the states and exercise all the transitions in a finite amount of time. If a system has infinite state, we cannot visit all its states in finite time. Although it may seem impractical to walk through all the states of an FSM in practice, research over the past 20 years has led us to efficient algorithms for exploring large state spaces.

The **ordered Boolean decision diagram (OBDD)** [Bry86] can be used to describe combinational Boolean functions. Techniques have been developed to describe state spaces in terms of OBDDs such that, in many cases, properties of those state spaces can be efficiently checked. OBDDs do not take away the basic NP-completeness of combinational and state space search problems; in some cases the OBDDs can become very large and slow to evaluate. But in many cases they run very fast and even in pathological cases can be faster than competing methods. OBDDs allow us to perform many checks that are useful tests of the correctness of practical systems.

- **Product machines**—It is often easier to express complex functions as systems of communicating machines. However, hidden bugs may lurk in the communication between those components. Building the product of the communicating machines is the first step in many correctness checks.

- **Reachability**—Many bugs manifest themselves as inabilities to reach certain states in the machine. In some cases, unreachable states may simply describe useless but unimportant behavior. In other cases, unreachable states may signal a missing feature in the system.

**Nondeterministic FSMs**, also known as nondeterministic finite automata (NFAs), are used to describe some types of systems. An example is shown in

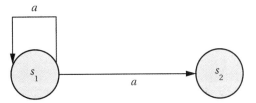

**Figure 1-18**  *A nondeterministic FSM.*

Figure 1-18: two transitions out of state $s_1$ have the same input label. One way to think about this model is that the machine nondeterministically chooses a transition such that future inputs will cause the machine to be in the proper state; another way to think about execution is that the machine follows all possible transitions simultaneously until future inputs cause it to prune some paths. It is important to remember that nondeterministic automata are not formally more expressive than deterministic FSMs. An algorithm can transform any NFA into an equivalent deterministic machine. But NFAs can be exponentially smaller than its equivalent deterministic machine. This is a simple but clear example of the stylistic aspect of expressiveness.

*control-oriented languages*

A number of languages have been developed to describe control. Statecharts is a well-known example. We will discuss Statecharts in more detail in Section 3.5.3.

*Turing machine*

The **Turing machine** is the most well-known infinite-state model for computation. (Church developed his lambda calculus first, but the Turing machine more closely models the operation of practical computing machines.) As illustrated in Figure 1-19, the Turing machine itself consists of a program, a read head, and a state. The machine reads and writes a tape that has been divided into

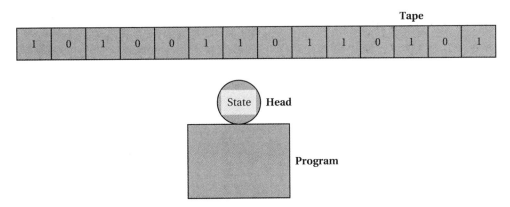

**Figure 1-19**  *A Turing machine.*

cells, each of which contains a symbol. The tape can move back and forth underneath the head; the head can both read and write symbols on the tape. Because the tape may be of infinite length, it can describe infinite-state computations. An operating cycle of a Turing machine consists of the following steps.

1. The machine uses the head to read the symbol in the tape cell underneath the head.

2. The machine erases the symbol on the cell underneath the head.

3. The machine consults its program to determine what to do next. Based on the current state and the symbol that was read, the machine may write a new symbol and/or move the tape.

4. The machine changes its state as described by the program.

The Turing machine is a powerful model that allows us to demonstrat the capabilities and limits of computability. However, as we noted previously, finite state enables verification of many important aspects of real programs even though the basic programming model is more limited. For example, one of the key results of theoretical computer science is the **halting problem**—the Turing model allows us to confirm that we cannot, in general, show that an arbitrary program will halt in a finite amount of time. The failure to ensure that programs will halt makes it impossible to verify many important problems of programs on infinite-state systems. In contrast, because we can visit all the states of a finite-state system in finite time, important properties become more tractable.

### 1.5.3 Control Flow and Data Flow Models

Control and data are basic units of programming. Although control and data are fundamentally equivalent, we tend to think of data operations, such as arithmetic, as more regular, and control as less regular and more likely to involve state.

*control flow graph*

A basic model of control is the **control flow graph** (CFG), as shown in Figure 1-20. The nodes in the graph are either unconditionally executed operations (the rectangles) or conditions (the diamond). The control flow graph has a single thread of control, which can be thought of as a program counter moving through the program. The CFG is a finite-state model of computation. Many compilers model a program using a **control data flow graph** (CDFG), which adds data flow models that we will use to describe the operations of the unconditional nodes and the decisions in the conditional nodes.

*basic data flow graphs*

A basic model of data is the **data flow graph** (DFG), an example of which is shown in Figure 1-21. Like the task graph, the data flow graph consists of nodes and directed edges, where the directed edges represent data dependencies. The nodes in the DFG represent the data operations, such as arithmetic

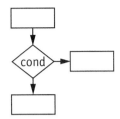

**Figure 1-20**  *A control flow graph.*

operations. Some edges in the DFG terminate at a node but do not start at one; these sources provide inputs. Similarly, sinks start at a node but do not terminate at one. (An alternative formulation is to provide three types of nodes: operator, input, and output.)

We require that DFGs be trees—they cannot have cycles. This makes the graphs easier to analyze but does limit their uses. Basic DFGs are commonly used in compilers.

The DFG is finite-state. It describes parallelism in that it defines only a partial order on the operations in the graph. Whether we execute those operations one at a time or several at once, any order of operations that satisfies the data dependencies is acceptable.

*streams and firing rules*    We can use streams to model the behavior of the DFG. Each source in the data flow graph has its own stream, and each sink of the graph is a stream as well. The nodes in the DFG use **firing rules** to determine their behavior. The simplest firing rule is similar to the operation of finite-state machines: firing consumes a token on each of the node's input streams and generates one token on its output; we will call this the "standard data flow firing rule." One way to introduce conditions into the DFG is with a conditional node with $n + 1$ terminals: data inputs $d_0, d_1, \ldots$ and control input $k$. When $k = 0$, data input $d_0$ is consumed and sent to the output; when $k = 1$, $d_1$ is consumed and transferred to the

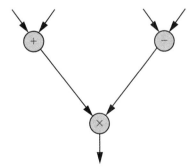

**Figure 1-21**  *A data flow graph.*

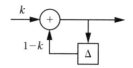

**Figure 1-22** *A signal flow graph.*

output, and so on. In this firing rule, not all of the inputs to the node consume a token at once.

*signal flow graphs*

A slightly more sophisticated version of data flow is the **signal flow graph** (**SFG**), commonly used in signal processing. As shown in Figure 1-22, the signal flow graph adds a new type of node generally called a **delay** node. As signified by the $\Delta$ symbol, the delay node delays a stream by $n$ (by default, one) time steps. Given a stream $S$, the result of a delay operator is $\Delta(t) = S(t-1)$. Edges in the SFG may be given weights that indicate that the value given to a node is to be multiplied by the weight. We also allow SFGs to have cycles. SFGs are commonly used to describe digital filters.

*synchronous data flow*

A more sophisticated data flow model is the **synchronous data flow** (**SDF**) model introduced by Lee and Messerschmitt [Lee87]. Synchronous data flow graphs allow feedback and provide methods for determining when a system with feedback is in fact legal. A simple SDF graph is shown in Figure 1-23. As with basic data flow graphs, nodes define operations and directed edges define the flow of data. The data flowing along the edges can be modeled as streams. Each edge has two labels: $r_o$ describes the number of tokens produced per invocation while $r_i$ gives the number of tokens consumed per invocation. Each edge may also be labeled with a delay $\delta$ that describes the amount of time between when a token is produced at the source and when it is consumed at the edge; by convention the default delay is $0S$.

*Kahn process networks*

Lee and Parks [Lee95] identified the networks of **Kahn processes** as important models for systems of communicating processes. Kahn processes can be used to build networks of communicating processes. Based on certain properties of the Kahn process, we can determine some important properties of the network. We can prove these properties without making use of the concept of time in the wall clock sense. The inputs and outputs of a Kahn process are modeled as streams, which define sequential patterns but do not define a time base.

A Kahn process is shown in Figure 1-24. The process itself is connected to its inputs by infinite-size buffers. The process maps its input streams to output

**Figure 1-23** *A simple SDF graph.*

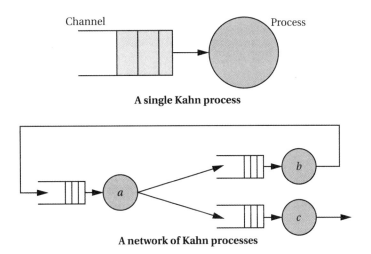

**Figure 1-24** *A single Kahn process and a network of Kahn processes.*

streams. A process can have one or more inputs and one or more outputs. If $X$ is a stream, then $F(X)$ is the output of a Kahn process when given that stream. One important property of a Kahn process is **monotonicity**.

$$X \in X' \Rightarrow F(X) \in F(X'). \qquad \text{(EQ 1-6)}$$

The behavior of a monotonic process is physical in the sense that adding more inputs will not cause it to mysteriously generate fewer outputs.

A network of Kahn processes, also shown in Figure 1-24, equates the input and output streams of processes in the network; for example, the output of process $a$ is equal to the input of process $b$ as well as the input of process $c$. If $I$ is the input stream to a network and $X$ is the set of internal streams and outputs, then the fixed point behavior of the network is

$$X = F(X, I). \qquad \text{(EQ 1-7)}$$

Kahn showed that a network of monotonic processes is itself monotonic. This means that we can compose monotonic processes without worrying about the network becoming nonmonotonic.

### 1.5.4  Parallelism and Communication

Parallelism is a fundamental concept in computer science and of great practical importance in embedded systems. Many embedded systems perform many tasks simultaneously. The real parallelism embodied in the hardware must be matched by apparent parallelism in the programs.

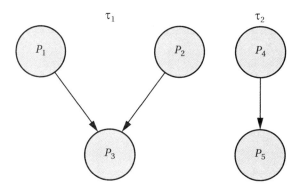

**Figure 1-25** *A task graph.*

*parallelism and architecture*

We need to capture parallelism during the early stages of design so that we can use it to optimize the design. Parallel algorithms describe time as partially ordered—the exact sequence of operations is not determined up front. As we bind operations to the architecture, we move the description toward a totally ordered description (although some operations may be left partially ordered to be managed by the operating system). Different choices for ordering require different amounts of hardware resources, affecting cost and power consumption.

*task graphs*

A simple model of parallelism is the **task graph**, as shown in Figure 1-25. The nodes in the task graph represent **processes** or **tasks** while the directed edges represent data dependencies. In the example, process $P_4$ must complete before $P_5$ can start. Task graphs model concurrency because sets of tasks that are not connected by data dependencies may operate in parallel. In the example, $\tau_1$ and $\tau_2$ are separate components of the graph that can run independently. Task graphs are often used to represent multirate systems. Unless we expose the computation within the processes, a task graph is less powerful than a Turing machine. The basic task graph cannot even describe conditional behavior. Several extended task graphs have been developed that describe conditions but even these are finite-state machines.

*Petri nets*

The **Petri net** [Mur89] is one well-known parallel model of computation. Petri nets were originally considered to be more powerful than Turing machines, but later work showed that the two are in fact equivalent. However, Petri nets explicitly describe parallelism in a way that makes some types of systems easier to specify. An example Petri net is shown in Figure 1-26. A net is a weighted, directed bipartite graph. One type of node is the **place**; the other type is a **transition**. Arcs connect places and transitions; an arc is weighted with a non-negative integer. There are no arcs between two places or two transitions.

The state of the executing system is defined by **tokens** that define a **marking**. The tokens move around the net in accordance with firing rules. In general, a place can hold zero, one, or more than one tokens.

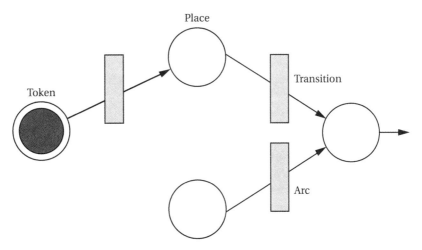

**Figure 1-26** *A Petri net.*

The Petri net's behavior is defined by a sequence of markings, each defining a state of the net. The **firing rule** or **transition rule** determines the next state given the current state. A transition is **enabled** if each input place of the transition is marked with at least as many tokens as are specified by the weight of each incoming arc. Enabled transitions may fire but are not required to do so. Firing removes tokens from the places that feed the transition equal to the weight of the arc from the place to the transition and adds the same number of tokens to each output place equal to the weight of the arc from the transition to the place.

Petri nets have been used to study many problems in parallel programming. They are sometimes used to write parallel programs but are not often used directly as programs. However, the notion of multiple tokens is a powerful one that serves us well in many types of programs.

*communication styles*    Useful parallelism necessarily involves communication between the parallel components of the system. Different types of parallel models use different styles of communication. These styles can have profound implications on the efficiency of the implementation of communication. We can distinguish two basic styles of communication: **buffered** and **unbuffered**. A buffered communication assumes that memory is available to store a value if the receiving process is temporarily not ready to receive it. An unbuffered model assumes no memory in between the sender and the receiver.

*communication in FSMs*    Even a simple model like the FSM can exhibit parallelism and communication. Figure 1-27 shows two communicating FSMs. Each machine, $M_1$ and $M_2$, has an input from the outside world and an output to the outside world. But each has one output connected to the input of the other machine. The behavior of each machine therefore depends on the behavior of the other machine. As we

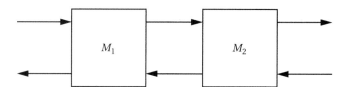

**Figure 1-27** *Two communicating FSMs.*

noted before, the first step in analyzing the behavior of such networks of FSMs is often to form the equivalent product machine.

*synchronous languages*

Communicating FSM languages such as Esterel [Ben91] have been used for software as well as hardware. As we will see in Chapter 3, each process in an Esterel program is considered as finite-state machine, and the behavior of the system of process is determined by building the product of the component machines. Esterel has been widely used to program avionics and other critical applications.

The communicating FSMs of Figure 1-27 communicate without buffers. A buffer would correspond to a register (in hardware) or variable (in software) in between an output on one machine and the corresponding input on the other machine. However, we can implement both synchronous and asynchronous behavior using this simple unbuffered mechanism as shown in Figure 1-28. Synchronous communication simply has one machine throw a value to the other machine. In the figure, the synchronously communicating $M_1$ sends *val* to $M_2$

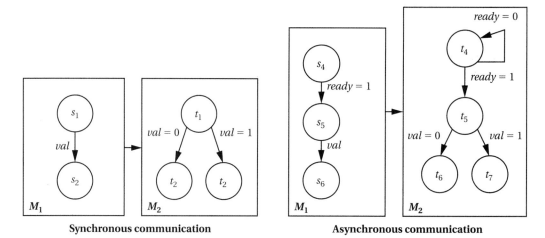

**Figure 1-28** *Synchronous and asynchronous communication in FSMs.*

without checking whether $M_2$ is ready. If the machines are designed properly, this is very efficient, but if $M_1$ and $M_2$ fall out of step, then $M_2$ will misbehave because *val* is either early or late. Asynchronous communication uses a handshake. On the right side of the figure, the asynchronous $M_1$ first sends a ready signal, then a value. $M_2$ waits for the ready signal before looking for *val*. This requires extra states but does not require that the machines move in lockstep.

*blocking versus nonblocking*
Another fundamental distinction between communication methods, involves **blocking** versus **nonblocking** behavior. In **blocking communication**, the sending process blocks, or waits until the receiving process has the data. **Nonblocking communication** does not require the sender to wait for the receiver to receive the data. If there are no buffers between the sender and receiver, and the receiver is not ready, nonblocking communication will drop data. Adding a buffer allows the sender to move on even if the receiver is not ready, assuming that the buffer is not already full. An infinite-size buffer allows unlimited nonblocking communication.

*buffering and communication*
A natural question in the case of buffered communication concerns the size of the buffer required. In some systems, an infinite-size buffer is required to avoid losing data. In a multirate system in which the sender may always produce data faster than the consumer, the buffer size may grow indefinitely. However, it may be possible to show that the producer cannot keep more than some finite number of elements in the buffer even in the worst case. If we can prove the size of the buffer required, we can create a less-expensive implementation. Proving that the buffer is finite also tells us that it is possible to build a system in which the buffer never overflows. As with other problems, proving buffer sizes is easier in finite-state systems.

### 1.5.5 Sources and Uses of Parallelism

*varieties of parallelism*
One of the benefits of using a programming language or model of computation suited to a problem is that it may be easier to identify and extract opportunities for parallelism from the application. Concurrent hardware enables us to perform operations that take advantage of the independence of the operations we want to perform. Parallelism may be found at many different levels of abstraction.

*instruction-level parallelism*
**Instruction-level parallelism** is exploited by high-performance microprocessors. Instruction-level parallelism in its purest form is truly at the instruction level, such as load, stores, and ALU operations. The instruction-level operations are not visible in the source code and so cannot be manipulated by the programmer.

*data parallelism*
**Data-level parallelism** can be found in C or Fortran programs by optimizing compilers. Data parallelism on a small scale can be found in a basic block of a program. Larger-scale data parallelism can be found in a nest of loops that perform array calculations.

*task parallelism*

**Task-level parallelism** can be found in many applications. It is particularly important in embedded systems because these systems often perform several different types of computation on data streams. In many ways, task-level parallelism is easy to exploit since tasks can be allocated to processors. However, task structure is not easily conveyed in C; programmers often resort to programming conventions combined with calls to interprocess communication routines to define tasks. More abstract programming models may help clarify the task structure of an application.

*static versus dynamic*

Some types of parallelism can be found statically, by examining the program. Other opportunities can be found only dynamically, by executing the program. Static parallelism is easier to implement but does not cover all important sources of parallelism (at least, not in a Turing-complete model). Dynamic discovery of parallelism can be performed at many levels of abstraction: instruction, data/control, task, and so on.

## 1.6 Reliability, Safety, and Security

This section looks at aspects of reliable system design that are particularly important to embedded system design. Reliability, safety, and security are closely related.

- **Reliable (or dependable) system design** is concerned with making systems work even in the face of internal or external problems. Reliable system design most often assumes that problems are not caused maliciously.

- **Safety-critical system design** studies methods to make sure systems operate safely, independent of the cause of the problem.

- **Security** is concerned largely with malicious attacks.

**Figure 1-29** *Dependability and security as described by Avizienis et al. [Avi04].*

Avizienis et al. [Avi04] describe the relationship between dependability and security as shown in Figure 1-29. Dependability and security are composed of several attributes:

■ **Availability** of correct service

■ **Continuity** of correct service

■ **Safety** from catastrophic consequences on users and their environment

■ **Integrity** from improper system alterations

■ **Maintainability** through modifications and repairs

■ **Confidentiality** of information

Embedded systems are increasingly subject to malicious attack. But whatever the source of the problem, many embedded systems must operate properly in the presence of faults.

### 1.6.1  Why Reliable Embedded Systems?

*applications demand reliability*

Certainly many embedded systems do not need to be highly reliable. Some consumer electronics devices are so inexpensive as to be nearly disposable. Many markets do not require highly reliable embedded computers. But many embedded computers must be built to be highly reliable:

■ automotive electronics;

■ avionics;

■ medical equipment;

■ critical communications.

Embedded computers may also handle critical data, such as purchasing data or medical information.

The definition of reliability can vary widely with context. Certainly, computer systems that run for weeks at a time without failing are not unknown. Telephone switching systems have been designed to be down for less than 30 seconds per year.

*new problems*

The study of reliable digital system design goes back several decades. A variety of architectures and methodologies have been developed to allow digital systems to operate for long periods with very low failure rates. What is the difference between the designs of traditional reliable computers and reliable embedded systems?

First, reliable embedded computers are often distributed systems. Automotive electronics, avionics, and medical equipment are all examples of distributed embedded systems that must be highly reliable. Distributed computing can work to our advantage when designing reliable systems, but distributed computers can also be very unreliable if improperly designed.

Second, embedded computers are vulnerable to many new types of attacks. Reliable computers were traditionally servers or machines that were physically inaccessible—physical security has long been a key strategy for computer security. However, embedded computers generally operate in unprotected environments. This allows for new types of faults and attacks that require new methods of protection.

### 1.6.2   Fundamentals of Reliable System Design

*sources of faults*   Reliable systems are designed to recover from **faults**. A fault may be **permanent** or **transient**. A fault may have many sources, some of which are the following.

- **Physical faults** are caused by manufacturing defects, radiation hazards, and so on.

- **Design faults** are the result of improperly designed systems.

- **Operational faults** come from human error, security breaches, poorly designed human–computer interfaces, and so on.

While the details of how such faults occur and how they affect the system may vary, the system's users do not really care what caused a problem, only that the system reacted properly to it. Whether a fault comes from a manufacturing defect or a security problem, the system must react in such a way as to minimize the fault's effect on the user.

*system reliability metrics*   Users judge systems by how reliable they are, not by the problems that cause them to fail. Several metrics are used to quantify system reliability [Sie98].

**Mean time to failure** (**MTTF**) is one well-known metric. Given a set of perfectly functioning systems at time 0, MTTF is the expected time for the first system in that set to fail. Although it is defined for a large set of systems, it is also often used to characterize the reliability of a single system. The mean time to failure can be calculated by

$$MTTF = \int_{0}^{\infty} R(t)\,dt \qquad \text{(EQ 1-8)}$$

where *R(t)* is the reliability function of the system.

The **reliability function** of a system describes the probability that the system will operate correctly in the time period $[0, t]$. $R(0) = 1$ and $R(t)$ monontonically decreases with time.

The **hazard function** $z(t)$ is the failure rate of components. For a given probability function, the hazard function is defined as

$$z(t) = \frac{pdf}{1 - CDF}. \tag{EQ 1-9}$$

*characterizing*
*faults*

Faults can be measured empirically or modeled by a probability distribution. Empirical studies are usually the basis for choosing an appropriate probability distribution. One common model for failures is exponential distribution. In this case, the hazard function is

$$z(t) = \hat{\lambda}. \tag{EQ 1-10}$$

Another function used to model failures is the Weibull distribution:

$$z(t) = \alpha\lambda(\lambda t)^{\alpha - t}. \tag{EQ 1-11}$$

In this formula, $\alpha$ is known as the shape parameter and $\lambda$ is known as the scale parameter. The Weibull distribution normally must be solved numerically.

A distribution that is observed empirically for many hardware components is the **bathtub function** shown in Figure 1-30. The bathtub curve gets its name from its similarity to the cross-section of a bathtub. Hardware components generally show infant mortality in which marginal components fail quickly, then a long period with few failures, followed by a period of increased failures due to long-term wear mechanisms.

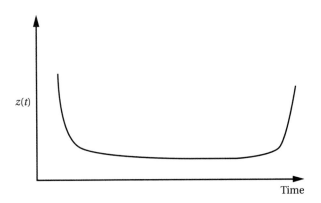

**Figure 1-30** *A bathtub function.*

*actions after faults*

The system can do many things after a fault. Generally several of these actions are taken in order until an action gets the system back into running condition. Actions from least to most severe include the following.

- **Fail**—All too many systems fail without trying to even detect an error.

- **Detect**—An error may be detected. Even if the system stops at this point, the diagnostic information provided by the detector can be useful.

- **Correct**—An error may be corrected. Memory errors are routinely corrected. A simple correction causes no long-term disturbance to the system.

- **Recover**—A recovery may take more time than a simple correction. For example, a correction may cause a noticeable pause in system operation.

- **Contain**—The system may take steps to ensure that a failure does not corrupt a large part of 17. This is particularly true of software or hardware failures that can, for example, cause large parts of memory to change.

- **Reconfigure**—One way to contain a fault is to reconfigure the system so that different parts of the system perform some operations. For example, a faulty unit may be disabled and another unit enabled to perform its work.

- **Restart**—Restarting the system may be the best way to wipe out the effects of an error. This is particularly true of transient errors and software errors.

- **Repair**—Either hardware or software components can be modified or replaced to repair the system.

*reliability methods*

Many techniques have been developed to make digital systems more reliable. Some are more applicable to hardware, others to software, and some may be used in both hardware and software.

*error-correction codes*

Error-correction codes were developed in the 1950s, starting with Hamming, to both detect and correct errors. They are widely used throughout digital systems to identify and correct transient or permanent errors. These codes introduce redundant information in a way such that certain types of errors can be guaranteed to be detected or corrected. For example, a code that is single-error correcting/double-error detecting can both detect and correct an error in a single bit and detect, but not correct, two bit errors.

*voting systems*

Voting schemes are often used to check at higher levels of abstraction. One well-known voting method is **triple modular redundancy**, illustrated in Figure 1-31. The computation unit $C$ has three copies, $C_1$, $C_2$, and $C_3$. All three units receive the same input. A separate unit compares the results generated by each input. If at least two results agree, then that value is chosen as correct by the voter. If all three results differ, then no correct result can be given.

*watchdog timers*

The **watchdog timer** is widely used to detect system problems. As shown in Figure 1-32, the watchdog timer is connected to a system that it watches. If the

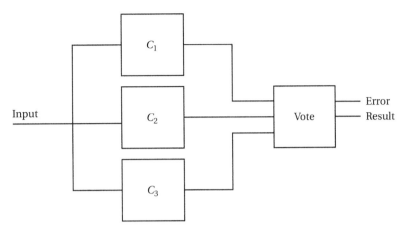

**Figure 1-31** *Triple modular redundancy.*

watchdog timer rolls over, it generates a *done* signal that should be attached to an error interrupt in the system. The system should be designed so that, when running properly, it always resets the timer before it has a chance to roll over. Thus, a *done* signal from the watchdog timer indicates that the system is somehow operating improperly. The watchdog timer can be used to guard against a wide variety of faults.

*design diversity*     **Design diversity** is a design methodology intended to reduce the chance that certain systematic errors creep into the design. When a design calls for several instances of a given type of module, different implementations of that module are used rather than using the same type of module everywhere. For example, a system with several CPUs may use several different types of CPUs rather than use the same type of CPU everywhere. In a triple modular redundant system, the components that produce results for voting may be of different implementations to decrease the chance that all embody the same design error.

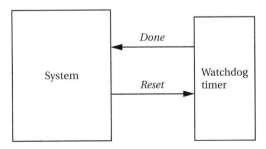

**Figure 1-32** *Watchdog timer.*

### 1.6.3 Novel Attacks and Countermeasures

*physical access*

A key reason that embedded computers are more vulnerable than general-purpose computers is that many embedded computers are physically accessible to attackers. Physical security is an important technique used to secure the information in general-purpose systems—servers are physically isolated from potential attackers. When embedded computers with secure data are physically available, the attacker can gain a great deal more information about the hardware and software. This information not only can be used to attack that particular node but also helps the attacker develop ways to interfere with other nodes of that model.

*Internet attacks*

Some attacks on embedded systems are made much easier by Internet access. Many embedded systems today are connected to the Internet. Viruses can be downloaded, or other sorts of attacks can be perpetrated via the Internet. Siewiorek et al. [Sie04] argue that global volume is a key trend in reliable computing systems. They point out that hundreds of millions of networked devices are sold every year, primarily to users with little or no formal training. The combination of large numbers of devices and untrained users means that many tasks formerly performed in the privacy of a machine room must now be automated and reliably delivered to the masses and that these systems must be designed to shield against both faults and malicious attacks.

*attacks on automobiles*

But many devastating problems can be caused even without Internet access. Consider, for example, attacks on automobiles. Most modern cars uses microprocessors to control their engines, and many other microprocessors are used throughout the car. The software in the engine controller could, for example, be changed to cause the car to stall under certain circumstances. This would be annoying or occasionally dangerous when performed on a single car. If a large number of cars were programmed to all stall at the same time, the resulting traffic accidents could cause significant harm. This sort of programmed accident is arguably worse if only some of the cars on the road have been programmed to stall.

Clearly, a stalling accident could be perpetrated on a wider scale if automobiles provided Internet access to the engine controller software. Prototype cars have demonstrated Internet access to at least part of the car's internal network. However, Internet-enabled cars are not strictly necessary. Auto enthusiasts have reprogrammed engine controllers for more than 20 years to change the characteristics of their engines. A determined attacker could spread viruses through auto repair shops; adding Internet access to the internals of automobiles would open up attacks to a wider variety of perpetrators.

*battery attack*

One novel category of attack is the **battery attack.** This attack tries to disable the node by draining its battery. If a node is operated by a battery, the node's power management system can be subverted by network operations. For example, pinging a node over the Internet may be enough to cause it to operate more often than intended and drain its battery prematurely.

Battery attacks are clearly threats to battery-operated devices such as cell phones and PDAs. Consider, for example, a cell phone virus that causes it to repeatedly make calls. Cell phone viruses have already been reported [Jap05]. But many other devices use batteries even though they also receive energy from the power grid. The battery may be used to run a real-time clock (as is done in many PCs) or to maintain other system states. A battery attack on this sort of device could cause problems that would not be noticed for quite some time.

*QoS attacks*

**Denial-of-service attacks** are well known in general-purpose systems, but real-time embedded systems may be vulnerable to **quality-of-service (QoS) attacks**. If the network delivers real-time data, then small delays in delivery can cause the data to be useless. If that data is used for real-time control, then those small delays can cause the system to fail. We also refer to this threat as a **timing attack** because it changes the real-time characteristics of the system. A QoS or timing attack is powerful because its effects are not limited to just information. The dynamics of the system being controlled help to determine the response of the system. A relatively small change in timing can cause a great deal of damage if a large, heavy, fast-moving object is being controlled.

*attacks on sensor networks*

Wood and Stankovic [Woo02] identified a number of ways, which are briefly described in the following list, to perform denial-of-service attacks on sensor networks at different levels of the network hierarchy.

- **Physical layer**—Jamming, tampering

- **Link layer**—Collision, exhaustion, unfairness

- **Network and routing layer**—Neglect and greed, horning, misdirection, black holes, authorization, probing, redundancy

- **Transport layer**—Flooding, desynchronization

*power attack*

An example of an attack that is much more easily used against embedded computers than general-purpose computers is the **power attack**. Kocher et al. [Koc99] showed that measurements of the power supply current of a CPU can be used to determine a great deal about the processor's internal activity. They developed two methods of power attacks. **Simple power analysis** inspects a trace manually and tries to determine the location of program actions, such as branches, based on knowledge of the power consumption of various CPU operations. Based on program actions, the attacker then deduces bits of the key. **Differential power analysis** uses correlation to identify actions and key bits. This attack was originally aimed at smart cards, which draw their power from the external card reader, but it can be applied to many embedded systems.

*physical security*

In some cases, it may be possible to build tamper-resistant embedded systems. Making the electronic devices difficult to detect and analyze slows down attackers. Limiting information within a chip also helps deter attackers from revealing data.

**Consumer Electronics Architectures**

Consumer electronics devices are increasingly complex and rely on embedded computers to provide services that are not necessarily tied to the core function of the device. Music players may, for example, store files or perform cryptography.

Consumer electronics devices may be connected into networks to make them easier to use and to provide access to audio and video data across the home. This section looks at networks used in consumer devices, then considers the challenges of integrating networks into consumer devices.

### 1.7.1 Bluetooth

*personal area networks*

Bluetooth is a **personal area network** designed to connect devices in close proximity to a person. The Bluetooth radio operates in the 2.5 GHz spectrum. Its wireless links typically operate within 2 meters, although advanced antennas can extend that range to 30 meters. A Bluetooth network can have one master and up to seven active slaves; more slaves can be parked for a total of 255. Although its low-level communication mechanisms do require master–slave synchronization, the higher levels of Bluetooth protocols generally operate as a peer-to-peer network, without masters or slaves.

*transport group protocols*

Figure 1-33 shows the **transport group protocols**, which belong to layers 1 and 2 of the OSI model.

- The physical layer provides basic radio functions.

- The **baseband** layer defines master–slave relationships and frequency hopping.

- The **link manager** provides mechanisms for negotiating link properties such as bandwidth and quality-of-service.

- The **logical link control and adaptation protocol** (**L2CAP**) hides baseband-layer operations such as frequency hopping.

*physical layer*

The Bluetooth radio transmits using frequency-hopping spread spectrum, which allows several radios to operate in the same frequency band without interference. The band is divided into 79 channels that are 1 MHz wide; the Bluetooth radio hops between these frequencies at a rate of 1,600 hops/per second. The radio's transmission power can also be controlled.

*baseband layer*

The baseband layer chooses frequency hops according to a pseudorandom sequence that is agreed on by the radios; it also controls the radio signal strength to ensure that the receiver can properly decode the spread spectrum signal. The baseband layer also provides medium access control, determining packet types

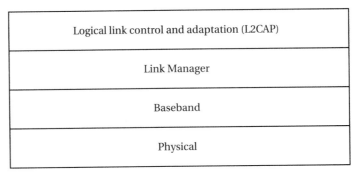

**Figure 1-33** *Bluetooth transport protocols.*

and processing. It controls the radio power, provides a real-time clock, and provides basic security algorithms.

*link manager*    The link manager builds on the baseband layer to provide several functions. It schedules transmissions, choosing which data packets to send next. Transmission scheduling takes QoS contracts into account. It manages overall power consumption. The link manager also manages security and encrypts transmissions as specified.

*L2CAP layer*    The L2CAP layer serves as an interface between general-purpose protocols to the lower levels of the Bluetooth stack. Primarily, it provides asynchronous transmissions. It also allows higher layers to exchange QoS information.

*middleware group protocols*    The **middleware group protocol** provides several widely used protocols. It provides a serial port abstraction for general-purpose communication and protocols to interoperate with IrDA infrared networks. It provides a service discovery protocol. In addition, because Bluetooth is widely used for telephone headsets, it provides a telephony control protocol.

*RFCOMM*    The Bluetooth serial interface is known as RFCOMM. It multiplexes several logical serial communications onto the radio channel. Its signals are compatible with the traditional RS-232 serial standard. It provides several enhancements, including remote status and configuration, specialized status and configuration, and connection establishment and termination. RFCOMM can emulate a serial port within a single device to provide seamless data service whether the ends of the link are on the same processor or not.

*service discovery protocol*    The service discovery protocol allows a Bluetooth client device to determine whether a server device in the network provides a particular service. Services are defined by **service records**, which consists of a set of <ID,value> attributes. All service records include a few basic attributes such as class and protocol stack information. A service may define its own attributes, such as capabilities. To discover a service, the client asks a server for a type of service. The server then responds with a service record.

|         | Bandwidth | Band    |
|---------|-----------|---------|
| 802.11b | 11 Mbps   | 2.4 GHz |
| 802.11a | 54 Mbps   | 5 GHz   |
| 802.11g | 802.11g   | 2.4 GHz |

**Table 1-1** *802.11 specifications*

### 1.7.2 WiFi

The WiFi family of standards (*http://grouper.ieee.org/groups/802/11, http://www.wi-fi.org*) provides wireless data communication for computers and other devices. WiFi is a family of standards known as 802.11 from the IEEE 802 committee. The original 802.11 specification was approved in 1997. An improved version of it, known as 802.11b, was presented in 1999. This standard used improved encoding methods to increase the standard's bandwidth. Later standards include 802.11a, which provided substantially wider bandwidth, and 802.11g, which extended 802.11b. Table 1-1 compares the properties of these networks.

Full-duplex communication requires two radios, one for each direction. Some devices use only one radio, which means that a device cannot transmit and receive simultaneously.

### 1.7.3 Networked Consumer Devices

Networked consumer devices have been proposed for a variety of functions, particularly for home entertainment. These systems have not yet entirely fulfilled their potential. A brief survey helps us understand the challenges in building such systems.

*network organization*

Figure 1-34 shows a typical organization of an entertainment-oriented home network.

■ The PC acts as a server for file storage of music, images, movies, and so on. Today's disk drives are large enough to hold substantial amounts of music or images.

■ Some devices may be permanently attached to the PC. For example, the USB port can be used to send audio to an audio receiver for high-quality amplification.

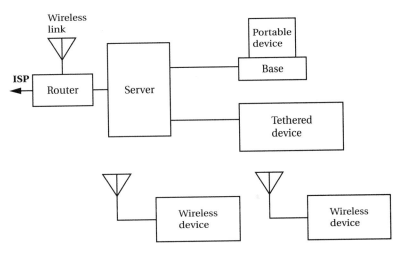

**Figure 1-34** *Networked home entertainment devices.*

- Mobile devices, such as portable music players, can dock with the PC through a base. The PC is used to manage the device.

- Other devices can connect via wireless links. They may connect to the server or to each other. For example, digital video recorders may have their own storage and stream video to other devices.

Several companies have proposed home server devices for audio and video. Built from commodity hardware, these servers provide specialized interfaces for detailing with media. They may also include capture subsystems, such as DVD drives, for reading movies from DVDs.

*configuration*     A key challenge in the design of home entertainment networks is configurability. Consumers do not want to spend time configuring their components for operation on their networks; in many cases, the devices do not have keyboards so configuration is very difficult. Many levels of the network hierarchy must be configured. Clearly, physical and link-level parameters must be configured. But another important aspect of configuration is service discovery and configuration. Each device added to the network must be able to determine which other devices it can work with, which services it can get from other devices, and which services it needs to provide to the rest of the network. Service discovery protocols help devices adapt to the network.

*software*
*architecture*     Java has been used to develop middleware for consumer networks. Java can be efficiently executed on a number of different platforms, which not only simplifies software development but also enables devices to trade Java code to provide services.

## 1.7.4 High-Level Services

Today's consumer devices must provide many advanced services. Some of the services were originally developed for the Internet and are now being pushed down into small devices. Other services are unique to consumer applications.

*service discovery*

**Service discovery** mechanisms have been used on the Internet for quite some time and are now used to simplify the configuration of networks of consumer devices. A service discovery mechanism is a protocol and a data schema. The data schema is used by devices on the network to describe the services they provide. The protocol allows devices to search for nodes on the network that provide the services they desire.

The next example describes the Jini service discovery protocol.

---

**Example 1-7**

*Jini*

Jini (*http://www.jini.org*) [Shi05] is a Java-based network service discovery system. Services are defined by a Java interface type. As such, it need not define an explicit communication protocol.

Jini **lookup services** hold **service proxies** that describe services available on the network. Clients can download these service proxies. The Jini discovery protocol is the method by which Jini services and clients communicate. A service uses the **join protocol** to add itself to the lookup service. It may use either multicast or unicast, depending on the network environment. Generally multicast is used in local area networks and unicast is used in wide area networks.

The service proxy is an implementation of the Java interface type for a particular service. It provides the graphical user interface, the communication protocol necessary to talk to the device, and the device driver.

A client obtains a **lease** for a given service. A lease may be exclusive or shared. The lease is a loose contract that provides the service to the client for a given time period. The timeout implicit in a lease allows the network to recover from a variety of problems.

---

*digital rights management*

**Digital rights management (DRM)** is a newer type of service that has evolved for multimedia applications. **DRM** may be used on PCs or consumer devices; in some cases, a PC is used to manage rights for a handheld device. **DRM** is a protocol that enforces the terms of a license agreement. Because digital media can be copied, copyright owners and media companies have demanded that certain steps be used to limit the ways in which music, movies, and other

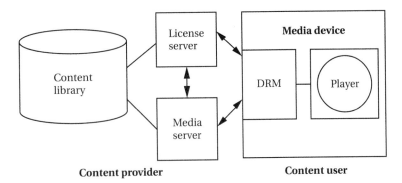

**Figure 1-35** *Architecture of a digital rights management system.*

types of copyrighted material are used in computer systems. A copyrighted work may be sold with a number of restrictions: how many times it can be played, how many machines it can be played on, expiration date, and so on. DRM determines the rights associated with a copyrighted work and enforces those rights on the device.

Digital rights management makes use of cryptography but is itself much more than cryptography. Once an encrypted work has been decrypted, it can be used and modified freely. The DRM system may encrypt both the content and its associated rights information, but it enforces those rights throughout the life of the content and the device on which it is used.

Figure 1-35 illustrates the architecture of a DRM system. The content provider maintains a license server as well as the infrastructure necessary to distribute the copyrighted material itself. A digital rights management module is installed in each media device. The DRM module communicates with the license server to obtain the rights associated with a particular piece of content. The DRM module also communicates with the subsystems in the media device that use the content to ensure that the available rights are enforced.

The next example describes the Windows Media Rights Manager.

## Example 1-8

*Windows Media Rights Manager*

Windows Media Rights Manager is used in Windows Media Player and other multimedia software to enforce digital rights management.

A copyrighted work to be used with Windows Media Rights Manger is packaged by encrypting the content. The key is contained in a license object that is encrypted and separately distributed. A license server authenticates requests for licenses, perhaps by checking for payment or other permissions. The license request may be triggered automatically when the content is first requested to be played, or the license may be requested manually.

Licenses provided by the Windows Media Rights Manager can specify a number of conditions on use, such as expiration date, number of plays, whether the content can be played on a Secure Digital Music Initiative-compliant player, and whether the license can be backed up and restored.

---

## 1.8 Summary and a Look Ahead

The designers of high-performance embedded computing systems are required to master several skills. They must be expert at system specification, not only in the informal sense but also in creating executable models. They must understand the basic architectural techniques for both hardware and software. They must be able to analyze performance and energy consumption for both hardware and software. And they must be able to make trade-offs between hardware and software at all stages in the design process.

*remainder of this book*
The rest of this book will proceed roughly bottom-up from simpler components to complex systems. Chapters 2 through 4 concentrate on single processor systems:

- Chapter 2 will cover CPUs (including the range of microarchitectures available to embedded system designers), processor performance, and power consumption.

- Chapter 3 will look at programs, including languages and design and how to compile efficient executable versions of programs.

- Chapter 4 will study real-time scheduling and operating systems.

Chapters 5 through 7 concentrate on problems specific to multiprocessors:

- In Chapter 5 we will introduce a taxonomy of multiprocessor hardware architectures and the sorts of multiprocessor structures that are useful in optimizing embedded system designs.

- In Chapter 6 we will look at software for multiprocessors.

- Chapter 7 will describe methods for hardware/software co-design, which produces application-specific multiprocessors.

## What We Have Learned

■ Many embedded computing systems are based on standards. The form in which the standard is expressed affects the methodology used to design the embedded system.

■ Embedded systems are vulnerable to new types of security and reliability threats. Embedded computers that perform real-time control pose particular concerns.

## Further Reading

The website *http://www.chiariglione.org* includes an excellent description of MPEG. The team of Lee and Sangiovanni-Vincentelli created the study of models of computation for embedded computing. Siewiorek and Swarz [Sie96] is the classical text on reliable computer system design. Storey [Sto96] provides a detailed description of safety-critical computers. Lee's [Lee **DATE**] book describes digital communication. Ravi et al. [Rav04] survey security challenges and techniques for embedded systems.

## Questions

**Q1-1**   What are the essential characteristics of embedded computing systems?

**Q1-2**   Using commercially available products, give two examples of the following.

   a. Embedded hardware architectures.

   b. Embedded software architectures.

**Q1-3**   Which part of a digital radio provides the most exploitable parallelism: the demodulator or the error corrector? Explain.

**Q1-4**   Can Turbo codes be decoded on a hard real-time deadline? Explain.

**Q1-5**   Draw a data flow diagram for a 4-input, 4-output DCT computation.

**Q1-6**   A video compressor performs motion estimation on $16 \times 16$ macroblocks; the search field is 31 pixels vertically and 41 pixels horizontally.

   a. If we search every point in the search area, how many SAD operations must we perform to find the motion vector for one macroblock?

   b. If we search 16 points in the search area, how many SAD operations must we perform to find the motion vector for one macroblock?

**Q1-7**   Which is more important in an embedded system: throughput or latency? Explain.

**Q1-8** Are hardware designer productivity and software designer productivity related in an embedded system design? Explain.

**Q1-9** Why was the spiral development model considered an improvement on the waterfall model?

**Q1-10** What are the important characteristics of:

a. A software design methodology for embedded computing systems.

b. A hardware design methodology.

c. A complete hardware/software methodology.

**Q1-11** If we use a reference implementation of a standard as the starting point for the implementation of our embedded system for that standard, can we also use the reference implementation to verify the behavior of our design? Explain.

**Q1-12** What are the essential properties of a data flow graph?

**Q1-13** Is it possible to describe the behavior of a DAG-style data flow graph as a finite-state machine? Explain.

**Q1-14** What are the essential properties of a Petri net?

**Q1-15** A pair of processes communicate via a fixed-size buffer. How would you verify that the programs never overflow the buffer? Explain.

**Q1-16** Describe how each of the dependability and security attributes given in Figure 1-29 apply to:

a. An automotive electronics system.

b. A cell phone.

**Q1-17** Plot computation versus communication energy in a wireless network. State your assumptions.

a. Determine the computation and communication required for a node to receive two 16-bit integers and multiply them together.

b. Plot total system energy as a function of computation versus communication energy.

**Q1-18** Modify (EQ 1-8) to compute the MTTF of an embedded computing network with $n$ nodes and a communication bus.

**Q1-19** Which of the actions after faults described in Section 1.6.2 apply to a CD player that has failed to properly read a section of a CD?

**Q1-20** What sorts of embedded systems are vulnerable to battery attacks?

**Q1-21** You are designing a portable media player that must include a digital rights management module. Should you implement the DRM functions on a general-purpose processor or on a specialized cryptoprocessor? Explain.

## Lab Exercises

**L1-1**   Select a device of your choice and determine whether it uses embedded computers. Determine, to the extent possible, the internal hardware architecture of the device.

**L1-2**   Estimate the amount of code includedin a device with an embedded computer.

**L1-3**   How much computation must be done to demodulate a cdma2000 signal?

**L1-4**   How much computation must be done to decompress an MPEG-4 video signal at QCIF ($176 \times 120$) resolution?

**L1-5**   Identify an example embedded computing system that could be described using two different communicating models of computation.

**L1-6**   Develop a system architecture for an Internet-enabled home heating and air conditioning system that is designed to prevent attacks. Consider both Internet attacks and physical attacks.

*Chapter*

# 2

# **CPUs**

- Architectural mechanisms for embedded processors
- Parallelism in embedded CPUs
- Code compression and bus encoding
- Security mechanisms
- CPU simulation
- Configurable processors

## **2.1** **Introduction**

Computer processing units (CPUs) are at the heart of embedded systems. Whether we use one CPU or combine several to build a multiprocessor, instruction set execution provides the combination of efficiency and generality that makes embedded computing powerful.

A number of CPUs have been designed especially for embedded applications or adapted from other uses. We can also use design tools to create CPUs to match the characteristics of an application. In either case, a variety of mechanisms can be used to match the CPU characteristics to the job at hand. Some of these mechanisms are borrowed from general-purpose computing; others have been developed especially for embedded systems.

This chapter begins with a brief introduction to the CPU design space. We then look at the major categories of processors: RISC and DSP in Section 2.3; and VLIW, superscalar, and related methods in Section 2.4. Section 2.5 considers novel variable-performance techniques such as better-than-worst-case design. In Section 2.6 we study the design of memory hierarchies. Section 2.7 looks at additional CPU mechanisms such as code compression and bus encoding. Section 2.8 surveys techniques for CPU simulation. Section 2.9 introduces some methodologies and techniques for the design of custom processors.

# 2.2   Comparing Processors

Choosing a CPU is one of the most important tasks faced by an embedded system designer. Fortunately, designers have a wide range of processors to choose from, allowing them to closely match the CPU to a problem's requirements. They can even design their own CPU. This section briefly looks at the metrics used to evaluate embedded CPUs, before going on to look at some CPUs in more detail.

## 2.2.1   Evaluating Processors

We can judge processors in several ways. Many of these are metrics. However, some evaluation characteristics are harder to quantify.

*performance*    **Performance** is a key characteristic of processors. Different fields tend to use the term "performance" in different ways—for example, image processing tends to use the word to mean image quality. Computer system designers use *performance* to denote the rate at which programs execute.

We can look at computer performance more microscopically, in terms of a window of a few instructions, or macroscopically over large programs. In the microscopic view, we consider either latency or throughput. Figure 2-1 is a

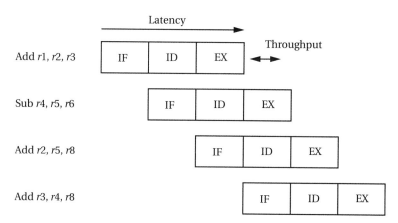

**Figure 2-1** *Latency and throughput in instruction execution.*

simple pipeline diagram that shows the execution of several instructions. In the figure, *latency* refers to the time required to execute an instruction from start to finish, while *throughput* refers to the rate at which instructions are finished. Even if it takes several clock cycles to execute an instruction, the processor may still be able to finish one instruction per cycle.

At the program level, computer architects also speak of **average performance** or **peak performance**. Peak performance is often calculated assuming that instruction throughput proceeds at its maximum rate and all processor resources are fully utilized. There is no easy way to calculate average performance for most processors; it is generally measured by executing a set of benchmarks on sample data.

However, embedded system designers often talk about program performance in terms of **worst-case** (or sometimes **best-case**) **performance**. This is not simply a characteristic of the processor; it is determined for a particular program running on a given processor. As discussed in later chapters, it is generally determined by analysis because of the difficulty of determining an input set that should be used to cause the worst-case execution.

*cost*

*Cost* is another important measure of processors. In this case, we mean the purchase price of the processor. In VLSI design, cost is often measured in terms of the silicon area required to implement a processor, which is closely related to chip cost.

*energy and power*

**Energy** and **power** are key characteristics of CPUs. In modern processors, energy and power consumption must be measured for a particular program and data for accurate results. Modern processors use a variety of techniques to manage energy consumption on-the-fly, meaning that simple models of energy consumption do not provide accurate results.

*nonmetric characteristics*

There are other ways to evaluate processors that are more difficult to measure. **Predictability** is an important characteristic for embedded systems—when designing real-time systems, we want to be able to predict execution time. Because predictability is affected by so many characteristics, ranging from the pipeline to the memory system, it is difficult to come up with a simple predictability model.

*Security* is also an important characteristic of all processors, including embedded processors. Security is inherently unmeasurable because of the fact that we do not know of a successful attack on a system; this does not mean that such an attack cannot exist.

## 2.2.2  A Taxonomy of Processors

We can classify processors along several dimensions. These dimensions interact somewhat, but they help us to choose a processor type based on problem characteristics.

*Flynn's categories*

Flynn [Fly72] created a well-known taxonomy of processors. He classifies processors along two axes: the amount of data being processed and the number of instructions being executed. This taxonomy includes the following categories:

- **Single-instruction, single-data** (**SISD**)—This is more commonly known today as a RISC processor. A single stream of instructions operates on a single set of data.

- **Single-instruction, multiple-data** (**SIMD**)—These machines include several processing elements, each with its own data. However, they all perform the same operations on their data in lockstep. A single program counter can be used to describe execution of all the processing elements.

- **Multiple-instruction, multiple-data** (**MIMD**)—Several processing elements have their own data and their own program counters. The programs do not have to run in lockstep.

- **Multiple-instruction, single-data** (**MISD**)—Few, if any, commercial computers fit this category.

*RISC versus CISC*

**Instruction set style** is one basic characteristic. The RISC/CISC divide is well known. The origins of this dichotomy are related to performance—RISC processors were devised to make processors more easily pipelineable, increasing their throughput. However, instruction set style also has implications for code size, which can be important for cost, and sometimes performance and power consumption as well (through cache utilization). CISC instruction sets tend to give smaller programs than RISC, and tightly encoded instruction sets still exist on some processors that are destined for applications that need small object code.

*single issue versus multiple issue*

**Instruction issue width** is an important aspect of processor performance. Processors that can issue more than one instruction per cycle generally execute programs faster. They do so at the cost of increased power consumption and higher cost.

*static versus dynamic scheduling*

A closely related characteristic is how instructions are issued. **Static scheduling** of instructions is determined when the program is written. In contrast, **dynamic scheduling** determines which instructions are issued at runtime. Dynamically scheduled instruction issue allows the processor to take data-dependent behavior into account when choosing how to issue instructions. **Superscalar** is a common technique for dynamic instruction issue. Dynamic scheduling generally requires a much more complex and costly processor than static scheduling.

*vectors and threads*

Instruction issue width and scheduling mechanisms are only one way to provide parallelism. Many other mechanisms have been developed to provide new types of parallelism and concurrency. **Vector processing** uses instructions that perform on one- or two-dimensional arrays, generally performing operations common in linear algebra. **Multithreading** is a fine-grained concurrency mechanism that allows the processor to quickly switch between several threads of execution.

### 2.2.3  Embedded versus General-Purpose Processors

General-purpose processors are just that—they are designed to work well in a variety of contexts. Embedded processors must be flexible, but they often can be tuned to a particular application. As a result, some of the design precepts that are commonly followed in the design of general-purpose CPUs do not hold for embedded computers. In addition, given the large number of embedded computers sold each year, many application areas make it worthwhile to spend the time to create a customized architecture. Not only are billions of 8-bit processors sold each year, but also hundreds of millions of 32-bit processors are sold for embedded applications. Cell phones alone make the largest single application of 32-bit CPUs.

*RISC versus embedded*

One tenet of RISC design is single-cycle instructions—an instruction spends one clock cycle in each pipeline stage. This ensures that other stages do not stall while waiting for an instruction to finish in one stage. However, the most fundamental goal of processor design is efficient application performance, which can be attained in a number of ways.

One of the consequences of the emphasis on pipelining in RISC is simplified instruction formats that are easy to decode in a single cycle. However, simple instruction formats result in increased code size. The Intel Architecture has a large number of CISC-style instructions with reduced numbers of operands and tight operation coding. Intel Architecture code is among the smallest code available when generated by a good compiler. Code size can affect performance—larger programs make less efficient use of the cache. We discuss code compression in Section 2.7.1, which automatically generates tightly coded instructions; several techniques have been developed to reduce the performance penalty associated with complex instruction decoding steps.

## 2.3  RISC Processors and Digital Signal Processors

In this section, we look at the workhorses of embedded computing, RISC and DSP. Our goal is not to exhaustively describe any particular embedded processor; that task is best left to data sheets and manuals. Instead, we try to describe important aspects of these processors, compare and contrast RISC and DSP approaches to CPU architecture, and consider the different emphases of general-purpose and embedded processors.

### 2.3.1 RISC Processors

Today, the term *RISC* is often used to mean single-issue processor. The term originally came from the comparison to complex instruction set (CISC) architectures. We will consider both aspects of the term.

*pipeline design*    A hallmark of RISC architecture is pipelining. General-purpose processors have evolved longer pipelines as clock speeds have increased. As the pipelines grow longer, the control required for their proper operation becomes more complex. The pipelines of embedded processors have also grown considerably longer with more sophisticated control, as illustrated by the ARM family [Slo04]:

■ The ARM7 uses a three-stage pipeline with fetch, decode, and execute stages. This pipeline requires only very simple control.

■ The ARM9 uses a five-stage pipeline with fetch, decode, ALU, memory access, and register write stages. It does not perform branch prediction.

■ The ARM11 has an eight-stage pipeline. Its structure is shown in Figure 2-2. It performs dynamic branch prediction to make up for the six-cycle penalty of a mispredicted branch. The pipeline has several independent completion stages and its control allows instructions to complete out of order.

The MIPS architecture (*http://www.mips.com*) includes several families. The MIPS32 4K family has a five-stage pipeline. The MIPS32 4KE family includes a DSP application-specific extension. The MIPS32 4KS family is designed for security applications; it includes features to resist power attacks, cryptographic enhancements, and so on.

The PowerPC family is offered by several vendors. The PowerPC 400 series [Ext05] is offered by AMCC and includes several members with varying

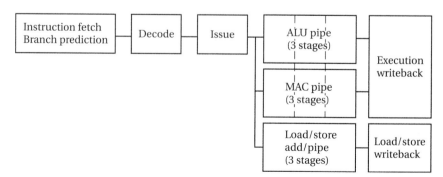

**Figure 2-2** *The ARM11 pipeline [ARM05].*

configurations. Freescale Semiconductor (*http://www.freescale.com*) offers several PowerPC models; the MPC7410, for example, has two integers and one double-precision floating-point unit and can issue two instructions plus one branch per cycle. The IBM PowerPC 970FX [IBM05] is designed for high-frequency operation; it requires sixteen pipeline stages for most fixed-point register-to-register operations, for example.

### 2.3.2  Digital Signal Processors

**Digital signal processor (DSP)**[*] is often used today as a marketing term. However, its original technical meaning still has some utility. The AT&T DSP-16 was the first DSP. As illustrated in Figure 2-3 it introduced two features that define digital signal processors. First, it had an onboard multiplier and provided a multiply–accumulate instruction. At the time the DSP-16 was designed, silicon was still expensive, and the inclusion of a multiplier was a major architectural decision. The multiply–accumulate instruction computes

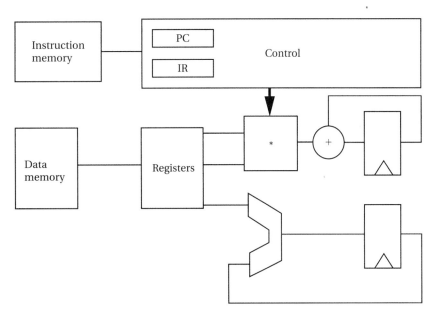

**Figure 2-3**  *A DSP with multiply–accumulate unit and Harvard-architecture.*

---

[*] Unfortunately, the literature uses DSP to mean both digital signal processor (a machine) and digital signal processing (a branch of mathematics).

dest = src1*src2 + src3, a common operation in digital signal processing. Defining the multiply–accumulate instruction made the hardware somewhat more efficient because it eliminated a register, improved code density by combining two operations into a single instruction, and improved performance. Second, the DSP-16 used a Harvard-architecture with separate data and instruction memories. The Harvard structure meant that data accesses could rely on consistent bandwidth from the memory, which is particularly important for sampled-data systems.

Some of the trends evident in RISC architectures also make their way into digital signal processors. For example, high-performance DSPs have very deep pipelines to support high clock rates. A major difference between modern processors used in digital signal processing versus other applications is in both register organization and opcodes. RISC processors generally have large, regular register files, which help simplify pipeline design as well as programming. Many DSPs, in contrast, have smaller general-purpose register files and many instructions that must use only one or a few selected registers. The accumulator is still a common feature of DSP architectures, and other types of instructions may require the use of certain registers as sources or destinations for data. DSPs also often support specialized instructions for digital signal processing operations, such as multiply–accumulate, Viterbi encoding/decoding, and so on.

The next example studies a family of high-performance DSPs.

---

## Example 2-1

*The Texas Instruments C5x DSP Family*

The C5x family [Tex01a; Tex01b] is an architecture for high-performance signal processing. The C5x supports the following features.

- A 40-bit arithmetic unit, which may be interpreted as 32-bit values plus 8 guard bits for improved rounding control. The architecture logic unit (ALU) can also be split to perform two 16-bit operands.

- A barrel shifter performs arbitrary shifts for the ALU.

- A $17 \times 17$ multiplier and adder can perform multiply–accumulate operations.

- A comparison unit compares the high- and low-accumulator words to help accelerate Viterbi encoding/decoding.

- A single-cycle exponent encoder can be used for wide-dynamic-range arithmetic.

- Two dedicated address generators perform address calculations.

The C5x includes a variety of registers, as follows.

- Status registers include flags for arithmetic results, processor status, and so on.

- Auxiliary registers are used to generate 16-bit addresses.

- A temporary register can hold a multiplicand or a shift count.

- A transition register is used for Viterbi operations.

- The stack pointer holds the top of the system stack.

- A circular buffer size register is used for circular buffers common in signal processing.

- Block-repeat registers help implement block-repeat instructions.

- Interrupt registers provide the interface to the interrupt system.

The C5x family defines a variety of addressing modes, as follows.

- The *ARn* mode performs indirect addressing through the auxiliary registers.

- The *DP* mode performs direct addressing from the *DP* register.

- The *K23* mode uses an absolute address.

- Bit instructions provide bit-mode addressing.

The RPT instruction provides single-instruction loops. The instruction provides a repeat count that determines the number of times the instruction that follows is executed. Special registers control the execution of the loop.

The C5x family includes several implementations. The C54x is a lower-performance implementation, while the C55x is a higher-performance implementation. The C54x pipeline has the following six stages.

1. Program prefetch sends the PC value on the program bus.

2. Fetch loads the instruction.

3. The decode stage decodes the instruction.

4. The access step puts operand addresses on the busses.

5. The read step gets the operand values from the bus.

6. The execute step performs the operations.

The C55x microarchitecture includes three data read and two data write busses in addition to the program read bus.

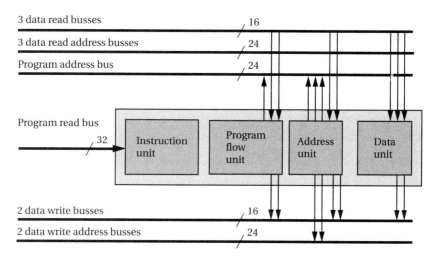

The C55x pipeline, which is divided into two stages as shown here, is longer than that of the C54x, and it has a more complex structure. The fetch stage takes four clock cycles; the execute stage takes seven or eight cycles.

During fetch, the prefetch 1 stage sends an address to memory, while prefetch 2 waits for the response. The fetch stage gets the instruction. Finally, the predecode stage sets up decoding.

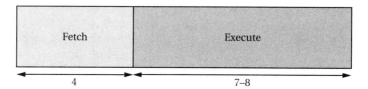

During execution, the decode stage decodes a single instruction or instruction pair. The address stage performs address calculations. Data-access stages send data addresses to memory. The read cycle gets the data values from the bus. The execute stage performs operations and writes registers. Finally, the W and W+ stages write values to memory.

The C55x includes three computation units and fourteen operators. In general, the machine can execute two instructions per cycle. However, some combinations of operations are not legal due to resource constraints.

---

A **co-processor** is an execution unit controlled by the processor's execution unit. (In contrast, an *accelerator* is controlled by registers and is not assigned opcodes.) Co-processors are used in both RISC processors and DSPs, but DSPs include some particularly complex co-processors. Co-processors can be used to extend the instruction set to implement common signal-processing operations. In some cases, the instructions provided by co-processors can be integrated easily into other code. In other cases, the co-processor is designed to execute a particular stream of instructions, and the DSP acts as a sequencer for a complex, multicycle operation.

The next example looks at some co-processors for digital signal processing.

---

## Example 2-2

*TI C55x Co-processor*

The C55x provides three co-processors for use in image processing and video compression: one for pixel interpolation, one for motion estimation, and one for DCT/IDCT computation.

The pixel interpolation co-processor supports half-pixel computations that are often used in motion estimation. Given a set of four pixels, *A*, *B*, *C*, and *D* (as shown in the following figure), we want to compute the intermediate pixels *U*, *M*, and *R*.

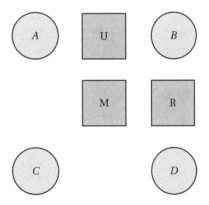

Two instructions support this task. The first one loads pixels and computes

ACy = copr(K8,AC,Lmem)

K8 is a set of control bits. The other loads pixels, computes, and stores, as follows.

ACy = copr(K8,ACx,Lmem) || Lmem = ACz

The motion estimation co-processor is built around a stylized usage pattern. It supports full search and three heuristic search algorithms: three-step, four-step, and four-step with half-pixel refinement. It can produce either one motion vector for a $16 \times 16$ macroblock or four motion vectors for four $8 \times 8$ blocks. The basic motion estimation instruction has this form

[ACx,ACy] = copr(K8,ACx,ACy,Xmem,Ymem,Coeff)

where ACx and ACy are the accumulated sum-of-differences, K8 is a set of control bits, and Xmem and Ymem point to odd and even lines of the search window.

The DCT co-processor implements functions for one-dimensional DCT and IDCT computation. The unit is designed to support $8 \times 8$ DCT/IDCT, and a particular sequence of instructions must be used to ensure that data operands are available at the required times. The co-processor provides three types of instructions: load, compute, and transfer to accumulators; compute, transfer, and write to memory; and special.

As shown in the following figure, several iterations of the DCT/IDCT loop are pipelined in the co-processor when the proper sequence of instructions is used.

## **2.4**  Parallel Execution Mechanisms

In this section, we look at various ways that processors perform operations in parallel. We consider very long instruction word and superscalar processing, subword parallelism, vector processing, and thread-level parallelism. We end this section with a brief consideration of the available parallelism in some embedded applications.

### 2.4.1  Very Long Instruction Word Processors

**Very long instruction word** (**VLIW**) architectures were originally developed as general-purpose processors but have seen widespread use in embedded systems. VLIW architectures provide instruction-level parallelism with relatively low hardware overhead.

*VLIW basics*    Figure 2-4 shows a simplified version of a VLIW processor to introduce the basic principles of the technique. The execution unit includes a pool of function units connected to a large register file. Using today's terminology for VLIW machines, we say the execution unit reads a **packet** of instructions—each instruction in the packet can control one of the function units in the machine. In an ideal VLIW machine, all instructions in the packet are executed simultaneously; in modern machines, it may take several cycles to retire all the instructions in the packet. Unlike a superscalar processor, the order of execution is determined by the structure of the code and how instructions are grouped into packets; the next packet will not begin execution until all the instructions in the current packet have finished.

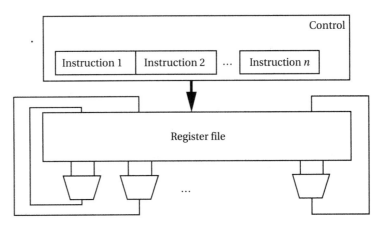

**Figure 2-4** *Structure of a generic VLIW processor.*

Because the organization of instructions into packets determines the schedule of execution, VLIW machines rely on powerful compilers to identify parallelism and schedule instructions. The compiler is responsible for enforcing resource limitations and their associated scheduling policies. In compensation, the execution unit is simpler because it does not have to check for many resource interdependencies.

The ideal VLIW is relatively easy to program because of its large, uniform register file. The register file provides a communication mechanism between the function units since each function unit can read operands from and write results to any register in the register file.

*split register files*    Unfortunately, it is difficult to build large, fast register files with many ports. As a result, many modern VLIW machines use partitioned register files, as shown in Figure 2-5. In the figure, the registers have been split into two register files, each of which is connected to two function units. The combination of a register file and its associated function units is sometimes called a **cluster**. A cluster bus can be used to move values between the register files. Register file-to-register file movement is performed under program control using explicit instructions. As a result, partitioned register files make the compiler's job more difficult. The compiler must partition values among the register files, determine when a value has to be copied from one register file to another, generate the required move instructions, and adjust the schedules of the other operations to wait for the values to appear. However, the characteristics of VLIW circuits often require designing partitioned register file architectures.

*uses of VLIW*    VLIW machines have been used in applications with a great deal of data parallelism. The Trimedia family of processors, for example, was designed for use in video systems. Video algorithms often perform similar operations on several pixels at time, making it relatively easy to generate parallel code.

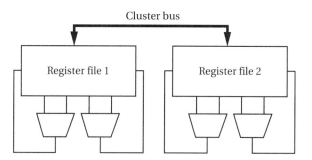

**Figure 2-5** *Split register files in a VLIW machine.*

VLIW machines have also been used for signal processing and networking. Cell phone baseband systems, for example, must perform the same signal processing on many channels in parallel; the same instructions can be performed on separate data streams using VLIW architectures. Similarly, networking systems must perform the same or similar operations on several packets at the same time.

Example 2-3 describes a VLIW digital signal processor. Example 2-4 describes another VLIW machine.

## Example 2-3

*Texas Instruments C6x VLIW DSP*

The TI C6x is a VLIW processor designed for digital signal processing. Here is the block diagram of the C6x chip.

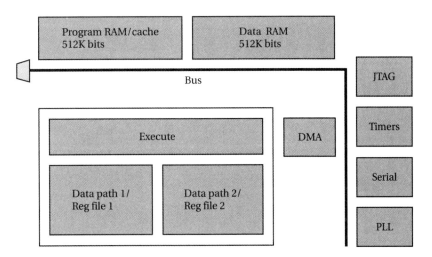

The chip includes an onboard program and a data RAM as well as standard devices and DMA. The processor core includes two clusters, each with the same configuration. Each register file holds 16 words. Each data path has eight function units: two load units, two store units, two data address units, and two register file cross paths.

**Example 2-4**

*Freescale Starcore SC140 VLIW Core*

The Starcore architecture was jointly designed by Motorola (now Freescale Semiconductor) and Agere. The SC140 (http://www.freescale.com) is an implementation of the Starcore architecture; the SC140 is a core that can be used in chip designs.

Like the C6x, the SC140 is organized into two clusters. But unlike the C6x, the two clusters in the SC140 perform different functions. One cluster is for data operations; it includes four data ALUs and a register file. The other cluster is for address operations; it includes two address operation units and its own register file.

The MC8126 is a chip that includes four SC140 cores along with shared memory.

## 2.4.2 Superscalar Processors

Superscalar processors issue more than one instruction per clock cycle. Unlike VLIW processors, they check for resource conflicts on-the-fly to determine which combinations of instructions can be issued at each step. Superscalar architectures dominate desktop and server architectures. Superscalar processors are not as common in the embedded world as in the desktop/server world. Embedded computing architectures are more likely to be judged by metrics, such as operations per watt, rather than raw performance.

*example superscalar embedded processors*

A surprising number of embedded processors do, however, make use of superscalar instruction issue, though not as aggressively as do high-end servers. The embedded Pentium processor is a two-issue, in-order processor. It has two pipes: one for any integer operation and another for simple integer operations. We saw in Section 2.3.1 that other embedded processors also use superscalar techniques.

## 2.4.3 SIMD and Vector Processors

Many applications present data-level parallelism that lends itself to efficient computing structures. Furthermore, much of this data is relatively small, which allows us to build more parallel-processing units to soak up more of that available parallelism.

*data operand*
*sizes*

A variety of studies have shown that many of the variables used in most programs have small dynamic ranges. Figure 2-6 shows the results of one such study by Fritts [Fri00]. He analyzed the data types of programs in the Media-Bench benchmark suite [Lee97]. The results show that 8-bit (byte) and 16-bit (halfword) operands dominate this suite of programs. If we match the function unit widths to the operand sizes, we can put more function units in the available silicon than if we simply used wide-word function units to perform all operations.

*subword*
*parallelism*

One technique that exploits small operand sizes is **subword parallelism** [Lee94]. The processor's ALU can operate in normal mode, or it can be split into several smaller ALUs. An ALU can easily be split by breaking the carry chain so that bit slides operate independently. Each subword can operate on independent data; the operations are all controlled by the same opcode. Because the same instruction is performed on several data values, this technique is often referred to as a form of SIMD.

*vectorization*

Another technique for data parallelism is **vector processing**. Vector processors have been used in scientific computers for decades; they use specialized instructions designed to efficiently perform operations such as dot products on vectors of values. Vector processing does not rely on small data values, but vectors of smaller data types can perform more operations in parallel on available hardware, particularly when subword parallelism methods are used to manage data path resources.

The next example describes a widely used vector processing architecture.

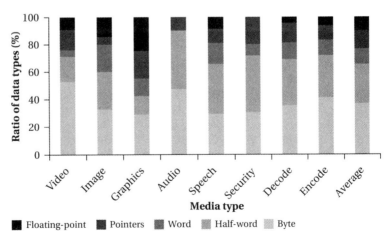

**Figure 2-6**  *Operand sizes in MediaBench benchmarks. From Fritts [Fri00].*

---

## Example 2-5

*Motorola AltiVec Vector Architecture*

The AltiVec vector architecture [Ful98] was defined by Motorola (now Freescale Semiconductor) for the PowerPC architecture. AltiVec provides a 128-bit vector unit that can be divided into operands of several sizes: four operands of 32 bits, eight operands of 16 bits, or sixteen operands of 8 bits. A register file provides thirty-two 128-bit vectors to the vector unit. The architecture defines a number of operations, including logical and arithmetic operands within an element as well as inter-element operations such as permutations.

---

## 2.4.4   Thread-Level Parallelism

Processors can also exploit thread- or task-level parallelism. It may be easier to find thread-level parallelism, particularly in embedded applications. The behavior of threads may be more predictable than instruction-level parallelism.

*varieties of multithreading*    Multithreading architectures must provide separate registers for each thread. But because switching between threads is stylized, the control required for multithreading is relatively straightforward. **Hardware multithreading** alternately fetches instructions from separate threads. On one cycle, it fetches several instructions from one thread, fetching enough instructions to be able to keep the pipelines full in the absence of interlocks. On the next cycle, it fetches instructions from another thread. **Simultaneous multithreading** (**SMT**) fetches instructions from several threads on each cycle rather than alternating between threads.

The next example describes a multithreading processor designed for cell phones.

---

## Example 2-6

*Sandbridge Sandblaster Multithreaded CPU*

The Sandblaster processor [Glo03; Glo05] is designed for mobile communications. It processes four threads, as depicted in the following figure.

The Sandblaster uses 64-bit compound instructions that efficiently but non-orthogonally allows multiple operations to be specified in an instruction. A 4 × 16-bit vector unit is time-scheduled among threads. The machine is fully interlocked, blocking operations based on resource constraints. The architecture is multithreaded using a technique called **token-triggered threading**. This method allows several hardware contexts to execute simultaneously, but only one context at a time can issue an instruction on a cycle boundary. On each cycle, a token indicates the next context to execute, allowing both round-robin or non-round-robin scheduling of threads.

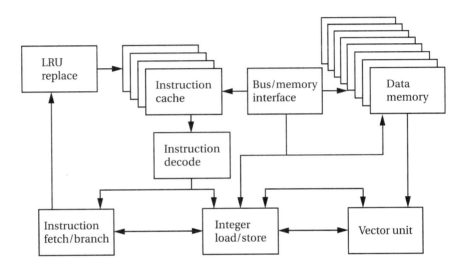

*From:* Glossner et al. [Glo03] © 2003 IEEE.

## 2.4.5 Processor Resource Utilization

The choice of processor architecture depends in part on the characteristics of the programs to be run on the processor. In many embedded applications, we can leverage our knowledge of the core algorithms to choose effective CPU architectures. However, we must be careful to understand the characteristics of those applications. As an example, many researchers assume that multimedia

*measurements on multimedia benchmarks*

algorithms exhibit embarrassing levels of parallelism. Experiments show that this is not necessarily the case.

Tallu et al. [Tal03] evaluated the instruction-level parallelism available in multimedia applications. As shown in Figure 2-7, they evaluated several different processor configurations using SimpleScalar. They measured nine benchmark programs on the various architectures. The bar graphs show the instructions per cycle for each application; most applications exhibit fewer than four instructions per cycle.

Fritts [Fri00] studied the characteristics of loops in the MediaBench suite [Lee97]. Figure 2-8, shows two measurements; in each case, results are shown with the benchmark programs grouped into categories based on their primary function. The first measurement shows the average number of iterations of a

| Parameters | 2-way | 4-way | 8-way | 16-way |
|---|---|---|---|---|
| Feich width, decode width, issue width, and common width | 2 | 4 | 8 | 16 |
| RUU Size | 32 | 64 | 128 | 256 |
| Load store queue | 16 | 32 | 64 | 128 |
| Integer ALUs (latency/recovery = 1/J) | 2 | 4 | 8 | 16 |
| Integer Multipliers (latency/recovery = 3/I) | 1 | 2 | 4 | 8 |
| Load Store ports (latency/recovery = 1/J) | 2 | 4 | 8 | 16 |
| L1 I-cache (size in KB, bit time, associativity, block size in bytes) | 16,1,4,32 | 16,1,4,32 | 16,1,4,32 | 32,1,4,64 |
| L1 D-cache (size in KB, bit time, associativity, block size in bytes) | 16,1,4,32 | 16,1,4,32 | 16,1,4,32 | 16,1,4,32 |
| L2 unified cache (size in KB, bit time, associativity, block size) | 256,6,4,64 | 256,6,4,64 | 256,6,4,64 | 256,6,4,64 |
| Main memory width | 64 bits | 128 bits | 256 bits | 256 bits |
| Main memory latency (first chunk, next chunk) | 65, 4 | 65, 4 | 65, 4 | 65, 4 |
| Branch predictor-bimodal (size, BTH size) | 2K, 2K | 2K, 2K | 2K, 2K | 2K, 2K |
| **SIMD ALUs** | 2 | 4 | 8 | 16 |
| **SIMD Multipliers** | 1 | 2 | 4 | 8 |

**Processor configurations**

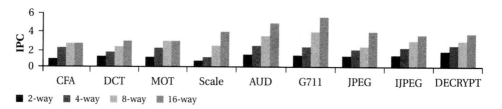

| | CFA | DCT | MOT | Scale | AUD | G711 | JPEG | IJPEG | DECRYPT |
|---|---|---|---|---|---|---|---|---|---|
| 4-way | <1% | <1% | <1% | <2% | <4% | <1% | <1% | <1% | <1% |
| 8-way | <1% | <1% | <1% | <3% | <1% | <1% | <1% | <1% | <1% |
| 16-way | <1% | <1% | <1% | <1% | <1% | <1% | <1% | <1% | <1% |

**Results**

**Figure 2-7** *An evaluation of the available parallelism in multimedia applications. From Talla et al. [Tal03] © 2003 IEEE.*

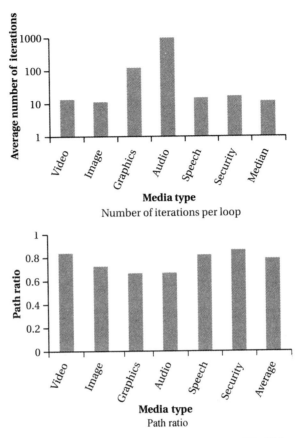

**Figure 2-8** *Dynamic behavior of loops in MediaBench. After Fritts [Fri00].*

loop; fortunately, loops on average are executed many times. The second measurement shows **path ratio**, which is defined as

$$\frac{Number\ of\ loop\ body\ instructions\ executed}{Total\ number\ of\ instructions\ in\ loop\ body} \times 100 .\qquad \text{(EQ 2-1)}$$

Path ratio measures the percentage of a loop's instructions that are actually executed. The average path ratio over all the MediaBench benchmarks was 78%, which means that 22% of the loop instructions were not executed.

*multimedia*
*algorithms*

These results should not be surprising given the nature of modern embedded algorithms. Modern signal-processing algorithms have moved well beyond filtering. Many algorithms use control to improve performance. The large specifications for multimedia standards naturally result in complex programs.

*implications for CPUs*

To take advantage of the available parallelism in multimedia and other embedded applications, we need to match the processor architecture to the application characteristics. These experiments suggest that processor architectures must exploit parallelism at several levels of abstraction.

## 2.5 Variable-Performance CPU Architectures

Because so many embedded systems must meet real-time deadlines, predictable execution time is a critical feature of the components used in them. However, traditional computer architecture designs have emphasized average performance over worst-case performance, producing processors that are fast on average but whose worst-case performance is hard to bound. This often leads to conservative designs of both hardware (oversized caches, faster processors) and software (simplified coding, restricted use of instructions).

As both power consumption and reliability have become even more important, new techniques have been developed that make processor behavior extremely complex. Those techniques are finding their way into embedded processors even though they make designs more difficult to analyze. This section surveys two important developments: dynamic voltage and frequency scaling and better-than-worst-case design. We explore the implications of these features and how to use them to advantage in later chapters.

### 2.5.1 Dynamic Voltage and Frequency Scaling

*DVFS*

**Dynamic voltage and frequency scaling (DVFS)** [Wei94] is a popular technique for controlling CPU power consumption that takes advantage of the wide operating range of CMOS digital circuits. Unlike many other digital circuit families, CMOS circuits can operate at a wide range of voltages [Wol02]. Furthermore, CMOS circuits operate more efficiently at lower voltages.

*CMOS circuit characteristics*

The delay of a CMOS gate is close to linear function of power supply voltage [Gon97]. The energy consumed during operation of the gate is proportional to the square of the operating voltage

$$E \propto CV^2. \tag{EQ 2-2}$$

The speed–power product for CMOS (ignoring leakage) is also $CV^2$. Therefore, by lowering the power supply voltage, we can reduce energy consumption by $V^2$ while reducing performance by only $V$.

Because we can operate CMOS logic at many different points, a CPU can be operated within an envelope. Figure 2-9 illustrates the relationship between power supply voltage ($V$), operating speed ($T$), and power ($P$).

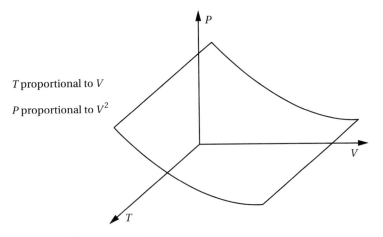

$T$ proportional to $V$

$P$ proportional to $V^2$

**Figure 2-9** *The voltage/speed/power operating space.*

*DVFS architecture*

An architecture for dynamic voltage and frequency scaling operates the CPU within this space under a control algorithm. Figure 2-10 shows the architecture of a DVFS architecture. The clock and power supply are generated by circuits that can supply a range of values; these circuits generally operate at discrete points rather than at continuously varying values. Both the clock generator and voltage generator are operated by a controller that determines when the clock frequency and voltage will change and by how much.

*DVFS control strategy*

A DVFS controller must operate under constraints in order to optimize a design metric. The constraints are related to clock speed and power supply voltage: not only their minimum and maximum values, but also how quickly clock

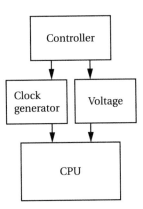

**Figure 2-10** *Dynamic voltage and frequency scaling (DVFS) architecture.*

speed or power supply voltage can be changed. The design metric may be either to maximize performance given an energy budget or to minimize energy given a performance bound.

While it is possible to encode the control algorithm in hardware, the control method is generally set at least in part by software. Registers can set the value of certain parameters. More generally, the complete control algorithm can be implemented in software.

The next example describes voltage scaling features in a modern embedded processor.

---

**Example 2-7**

*Dynamic Voltage and Frequency Scaling in the Intel XScale*

The Intel XScale [Int00] is compliant with ARM version 5TE. Operating voltage and clock frequency can be controlled by setting bits CP 14, registers 6 and 7, respectively. Software can use this programming model interface to implement a selected DVFS policy.

---

## 2.5.2  Better-Than-Worst-Case Design

Digital systems are traditionally designed as synchronous systems governed by clocks. The clock period is determined by careful analysis so that values are stored into registers properly, with the clock period extended to cover the worst-case delay. In fact, the worst-case delay is relatively rare in many circuits and the logic sits idle for some period most of the time.

*Razor Micro-architecture*

**Better-than-worst-case design** is an alternative design style in which logic detects and recovers from errors, allowing the circuit to run most of the time at a higher speed. The Razor architecture [Ern03] is one architecture for better-than-worst-case performance.

Razor uses a specialized register, shown in Figure 2-11, that measures and evaluates errors. The system register holds the latched value and is clocked at the higher-than-worst-case clock rate. A separate register is clocked separately and slightly behind the system register. If the results stored in the two registers are different, then an error occurred, probably due to timing. The XOR gate measures that error and causes the latter value to replace the value in the system register.

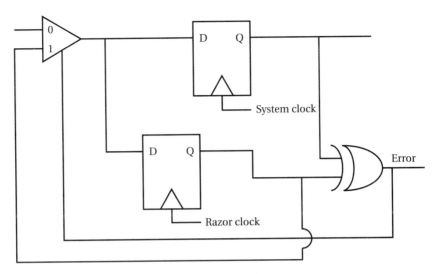

**Figure 2-11** *A Razor latch.*

The Razor microarchitecture does not cause an erroneous operation to be recalculated in the same stage. Rather, it forwards the operation to a later stage. This avoids having a stage with a systematic problem stall the pipeline with an indefinite number of recalculations.

## 2.6  Processor Memory Hierarchy

The memory hierarchy is a critical determinant of overall system performance and power consumption. This section reviews some basic concepts in the design of memory hierarchies and how they can be exploited in the design of embedded processors. We start by introducing a basic model of memory components that can be used to evaluate various hardware and software design strategies. We then consider the design of register files and caches. We end with a discussion of scratch pad memories, which have been proposed as adjuncts to caches in embedded processors.

### 2.6.1  Memory Component Models

To evaluate some memory design methods, we need models for the physical properties of memories: area, delay, and energy consumption. Because a variety

*memory block*
*structure*

of structures at different levels of the memory hierarchy are built from the same components, we can use a single model throughout the memory hierarchy and for different types of memory circuits.

Figure 2-12 shows a generic structural model for a two-dimensional memory block. This model does not depend on the details of the memory circuit and so applies to various types of dynamic RAM, static RAM, and read-only memory. The basic unit of storage is the **memory cell**. Cells are arranged in a two-dimensional array. This memory model describes the relationships between the cells and their associated access circuitry.

Within the memory core, cells are connected to row and bit lines that provide a two-dimensional addressing structure. The row line selects a one-dimensional row of cells, which then can be accessed (read or written) via their bit lines. When a row is selected, all the cells in that row are active. In general, there may be more than one bit line, since many memory circuits use both the true and complementary forms of the bit.

The row decoder circuitry is a demultiplexer that drives one of the *n* row lines in the core by decoding the *r* bits of row address. A column decoder selects a *b*-bit wide subset of the bit lines based on the *c* bits of column address. Some memories also require precharge circuits to control the bit lines.

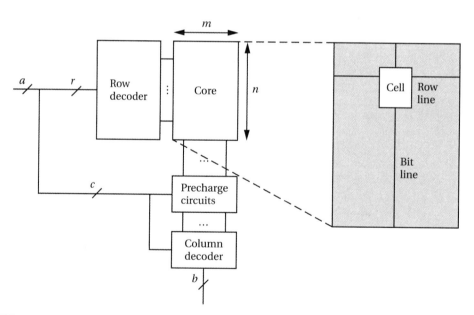

**Figure 2-12** *Structural model of a memory block.*

*area model*    The area model of the memory block has the following components for the elements of the block model.

$$A = A_r + A_x + A_p + A_c \qquad \text{(EQ 2-3)}$$

The row decoder area is

$$A_r = a_r n, \qquad \text{(EQ 2-4)}$$

where $a_r$ is the area of a one-bit slice of the row decoder. The core area is

$$A_x = a_x mn, \qquad \text{(EQ 2-5)}$$

where $a_x$ is the area of a one-bit core cell, including its share of the row and bit lines. The precharge circuit area is

$$A_p = a_p n, \qquad \text{(EQ 2-6)}$$

where $a_p$ is the area of a one-bit slice of the precharge circuit. The column decoder area is

$$A_c = a_c n, \qquad \text{(EQ 2-7)}$$

where $a_c$ is the area of a one-bit slice of the column decoder.

*delay model*    The delay model of the memory block follows the flow of information in a memory access. Some of its elements are independent of $m$ and $n$ while others depend on the length of the row or column lines in the cell:

$$\Delta = \Delta_{setup} + \Delta_r + \Delta_x + \Delta_{bit} + \Delta_c. \qquad \text{(EQ 2-8)}$$

$\Delta_{setup}$ is the time required for the precharge circuitry. It is generally independent of the number of columns but may depend on the number of rows due to the time required to precharge the bit line. $\Delta$ is the row decoder time, including the row line propagation time. The delay through the decoding logic generally depends on the value of $m$, but the dependence may vary due to the type of decoding circuit used. $\Delta_x$ is the reaction time of the core cell itself. $\Delta_{bit}$ is the time required for the values to propagate through the bit line. $\Delta_c$ is the delay through the column decoder, which once again may depend on the value of $n$.

*energy model*    The energy model must include both static and dynamic components. The dynamic component follows the structure of the block to determine the total energy consumption for a memory access.

$$E_D = E_r + E_x + E_p + E_c, \qquad \text{(EQ 2-9)}$$

given the energy consumptions of the row decoder, core, precharge circuits, and column decoder. The core energy depends on the values of $m$ and $n$ due to the row and bit lines. The decoder circuitry energy also depends on $m$ and $n$, though the details of that relationship depend on the circuits used.

The static component $E_S$ models the standby energy consumption of the memory. The details vary for different types of memories, but the static component can be significant. The total energy consumption is

$$E = E_D + E_S. \tag{EQ 2-10}$$

*multiported memories*

This model describes a single-port memory in which a single read or write can be performed at any given time. A **multiport memory** accepts multiple addresses and data for simultaneous accesses. Some aspects of the memory block model extend easily to multiport memories. However, delay for a multiport memory is a nonlinear function of the number of ports. The exact relationship depends on the detail of the core circuit design, but the memory cell core circuits introduce nonlinear delay as ports are added to the cell. Figure 2-13 shows the results of one set of simulation experiments that measured the delay of a multiport SRAM as a function of the number of ports and memory size [Dut98].

*cache models*

Energy models for caches are particularly important in CPU and program design. Kamble and Ghose [Kam97] developed an analytical model of power consumption in caches. Given an $m$-way set associative cache with a capacity of $D$ bytes, a tag size of $T$ bits and a line size of $L$ bytes, with $St$ status bits per block frame, they divide the cache energy consumption into several components.

- **Bit line energy**

$$\begin{aligned} E_{bit} = 0.5\, V^2_{DD}\, [N_{bit,pr} \cdot C_{bit,pr} + N_{bit,w} \cdot C_{bit,rw} \\ + N_{bit,r} \cdot C_{bit,rw} + m(8L + t + St)\, CA\, (C_{g,Qpa} \\ + C_{g,Qpa} + C_{g,Qpa})], \end{aligned} \tag{EQ 2-11}$$

where $N_{bit,pr}$, $N_{bit,r}$, and $N_{bit,w}$ are the number of bit line transitions due to precharging, reads, and writes; $C_{bit,pr}$ and $C_{bit,rw}$ are the capacitance of the bit lines during precharging and read/write operations; and $CA$ is the number of cache accesses.

- **Word line energy**

$$E_{word} = V^2_{DD} \cdot CA \cdot m(8L + t + St)\, (2C_{g,Q1} + C_{wordwire}), \tag{EQ 2-12}$$

where $C_{g,Q1}$ is the gate capacitance of the access transistor for the bit line and $C_{wordwire}$ is the capacitance of the word line.

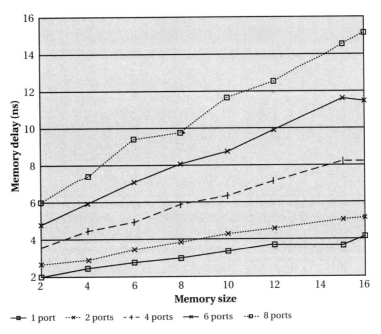

**Figure 2-13** *Memory delay as a function of number of ports. From Dutta et al. [Dut98]*
*© 1998 IEEE.*

- **Output line energy**—Total output energy is divided into address and data
  line dissipation and may occur when driving lines either toward the CPU or
  toward memory. The *N* values are the number of transitions (*d2m* for data to
  memory, *d2c* for data to CPU, for example), and the *C* values are the corresponding capacitive loads.

$$E_{aoutput} = 0.5\ V^2_{DD}\ (N_{out,a2m}C_{out,a2m} + N_{out,a2c}C_{out,a2c}) \qquad \text{(EQ 2-13)}$$

$$E_{doutput} = 0.5\ V^2_{DD}\ (N_{out,d2m}C_{out,d2m} + N_{out,d2c}C_{out,d2c}) \qquad \text{(EQ 2-14)}$$

- **Address input lines**

$$E_{ainput} = 0.5\ V^2_{DD}N_{ainput}[(m + 1)2SC_{in,dec} + C_{awire}], \qquad \text{(EQ 2-15)}$$

where $N_{ainput}$ is the number of transitions in the address input lines, $C_{in,dec}$ is
the gate capacitance of the first decoder level, and $C_{awire}$ is the capacitance
of the wires that feed the RAM banks.

Kamble and Ghose developed formulas to derive the number of transitions in
various parts of the cache based on the overall cache activity.

Shiue and Chakrabarti [Shi89b] developed a simpler cache model that they showed gave results similar to the Kamble and Ghose model. Their model used several definitions: *add_bs* is the number of transitions on the address bus per instruction; *data_bs* is the number of transitions on the data bus per instruction; *word_line_size* is the number of memory cells on a word line; *bit_line_size* is the number of memory cells in a bit line; *Em* is the energy consumption of a main memory access; $\alpha$, $\beta$, $\gamma$ are technology parameters. The energy consumption is given by

$$Energy = hit\_rate * energy\_hit + miss\_rate * energy\_miss \quad \text{(EQ 2-16)}$$

$$Energy\_hit = E\_dec + E\_cell \quad \text{(EQ 2-17)}$$

$$Energy\_miss = E\_dec + E\_cell + E\_io + E\_main$$
$$= Energy\_hit + E\_io + E\_main \quad \text{(EQ 2-18)}$$

$$E\_dec = \alpha * add\_bs \quad \text{(EQ 2-19)}$$

$$E\_+dell = \beta * word\_line\_size * bit\_line\_size \quad \text{(EQ 2-20)}$$

$$E\_io = \gamma * (data\_bs * cache\text{-}line\_size + add\_bs) \quad \text{(EQ 2-21)}$$

$$E\_main = \gamma * data\_bs * cache\_line\_size$$
$$+ Em * cache\_line\_size \quad \text{(EQ 2-22)}$$

*busses*
We may also want to model the bus that connects the memory to the remainder of the system. Busses present large capacitive loads that introduce significant delay and energy penalties.

*memory arrays*
Larger memory structures can be built from memory blocks. Figure 2-14 shows a simple wide memory in which several blocks are accessed in parallel from the same address lines. A set-associative cache could be constructed from

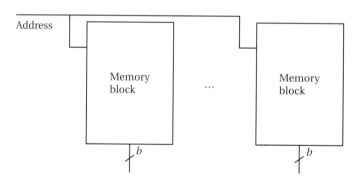

**Figure 2-14** *A memory array built from memory blocks.*

this array—for example, by a multiplexer that selects the data from the block that corresponds to the appropriate set. Parallel memories can be built by feeding separate addresses to different memory blocks.

## 2.6.2 Register Files

The register file is the first stage of the memory hierarchy. Although the size of the register file is fixed when the CPU is predesigned, if we design our own CPUs then we can select the number of registers based on the application requirements. Register file size is a key parameter in CPU design that affects code performance and energy consumption as well as the area of the CPU.

*sweet spot in register file design*

Register files that are either too large or too small relative to the application's needs mean extra costs. If the register file is too small, the program must **spill** values to main memory: the value is written to main memory and later read back from main memory. Spills cost both time and energy because main memory accesses are slower and more energy-intense than register file accesses. If the register file is too large, then it consumes static energy as well as taking extra chip area that could be used for other purposes.

*register file parameters*

The most important parameters in register file design are number of words and number of ports. Word width affects register file area and energy consumption but is not closely coupled to other design decisions. The number of words more directly determines area, energy, and performance. The number of ports is important because, as noted before, delay is a nonlinear function of the number of ports. This nonlinear dependency is the key reason that many VLIW machines use partitioned register files.

Wehmeyer et al. [Weh01] studied the effects of varying register file size on program dynamic behavior. They compiled a number of benchmark programs and used profiling tools to analyze their behavior. Figure 2-15 shows performance and energy consumption as a function of register file size. In both cases, overly small register files result in nonlinear penalties whereas large register files present little benefit.

## 2.6.3 Caches

Cache design has received a lot of attention in general-purpose computer design. Most of the lessons apply to embedded computers as well, but because we may design the CPU to meet the needs of a particular set of applications, we can pay extra attention to the relationship between the cache configuration and the programs that use it.

*sweet spot in cache design*

As with register files, caches have a sweet spot that is neither too small nor too large. Li and Henkel [Li98] measured the influence of caches on energy con-

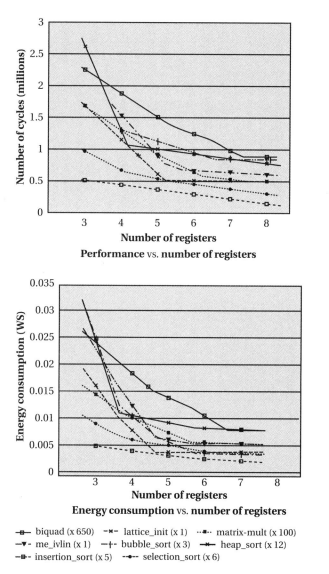

**Figure 2-15** *Performance and energy consumption as a function of register file size. From Wehmeyer et al. [Weh01] © 2001 IEEE.*

sumption in detail. Figure 2-16 shows the energy consumption of a CPU running an MPEG encoder. Energy consumption has a global minimum: too-small caches result in excessive main memory accesses; too-large caches consume excess static power.

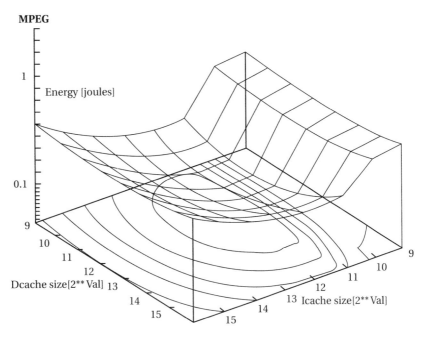

**Figure 2-16** *Energy consumption versus instruction/data cache size for an MPEG benchmark program. From Li and Henkel [Li98] © 1998 ACM. Reprinted by permission.*

*cache parameters and behavior*

The most basic cache parameter is total cache size. Larger caches can hold more data or instructions at the cost of increased area and static power consumption. Given a fixed number of bits in the cache, we can vary both the set associativity and the line size. Splitting a cache into more sets allows us to independently reference more locations that map onto similar cache locations at the cost of mapping more memory addresses into a given cache line. Longer cache lines provide more prefetching bandwidth, which is useful in some algorithms but not others.

*cache parameter selection*

Line size affects prefetching behavior—programs that access successive memory locations can benefit from the prefetching induced by long cache lines. Long lines can also, in some cases, provide reuse for very small sets of locations. **Set-associative caches** are most effective for programs with large working sets or working sets made of several disjoint sections.

Panda et al. [Pan99] developed an algorithm to explore the memory hierarchy design space and to allocate program variables within the memory hierarchy. They allocated frequently used scalar variables to the register file. They used the following classification of Wolfe and Lam [Wol91a] to analyze the behavior of arrays.

- **Self-temporal** reuse—The same array element is accessed in different loop iterations.

- **Self-spatial** reuse—The same cache line is accessed in different loop iterations.

- **Group-temporal** reuse—Different parts of the program access the same array element.

- **Group-spatial** reuse—Different parts of the program access the same cache line.

This classification system treats temporal reuse (the same data element) as a special case of spatial reuse (the same cache line). It divides memory references into equivalence classes, with each class containing a set of references with self-spatial and group-spatial reuse. The equivalence classes allowed Panda et al. to estimate the number of cache misses required by those references. They assume that spatial locality can result in reuse if the number of memory references in the loop is less than the cache size. Group-spatial locality is possible when a row fits into a cache and the other data elements used in the loop are smaller than the cache size. Two sets of accesses are compatible if their index expressions differ by a constant.

Gordon-Ross et al. [Gor04] developed a method to optimize multilevel cache hierarchies. They adjusted cache size, then line size, then associativity. They found that the configuration of the first-level cache affects the required configuration for the second-level cache—different first-level configurations cause different elements to miss the first-level cache, causing different behavior in the second-level cache. To take this effect into account, they alternately chose cache size for each level, then line size for each level, and finally associativity for each level.

*configurable caches*

Several groups, such as Balasubramonian et al. [Bal03], have proposed **configurable caches** whose configuration can be changed at runtime. Additional multiplexers and other logic allow a pool of memory cells to be used in several different cache configurations. Registers hold the configuration values that control the configuration logic. The cache has a configuration mode in which the cache parameters can be set; the cache acts normally in operation mode between configurations. The configuration logic incurs an area penalty as well as static and dynamic power consumption penalties. The configuration logic also increases the delay through the cache. However, it allows the cache configuration to be adjusted for different parts of the program in fairly small increments of time.

### 2.6.4 Scratch Pad Memories

A cache is designed to move a relatively small amount of memory close to the processor. Caches use hardwired algorithms to manage the cache con-

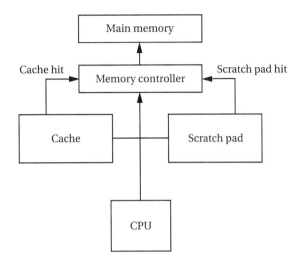

**Figure 2-17** *A scratch pad memory in a system.*

tents—hardware determines when values are added or removed from the cache. Software-oriented schemes are an alternative way to manage close-in memory.

*scratch pads*    As shown in Figure 2-17, a **scratch pad** memory [Pan00] is located parallel to the cache. However, the scratch pad does not include hardware to manage its contents. The CPU can address the scratch pad to read and write it directly. The scratch pad appears in a fixed part of the processor's address space, such as the lower range of addresses. The size of the scratch pad is chosen to fit on-chip and provide a high-speed memory. Because the scratch pad is a part of memory, its access time is predictable, unlike accesses to a cache. Predictability is the key attribute of a scratch pad.

Because the scratch pad is part of the main memory space, standard read and write instructions can be used to manage the scratch pad. Management requires determining what data is in the scratch pad and when it is removed from the cache. Software can manage the cache using a combination of compile-time and runtime decision making. We will discuss management algorithms in more detail in Section 3.3.4.

## 2.7  Additional CPU Mechanisms

This section covers other topics in the design of embedded processors. We start with a discussion of code compression—an architectural technique that uses compression algorithms to design custom instruction encodings. Based on that discussion, we consider architectures that compress both code and data. We next describe methods to encode bus traffic to reduce power consumption of address and data busses. We end with a survey of security-related mechanisms in processors.

## 2.7.1    Code Compression

Code compression is one way to reduce object code size. Compressed instruction sets are not designed by people, but rather by algorithms. We can design an instruction set for a particular program, or we can use algorithms to design a program based on more general program characteristics. Surprisingly, code compression can improve performance and energy consumption as well.

The next two examples describe two approaches to compact code: a commercially available code compression system and a hand-designed compact instruction set.

---

## Example 2-8

*IBM CodePack*

The IBM CodePack architecture was implemented on some models of PowerPC [Kem98]. CodePack uses Huffman compression on each 16-bit half of a 32-bit instruction; instructions are divided into blocks of 64 bytes. CodePack achieved compression ratios of 55% to 65%. A branch table is used to translate addresses. The K bit to the TLB indicates whether a page in memory holds compressed instructions.

---

## Example 2-9

*ARM Thumb Instruction Set*

The ARM Thumb instruction set is an extension to the basic ARM instruction set; any implementation that recognizes Thumb instructions must also be able to interpret standard ARM instructions. Thumb instructions are 16 bits long.

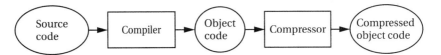

**Figure 2-18** *How to generate a compressed program.*

*executing*
*compressed code*     Wolfe and Chanin [Wol92] proposed code compression and developed the first method for executing compressed code. Relatively small modifications to both the compilation process and the processor allow the machine to execute code that has been compressed by lossless compression algorithms. Figure 2-18 shows their compilation process. The compiler itself is not modified. The object code (or perhaps assembly code in text form) is fed into a compression program that uses lossless compression to generate a new, compressed object file that is loaded into the processor's memory. The compression program modifies the instruction but leaves data intact. Because the compiler need not be modified, compressed code generation is relatively easy to implement. Wolfe and Chanin used Huffman's algorithm [Huf52] to compress code.

*Huffman coding*     Huffman's algorithm was the first modern one for code compression. It requires an alphabet of symbols and the probabilities of occurrence of those symbols. As shown in Figure 2-19, a **coding tree** is built based on those probabilities. Initially, we build a set of subtrees, each having only one leaf node for a symbol. The score of a subtree is the sum of the probabilities of all its leaf nodes. We repeatedly choose the two lowest-score subtrees and combined them into a new subtree, with the lower-probability subtree taking the 0 branch and the higher-probability subtree taking the 1 branch. We continue combining sub-

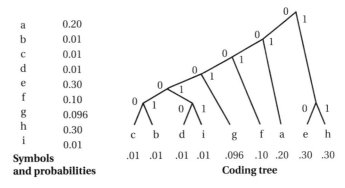

**Figure 2-19** *Huffman coding.*

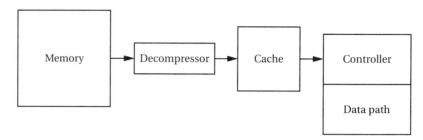

**Figure 2-20**   *The Wolfe and Chanin architecture for executing compressed code.*

trees until we have formed a single large tree. The code for a symbol can be found by following the path from the root to the appropriate leaf node, noting the encoding bit at each decision point.

*microarchitecture with code decompression*
Figure 2-20 shows the structure of a CPU modified to execute compressed code using the Wolfe and Chanin architecture. A decompression unit is added between the main memory and the cache. The decompressor intercepts instruction reads (but not data reads) from the memory and decompresses instructions as they go into the cache. The decompressor generates instructions in the CPU's native instruction set. The processor execution unit itself does not have to be modified because it does not see compressed instructions. The relatively small changes to the hardware make this scheme easy to implement with existing processors.

*compressed code blocks*
As illustrated in Figure 2-21, hand-designed instruction sets generally use a relatively small number of distinct instruction sizes and typically divide instructions on word or byte boundaries. Compressed instructions, in comparison, can be of arbitrary length. Compressed instructions are generally generated in blocks. The compressed instructions are packed bit-by-bit into blocks, but the blocks start on more natural boundaries, such as bytes or words. This leaves empty space in the compressed program that is overhead for the compression process.

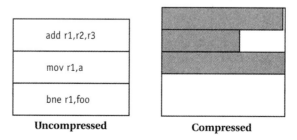

**Figure 2-21**   *Compressed versus uncompressed code.*

The block structure affects execution. The decompression engine decompresses code a block at a time. This means that several instructions become available in short order, although it generally takes several clock cycles to finish decompressing a block. Blocks effectively lengthen prefetch time.

Block structure also affects the compression process and the choice of a compression algorithm. Lossless compression algorithms generally work best on long blocks of data. However, longer blocks impede efficient execution because programs are not executed sequentially from beginning to end. If the entire program were a single block, we would decompress the entire block before execution, which would nullify the advantages of compression. If blocks are too short, the code will not be sufficiently compressed to be worthwhile.

*Wolfe and Chanin evaluation*

Figure 2-22 shows Wolfe and Chanin's comparison of several compression methods. They compressed several benchmark programs in four different ways: using the UNIX *compress* utility; using standard Huffman encoding on 32-byte blocks of instructions; using a Huffman code designed specifically for that program; using a bounded Huffman code, which ensures that no byte is coded in a symbol longer than 16 bits, once again with a separate code for each program; and with a single bounded Huffman code computed from several test programs and used for all the benchmarks.

Wolfe and Chanin also evaluated the performance of their architecture on the benchmarks using three different memory models: programs stored in EPROM with 100 ns memory access time; programs stored in burst-mode EPROM with

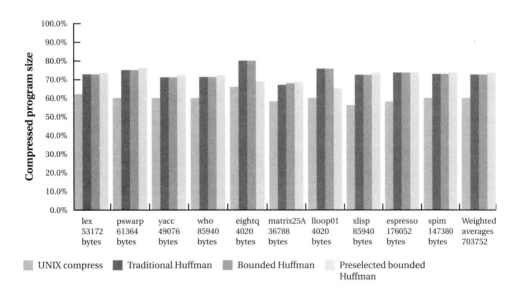

**Figure 2-22** *Comparison of code compression efficiency. From Wolfe and Chanin [Wol92] © 1992 IEEE.*

three cycles for the first access and one cycle for subsequent sequential accesses; and static-column DRAM with four cycles for the first access and one cycle for subsequent sequential accesses, based on 70 ns access time. They found that system performance improved when compressed code was run from slow memories and that system performance slowed down about 10% when executed from fast memory.

*branches in compressed code*

If a branch is taken in the middle of a large block, we may not use some of the instructions in the block, wasting the time and energy required to decompress those instructions. As illustrated in Figure 2-23, branches and branch targets may be at arbitrary points in blocks. The ideal size of a block is related to the distances between branches and branch targets. Compression also affects jump tables and computed branch tables [Lef97].

*branch tables*

The locations of branch targets in the uncompressed code must be adjusted in the compressed code because the absolute locations of all the instructions move as a result of compression. Most instruction accesses are sequential, but branches may go to arbitrary locations given by labels. However, the location of the branch has moved in the compressed program. Wolfe and Chanin proposed that **branch tables** be used to map compressed locations to uncompressed locations during execution (see Figure 2-24). The branch table would be generated by the compression program and included in the compressed object code. It would be loaded into the branch table at the start of execution (or after a context switch) and used by the CPU every time an absolute branch location needed to be translated.

*branch patching*

An alternative to branch tables, proposed by Lefurgy et al. [Lef97], is **branch patching**. This method first compresses the code, doing so in a way that branch instructions can still be modified. After the locations of all the instructions are known, the compression system modifies the compressed code. It

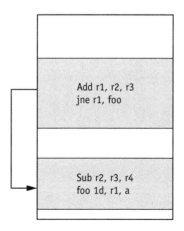

**Figure 2-23** *Branches and blocks in compressed code.*

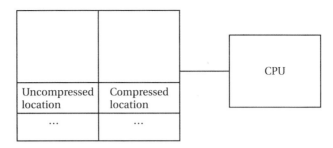

**Figure 2-24** *Branch tables for branch target mapping.*

changes all the branch instructions to include the address of the compressed branch target rather than the uncompressed location. This method uses a slightly less efficient encoding for branches because the address must be modifiable, but it also eliminates the branch table. The branch table introduces several types of overhead: it is large, with one entry for each branch target; it consumes a great deal of energy; and accessing the branch table slows down execution of branches. The branch patching scheme is generally considered to be the preferred method.

*code compression metrics*

We can judge code compression systems by several metrics. The first is code size, which we generally measure by **compression ratio**.

$$K = \frac{Compressed\ code\ size}{Uncompressed\ code\ size}. \tag{EQ 2-23}$$

Compression ratio is measured independent of execution; in Figure 2-21, we would compare the size of the uncompressed object code to the size of the compressed object code. For this result to be meaningful, we must measure the entire object code, including data. It also includes artifacts in the compressed code itself, such as empty space and branch tables.

*block size versus compression ratio*

The choice of block size is a major decision in the design of a code compression algorithm. Lekatsas and Wolf [Lek99c] measured compression ratio as a function of block size. These results, shown in Figure 2-25, reveal that very small blocks do not compress well, but that compression ratio levels off for even moderately sized blocks.We can also judge code compression systems by performance and power consumption.

*variable-length codewords*

Lefurgy et al. [Lef97] used variable-length codewords. They used the first four bits to define the length of the compressed sequence. They used code words of 8, 12, 16, and 36 bits. They found that they obtained the best results when they used a compression method that could encode single instructions efficiently. They also compared their method to the results of compiling for the ARM Thumb instruction set. They found that Thumb code was superior to compressed ARM code for programs smaller than 40 KB but that compressing ARM

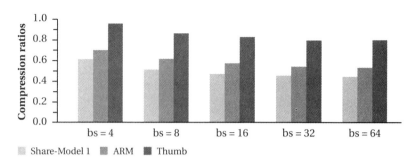

**Figure 2-25**  *Compression ratio versus block size (in bytes) for one compression algorithm. From Lekatsas and Wolf [Lek99b] © 1999 IEEE.*

programs was superior for large programs. They surmised that small programs had insufficient repeated instructions to benefit from compression.

*field-based encoding*

Ishiura and Yamaguchi [Ish98b] automatically extracted fields from the program's instructions to optimize encoding. Their algorithm breaks instructions into fields of one bit, then combines fields to reduce the overall cost of the decoder.

Larin and Conte [Lar99] proposed tailoring the instruction format to the program's utilization of instructions. They used fields defined in the original instruction set, but tailored the encodings of these fields to the range of values found in the program. Programs that used only a subset of possible values for a particular field could use fewer bits for that field. They found that this method resulted in a much smaller decoder than was required for Huffman decoding. They also considered modifications to the instruction cache controller to hold compressed instructions in variable-sized blocks.

*pre-cache versus post-cache decompression*

The Wolfe and Chanin architecture compresses blocks as they come into the cache. This means that each block needs to be decompressed only once but it also means that the cache is filled with uncompressed instructions. Larin and Conte [Lar99] and Lekatsas et al. [Lek00a] proposed **post-cache decompression** in which instructions are decompressed between the cache and CPU, as shown in Figure 2-26. This architecture requires instructions in a block to be decompressed many times if they are repeatedly executed, such as in a loop, but it also leaves compressed instructions in the cache. The post-cache architecture effectively makes the cache larger because the instructions take up less room. Architects can use a smaller cache either to achieve the same performance or to achieve a higher cache hit rate for a given cache size. This gives the architect trade-offs among area, performance, and energy consumption (since the cache consumes a large amount of energy). Surprisingly, the post-cache architecture can be considerably faster and consume less energy even when the overhead of repeated decompressions is taken into account.

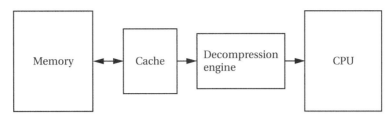

**Figure 2-26** *A post-cache decompression architecture.*

Benini et al. [Ben01a] developed a combined cache controller and code decompression engine. They aligned instructions so that they do not cross cache line boundaries and instructions at branch destinations are word-aligned. Their method gave a compression ratio of 72% and energy savings average of 30%.

Corliss et al. [Cor05] proposed dynamic instruction stream editing (DISE) for post-cache decompression. DISE is a general facility for on-the-fly instruction editing; it macroexpands instructions that match certain patterns into parameterized sequences of instructions. Because this operation is performed after fetching the instruction from the cache, it can be used for post-cache decompression. Some parameters of the compressed instruction are saved as non-opcode bits of the codeword.

*data compression algorithms and code compression*

Many data compression algorithms were originally developed to compress text. Code decompression during execution imposes very different constraints: high performance, small buffers, low energy consumption. Code compression research has studied many different compression algorithms to evaluate their compression abilities in small blocks, decoding speed, and other important properties.

*dictionary-based encoding*

Yoshida et al. [Yos97] used a dictionary to encode ARM instructions. Their transform table mapped a compressed code for an instruction back to the original instruction. The mapping included opcode and operand fields. They proposed this formula for the **power reduction ratio** of their full instruction compression scheme:

$$P_{f/o} = 1 - \frac{N\lceil \log n \rceil + knm}{Nm}.$$  (EQ 2-24)

where $N$ is the number of instructions in the original program, $m$ is the bit width of those instructions, $n$ is the number of compressed instructions, and $k$ is the ratio of the power dissipation of on-chip memory to external memory.

Yoshida et al. also proposed subcode encoding that did not encode some operand values.

*arithmetic coding*

Arithmetic coding was proposed by Whitten et al. [Whi87] as a generalization of Huffman coding, which can make only discrete divisions of the coding

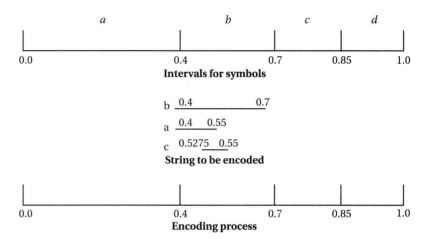

**Figure 2-27** *Arithmetic coding.*

space. Arithmetic coding, in contrast, uses real numbers to divide codes into arbitrarily small segments; this is particularly useful for sets of symbols with similar probabilities. As shown in Figure 2-27, the real number line [0,1] can be divided into segments corresponding to the probabilities of the symbols. For example, the symbol *a* occupies the interval [0,0.4]. Any real number in a symbol's interval can be used to represent that symbol. Arithmetic coding selects values within those ranges so as to encode a string of symbols with a single real number.

A string of symbols is encoded using this algorithm:

```
low = 0; high = 1; i = 0;
while (i < strlen(string)) {
    range = high − low;
    high = low + range*high_range(string[i]);
    low = low + range*low_range(string[i]);
}
```

An example of arithmetic coding is shown at the bottom of Figure 2-27. The range is repeatedly narrowed to represent the symbols and their sequence in the string arithmetic coding and Markov models.

*arithmetic coding and Markov models*

Lekatsas and Wolf [Lek98, Lek99c] combined arithmetic coding and **Markov models**. Arithmetic coding provides more efficient codes than Huffman coding but requires more careful coding. Markov models allow coding to take advantage of the relationships between strings of symbols.

| Example interval machine for N = 8 | | | |
|---|---|---|---|
| State | P(MPS) | LPS | MPS |
| [ 0,8) | 7/8 | 000, [0,8) | −, [1,8) |
| | 6/8 | 00, [0,8) | −, [2,8) |
| | 4/8 | 0, [0,8) | 1, [0,8) |
| [1,8) | 6/7 | 001, [0,8) | −, [2,8) |
| | 5/7 | 0f, [0,8) | −, [3,8) |
| | 4/7 | 0, [2,8) | 1, [0,8) |
| [2,0) | 5/6 | 010, [0,8) | −, [3,8) |
| | 4/6 | 01, [0,8) | 1, [0,8) |
| [3,8) | 4/5 | 011, [0,8) | 1, [0,8) |
| | 3/5 | ff, [0,8) | 1, [2,8) |

**Figure 2-28** *An example of table-based arithmetic decoding. From Lekatsas and Wolf [Lek99c]* © *1999 IEEE.*

*fixed-point method for arithmetic coding*

A straightforward implementation of an arithmetic coder would require floating-point arithmetic but a floating-point arithmetic unit is too slow, too large, and too energy-intense to be used in the instruction decode path. Howard and Vitter [How92] developed a table-based algorithm for arithmetic compression that requires only fixed-point arithmetic; an example is shown in Figure 2-28. The table encodes the segments into which the number line has been divided by the code.

*Markov models*

Markov models are well-known statistical models. We use Markov models in data compression to model the conditional probabilities of symbols—for example, the probability that $z$ follows $a$, as compared to the probability of $w$ following $a$. As shown in Figure 2-29, each possible state in the sequence is modeled by a state in the Markov model. A transition shows possible moves between states, with each transition labeled by its probability. In the example, states model the sequences $az$ and $aw$.

The Markov model describes the relationship between the bits in an instruction. As shown in Figure 2-30, each state has two transitions, one for a zero bit and one for a one bit. Any particular instruction defines a trajectory through the Markov model. Each state is marked with the probability of the most probable bit and whether that bit is 0 or 1. The largest possible model for a block of $b$ bits has $2^b$ states, which is too large. We can limit the size of the model in two ways:

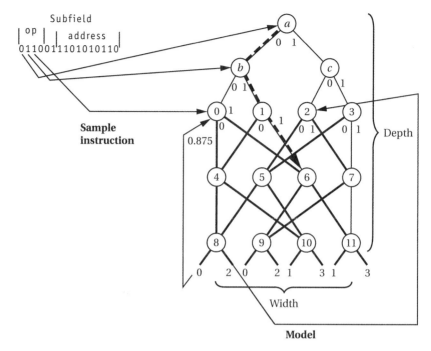

**Figure 2-29** *A Markov model of an instruction.*

(1) limit the width by wrapping around transitions so that a state may have more than one incoming transition, and (2) limit the depth in a similar way by cutting off the bottom of the model and wrapping around transitions to terminate at existing states. The depth of the model should divide the instruction size evenly or be a multiple of the instruction size so that the root state always falls on the start of an instruction.

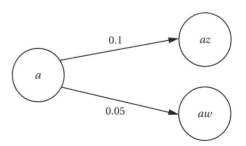

**Figure 2-30** *A Markov model for conditional character probabilities.*

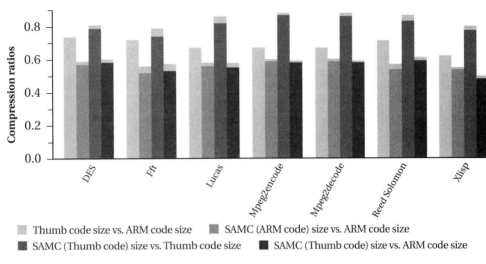

Thumb code size vs. ARM code size    SAMC (ARM code) size vs. ARM code size

SAMC (Thumb code) size vs. Thumb code size    SAMC (Thumb code) size vs. ARM code size

**Figure 2-31** *SAMC versus ARM and Thumb from Lekatsas and Wolf [Lek99].*

Lekatsas and Wolf compared SAMC to both ARM and Thumb. As shown in Figure 2-31, SAMC created smaller programs than Thumb—compressed ARM programs were smaller than Thumb, and compressed Thumb programs were also smaller.

*variable-to-fixed encoding*

Xie et al. [Xie02] used Tunstall coding [Tun67] to create fixed-sized code blocks from variable-sized segments of program text. Tunstall coding creates a coding tree with $2^N$ leaf nodes and assigns an equal-length code to each leaf node. Because the depth of the tree varies at different points, the input sequences that generate the leaf nodes, as described by paths from the root to leaves, can vary. This allows several parallel decoders to independently decode different segments of the compressed data stream. Xie et al. added a Markov model to the basic Tunstall method to improve the resulting compression ratio. Variable-to-fixed encoding means that the decoder can fetch fixed-length blocks to decode into variable-length code segments. The parallel coder cannot be used with Markov models since the current block must be decoded to know which code-book to use for the next block. They also showed that the choice of codewords, which was arbitrary in Tunstall's method, affects the energy consumption of the decoder by reducing bit toggling on the compressed instruction bus. Figure 2-32 shows the results of compressing code for a TI TMS320C6x processor using both basic Tunstall coding and a $32 \times 4$ Markov model. The compression ratio is not as good as some other encoding methods but may be offset by the simplified decoder.

*software-based decompression*

Several groups have proposed code compression schemes that use software routines to decompress code. Liao et al. [Lia95] used dictionary-based methods.

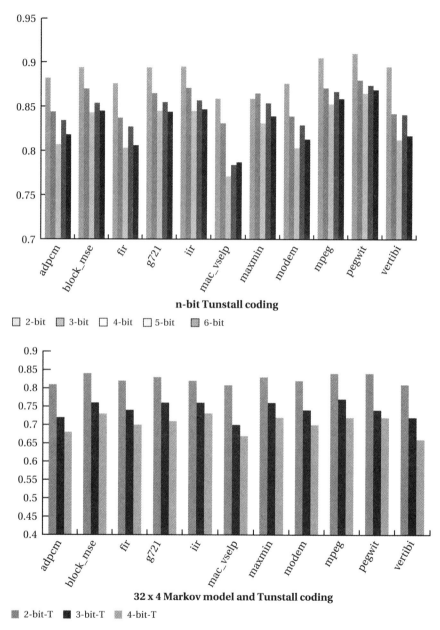

**Figure 2-32** *Code compression using variable-to-fixed coding for the TI TMS320C6x processor. From Xie et al. [Xie02] © 2002 IEEE.*

They identified common code sequences and placed them into a dictionary. Instances of the compressed sequences were replaced by a call/return to a mini-subroutine that executed the code. This method allowed code fragments to have branches as long as the block had a unique exit point. They also proposed a hardware implementation of this method that did not require an explicit return. They found instruction sequences by dividing the code into basic blocks by comparing blocks against each other and themselves at every possible region of overlap. They reported an average compression ratio of 70%.

Kirovski et al. [Kir97] proposed a **procedure cache** for software-controlled code compression. The procedure cache sits parallel to the instruction and data caches. The procedure cache is large enough to hold an entire decompressed procedure. Rather than directly embedding procedure addresses in subroutine call instructions, they use a table to map procedure identifiers in the code to the location of compressed procedures in memory. In addition to decompressing procedures, their handler also managed free space and reduced fragmentation in the procedure cache. This means that a calling procedure might be expunged from the procedure cache while it is waiting for a subroutine to return (consider, for example, a deep nest of procedure calls). The procedure call stores the identifier for the calling procedure, the address of the start of the calling procedure at the time it was called, and the offset of the call from the start of the calling procedure.

Lefurgy et al. [Lef00] proposed adding a mechanism to allow software to write into the cache: an exception is raised on a cache miss; an instruction cache modification instruction allows the exception handler to write into the cache. They also proposed adding a second register file for the exception handler to reduce the overhead of saving and restoring registers. They use a simple dictionary-based compression algorithm. Every compressed instruction is represented by a 16-bit index. They also experimented with the compression algorithm used by IBM CodePack. In addition, these authors developed an algorithm for selectively compressing programs by measuring the cache misses on sample executions and selecting the most frequently missing sections of code for compression.

Figure 2-33 shows the results of their experiments with instruction cache size. Lefurgy et al. tested both their dictionary compression algorithm and the CodePack algorithm for several different cache sizes: 4KB, 16KB, and 64KB; they tested these cache sizes both with a single register file and with the added register file for the exception handler. Figure 2-34 shows the performance of selectively compressed programs relative to uncompressed code. The plots show relative performance as a function of the percentage of the program that has been compressed for several benchmarks. In several cases (notably ijpeg, mpeg2enc, perl, and pegwit), the compressed program was somewhat faster, a fact that they attribute to changes in cache behavior due to different procedure placement in the compressed versus uncompressed programs.

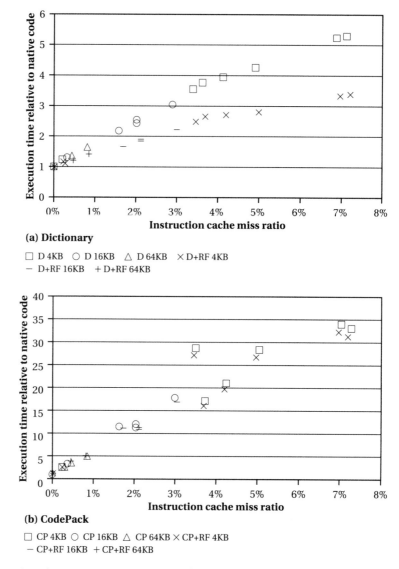

(a) Dictionary

    □ D 4KB   ○ D 16KB  △ D 64KB  × D+RF 4KB
    − D+RF 16KB  + D+RF 64KB

(b) CodePack

    □ CP 4KB ○ CP 16KB △ CP 64KB × CP+RF 4KB
    − CP+RF 16KB + CP+RF 64KB

**Figure 2-33** *Execution time versus instruction cache miss ratio. From Lefurgy et al. [Lef00] © 2000 IEEE.*

Chen et al. [Che02] proposed software-controlled code compression for Java. This method compresses read-only data, which includes virtual machine binary code and Java class libraries. Read-only data is put in a scratch-pad memory on decompression. Compression allows some blocks in the on-chip memory system to be turned off and others to be operated in low-power modes.

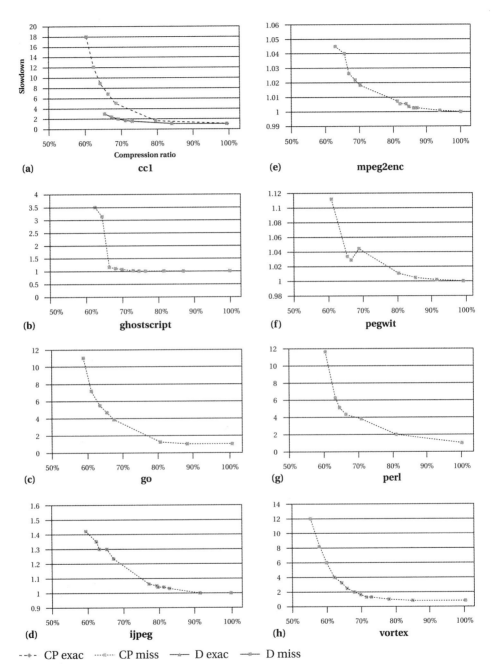

**Figure 2-34**  *Relative performance of selective compression. From Lefurgy et al. [Lef00] © 2000 IEEE.*

### 2.7.2   Code and Data Compression

Given the success of code compression, it is reasonable to consider compressing both code and data and decompressing them during execution. However, maintaining compressed data in memory is more difficult. While instructions are (for the most part) only read, data must be both read and written. This requires that we be able to compress on-the-fly as well as decompress, leading to somewhat different trade-offs for code/data compression than for code compression.

*Lempel–Ziv coding*

**Lempel–Ziv coding** [Ziv77] has been used for joint code/data compression. It builds a dictionary for coding in a way that it does not have to send the dictionary along with the compressed text. As shown in Figure 2-35, the transmitter uses a buffer to recognize repeated strings in the input text; the receiver keeps its own buffer to record repeated strings as they are received so that they can be reused in later steps of the decoding process. The Lempel–Ziv coding process is illustrated in Figure 2-36. The compressor scans the text from first to last character. If the current string, including the current character, is in the buffer, then no text is sent. If the current string is not in the buffer, it is added to the buffer. The sender then transmits a token for the longest recognized string (the current string minus the last character) followed by the new character.

*Lempel–Ziv– Welch coding*

**The Lempel–Ziv–Welch (LZW)** algorithm [Wel84] uses a fixed-size buffer for the Lempel–Ziv algorithm. LZW coding was originally designed for disk drive compression, in which the buffer is a small RAM; it is also used for image encoding in GIF format.

*MXT memory system*

Tremaine et al. [Tre01] developed the MXT memory system to make use of compressed data and code. A level 3 cache is shared among several processors; it talks to main memory and to I/O devices. Data and code are uncompressed as they move from main memory to the L3 cache and compressed when they move back to main memory. MXT uses a derivative of the 1977 Lempel–Ziv algorithm. A block to be compressed is divided into several equal-sized parts, each of which is compressed by an independent engine. All the compression engines share the same dictionaries. Typically, one-kilobyte blocks are divided into four 256-byte blocks for compression. The decompressor also uses four engines.

*compression for energy savings*

Benini et al. [Ben02] developed a data compression architecture with a compression/decompression unit between cache and main memory. They evaluated

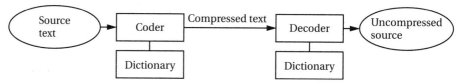

**Figure 2-35** *Lempel–Ziv coding.*

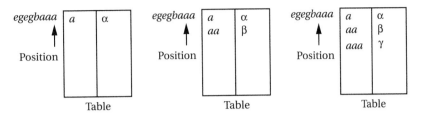

**Figure 2-36** *An example of Lempel–Ziv coding.*

several different compression algorithms and evaluated them for both compression ratio and energy savings. One algorithm they tested was a simple dictionary-based compression algorithm that stored the $n$ most frequent words and their codes in a dictionary. This algorithm gave an average of 35% less energy consumption.

*compression and encryption*

Lekatsas et al. [Lek04] developed an architecture that combined compression and encryption of data and code. The encryption method must support random access of data so that large blocks do not need to be decrypted to allow access to a small piece of data. Their architecture modifies the operating system to place compression and encryption operations at the proper points in the memory access process; the system designer can use a variety of different compression or encryption algorithms. A table maps uncompressed addresses to locations in compressed main memory.

### 2.7.3   Low-Power Bus Encoding

The busses that connect the CPU to the caches and main memory account for a significant fraction of all the energy consumed by the CPU. These busses are both wide and long, giving them large capacitance to switch. The busses also are used frequently, inducing many switching events on their large capacitance.

*bus encoding*

A number of **bus encoding** systems have been developed to reduce bus energy consumption. As shown in Figure 2-37, information to be placed on the bus is first encoded at the transmitting end and then decoded at the receiving end. The memory and CPU do not know that the bus data is being encoded. Bus encoding schemes must be invertible—we must be able to losslessly recover the data at the receiving end. Some schemes require **side information**, usually a small number of bits to help decode. Other schemes do not require side information to be transmitted alongside the bus.

*metrics*

The most important metric for a bus encoding scheme is energy savings. Because the energy itself depends on the physical and electrical design of the bus, we usually measure energy savings using **toggle counts**. Because bus energy is proportional to the number of transitions on each line in the bus, we

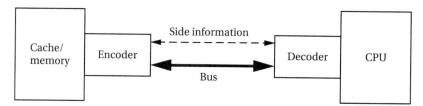

**Figure 2-37** *Microarchitecture of an encoded bus.*

can use toggle count as a relative energy measure. Toggle counts measure toggles between successive bits on a given bus signal. Because crosstalk reduces power consumption too, some schemes also look at the values of physically adjacent bus signals. We are interested, in addition, to the time, energy, and area overhead of the encoder and decoder. All these metrics must include the toggle counts and other costs of any side information used for bus encoding.

*bus-invert coding*

Stan and Burleson proposed **bus-invert coding** [Sta95] to reduce the energy consumption of busses. This scheme takes advantage of the correlation between successive values on the bus. A word on the bus may be transmitted either in its original form or inverted form to reduce the number of transitions on the bus.

As shown in Figure 2-38, the transmitter side of the bus (for example, the CPU) stores the previous value of the bus in a register so that it can compare the current bus value to the previous value. It then computes the number of bit-by-bit transitions using the function majority $(XOR(B^t, B^{t-1}))$, where $B^t$ is the bus value at time $t$. If more than half the bits of the bus change value from time $t$ to time $t-1$, then the inverted form of the bus value is transmitted, otherwise the

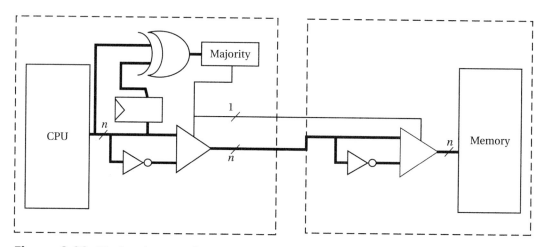

**Figure 2-38** *The bus-invert coding architecture.*

original form of the bus value is transmitted. One extra line of side information is used to tell the receiver whether it needs to re-invert the value.

Stan and Burleson also proposed breaking the bus into fields and applying bus-invert coding to each field separately. This approach works well when data is naturally divided into sections with correlated behavior.

*working-zone encoding*

Musoll et al. [Mus98] developed **working-zone encoding** for address busses, as illustrated in Figure 2-39. Their method is based on the observation that a large majority of the execution time of programs is spent within small ranges of addresses, such as during the execution of loops. They divide program addresses into sets known as **working zones**. When an address on the bus falls into a working zone, the offset from the base of the working zone is sent in a one-hot code. Addresses that do not fall into working zones are sent in their entirety. (See Figure 2-39.)

*address bus encoding*

Benini et al. [Ben98] developed a method for address bus encoding. They cluster address bits that are correlated, create efficient codes for those clusters, then use combinational logic to encode and decode those clustered signals.

```
for 1 ≤ i ≤ H + M do △₁ = current - Pref₁        (1)
if ∃△ᵣ such that −n/2 ≤ △ᵣ ≤ n/2 − 1 then
   offset = △ᵣ
   Pref_miss = 0
   ident = r
   if offset = prev_offᵣ then
      word = prev_sent
   else
      word = transition−signaling[one-hot(offset)]
   Prefᵣ = current
   Prev_offᵣ = offset
   Prev_ident = r
   if H + 1 ≤ r ≤ H + M then
      prefⱼ = current  (1 ≤ j ≤ H)              (2)
      prev_offⱼ = offset
else
   Pref_miss = 1
   ident = prev_ident                           (3)
   word = current
   if M ≠ 0 then
     Prefⱼ = current  (H + 1 ≤ j ≤ H + M)        (2)
   else
     Prefⱼ = current  (1 ≤ j ≤ H)               (2)
     (leave prev_offⱼ as before)                (4)
Prev_sent _ word
```

```
if pref_miss = 0 then
   xor = prev_received XOR word
   if xor = 0 then
      current = Pref_ident + prev_off_ident
      (leave prev_off_ident as before)
   else
      current = Pref_ident + one-hot-retrieve(xor)
      prev_off_ident = one-hot-retrieve(xor)
   Pref_ident = current
   if ident > H then
      Prefⱼ = current, (1 ≤ j ≤ H)              (2)
      if xor = 0 then
         (leave prev_offⱼ as before)
      else
         prev_offⱼ = one-hot-retrieve(xor)
else
   current = word
   Prefⱼ = current
   (leave prev_offⱼ as before)                  (4)
prev_received = word
```

(1) Active working zone search; in this work, fully associative
(2) Replacement algorithm; in this work, LRU
(3) ident is don't care; its previous value is sent
(4) prev_off is not modified since no previous offset is known

**Figure 2-39** *Working-zone encoding and decoding algorithms. From Musoll et al. [Mus98] © 1998 IEEE.*

They compute correlations of **transition variables** as

$$\eta_i^{(t)} = [x_i^{(t)} \cdot (x_i^{(t-1)})'] - [(x_i^{(t)})'x_i^{(t-1)}], \qquad \text{(EQ 2-25)}$$

where $\eta_i^{(t)}$ is 1 if bit $i$ makes a positive transition, $-1$ if it makes a negative transition, and 0 if it does not change. They compute correlation coefficients of this function for the entire address stream of the program.

To ensure that the encoding and decoding logic is not too large, we must control the sizes of the clusters chosen. Benini et al. use a greedy algorithm to create clusters of signals with controlled maximum sizes. They use logic synthesis techniques to design efficient encoders and decoders for the clusters. Table 2-1 shows the results of experiments by Benini et al. comparing their method to working-zone encoding.

*dictionary-based*
*bus encoding*      Lv et al. [Lv03] developed a bus encoding method that uses dictionaries. This method is designed to consider both correlations between successive values and correlations between adjacent bits. They use a simple model of energy consumption for a pair of lines: the function $ENS(V^t, V^{t-1})$ is 0 if both lines stay the same, is 1 if one of the two lines changes, and is 2 if both lines change. They then model energy in terms of transition ($ET$) and interwire ($EI$) effects as

$$ET(k) = C_L V_{DD}^2 \sum_{0 \le i \ \le N-1} ENS(V_i((k-1), V_i(k))), \qquad \text{(EQ 2-26)}$$

$$EI(k) = C_L V_{DD}^2$$

$$\times \sum_{0 \le i \ \le N-2} ENS(V_i((((k-1), V_{i+1}(k)), V_i(k)), V_{i+1}(k))), \quad \text{(EQ 2-27)}$$

$$EN(k) = ET(k) + EI(k). \qquad \text{(EQ 2-28)}$$

*EN(k)* gives the total energy on the $k^{th}$ bus transaction.

Bus dictionary encoding makes sense because many values are repeated on busses. Figure 2-40 shows the frequency of the ten most common patterns in a set of benchmarks. A very small number of patterns clearly accounts for a majority of the bus traffic in these programs. This means that a small dictionary can be used to encode many of the values that appear on the bus.

Figure 2-41 shows the architecture of the dictionary-based encoding scheme. Both the encoder and decoder have small dictionaries built from static RAM. Not all the word is used to form the dictionary entry; only the upper bits of the word are used to match. The remaining bits of the word are sent unencoded. They divide the bus into three sections: the upper part of width *N-wi-w0*, the index part of width *wi*, and the bypassed part of width *wo*. If the upper part of

| Benchmark | Length | Binary transitions | Benini et al. transitions | Benini savings | Working-zone transitions | Working-zone savings |
|---|---|---|---|---|---|---|
| Dashboard | 84,918 | 619,690 | 443,115 | 28.4% | 452,605 | 26.9% |
| DCT | 13,769 | 48,917 | 31,472 | 35.6% | 36,258 | 25.8% |
| FFT | 23,441 | 138,526 | 85,653 | 38.1% | 99,814 | 27.9% |
| Matrix multiplication | 22,156 | 105,947 | 60,654 | 42.7% | 72,881 | 31.2% |
| Vector–vector multiplication | 19,417 | 133,272 | 46,838 | 64.8% | 85,473 | 35.8% |

**Table 2-1** *Experimental evaluation of address encoding using the Benini et al. method. From Benini et al. [Ben98] © 1998 IEEE.*

the word to be sent is in the dictionary, the transmitter sends the index and the bypassed part. When the upper part is not used, those bits are put into a high-impedance state to save energy. Side information tells when a match is found. Some results are summarized in Figure 2-42; Lv et al. found that this dictionary-based scheme saved about 25% of bus energy on data values and 36% on

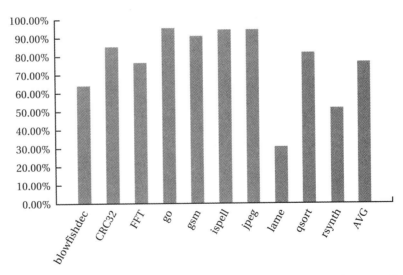

**Figure 2-40** *Frequency of the ten most common patterns in a set of benchmarks. From Lv et al. [Lv03] © 2003 IEEE.*

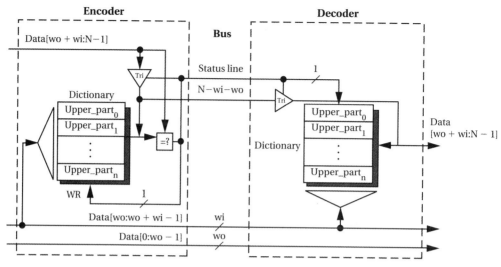

**Figure 2-41** *Architecture of the Lv et al. dictionary-based bus encoder. From Lv et al. [Lv03] © 2003 IEEE.*

address values at a cost of two additional bus lines for side information and about 4,400 gates.

### 2.7.4 Security

As we saw in Section 1.6, security is composed of many different attributes: authentication, integrity, and so on. Embedded processors require the same basic

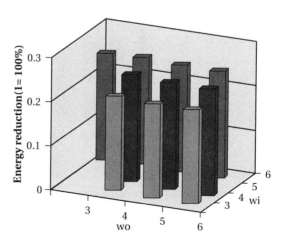

**Figure 2-42** *Energy savings of dictionary-based code compression. From Lv et al. [Lv03] © 2003 IEEE.*

security features seen in desktop and server systems, and they must guard against additional attacks.

*cryptography and CPUs*

Cryptographic operations are used in key-based cryptosystems. Cryptographic operations, such as key manipulation, are part of protocols used to authenticate data, users, and transactions. Cryptographic arithmetic requires very long word operations and a variety of bit- and field-oriented operations. A variety of instruction set extensions have been proposed to support cryptography. Co-processors also can be used to implement these operations.

*varieties of attacks*

Embedded processors must also guard against attacks. Attacks used against desktop and server systems—Trojan horses, viruses, and so on—can be used against embedded systems. Because users and adversaries have physical access to the embedded processor, new types of attacks are also possible. **Side channel attacks** use information leaked from the processor to determine what the processor is doing.

*smart cards*

**Smart cards** are an excellent example of a widely used embedded system with stringent security requirements. Smart cards are used to carry highly sensitive data such as credit and banking information or personal medical data. Tens of millions of smart cards are in use today. Because the cards are held by individuals, they are vulnerable to a variety of physical attacks, either by third parties or by the card holder.

The dominant smart card architecture is called the **self-programmable one-chip microcomputer (SPOM)** architecture. The electrically programmable memory allows the processor to change its own permanent program store.

*self-reprogramming architecture*

SPOM architectures allow the processor to modify either data or code, including the code being executed. Such changes must be done carefully to ensure that the memory is changed correctly and CPU execution is not compromised. Figure 2-43 shows an architecture for self-reprogramming [Ugo83]. The memory is divided into two sections: both may be EPROM or one may be ROM, in which case the ROM section of the memory cannot be changed. The address and data are divided among the two programs. Registers are used to hold the addresses during the memory operation as well as to hold the data to be read or written. One address register holds the address to be read/written while the other holds the address of a program segment that controls the memory operation.

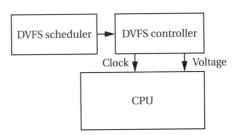

**Figure 2-43** *A DVFS-based attack to protect against power attack.*

Control signals from the CPU determine the timing of the memory operation. Segmenting the memory access into two parts allows arbitrary locations to be modified without interfering with the execution of the code that governs the memory modification. Because of the registers and control logic, even the locations that control the memory operation can be overwritten without causing operational problems.

The next two examples introduce security features on two embedded processor families.

---

## Example 2-10

*SmartMIPS*

The SmartMIPS extensions to the MIPS32 architecture [MIP05] are designed for smart card systems. It provides instruction set extensions for cryptographic operations; these operations are designed to be useful in a number of different cryptographic algorithms and key sizes. It also provides a memory management unit that allows the operating system and applications to be separated, as well as page protection attributes.

---

## Example 2-11

*ARM SecurCore*

SecurCore [ARM05b] is a series of processors designed for smart cards and related applications. They support cryptographic operations using the SafeNet cryptographic co-processor. The SafeNet EIP-25 coprocessor [ARM05c] can perform 1024-bit modular exponentiation and supports keys up to 2,048 bits. They provide memory management units that allow the operating system to manage access capabilities.

---

*SAFE-OPS*

The SAFE-OPS architecture [Zam05] is designed to validate the state of embedded software and protect against software modifications. The compiler embeds a **watermark**—a verifiable identifier—into the code using register assignment. If each register is assigned a symbol, then the sequence of registers used in a section of code represents the watermark for that code. An FPGA attached to the system bus can monitor the instruction stream and extract the watermark during execution. If the watermark is invalid, then the FPGA can signal an exception or otherwise take action.

*power attacks*    Side channel attacks, as mentioned previously, use information emitted from the processor to determine the processor's internal state. Electronic systems typically emit electromagnetic energy that can be used to infer some of the circuit's activity. Similarly, the dynamic behavior of the power supply current can be used to infer internal CPU state. Kocher et al. [Koc99] showed that, using a technique they call **differential power analysis**, measurements of the power supply current into a smart card could be used to identify the cryptosystem key stored in the smart card.

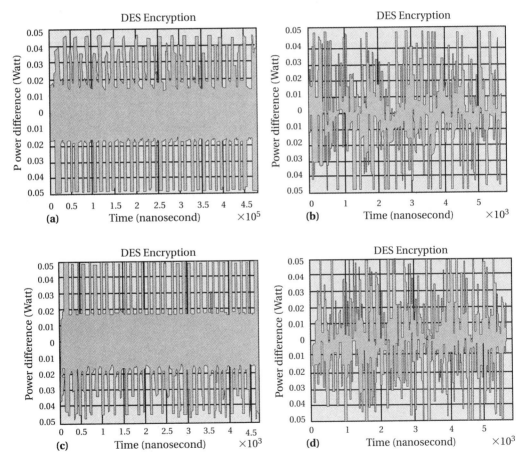

**Figure 2-44**  *Traces without and with DVFS protection. From Yang et al. [Yan05] © 2005 ACM Press.*

*countermeasures*    Countermeasures have been developed for power attacks. Yang et al. [Yan05] used dynamic voltage and frequency scaling to mask operations in processors, as shown in Figure 2-44. They showed that proper design of a DVFS schedule can make it substantially more difficult for attackers to determine internal states from the processor power consumption. The figure compares traces without dynamic voltage and frequency scaling (**a** and **c**) and traces with DVFS-based protection (**b** and **d**).

## 2.8    CPU Simulation

CPU simulators are essential to computer system design. CPU architects use simulators to evaluate processor designs before they are built. System designers use simulators for a variety of purposes: analyzing the performance and energy consumption of programs, simulating multiprocessors before and after they are built, and system debugging.

The term "CPU simulator" generally is used broadly to mean any method of analyzing the behavior of programs on processors. We can classify CPU simulation methods along several lines:

- **Performance versus energy/power**—Simulating the energy or power consumption of a processor requires accurate simulation of its internal behavior. Some types of performance-oriented simulation, in contrast, can perform a less detailed simulation and still provide reasonably accurate results.

- **Temporal accuracy**—By simulating more details of the processor, we can obtain more accurate timings. More accurate simulators take more time to execute.

- **Trace versus execution**—Some simulators analyze a trace taken from a program that executes on the processor. Others analyze the program execution directly.

- **Simulation versus direct execution**—Some execution-based systems directly execute on the processor being analyzed while others use simulation programs.

Simulation is generally driven by programs and data. To obtain useful results from simulation, we need to simulate the right programs that are working on reasonable input data. The application code itself is the best way to exercise an embedded system, but benchmark suites can help evaluate architectures when we do not yet have the code.

Engblom [Eng99b] compared the SPECInt95 benchmarks with the properties of several proprietary embedded programs (totaling 334,600 lines of C code) and concluded that embedded software has very different characteristics than the SPECInt benchmark set. The analysis was based on static analysis of the program using an intermediate representation of the programs to minimize differences introduced by coding methods. Some of this author's results are summarized in Figure 2-45. He found that dynamic data structures were more

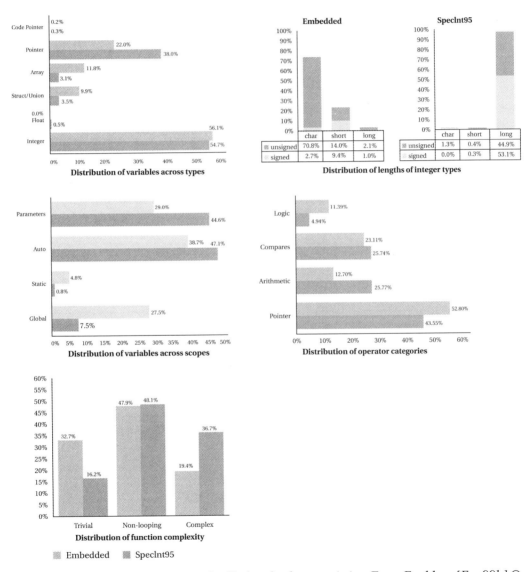

**Figure 2-45** *SPECInt95 versus embedded code characteristics. From Engblom [Eng99b] © 1999 ACM Press.*

common in SPECInt95, and arrays and structs were more common in embedded programs. SPECInt95 used more 32-bit variables, while embedded programs used mostly smaller data; embedded programs also used many more unsigned variables. Embedded programs used more static and global variables. Embedded programs used more logic operations than did SPECInt95. Engblom also found that embedded programs had more trial functions that made no decisions and fewer complex functions with loops.

The next two examples introduce two sets of benchmarks for embedded computing applications.

## Example 2-12

*MediaBench*

MediaBench [Lee97] is a benchmark set designed to represent workloads for multimedia and communication applications. It includes several components, such as JPEG and MPEG, GSM speech encoding for cell phones, G.721 voice compression, the PGP cryptography package, and Ghostscript. The suite includes sample data as well as code.

## Example 2-13

*EEMBC DENBench*

The Embedded Microprocessor Benchmark Consortium (EEMBC)—(*http://www.eembc.org*)—develops and maintains benchmarks for a variety of embedded systems application areas. The DENBench suite [Lev05] is designed to characterize digital entertainment systems, both mobile and installed. DENBench is composed of four minisuites: MPEG EncodeMark, MPEG DecodeMark, CryptoMark, and ImageMark. The final score is the geometric mean of the four minisuites.

The next sections survey techniques for CPU simulation: first trace-based analysis, then direct execution, then simulators that model the CPU microarchitecture.

### 2.8.1  Trace-Based Analysis

Trace-based analysis systems do not directly operate on a program. Instead, they use a record of the program's execution, called a **trace**, to determine characteristics of the processor.

*tracing and analysis*

As shown in Figure 2-46, trace-based analysis gathers information from a running program. The trace is then analyzed after execution of the program being analyzed. The post-execution analysis is limited by the data gathered in the trace during program execution.

The trace can be generated in several different ways. The program can be instrumented with additional code that writes trace information to memory or a file. The instrumentation is generally added during compilation or by editing the object code. The trace data can also be taken by a process that interrupts the pro-

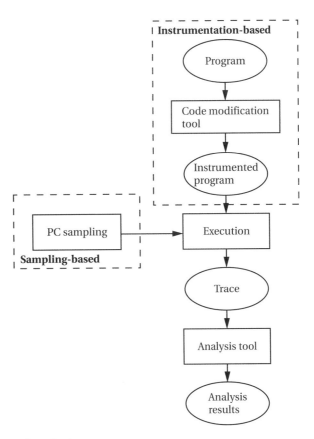

**Figure 2-46** *The trace-based analysis process.*

gram and samples its program counter (PC); this technique is known as **PC sampling**. The two techniques are not mutually exclusive.

The following profiling information can be taken on a variety of types of program information and at varying levels of granularity.

- **Control flow**—Control flow is useful in itself, and a great deal of other information can be derived from control flow. The program's branching behavior can generally be captured by recording branches; behavior within the branches can be inferred. Some systems may record function calls but not branches within a function.

- **Memory accesses**—Memory accesses tell us about cache behavior. The instruction cache behavior can be inferred from control flow. Data memory accesses are usually recorded by instrumentation code that surrounds each memory access.

*prof*

An early and well-known trace-based analysis tool is the UNIX prof command and its GNU cousin gprof [Fen98]. gprof uses a combination of instrumentation and PC sampling to generate the trace. The trace data can generate call-graph (procedure-level), basic-block-level, and line-by-line data.

*Dinero*

A different type of trace-based analysis tool is the well-known Dinero tool [Edl03]. Dinero is a cache simulator. It does not analyze the timing of a program's execution, rather it looks only at the history of references to memory. The reference memory history is captured by instrumentation within the program. After execution, the user analyzes the program behavior in the memory hierarchy using the Dinero tools. The user designs a cache hierarchy in the form of a tree and sets the parameters for the caches for analysis.

*trace sampling*

Traces can be sampled rather than recorded in full [Lah88]. A useful execution may require a great deal of data. Consider, for example, a video encoder that must process several frames to exhibit a reasonable range of behavior. The trace may be sampled by taking data for a certain number of instructions and then not recording information for another sequence of instructions. It is often necessary to warm up the cache before taking samples. The usual challenges of sampled data apply: an adequate length of sample must be taken at each point, and samples must be taken frequently enough to catch important behavior.

## 2.8.2 Direct Execution

*emulating architectures*

Direct execution-style simulation makes use of the host CPU in order to help compute the state of the target machine. Direct execution is used primarily for functional and cache simulation, not for detailed timing.

The various registers of the computer comprise its state; we need to simulate those target machine registers that are not defined in the host machine, but we can use the host machine's native state where appropriate. A compiler generates code for the simulation by adding instructions to compute the target state that has to be simulated. Because much of the simulation runs as native code on the host machine, direct execution can be very fast.

### 2.8.3  Microarchitecture-Modeling Simulators

*modeling detail and accuracy*

We can provide more detailed performance and power measurements by building a simulator that models the internal microarchitecture of the computer. Directly simulating the logic would provide even more accurate results but would be much too slow, preventing us from running the long traces that we need to judge system performance. Logic simulation also requires us to have the logic design, which is not generally available from the CPU supplier. But in many cases we can build a functional model of the microarchitecture from publicly available information.

Microarchitecture models can vary in the level of detail they capture about the microarchitecture. **Instruction schedulers** model basic resource availability but may not be cycle-accurate. **Cycle timers**, in contrast, model the architecture in more detail in order to provide cycle-by-cycle information about execution. Accuracy generally comes at the cost of somewhat slower simulation.

*modeling for simulation*

A typical model for a three-stage pipelined machine is shown in Figure 2-47. This model is not a register-transfer model in that it does not include the register file or busses as first-class elements. Those elements are instead subsumed into the models of the pipeline stages. The model captures the main units and paths that contribute to data and control flow within the microarchitecture.

*simulator design*

The simulation program consists of modules that correspond to the units in the microarchitectural model. Because we want them to run fast, simulators are typically written in a sequential language such as C, not in a simulation language such as Verilog or VHDL. Simulation languages have mechanisms to ensure that modules are evaluated in the proper order when the simulation state changes; when writing simulators in sequential languages, we must design the control flow in the program to ensure that all the implications of a given state change are properly evaluated.

*SimpleScalar*

SimpleScalar (*http://www.simplescalar.com*) is a well-known toolkit for simulator design. SimpleScalar provides modules that model typical components of CPUs as well as tools for data collection. These tools can be put together in various ways, modified, or added to in order to create a custom simulator. A machine description file describes the microarchitecture and is used to generate parts of the simulation engine as well as programming tools such as disassemblers.

*power simulation*

**Power simulators** take cycle-accurate microarchitecture simulators one step further in detail. Determining the energy/power consumption of a CPU generally requires even more accurate modeling than performance simulation. For example, a cycle-accurate timing simulator may not directly model the bus. But the bus is a major consumer of energy in a microprocessor, so a power simulator

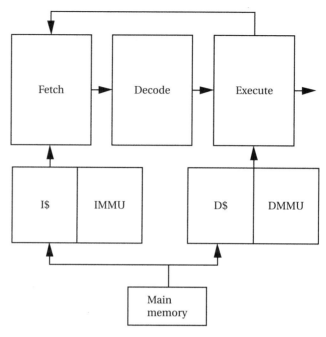

**Figure 2-47** *A microarchitectural model for simulation.*

needs to model the bus, as well as register files and other major structural components. In general, a power simulator must model all significant sources of capacitance in the processor since dynamic power consumption is directly related to capacitance. However, power simulators must trade-off accuracy for simulation performance just like other cycle-accurate simulators.

*Wattch and SimplePower*

The two best-known power simulators are Wattch [Bro00] and SimplePower [Ye00]. Both are built on top of SimpleScalar and add capacitance models for the major units in the microarchitecture.

## 2.9    Automated CPU Design

System designers have used custom processors to run applications at higher speeds for a time long. Custom processors were popular in the 1970s and 1980s thanks to bit-slice CPU components. Chips for data paths and controllers, such as the AMD 2910 series, could be combined and microprogrammed to implement a wide range of instruction sets. Today, custom integrated circuits and FPGAs offer complete freedom to designers who are willing to put the effort into creating a CPU architecture for their applications. Custom CPUs are often known as **application-specific instruction processors (ASIPs)** or **configurable processors**.

*why automate CPU design*

Custom CPU design is an area that cries out for methodological and tool support. System designers need help determining what sorts of modifications to the CPU are likely to be fruitful. They also need help implementing those modifications. Today, system designers have a wide range of tools available to help them design their own processors.

*axes of customization*

We can customize processors in several ways.

- Instruction sets can be adapted to the application.

  — New instructions can provide compound sets of existing operations, such as multiply–accumulate.

  — Instructions can supply new operations, such as primitives for Viterbi encoding or block motion estimation.

  — Instructions that operate on nonstandard operand sizes can be added to avoid masking and to reduce energy consumption.

  — Instructions not important to the application can be removed.

- Pipelines can be specialized to take into account the characteristics of function units used in new instructions, to implement specialized branch prediction schemes, and so on.

- Memory hierarchy can be modified by adding and removing cache levels, choosing a cache configuration, or choosing the banking scheme in a partitioned memory system.

- Busses and peripherals can be selected and optimized to meet bandwidth and I/O requirements.

*software tools*

ASIPs require customized versions of the tool chains that software developers have come to rely on. Compilers, assemblers, linkers, debuggers, simulators, and IDEs (integrated development environments) must all be modified to match the CPU characteristics.

*tool support*

Two major varieties of tools support customized CPU design. **Configuration tools** take the microarchitecture—instruction set, pipeline, memory hierarchy, and so on—as a specification and create the logic design of the CPU (usually as register–transfer Verilog or VHDL) along with the compiler and other tools for the CPU. **Architecture optimization tools** help the designer select a particular instruction set and microarchitecture based on application characteristics.

*early work*

The MIMOLA system [Mar84] is an early example of both architecture optimization and configuration. MIMOLA analyzed application programs to determine opportunities for new instructions. It then generated the structure of the CPU hardware and generated code for the application program for which the CPU was designed.

*in this section*      We defer a discussion of compilers for custom CPUs until the next chapter. This section concentrates on architecture optimization and configuration.

## 2.9.1 Configurable Processors

CPU configuration spans a wide range of approaches. Relatively simple generator tools can create simple adjustments to CPUs. Complex synthesis systems can implement a large design space of microarchitectures from relatively simple specifications.

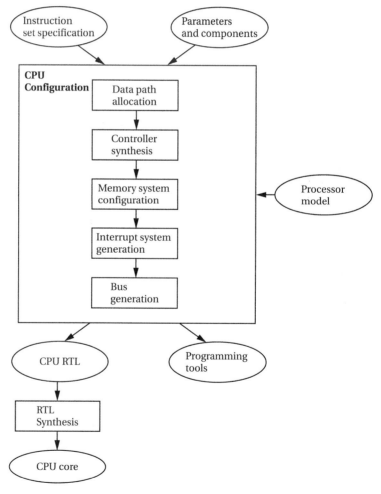

**Figure 2-48** *The CPU configuration process.*

Figure 2-48 shows a typical design flow for CPU configuration. The system designer can specify instruction set extensions as well as other system parameters such as cache configuration. The system also may accept designs for function units that will be plugged into the processor. Although it is possible to synthesize the microarchitecture from scratch, the CPU's internal structure is often built around a processor model that defines some basic characteristics of the generated processor. The configuration process has several steps, including allocation of the data path and control, memory system design, and I/O and bus design. Configuration results in both the CPU logic design and software tools (compiler, assembler, and so on) for the processor. Configurable processors are generally created in register–transfer form and used as soft IP. Standard register-transfer synthesis tools can be used to create a set of masks or FPGA configuration for the processor.

Several processor configuration systems have been created over the years by both academic and industrial teams. ASIP Meister [Kob03] is the follow-on system to PEAS. It generates Harvard-architecture machines based on estimations of area, delay, and power consumption during architecture design and micro-operation specification. The ARC family of configurable cores (*http://www.arc.com*) includes the 600 series with a five-stage pipeline and the 700 series with a seven-stage pipeline.

The next example describes a commercial processor configuration system.

---

## Example 2-14

*The Tensilica Xtensa Configurable Processor*

The Tensilica Xtensa configurable processor [Row05] is designed to allow a wide range of CPUs to be designed from a very simple specification. An Xtensa core can be customized in the following ways.

■ The instruction set can be augmented with basic ALU-style operations, wide instructions, DSP-style instructions, or co-processors.

■ The configuration of the caches can be controlled, memory protection and translation can be configured, DMA access can be added, and addresses can be mapped into special-purpose memories.

■ The CPU bus width, protocol, system registers, and scan chain can be optimized.

■ Interrupts, exceptions, remote debugging features, and standard I/O devices, such as timers, can be added.

The following figure illustrates the range of features in the CPU that can be customized. Instructions are specified using the TIE language. TIE allows the designer to declare an instruction using state declarations, instruction encodings and formats, and operation descriptions. For example, consider this simple TIE instruction specification (after Rowen):

```
Regfile LR 16 128 I
Operation add128
    { out LR sr, in LR ss, in LR st } {}
    { assign sr = st + ss; }
```

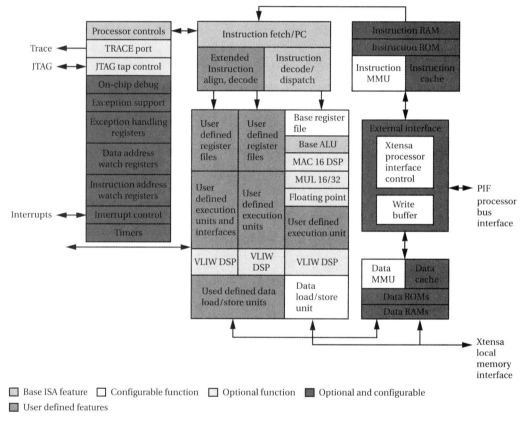

*Source:* From Tensilica [Ten04] © 2004 Tensilica, Inc.

The Regfile declaration defines a large register file named LR with 16 entries, each 128 bits wide. The add128 instruction description starts with a declaration of the arguments to the instruction; each of the arguments is declared to be in the

LR register file. It then defines the instruction's operation, which adds two elements of the LR register file and assigns it to a third register in LR.

New instructions can be used in programs with intrinsic calls that map onto instructions. For example, the code out[i]=add128(a[i],b[i]) makes use of the new instruction. Optimizing compilers can also map onto the new instructions.

EEMBC compared several processors on benchmarks for consumer electronics, digital signal processing, and networking. These results [Row05], shown in the following figure, confirm that custom, configurable processors can provide much higher performance than standard processors.

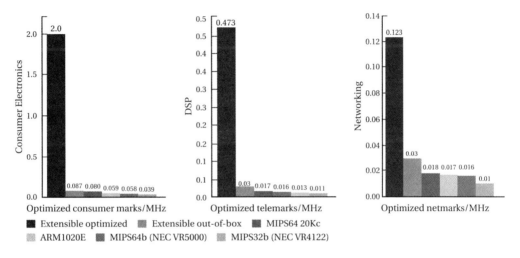

*Source:* From Tensilica [Ten04] © 2004 Tensilica, Inc.

To evaluate the utility of the configuration, Tensilica created the following customized processors for four different benchmark programs.

- DotProd—Dot product of two 2048-element vectors

- AES—Advanced Encryption Standard

- Viterbi—Viterbi trellis decoder

- FFT—256-point fast Fourier transform

A different CPU was designed for each benchmark.

The CPUs were implemented, measured, and compared to a baseline Xtensa processor without extensions. As shown in the following table, the performance, power, and energy consumption of the processors indicate that configuring customized processors can provide large energy savings [Ten04].

| Configuration | Metric | DotProd | AES | Viterbi | FFT |
|---|---|---|---|---|---|
| Reference processor | Area (mm$^2$) | 0.9 | 0.4 | 0.5 | 0.4 |
| | Cycles (K) | 12 | 283 | 280 | 326 |
| | Power (mW/MHz) | 0.3 | 0.2 | 0.2 | 0.2 |
| | Energy (μJ) | 3.3 | 61.1 | 65.7 | 56.6 |
| Optimized processor | Area (mm2) | 1.3 | 0.8 | 0.6 | 0.6 |
| | Cycles (K) | 5.9 | 2.8 | 7.6 | 13.8 |
| | Power (mW/MHz) | 0.3 | 0.3 | 0.3 | 0.2 |
| | Energy (μJ) | 1.6 | 0.7 | 2.0 | 2.5 |
| Energy improvement | | 2 | 82 | 33 | 22 |

*Source:* From Tensilica [Ten04] © 2004 Tensilica, Inc

The design of a processor for a 256-point FFT computation illustrates how different types of customizations contribute to processor efficiency. The following figure depicts the architecture for the processor [Ten04].

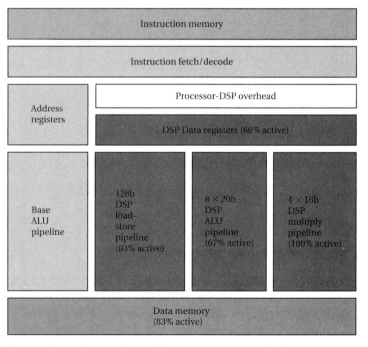

*Source:* From Rowen [Row05], personal communication.

When we analyze the energy consumption of the subsystems in the processor, we find that fine-grained clock gating contributed substantially to energy efficiency, followed by a reduction in processor-DSP overhead [Ten04].

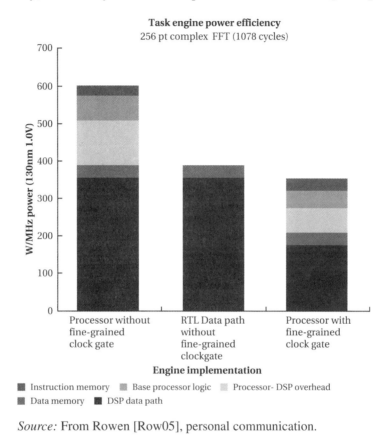

**Task engine power efficiency**
256 pt complex FFT (1078 cycles)

Engine implementation

■ Instruction memory   ■ Base processor logic   ■ Processor- DSP overhead
■ Data memory   ■ DSP data path

*Source:* From Rowen [Row05], personal communication.

The next example describes a configurable processor designed for media processing applications.

## Example 2-15

*The Toshiba MeP Core*

The MeP module [Tos05] is optimized for media processing and streaming applications. An MeP module can contain an MeP core, extension units, a data streamer, and a global bus interface unit. The MeP core is a 32-bit RISC processor. In addition to typical RISC features, the core can be augmented with optional instructions.

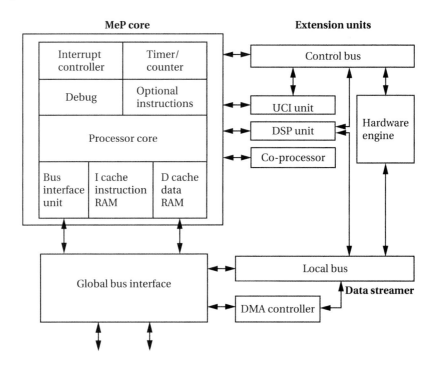

Extension units can be used for further enhancements. The user-custom instruction (UCI) unit adds single-cycle instructions while the DSP unit provides multicycle instructions. The co-processor unit can be used to implement VLIW or other complex extensions.

The data streamer provides DMA-controlled access to memory for algorithms that require regular memory access patterns. The MeP architecture uses a hierarchy of busses to feed data to the various execution units.

---

*CPU modeling*    Let us now look in more detail at models for CPU microarchitectures and how they are used to generate CPU configurations.

*LISA*    The LISA system [Hof01] generates ASIPs described in the LISA language. The language mixes structural and behavioral elements to capture the processor microarchitecture. Figure 2-49 shows example descriptions in the LISA language.

```
RESOURCE {
     PROGRAM_COUNTER int PC;
     REGISTER signed int R[0..7];
     DATA_MEMORY signed int RAM[0..255];
     PROGRAM_MEMORY unsigned int ROM[0..255];
     PIPELINE ppu_pipe = {FI; ID; EX; WB};
     PIPELINE_REGISTER IN ppu_pipe {
          bit[6] Opcode; short operandA; short operandB;
     };
}
```

**Memory model**

```
RESOURCE {
     REGISTER unsigned int R([0..7])6;
     DATA_MEMORY signed int RAM([0..15]);
};
```

```
OPERATION NEG_RM {
     BEHAVIOR USES (IN R[] OUT RAM[];) {
          RAM[address] = (−1) * R[index];
     }
}
```

**Resource model**

```
OPERATION COMPARE_IMM {
     DECLARE { LABEL index; GROUP src1, dest = {register}; }
     CODING {0b10011 index = 0bx[5] src1 dest }
     SYNTAX { "CMP" src1−"," index−"," dest }
     SEMANTICS { CMP (dest,src1,index) }
}
```

```
OPERATION register {
     DECLARE { LABEL index; }
     CODING { index = 0bx[4] }
     EXPRESSION { R[index] }
}
```

**Instruction set model**

```
OPERATION ADD {
     DECLARE { GROUP src1, src2, dest = {register}; }
     CODING { 0b10010 src1 src2 dest }
     BEHAVIOR { dest = src1 + src2; saturate(&dest); }
};
```

**Behavioral model**

**Figure 2-49** *Sample LISA modeling code. From Hoffman et al. [Hof01] © 2001 IEEE.*

The memory model is an extended version of the traditional programming model; in addition to the CPU registers, it also specifies other memories in the system. The resource model describes hardware resources as well as constraints on the usage of those resources. The USES clause inside an OPERATION specifies which resources are used by that operation. The instruction set model describes the assembly syntax, instruction coding, and the function of instructions. The behavioral model is used to generate the simulator; it relates hardware structures to the operations they perform.

Timing information comes from several parts of the model: the PIPELINE declaration in the resource section gives the structure of the pipeline; the IN keyword as part of an OPERATION statement assigns operations to pipeline stages; the ACTIVATION keyword in the OPERATION section launches other operations performed during the instruction. In addition, an ENTITY statement allows operations to be grouped together into functional units, such as an ALU made from several arithmetic and logical operators.

*LISA hardware generation*

LISA generates VHDL for the processor as a hierarchy of entities. The memory, register, and pipeline are the top-level entities. Each pipeline stage is an entity used as a component of the pipeline, while stage components, such as

ALUs, are described as entities. Grouping of operations into functional units are implemented as VHDL entities.

LISA generates VHDL for only some of the processors, leaving some entities to be implemented by hand. Some of the processor components must be carefully coded to ensure that register–transfer and physical synthesis will provide acceptable power and timing. LISA generates HDL code for the top-level entities (pipeline/registers/memory), the instruction decoder, and the pipeline decoder.

*PEAS/ASIP Meister*

PEAS-III [Ito00; Sas01] synthesizes a processor based on the following five types of description from the designer.

- Architectural parameters for number of pipeline stages, number of branch delay slots, and so on.

- Declaration of function units to be used to implement micro-operations.

- Instruction format definitions.

- Definitions of interrupt conditions and timing.

- Descriptions of instructions and interrupts in terms of micro-operations.

*PEAS pipeline structure*

Figure 2-50 shows the model used by PEAS-III for a single pipeline stage. The data path portion of a stage can include one or more function units that implement operations; a function unit may take one or more clock cycles to complete. Each stage has its own controller that determines how the function units are used and when data moves forward. The data path and controller both have registers that present their results to the next stage.

A pipeline stage controller may be in either the *valid* or *invalid* state. A stage may become invalid because of interrupts or other disruptions to the input of the instruction flow. A stage may also become invalid due to a multicycle operation, a branch, or other disruptions during the middle of instruction operation.

A pipeline model for the entire processor is built by concatenating several pipeline stages. The stages may also connect to other resources on both the data

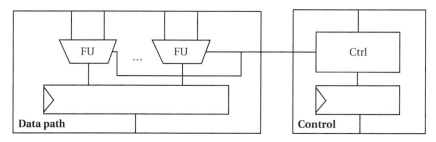

**Figure 2-50** *PEAS-III model of a pipeline stage.*

*PEAS hardware synthesis*

path or controller side. Data path stages may be connected to memory or caches. Controller stages may be connected to an interrupt controller that coordinates activity during exceptions.

PEAS-III generates two VHDL models, one for simulation and another for synthesis. The data path is generated in three phases. First, the structures required for each instruction are generated independently: the function unit resources, the ports on the resources, and the connections between those resources. The resource sets for the instructions are then merged. Finally, multiplexers and pipeline registers are added to control access to resources. After the data path stages are synthesized, the controllers can be generated. The controllers are synthesized in three stages.

1. The control signals required for the data path multiplexers and registers are generated.

2. The interlocks for multicycle operations are generated.

3. The branch control logic is synthesized.

The interrupt controller is synthesized based on the specifications for the allowed interrupts.

## 2.9.2   Instruction Set Synthesis

Instruction set synthesis designs the instruction set to be implemented by the microarchitecture. This topic has not received as much attention as one might think. Many researchers in the 1970s studied instruction set design for high-level languages. That work, however, tended to take the language, not particular programs, as the starting point. Instruction set synthesis requires, on the one hand, designers who are willing to create instructions that occupy a fairly small set of the static program size. This approach is justified when that small static code set is executed many times to create a large static trace.

Instruction set synthesis also requires the ability to automatically generate a CPU implementation, which was not practical in the 1970s. CPU implementation requires practical logic synthesis at a minimum as well as the CPU microarchitecture synthesis tools described earlier in this section.

*instruction set design space*

An experiment by Sun et al. [Sun04] demonstrates the size and complexity of the instruction set design space. They studied a BYTESWAP() program that swaps the order of bytes in a word. They generated all possible instructions for this program finding that 482 are possible. Figure 2-51 shows the execution time for the program with each possible instruction; the instructions are ordered arbitrarily across the $x$ axis. Even in this simple program, different instructions result in very different performance results.

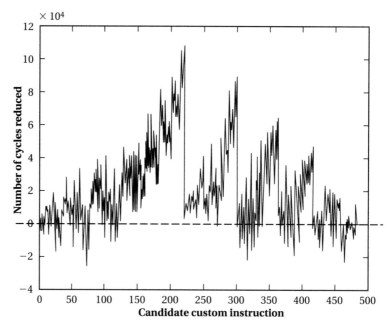

**Figure 2-51** *The instruction set design space for a small program. From Sun et al. [Sun04] ©
2004 IEEE.*

*instruction set
metrics*    Holmer and Despain [Hol91] formulated instruction set synthesis as an optimization problem, which requires selecting an optimization function to guide
the optimization process. They observed that, when designing instruction sets
manually, computer architects often apply a **1% rule**—an instruction that provides less than a 1% improvement in performance over the benchmark set is not
a good candidate for inclusion in the instruction set. They proposed this performance-oriented objective function:

$$100 \ln C + I, \qquad \text{(EQ 2-29)}$$

where $C$ is the number of cycles used to execute the benchmark set and $I$ is the
total number of instructions in the instruction set. The logarithm is the infinites-
imal form of $\Delta C / C$, and the $I$ term provides some benefit for adding a few
high-benefit instructions over many low-benefit ones. They also proposed an
objective function, one that incorporates code size:

$$100 \ln C + 20 \ln S + I, \qquad \text{(EQ 2-30)}$$

where $S$ is the static number of instructions. This form imposes a 5% rule for
code size improvements.

*instruction
formation*

Holmer and Despain identified candidate instructions using methods similar to the microcode compaction algorithms used to schedule micro-operations. They compiled a benchmark program into a set of primitive micro-operations. They then used a branch-and-bound algorithm to combine micro-operations into candidate instructions. Combinations of micro-operations were then grouped into instructions.

*instruction set
search
algorithms*

Huang and Despain [Hua95] also used an $n\%$ rule as a criterion for instruction selection. They proposed the use of simulated annealing to search the instruction set design space. Given a set of micro-operations that can be implemented in the data path, they use move operators to generate combinations of micro-operations. A move may displace a micro-operation to a different time step, exchange two micro-operations, insert a time step, or delete a time step. A move must be evaluated not only for performance but also to determine whether they violate design constraints, such as resource utilization.

*template
generation*

Kastner et al. [Kas02] use clustering to generate instruction templates and cover the program. Covering is necessary to ensure that the entire program can be implemented with instructions. Clustering finds subgraphs that occur frequently in the program graph and replaces those subgraphs with supernodes that correspond to new instructions.

Atasu et al. [Ata03] developed algorithms to find complex instructions. Figure 2-52 shows an operator graph from a section of the *adpcmde code* benchmark. Although the *M2* graph is large, the operators within it are fairly small; the entire *M2* subgraph implements a $16 \times 3$-bit multiplication, which is a good candidate for encapsulation in an instruction. Atasu et al. also argue that combining several disjoint graphs, such as *M2* and *M3*, into a single instruction is advantageous. Disjoint operations can be performed in parallel and so offer significant speedups. They also argue that multi-output operations are important candidates for specialized instructions.

A large operator graph must be convex to be mapped into an instruction. The graph identified by the dotted line in Figure 2-53 is not convex: input *b* depends on output *a*. In this case, the instruction would have to stall and wait for *b* to be produced before it could finish.

Atasu et al. found large subgraphs in the operator graph that maximize the speedup provided by the instruction. By covering the graph with existing instructions, we can count the number of cycles required to execute the graph without the new instruction. We can estimate the number of clock cycles required to execute the new instruction by fast logic synthesis that provides the critical path length, which we can then compare to the available cycle time. The authors use a branch-and-bound algorithm to identify cuts in the operator graph that define new instruction subgraphs.

Biswas et al. [Bis05] use a version of the Kernighan–Lin partitioning algorithm to find instructions. They point out that finding the maximum-size instruction does not always result in the best result. In the example of Figure 2-54, the

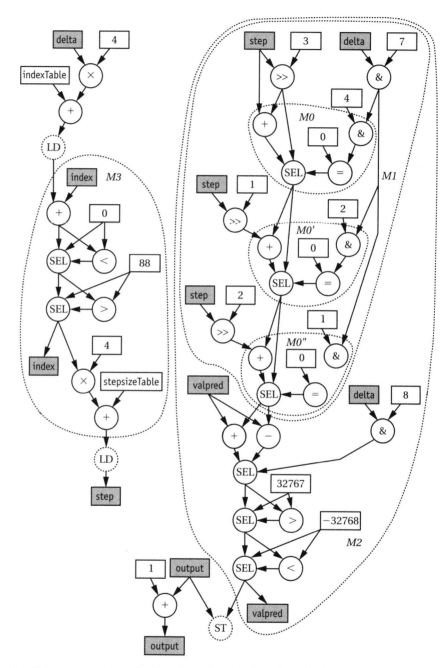

**Figure 2-52** *Candidate instructions in the adpcmde code benchmark. From Atasu et al.*
*[Ata03] © 2003 ACM Press. Reprinted by permission.*

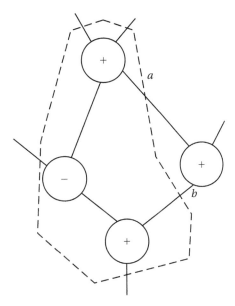

**Figure 2-53** *A nonconvex operator graph.*

*instructions in combination*

largest template (in the dotted line) can be used only three times in the computation, but the smaller graph (in the solid line) can be used six times.

Sun et al. [Sun04] developed an instruction set synthesis system that used the Tensilica Xtensa system to implement their choices. Their system generates TIE code that can be used to synthesize processors. They generate instructions from

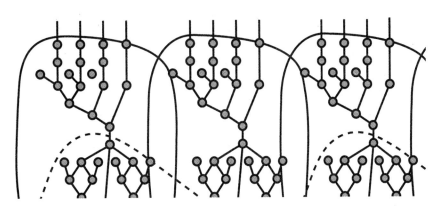

**Figure 2-54** *Instruction template size versus utilization. From Biswas et al. [Bis05] © 2005 IEEE Computer Society.*

programs by combining micro-instructions. They synthesize the register–transfer hardware for each candidate instruction, then synthesize logic and layout for that hardware to evaluate its performance and area. Sun et al. select a subset of all possible instructions for further evaluation based on their speedup and area potential. Based on this set of candidate instructions, they select a combination of instructions used to augment the processor instruction set. They use a branch-and-bound algorithm to identify a combination of instructions that minimizes area while satisfying the performance goal.

*large instructions*

Pozzi and Ienne [Poz05] developed algorithms to extract large operations as instructions. Larger combinations of micro-operations provide greater speedups for many signal processing algorithms. Because large blocks may require many memory accesses, they developed algorithms that generate multicycle operations from large data flow graphs. The authors identify mappings that require more memory ports than are available in the register file and add pipelining registers and sequencing to perform the operations across multiple cycles.

The next example describes a recent industrial instruction set synthesis system.

## Example 2-16

*The Tensilica Xpres Compiler*

The Xpres compiler [Ten04] designs instruction sets from benchmark programs. It creates TIE code and processor configurations that provide the optimizations selected from the benchmarks. Xpres looks for the following types of optimized instructions.

- **Operator fusion** creates new instructions out of combinations of primitive micro-operations.

- Vector/SIMD operations perform the same operation on vectors of 2, 4, or 8 subwords.

- Flix operations combine independent operations into a single instruction.

- Specialized operations may limit the source or destination registers or other operands. These specializations provide a tighter encoding for the operation that can be used to pack several operations into a single instruction.

The Xpres compiler searches the design space to identify instructions to be added to the architecture. It also allows the user to guide the search process.

*limited-precision arithmetic*

A related problem is the design of limited-precision arithmetic units for digital signal processing. Floating-point arithmetic provides high accuracy across a wide dynamic range but at a considerable cost in area, power, and performance. In many cases, if the range of possible values can be determined, finite-precision arithmetic units can be used. Mahlke et al. [Mah01] extended the PICO system to synthesize variable-bit-width architectures. They used rules, designer input, and loop analysis to determine the required bit width of variables. They used def-use analysis to analyze the propagation of bit widths.

Mahlke et al. clustered operations together to find a small number of distinct bit widths to implement the required accuracy with a small number of distinct units. They found that bit-width clustering was particularly effective when operations could be mapped onto multifunction units. The results of their synthesis experiments for a number of benchmarks are shown in Figure 2-55. The right bar shows hardware cost for bit-width analysis alone, while the left bar shows hardware cost after bit-width analysis and clustering. Each bar divides hardware cost into registers, function units, and other logic.

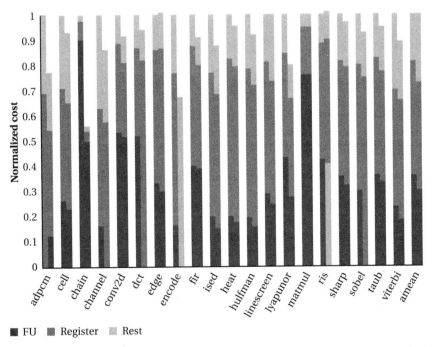

**Figure 2-55** *Cost of bit-width clustering for multifunction units. From Mahlke et al. [Mah01] © 2001 IEEE.*

The traditional way to determine the dynamic range of an algorithm is by simulation, which requires careful design of the input dataset as well as long runtimes. Fang et al. [Fan03] used affine arithmetic to analyze the numerical characteristics of algorithms. Affine arithmetic models the range of a variable as a linear equation. Terms in the affine model can describe the correlation between the ranges of other variables; accurate analysis of correlations allows the dynamic range of variables to be tightly bounded.

## 2.10 Summary

CPUs are at the heart of embedded computing. CPUs can be selected from a catalog for use or they can be custom-designed for the task at hand. A variety of architectural techniques are available to optimize CPUs for performance, power consumption, and cost; these techniques can be combined in a number of ways. Processors can be designed by hand; a variety of analysis and optimization techniques have been developed to help designers customize processors.

### What We Have Learned

- RISC and DSP approaches can be used in embedded CPUs. The design trade-offs for embedded processors lead to some different conclusions than are typical for general-purpose processors.

- A variety of parallel execution methods can be used; they must be matched to the parallelism available in the application.

- Encoding algorithms can be used to efficiently represent signals, data, and instructions in processors.

- Embedded processors are prone to many attacks that are not realistic in desktop or server systems.

- CPU simulation is an important tool for both processor design and software optimization. Several techniques, varying in accuracy and speed, can be used to simulate performance and energy consumption.

- CPUs can be designed to match the characteristics of the application for which they can be used. The instruction set, memory hierarchy, and other subsystems can all be specialized to the task at hand.

## Further Reading

Conte [Con92] describes both CPU simulation and its uses in computer design. Fisher et al. [Fis05] provides a detailed analysis of VLIW architectures for embedded computing. Rotenberg and Anantararaman's chapter in [Rot04] provides an excellent introduction to embedded CPU architectures. The SOS Research website (*http://www.sosresearch.org/caale/caalesimulators. html*) provides extensive information about CPU simulators. This chapter has made reference to U.S. patents, which are available online at *http://www.uspto.gov*. Witold Kinsner has created a good online introduction to smart cards at *http://www.ee.umanitoba.ca/~kinsner/whatsnew/tutorials/tu1999/smcards.html*.

## Questions

**Q2-1**  Identify possible instructions in matrix multiplication.

**Q2-2**  Identify possible instructions in the fast Fourier transform.

**Q2-3**  Compare and contrast performing a matrix multiplication using subword parallel instructions and vector instructions. How do the code fragments for the two approaches differ? How do these differences affect performance?

**Q2-4**  Compare the opportunities for parallelism in a Viterbi decoder. Would a superscalar CPU be able to find much more parallelism in a Viterbi decoder than would be found by a VLIW compiler?

**Q2-5**  Build a model for a two-way set-associative cache. The parameters of the cache are: line size $l$ (in bits), number of lines $n$. Show the block-level organization of the cache. Create formulas describing the area $A$, delay $D$, and energy $E$ of the cache based on the formulas for the block-level model.

**Q2-6**  Evaluate cache configurations for several block-motion estimation algorithms. The motion estimation search uses a $16 \times 16$ macroblock and a search area of $25 \times 25$. Each pixel is 8 bits wide. Consider full search and three-step search. The cache size is fixed at 4,096 bytes. Evaluate direct-mapped, 2-way, and 4-way set associative caches at three different line widths: 4 bytes, 8 bytes, and 16 bytes. Compute the cache miss rate for each case.

**Q2-7**  Draw a pipeline diagram for a processor that uses a code decompression engine. Not counting decode, the pipeline includes four stages. Assume that the code decompression engine requires four cycles for decoding. Show the execution of an addition followed by a branch.

**Q2-8** Use a Huffman code to encode these 5-bit opcodes: 00000, 00001, 10010, 10001, 00011. Show the Huffman coding tree and the codes for each opcode. Assume that all opcodes are equally probable.

**Q2-9** A hypothetical RISC processor uses different instruction formats for arithmetic operations and branches. An arithmetic operation includes an opcode and two register numbers. A conditional branch uses an opcode, one register number, and a branch offset.

   a. Compare the advantages and disadvantages of using Huffman coding to encode the entire instruction versus encoding each field in the instruction separately using Huffman coding.

   b. Compare the advantages and disadvantages of using dictionary-style coding to encode the entire instruction versus encoding each field in the instruction separately.

**Q2-10** If a cache is used for combined code and data compression, would a write-through or a write-back policy be preferable? Explain.

**Q2-11** Evaluate the energy savings of bus-invert coding on the address bus for the address sequences to the array $a[10][10]$, where $a$ starts at address 100. Changing one bit of the address bus consumes $e$ energy. Give the total savings for bus-invert coding versus an unencoded bus.

   a. Row-major sequential accesses to the array $a$.

   b. Column-major sequential access to $a$.

   c. Diagonal accesses such as those used for JPEG DCT encoding $(0,0 \rightarrow 1,0 \rightarrow 0,1 \rightarrow 2,0 \rightarrow 1,1 \rightarrow 0,2 \rightarrow \cdots)$.

**Q2-12** How do branches affect the effectiveness of bus-invert coding?

**Q2-13** How would you determine the proper dictionary size for a dictionary-based bus encoder?

**Q2-14** You are designing a configurable CPU for an embedded application. How would you choose the cache size and configuration?

**Q2-15** Design an algorithm to find convex subgraphs in an operator graph.

## Lab Exercises

**L2-1** Develop a SimpleScalar model for a DSP with a Harvard-architecture and multiply–accumulate instruction.

**L2-2** Use your SimpleScalar model to compare performance of a matrix multiplication routine with and without the multiply–accumulate instruction.

**L2-3**   Use simulation tools to analyze the effects of register file size on performance of motion estimation. Compare full search and three-step search.

**L2-4**   Develop a SimpleScalar model for a code decompression engine. Evaluate CPU performance as the decompression time varies from 1 to 10 cycles.

# Programs

- Code generation and back-end compilation
- Memory-oriented software optimizations
- Software performance analysis
- Programming models and languages

## 3.1 Introduction

This chapter looks at how to design and implement programs. By *program*, we mean a single executable. We will defer parallelism to later chapters, although this chapter does consider parallel specifications mapped onto sequential machines.

While embedded computing relies on the programming technology developed for the general-purpose world, many aspects of embedded programming are particularly challenging. Because we need to meet real-time deadlines, we must design software carefully, particularly when the processor includes a cache. We must also be able to accurately analyze the execution time of a program. Signal-processing systems are memory intensive, and streaming data in particular presents new challenges. Higher-level programming languages that provide useful abstractions and optimization tools are often used to design embedded software.

We will study embedded program design from the bottom up. We start in Section 3.2 by looking at the back end of compilers, which is where many of the optimizations required for embedded programs must take place. We then look at memory-oriented optimizations in Section 3.3 and study performance analysis

**155**

of software in Section 3.4. In Section 3.5 we consider various higher-level programming models for embedded applications.

## 3.2    Code Generation and Back-End Compilation

Embedded processors are often selected for their ability to execute particular algorithms, whether they are standard parts such as DSPs or ASIPs designed for a particular project. Back-end compiler phases are often keys to exploiting the relationship between the processor architecture and the application.

*general-purpose versus embedded compilers*

General-purpose compilers are designed to compile code for a wide range of purposes. Compilation speed is often important—when designing large software systems, programmers must be able to run through the write/compile/execute/debug cycle quickly. Software developers for embedded systems have somewhat different needs. Embedded software must often meet hard targets for execution time, energy consumption, or code size. As a result, a number of compilation algorithms developed for embedded systems are optimization algorithms; general-purpose compiler writers often have to balance the requirements of different users at the expense of precise constraint satisfaction. Embedded software developers may also be willing to wait longer for the compiler to run if it performs useful functions. While some stages may require fast write/compile/execute/debug cycles, other stages may require careful tuning to meet performance, size, or energy constraints. If the compiler can perform those tasks with minimal intercession by the programmer, then programmers generally are happy to wait for the compiler to do its work.

As illustrated in Figure 3-1, the major steps in code generation [Goo97] are as follows.

- **Instruction selection** determines which opcodes and modes are used to implement all the operations in the program. The abstract program must be covered by the selected instructions. They may also be selected to minimize program cost such as size or performance.

- **Register allocation** determines which registers are used to hold the values in the program. In a general-register machine, in which all instructions can operate on all registers, register allocation can be performed strictly after instruction selection. Many ASIPs and DSPs do not fit that model—some important instructions may work on only one or a few registers. In such cases, instruction selection must allocate critical values to registers, and the register-allocation phase allocates the remaining values to general-purpose or special-purpose registers.

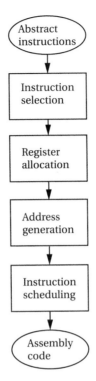

**Figure 3-1** *Phases in back-end code generation.*

- **Address generation** does not serve the same purpose as the code-placement steps described later in Section 3.2.5. Some instructions may use addressing modes that depend on properties of the addresses. For example, certain array-oriented instructions may work best at certain strides. Pre- or post-increment addressing can also be used to walk through the stack, providing data is put in the stack in the order in which it is used.

- **Instruction scheduling** is important in pipelined and parallel machines. CPUs with branch delay slots must fill those slots with appropriate instructions. VLIW processors also require instruction scheduling.

### 3.2.1 Models for Instructions

Instruction modeling is key to the design of ASIP compilers. When designing specialized instructions, we also need to design compilers that can make use of those instructions. We cannot in general rely on compiler designers to create

*twig*

*instruction selection as template matching*

handcrafted compilers for ASIPs. For compilers to adapt automatically to new instructions, we must describe those instructions in ways that allow the compiler to generate code.

To understand the problems of instruction selection for complex processors, let us consider the basic problem formulation and an algorithm to solve it. We will use the *twig* code generator of Aho et al. [Aho89] as an example, limiting ourselves to data flow operations.

We can formulate instruction selection as template matching. As shown in Figure 3-2, we generate data flow graphs for the program. We also represent the instructions in the processor architecture as data flow graphs of the same form. A template-matching algorithm selects instructions by matching the instruction templates to the program.

The generated assembly language code must satisfy the basic correctness constraint of covering the entire program. If the program data flow graph is not fully covered, then some operations are not implemented by instructions. Beyond correctness, the template-matching algorithm should optimize for some cost. The most basic cost is code size, but performance or energy may also be considered. The objectives may be specified by the programmer; the algorithm may make use of annotations, such as execution time or energy consumption, on the instruction templates.

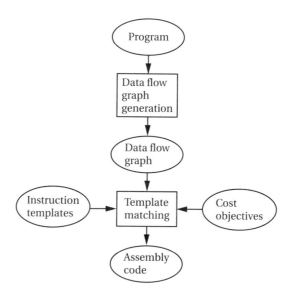

**Figure 3-2** *Instruction selection as template matching.*

*rewriting rules*        A tree-rewriting rule has the form

$$\text{replacement} \leftarrow \text{template \{ cost \} = action} \qquad \text{(EQ 3-1)}$$

where *template* is a tree, *replacement* is a single tree node, and *cost* and *action* are code fragments. Given a set of rules, *twig* generates a matching automaton that can find the low-cost match in a code segment that has been written in tree form.

*template-matching algorithm*        Figure 3-3 shows an example of a tree-rewriting rule [Aho89]. The tree on the left describes an increment instruction, while the tree on the right describes an addition instruction. The right side of the rule corresponds to the right side of the formula, while the result of the formula's left side corresponds to the left side of the rule. The cost and action code fragments are not shown in the figure. The cost code fragment can compute the cost of a given match using arbitrary code that can examine the state of the tree matching, cost tables, or other information. The action routine is executed when a match is identified; it could, for example, generate the required code.

The algorithm used by the automaton to generate code is based on dynamic programming. Costs are evaluated at each node to guide the dynamic programming process.

This tree-based approach must be extended to accommodate ASIP processors. Most important, ASIPs do not have general-purpose register files, and many of the important instructions use specialized registers.

*ASIP instruction description*        When designing code generators for existing machines, we only need to describe how the instruction modifies the programming model—the programmer-visible registers. When we generate ASIPs with custom instructions, we must describe the complete behavior of the instruction in the pipeline. PEAS-III [Kob02], for example, describes the pipeline resources used by the instruction along with the instruction format and registers. Leupers and Marwedel [Leu95] model instructions as register transfers interspersed with no-operations (NOPs).

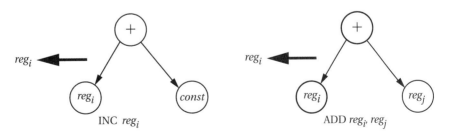

**Figure 3-3** *Example twig rewriting rules.*

Each register transfer is executed under its execution conditions, which are described as Boolean expressions. NOPs are used to preserve live values for later consumption.

### 3.2.2 Register Allocation

*register liveness*

The methods used for register allocation can be used, with some modification, for the allocation of many different types of resources. We want to allocate variables to registers as illustrated in Figure 3-4. In this case, the program variables *v1* and *v3* are never used at the same time, so they can both be assigned to register *R1*; similarly, *v2* and *v4* can both be assigned to *R1*. Two variables can be allocated to the same register if they are never **live** at the same time—that is, if the last use of one of the variables predates the first use of the other. Since we are assuming the schedule of operations, we know the times at which the variable values are needed.

Figure 3-5 shows the construction of a **variable lifetime chart** from a scheduled set of operations. The operations and their schedule provide the graduation of the time axis. Each variable is given its own column; a bar extends from the variable's **definition** to its last **use**. A horizontal line through the chart at any chosen time shows which variables are in use at that time.

The example of Figure 3-5 shows only straight-line code—no loops or branches. As a result, the variable lifetime chart has a simple structure. A more general representation for lifetimes is depicted as a **conflict graph**, as shown in Figure 3-6. Each variable is represented by a node. An edge joins two nodes if

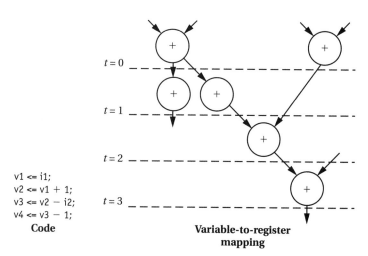

```
v1 <= i1;
v2 <= v1 + 1;
v3 <= v2 - i2;
v4 <= v3 - 1;
```
**Code**

**Figure 3-4** *Register allocation.*

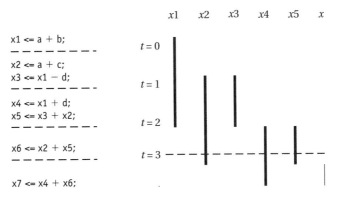

```
x1 <= a + b;
- - - - - - - -
x2 <= a + c;
x3 <= x1 - d;
- - - - - - - -
x4 <= x1 + d;
x5 <= x3 + x2;
- - - - - - - -
x6 <= x2 + x5;
- - - - - - - -
x7 <= x4 + x6;
```

**Figure 3-5** *Variable lifetime analysis.*

those variables have nonoverlapping lifetimes. An edge, therefore, identifies a pair of variables that can be allocated to the same register. The pairwise information is easy to generate from the schedule. However, to choose registers for the variables, we need to consider all the conflicts.

*clique*
A register is represented in this formulation by a **clique** of nodes, a clique being a set in which every pair of vertices is connected by an edge. To avoid defining a clique that is a subset of a larger clique, a clique must be the largest possible set of fully connected nodes. A graph and a set of cliques on it are shown in Figure 3-7. Depending on the structure of the graph, some cliques may be very small: two nodes connected by a single edge or an isolated node.

The fact that each node belongs to only one clique ensures that one variable is assigned to only one register. (So long as we keep the same value in both reg-

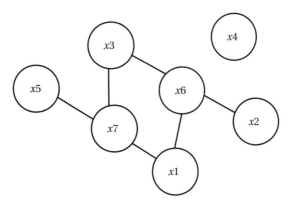

**Figure 3-6** *A conflict graph.*

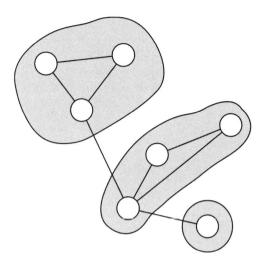

**Figure 3-7** *Cliques in a graph.*

isters, duplicating a variable does no harm and, if we have nonuniform interconnections between registers and function units, multiple copies may have some
advantage. However, in most cases, duplicating a variable only takes up space
that could be used by another variable.) We ensure that every variable has a register by requiring that every node in the graph be a member of a clique. Needless
to say, finding the cliques of a general graph is NP-hard.

*graph coloring*          Another way of viewing the problem is that we want to assign a **color** to
each node such that if two nodes are connected by an edge, they have different
colors. If each color denotes a distinct register, then forcing connected nodes to
have different colors ensures that variables with overlapping lifetimes have distinct registers.

While there are many possible colorings of the graph, they are not equally
good hardware designs. We actually want to solve a more general problem than
simply finding the cliques of the conflict graph. Using the simplest measure of
cost—the total number of registers required–***minimum cost allocation*** requires
the fewest cliques (or, in the graph-coloring world, the coloring with the fewest
colors). We can define the problem more formally: given an undirected graph
$G = \langle V, E \rangle$, we want to partition the graph into the smallest number of cliques
such that $\cup c_j = V$. Tseng and Siewiorek [Tse86] developed a heuristic algorithm
for finding the minimum size of the clique covering, in a conflict graph.

*VLIW register*           Register allocation in VLIW processors has additional implications for per-
*files*             formance beyond the general CPU case. VLIW register files are typically partitioned—each function unit in the data path can access only a subset of the
registers. When a function unit needs a value that is in a register it cannot access,

the value must be copied from one register file partition to another. Jacome and de Veciana [Jac99] developed methods to bound latency in VLIW processors with partitioned register files.

A data flow graph is bound to the function units and register files of a data path. They divide the problem into windows; the problem is defined by the start and finish steps for the window, the data path resource associated with the window, and the set of activities bound to that resource that we would like to schedule within the window's time range. An individual window is defined on a single operation in the data flow graph. These are used to construct basic windows, which group together operations that share the same resource and scheduling range. Basic windows are then combined into aggregated windows, which merge basic windows on the same data path resource but not necessarily the same time window. These windows can be scheduled using an algorithm that propagates delays in order to find the global feasible times for the windows.

### 3.2.3  Instruction Selection and Scheduling

Instruction selection becomes important when the processor has limited or irregular resources. Many DSPs have irregular register sets and operations, so instruction selection becomes very important for these machines. Limited or irregular processor resources are also influential when operations are performed. Instruction selection and scheduling may interact as a result of resource limitations.

As part of the FlexWare system, Liem et al. [Lie94] developed an instruction-generation system for ASIPs with irregular register files. Figure 3-8 shows the intermediate representation for programs, which includes both data and control flow aspects. Target instructions are described in the same basic format. Each instruction is annotated with register classes that identify how registers can communicate with each other. To cover the program graph with instructions, they use dynamic programming for the data flow segments and heuristics for the control flow parts of the graph.

The second-generation FlexWare compiler [Pau02] generates code in three main stages. It first uses rule-based techniques such as those just described to select instructions. It then performs peephole optimizations on the code. Finally, it compacts the code to create a schedule for the operations and generates assembly language.

The PEAS-III compiler generator as described in Kobayashi et al. [Kob02] creates mapping rules based on instruction descriptions. It classifies instructions into five categories: arithmetic/logical, control, load/store, stack manipulation, and special. The compiler generator creates scheduling information by tracing how each instruction uses pipeline resources, then calculating the latency and throughput of each instruction.

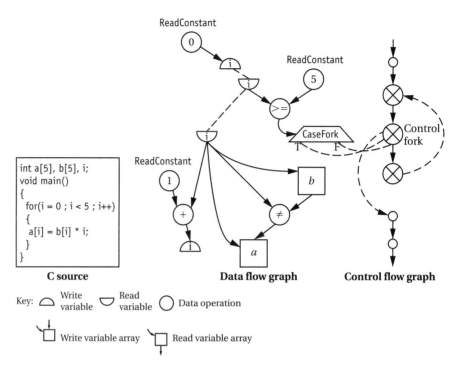

```
int a[5], b[5], i;
void main()
{
  for(i = 0 ; i < 5 ; i++)
  {
    a[i] = b[i] * i;
  }
}
```
**C source**

**Data flow graph**

**Control flow graph**

Key: ◠ Write variable   ◡ Read variable   ◯ Data operation

▢ Write variable array   ▢ Read variable array

**Figure 3-8** *Program representations for FlexWare. From Liem et al. [Lie94] © 1994 IEEE.*

*scheduling constraint modeling*

Mesman et al. [Mes97] developed a model for the constraints on code scheduling. Constraints determine the set of feasible times when operations can be scheduled; the feasible schedule space can be searched to find the desired schedule. Mesman et al. represent the set of constraints as a weighted directed graph. Vertices in the graph represent operations, and edges represent precedence relationships. The constraints can also be written as linear inequalities, as shown in Figure 3-9. Each node is constrained against the other. In this case, the pair of constraints can be rewritten as $a - b| \leq 1$.

Mesman et al. consider several types of constraints. Data dependencies are represented by a single edge whose weight is equal to the operation's execution time. If the data dependency is in a loop, the value must be consumed before the next iteration; a backward arc for each data dependency represents this requirement. Other types of latencies are also represented by single edges. Multicycle operations are represented using one node per stage of execution. They use 0–1 variable to model resource conflicts.

To solve the system of constraints and find a schedule, they add edges to the graph to fix the times of operations. For example, potential resource conflicts are avoided by adding an edge that ensures the operations are not scheduled at

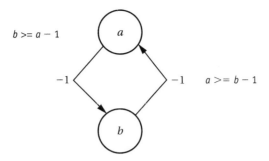

**Figure 3-9** *Constraint graphs and linear inequalities.*

the same time. Constraints are also added to ensure that all the operations in a subgraph have time to execute. In addition, edges can be added to make variable lifetimes sequential.

*combined instruction selection, register allocation, scheduling*

Araujo and Malik [Ara95] developed an optimal algorithm for instruction selection, register allocation, and scheduling on a class of architectures in which either one location or an unbounded number of those of a given class is available. The TI TMS320C25 is an example of this class, which Araujo and Malik call the **[1, ∞] class**. They define this class using a register transfer graph: each node in the graph is a register or main memory; a directed edge from one node to another indicates a possible data transfer, with a label on the edge that defines which instruction(s) can perform the transfer. An example of such a register transfer graph is shown in Figure 3-10: the *r3* register can be written from both

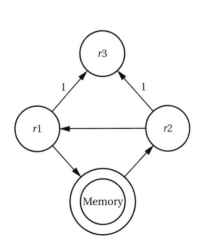

**Figure 3-10** *A register transfer graph that satisfies the [1, ∞] condition. From Araujo and Malik [Ara95] © 1995 ACM Press.*

*r1* and *r2* using the *l* instruction; all the cycles between *r1* and *r2* include the memory node. This condition ensures that values can be spilled to main memory when needed. Based on this property, Araujo and Malik showed that expression trees can always be scheduled without a memory spill.

They use a tree-grammar parser to select instructions and allocate registers; the patterns that define the instructions include the registers used by the instructions. They then use an *O(n)* algorithm, shown in Figure 3-11, to schedule the instructions.

```
GetUsage (u)
begin
    memset(n) = φ;
    regset(u) = φ;
    if match(u) is not memory
        regset(u) = match(u);
    foreach v in children(u)
        GetUsage(v);
        if match(v) is memory
            memset(u) = memset(u) ∪ {v};
        else
            memset(u) = memset(u) ∪ memset(v);
            regset(u) = regset(u) ∪ regset(v);
        endif;
    endfor;
end

OptSchedule (u)
begin
    foreach p in memset(u)
        OptSchedule(p);
    foreach v in children(u)
        FreeSchedule(v);
    emit(u);
end

FreeSchedule (u)
begin
    if match(u) is memory
        return;
    if u is not a leaf
        v₁ = unique(children(u));
        foreach w in children(v₁)
            FreeSchedule(w);
    endif;
    emit(u);
end
```

**Figure 3-11**  *The Araujo and Malik instruction-scheduling algorithm. From Araujo and Malik [Ara95] © 1995 ACM Press.*

### 3.2.4  Code Placement

The location of code in memory is important because it affects memory system performance. Simply moving a section of code or data from one address to another can speed up the program and reduce its energy consumption.

Figure 3-12 illustrates the code placement process. Assembly language uses relative addresses. Code placement assigns absolute addresses to optimize two types of memory access: cache access time and partitioned memory access. The result is absolute addresses that can be fed into a linker and loader.

Figure 3-13 illustrates the relationship between absolute addresses in main memory and cache lines. Many blocks of memory map into the same cache line. We cannot avoid all conflicts, but by moving one block we can avoid mapping that block to the same address as another block. If the blocks go to different cache lines, we are guaranteed that they will never conflict. A less strong form of code placement would assign two blocks that rarely conflict to the same cache line. If the amount of code that needs to remain in the cache is relatively small, then heuristics may be sufficient to avoid the major cache conflicts. In general, an optimization algorithm must balance the caching behavior of the blocks in a large program to find the least objectionable combination of cache conflicts.

Hwu and Chang [Hwu89] placed instructions to improve instruction cache performance. They analyzed traces to find the relative execution times of code

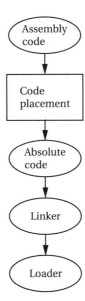

**Figure 3-12** *Post-assembly optimizations.*

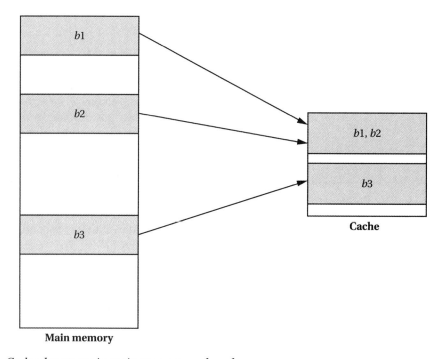

**Main memory**

**Figure 3-13** *Code placement in main memory and cache.*

sections. These authors inline expanded frequently called functions to eliminate function call overhead. They used a greedy algorithm to place frequently used traces in the program image.

McFarling [McF89] analyzed program structure in addition to using trace information to determine code segments that should be placed in noninterfering memory locations. He annotated the program with the average number of times that loops are executed, basic block size, and procedure call frequency. He then walked through the program to propagate labels, grouped together code segments based on their labels, and placed those code segments so that they would not interfere in the graph.

McFarling also studied procedure inlining [McF91]. He developed the following formula to estimate the number of cache misses in a loop.

$$s_l = \sum s_b \min(1, f), \qquad \text{(EQ 3-2)}$$

$$M_l = \max(0, l-1)\max(0, s_l - S), \qquad \text{(EQ 3-3)}$$

where $s_l$ is the effective loop body size, $s_b$ is the basic block size, $f$ is the average execution frequency of the block, $M_l$ is number of misses per loop instance, $l$ is the average number of loop iterations, and $S$ is the cache size. McFarling used the model to estimate the new cache miss rate when a procedure is inlined. He used a greedy algorithm to determine what functions to inline.

Pettis and Hansen [Pet90] evaluated several methods for determining code placement from profiling data. They profiled their programs using *gprof*. They positioned procedures such that the caller and callee were close to each other in the program, increasing the chance that they ended on the same page, reducing the size of the page working set, and decreasing the chance that they will knock each other out of the cache. They ordered procedures by building a call graph and weighting each edge with the number of times that the caller invokes the callee, then merging nodes connected by high-weight edges.

They also experimented with placement methods for basic blocks. Pettis and Hansen rearranged blocks from if-then-else code such that the most frequently executed path in the conditional takes advantage of the processor's branch prediction mechanism. They placed basic blocks by analyzing a control flow graph whose edges are annotated with the number of times that the given path is executed. A bottom-up algorithm examined the edges starting with the most heavily weighted edge and grouped nodes and edges into paths by adding heavily weighted edges to the path.

The authors also identified basic blocks that were never executed in the profile; they called these blocks **fluff**. The fact that a basic block does not appear in a profile does not mean that it is dead code that can be eliminated, since the input data set may not fully exercise the program. However, moving fluff blocks to separate procedures reduces the size of the procedures that include highly used code, improving their cache behavior. Their **procedure-splitting** algorithm added long branches to connect the nonfluff code to the fluff code.

Pettis and Hansen found that procedure positioning significantly reduced the number of long branches that were executed. They found that programs ran 1% to 6% faster even without using profiling data. They found that positioning basic blocks to generate more straight-line code sequences reduced the number of executed penalty branches by 42% and increased the number of instructions between branches from 6.19 to 8.08. They found that splitting procedures added a very small number of overhead instructions.

Tomiyama and Yasuura [Tom97] formulated trace placement as an integer linear programming problem. Their basic method increased code size between 13% and 30% on a series of benchmarks. They reduced code size by combining traces such that the size of a merged trace was a multiple of the cache line size, eliminating unused locations.

### 3.2.5 Programming Environments

When designing a custom processor, we need to create more than just a compiler to support the ASIP's programmers. We must also create a complete set of

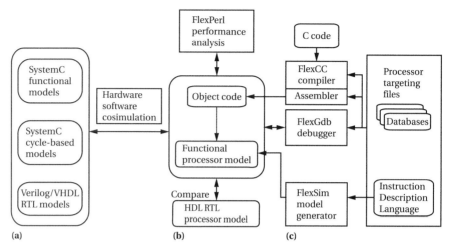

**Figure 3-14** *The FlexWare system. From [Pau02] © 2002 IEEE.*

programming tools: assembler, linker, loader, debugger, and graphical programming environment.

Figure 3-14 shows the elements of the FlexWare system [Pau02] including the application hardware (a), the ASIP hardware (b), and the embedded software and its development environment (c).

## 3.3   Memory-Oriented Optimizations

Memory is a key bottleneck in embedded systems. Many embedded computing applications spend a lot of their time accessing memory. The memory system is a prime determinant of not only performance but also energy consumption.

*types of memory optimizations*

Memory system optimizations can target any stage of the memory hierarchy. A large variety of techniques have been developed by both the general-purpose and embedded communities to optimize cache performance. More recently, optimization techniques for scratch pad memories have been developed. Optimizations can also target main memories, particularly when they are partitioned.

Memory system optimizations can target either data or instructions. Array optimizations are an important class of data-oriented optimizations. Control flow analysis leads to methods for improving the cache behavior of instructions.

Global memory analysis is particularly important in embedded systems. Many embedded systems are composed of many subsystems that pass data between themselves. The buffers between those subsystems must be carefully sized to avoid both buffer overflows and wasted memory.

```
for (i=0; i<N; i++)           for (i=1; i<N; i++)
    c[i] = a[i] + b[i];           c[i] = a[i] + c[i-1];
```
**Fully parallelizable**       **Loop-carried dependencies**

**Figure 3-15**  *Parallelism and constraints in loops.*


### 3.3.1  Loop Transformations

Some optimizations are applied early during compilation, without detailed knowledge of the target hardware. Such transformations try to expose parallelism that can be used by later stages. Loops are a prime candidate for such transformations since they may provide a great source for data parallelism. Loop transformations have been studied for decades for use in scientific programs and optimizing compilers. There is not enough space here to do this topic justice; we only introduce a few concepts that illustrate how this body of work can be used.

*ideal parallelism*    An ideal loop can be executed entirely in parallel. The code on the left side of Figure 3-15 has a loop body in which all the arrays are indexed only by $i$. Therefore, no loop iteration depends on any other iteration. As a result, all the loop bodies could be executed in parallel, in any order, without affecting the result. In the code on the right side of the figure, the $i^{th}$ iteration depends on the result of the $i - 1^{th}$ iteration. In this case, we cannot finish iteration $i$ until $i - 1$ has also finished, so these loop bodies must be done in the order in which they are enumerated by the loop. Data dependencies from one loop iteration to another are known as **loop-carried dependencies**.

*optimization strategy*    The compiler must schedule operations so that they do not violate the data dependencies—that is, the code does not try to use a value before it has been computed. In general, many possible schedules satisfy the data dependencies, provided that we have a way to enumerate those dependencies. While a single loop may provide some opportunities, a **loop nest** offers many possibilities for parallelism that require detailed analysis. As shown in Figure 3-16, a loop nest is a set of loops, one inside the other. A perfect loop nest has no conditionals inside the nest. An imperfect loop nest has conditionals that cause some statements in the nest to not be executed in some cases.

```
                                      for (i=0; i<N; i++)
    for (i=0; i<N; i++)                   for (j=0; j<M; j++)
        for (j=0; j<M; j++)                   if (i != j)
            for (k=0; k<L; k++)                   for (k=0; k<L; k++)
                c[k] = a[i][j] * b[k];               c[k]= a[i][j] * b[k];
```
**Perfect loop nest**                 **Imperfect loop nest**

**Figure 3-16**  *Loop nests.*

*types of loop transformations*

Loop and loop nests have many data dependencies—each operation in each iteration generates its own data dependency. However, we also know that the loop provides structure and regularity that we can exploit. Some possible transformations on loops and loop nests include:

- **Loop permutation** changes the order of the loops in the nest.

- **Index rewriting** changes the way the loop indexes are expressed.

- **Loop unrolling** creates several copies of a loop body and modifies the loop indexes appropriately.

- **Loop splitting** takes a loop with multiple operations and creates a separate loop for each operation; **loop fusion** performs the opposite.

- **Loop tiling** splits a loop into a nest of loops, with each inner loop working on a small block of data.

- **Loop padding** adds data elements to an array to change how the array maps into the memory system structure.

*polytope model*

The **polytope model** [Bac94; Dar98] is commonly used to represent and manipulate the data dependencies in loop nests. Figure 3-17 shows a loop nest. We can represent the loop nest as a matrix: each column in the matrix represents the iteration bounds of a loop.

The inner loop body modifies the values of $c$, creating a data dependency from $c[i][j]$ to $c[i][j+1]$. We represent each data element in the array as a node in a two-dimensional space, with the loop iteration variables forming the axes of the space. The nodes define a polytope in that space in a triangular shape. We add edges between the nodes that describe the loop-carried dependency between $c[i][j]$ and $c[i][j+1]$.

The points in the polytope fully describe all the loop-carried dependencies, but we have not yet reduced the complexity of that representation. We can use a

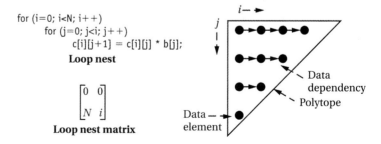

```
for (i=0; i<N; i++)
    for (j=0; j<i; j++)
        c[i][j+1] = c[i][j] * b[j];
```
**Loop nest**

$$\begin{bmatrix} 0 & 0 \\ N & i \end{bmatrix}$$

**Loop nest matrix**

**Figure 3-17** *Polytope representation of loop nests.*

**distance vector** that describes the direction and distance of a set of vectors. In this case, all the data dependencies are of the form $[i\, j] = [1\, 0]$.

Any set of loops that performs this computation must satisfy these loop-carried dependencies, but many schedules are, in general, possible. We can apply an ordering vector that describes the order in which the loops visit the nodes. We can use matrix algebra to manipulate the form of the loops.

*loop transformations and matrices*

For example, if we want to interchange the loops, putting $j$ in the outer loop and $i$ in the inner loop, we can multiply the loop nest matrix by an interchange matrix, as follows.

$$\begin{bmatrix} 0 & 0 \\ N & i \end{bmatrix} \cdot \begin{bmatrix} 0 & 1 \\ 1 & 0 \end{bmatrix} = \begin{bmatrix} 0 & 0 \\ i & N \end{bmatrix}. \qquad \text{(EQ 3-4)}$$

This gives the loop nest

```
for (j = 0; j < i; j ++)
   for (i = 0; i < N; i ++)
      c [i + 1][j ] = a[i ][j ]*b[j ];
```

Not all loop transformations are legal. Wolf and Lam [Wol91b] showed that a loop transformation is legal if all the transformed dependence vectors are lexicographically positive—that is, if they do not point backward in the iteration space.

*non-unimodular transformations*

Not all important loop transformations can be manipulated by matrix algebra. Loop tiling, for example, splits a large array into several smaller arrays to change the order in which the array elements are traversed. This transformation cannot be represented by matrix manipulations, but once a loop is tiled, the new loop nest can be analyzed using matrix methods.

Loop permutation and loop fusion [Wol96] can be used to reduce the time required to access matrix elements. Loop permutation reduces latency when it is used to change the order of array accesses to that used in the underlying data structure. Multidimensional arrays are stored by C in row-major format, so we want to access rows first. Figure 3-18 shows an example of loop permutation. Loop fusion (see example in Figure 3-19) allows references to the same array in different loops to be combined and reused.

```
for (j=0; j<M; j++)                    for (i=0; i<N; i++)
   for (i=0; i<N; i++)                    for (j=0; j<M; j++)
      x[i][j] = a[i][j] * b[j];             x[i][j] = a[i][j] * b[j];
      Original loop nest                     After loop permutation
```

**Figure 3-18** *An example of loop permutation.*

```
for (i=0; i<N; i++)
    x[i] = a[i] * b[i];               for (i=0; i<N; i++)
for (i=0; i<N; i++)                       for (j=0; j<M; j++)
    y[i] = a[i] * c[i];                       x[i][j] = a[i][j] * b[j];
       Original loops                       After loop fusion
```

**Figure 3-19**  *An example of loop fusion.*

*memory layout transformations*    The layout of array elements can also be modified to change the way that they map into the cache or a parallel memory system. For example, transposing a matrix is an alternative to loop permutation. Loops can also be padded to change how the data elements fall into cache lines. The wasted memory may be more than made up for by improved cache performance.

*loops and energy*    Given that the memory system is a major contributor to system power consumption, we would expect that loop transformations can either hurt or help the energy consumption of a program. Kandemir et al. [Kan00] studied the effects of compiler transformations on energy consumption by simulating different versions of several benchmark programs with SimplePower. Figure 3-20 summarizes their results. They experimented with different types of transformations on different benchmarks and measured the energy consumption of unoptimized and optimized code, testing several cache configurations for each program implementation.

One interesting result of these experiments is that, with the exception of loop unrolling, most optimizations increase the amount of energy consumed in the CPU core. Given the Kandemir et al. technology parameters, the increase in core energy consumption was more than offset by the reduced energy consumption in the memory system, but a different technology could result in net energy losses for such transformations. Any optimization strategy must balance the energy consumption of the memory system and the core. These experiments also show that increasing the cache size and associativity does come at the cost of increased static and dynamic energy consumption in the cache. Once again, losses were more than offset by gains in the rest of the memory system for these technology parameters, but a different technology could shift the balance.

## 3.3.2  Global Optimizations

Compilers apply a great many transformations. The order of transformations is important—some transformations enable other transformations, and some make it impossible to apply other transformations later. Optimization strategies have been developed for both general-purpose compilers and for embedded systems.

*real-time Java*    The **Real-Time Specification for Java** (**RTSJ**) [Bol00] is a standard version of Java that allows programmers to consider the temporal properties of their Java programs to determine whether they can meet deadlines. The designers of

| Program | Array Sizes | Hian Rate | Organizations |
|---|---|---|---|
| adi | 100*100*1 | 0.0010 | Linear transforms Sites |
| hydrosd/try | 100*1 | 0.0000 | Loop Fusion |
| hydrosd/try | 100*100*100*S | 0.2000 | Loop Fusion |
| hydro/necessity | 100*1 | 0.1100 | Loop Fusion |
| toatacy | 100*100 | 0.2400 | Scalar expansion |

**Benchmarks and optimizations**

| | Core Energy (J) | | Memory Energy (J) | | | |
|---|---|---|---|---|---|---|
| | | 1th | 1-way | 2-way | 4-way | 8-way |
| orig | 0.0043 | 1K | 0.1004 | 0.0015 | 0.0794 | 0.0772 |
| | | 2K | 0.1159 | 0.0780 | 0.0756 | 0.0757 |
| | | 4K | 0.1000 | 0.0783 | 0.0759 | 0.0760 |
| | | 3K | 0.0730 | 0.0681 | 0.0742 | 0.0766 |
| loop | 0.0054 | 1K | 0.1418 | 0.0640 | 0.5026 | 0.0466 |
| | | 2K | 0.0844 | 0.0493 | 0.0435 | 0.0436 |
| | | 4K | 0.0000 | 0.0441 | 0.0439 | 0.0440 |
| | | 3K | 0.0578 | 0.4283 | 0.0231 | 0.0251 |
| tile | 0.0052 | 1K | 0.1401 | 0.0731 | 0.0729 | 0.0288 |
| | | 2K | 0.0942 | 0.0640 | 0.0674 | 0.0488 |
| | | 4K | 0.0550 | 0.0426 | 0.0465 | 0.0457 |
| | | 3K | 0.0540 | 0.0226 | 0.0220 | 0.0221 |

**adi**

| | Core Energy (J) | | Memory Energy (J) | | | |
|---|---|---|---|---|---|---|
| | | | 1.Way | 2.Way | 4.Way | 8.Way |
| orign | 0.1503 | 1K | 3.4440 | 3.0333 | 2.1170 | 2.0734 |
| | | 2K | 3.3221 | 2.3311 | 1.3908 | 1.3014 |
| | | 4K | 1.6616 | 1.3948 | 6.0333 | 1.1133 |
| | | 8K | 1.3387 | 0.0373 | 0.1942 | 0.8732 |
| fiss | 0.1745 | 1K | 2.4086 | 4.4788 | 3.1001 | 3.2550 |
| | | 2K | 3.0100 | 8.7048 | 1.4469 | 1.2732 |
| | | 4K | 1.8087 | 1.4712 | 1.1003 | 1.1033 |
| | | 8K | 1.9887 | 0.0430 | 0.1362 | 0.8032 |

**nasa 7≠b trix**

| | Core Energy (J) | | Memory Energy (J) | | | |
|---|---|---|---|---|---|---|
| | | | 1.Way | 2.Way | 4.Way | 8.Way |
| orign | 0.0003 | 1K | 0.0200 | 0.0117 | 0.6070 | 0.0072 |
| | | 2K | 0.0130 | 0.0069 | 0.0000 | 0.0034 |
| | | 4K | 0.0056 | 0.0036 | 0.4051 | 0.0054 |
| | | 8K | 0.0338 | 0.0036 | 0.4055 | 0.0033 |
| fiss | 0.0005 | 1K | 0.0277 | 0.0102 | 0.0073 | 0.0063 |
| | | 2K | 0.0095 | 0.0034 | 0.0001 | 0.0063 |
| | | 4K | 0.0089 | 0.0030 | 0.0030 | 0.0030 |
| | | 8K | 0.0067 | 0.0030 | 0.4050 | 0.0030 |

**hydro 2d ≠ fct**

| | Core Energy (J) | | Memory Energy (J) | | | |
|---|---|---|---|---|---|---|
| | | | 1.Way | 2.Way | 4.Way | 8.Way |
| orign | 0.2713 | 1K | 3.4228 | 7.4466 | 6.8610 | |
| | | 2K | 0.0883 | 7.0487 | 7.0487 | 6.1011 |
| | | 4K | 7.6007 | 7.1870 | 0.3485 | 6.2203 |
| | | 8K | 3.4000 | 3.4774 | 0.5711 | 3.3755 |
| fiss | 0.2873 | 1K | 11.0321 | 10.1304 | 9.8536 | 9.2634 |
| | | 2K | 9.4603 | 9.4244 | 9.6897 | 9.7468 |
| | | 4K | 7.4571 | 6.07289 | 0.1112 | 3.10101 |
| | | 8K | 5.2204 | 3.2730 | 6.1806 | 3.2317 |

**nasa 7≠choles kg**

| | Core Energy (J) | | Memory Energy (J) | | | |
|---|---|---|---|---|---|---|
| | | 1th | 1-way | 2-way | 4-way | 8-way |
| orig | 0.0222 | 1K | 1.3934 | 0.0739 | 0.5858 | 0.5731 |
| | | 2K | 0.8384 | 0.0609 | 0.5706 | 0.5707 |
| | | 4K | 0.7920 | 0.5813 | 0.5716 | 0.5720 |
| | | 3K | 0.7111 | 0.5260 | 0.5301 | 0.5296 |
| loop | 0.2875 | 1K | 0.4256 | 0.0640 | 0.5278 | 0.9233 |
| | | 2K | 0.1753 | 0.0493 | 0.9223 | 0.9232 |
| | | 4K | 0.0228 | 0.0441 | 0.9253 | 0.9282 |
| | | 3K | 0.0924 | 0.4283 | 0.8005 | 0.3976 |

**tomca tv**

**Figure 3-20** *Simulation measurements of the effects of compiler transformations on energy consumption. From Kandemir et al. [Kan00] © 1998 ACM Press. Reprinted by permission.*

the standard identified three major features of Java that limit programmers' ability to determine a program's real-time properties: scheduling, memory management, and synchronization.

Java did not provide detailed specifications about scheduling. RTSJ requires a fixed-priority preemptive scheduler with at least 28 unique priorities. A RealtimeThread class defines threads that can be controlled by this scheduler.

Java uses garbage collection to simplify memory management for the general-purpose programmer but at the price of reduced predictability of memory systems. To improve the predictability of memory management, RTSJ allows programs to allocate objects outside the heap. A MemoryArea class allows programs to represent a memory area that is not garbage collected. It supports three types of objects: physical memory, which allows for the modeling of non-RAM memory components; immortal memory, which lives for the execution duration of the program; and scoped memory, which allows the program to manage memory objects using the syntactic scope of the object as an aid.

The RTSJ does not enforce priority-based synchronization, but it does provide additional synchronization mechanisms. The system queues all threads that are waiting for a resource so that they acquire the resource in priority order. Synchronization must implement a **priority inversion protocol** (see Section 4.2.2). RTSJ also provides a facility to handle asynchronous events, such as a hardware interrupt.

*general strategies*

Bacon et al. [Bac94] proposed a flow for optimizing compilers. Without going into all the details, we should consider some of their important steps.

- **Procedure restructuring** inlines functions, eliminates tail recursion, and so on.

- **High-level data flow optimization** reduces the strength of operations, moves loop-invariant code, and so on.

- **Partial evaluation** simplifies algebra, evaluates constants, and so on.

- **Loop preparation** peels loops and so on.

- **Loop reordering** interchanges, skews, and otherwise transforms loop nests.

A variety of lower-level transformations and code-generation steps complete the compilation process.

*strategies for streaming*

Catthoor et al. [Cat98] developed a methodology for streaming systems such as multi-media. This methodology is designed to manage global data flow and achieve an efficient implementation. The steps in the methodology include:

- **Memory-oriented data flow analysis and model extraction**, which analyzes loops to identify the memory requirements of the various phases of the program.

- **Global data flow transformations** to improve memory utilization.

- **Global loop and control flow optimizations** to eliminate system-level buffers and improve data locality.

- **Data reuse decisions for memory hierarchy** use caches to reduce energy consumption and improve performance.

- **Memory organization** designs the memory system and its ports.

- **In-place optimization** uses low-level techniques to reduce storage requirements.

### 3.3.3 Buffer, Data Transfer, and Storage Management

*buffer management*

Buffers are important because they mediate between subsystems. In many embedded applications, the various stages produce and consume data somewhat irregularly. As a result, we need buffers to make sure that all data makes it from the producer to the consumer. If the buffer is too small, data is lost. If the buffer is too large, then memory is wasted. Overly large buffers not only add to the manufacturing cost of the system, but they also consume both static and dynamic energy.

*problems with dynamic memory management*

A traditional approach is to use dynamic memory management—for example, the C library functions malloc() and free(). By allocating buffers of the proper size, we can avoid memory overflows. This approach may be difficult to verify, and *memory leaks*—memory that is allocated but never freed—may escape into production code. Just as important for embedded systems, the memory management routines themselves cost a great deal in both performance and energy consumption. Because the execution time of memory management routines is highly data-dependent, these routines make it difficult to meet real-time deadlines. A combination of static and dynamic buffer management techniques can make sure that buffers are properly sized at a much smaller runtime cost.

*data transfer and storage management*

Several groups at IMEC, including De Greef et al. [DeG95], Franssen et al. [Fra94], and Masselos et al. [Mas99], have developed methodologies and algorithms for data transfer and storage management. This line of work tries to restructure code to both minimize the required amount of buffer memory and to improve the performance of accesses to that buffer memory. Data transfer and storage management make use of many techniques, including loop transformations and control flow analysis. It requires analyzing the complete application to understand the dependencies between different sections of code, such as different loop nests, and to balance concerns across the entire program.

*loop transformations and buffering*

Panda et al. [Pan01] give some examples that illustrate how loop transformations can be used to improve buffer utilization. Consider the following code.

```
for (i = 0; i < N; ++i)
    for ( j = 0; j< = N–L; ++j )
        b[i ][j ] = 0;
for (i = 0; i < N; ++i )
    for ( j = 0; j < N – L; ++j )
        for (k = 0; k < L; ++k)
            b[i ][j ] + = a[i ][j + k]
```

This code causes buffering problems because both loop nests modify the b array. The first loop nest modifies all elements of b before the second loop nest has a chance to use those locations. If we combine the two loop nests, we can reuse the b elements much more easily.

```
for (i = 0; i < N; ++i )
    for ( j = 0; j < N – L; ++j )
        b[i ][j ] = 0;
        for (k = 0; k < L; ++k)
            b[i ][j ] + = a[i ][ j + k];
```

*buffer analysis*

Moving the first definition of *b* closer to its next use makes it much easier for lower-level optimizations to take advantage of mechanisms such as prefetching.

Panda et al. [Pan01] also showed that loop analysis can be used to help analyze buffers more explicitly. They added signal copies to the code to make data reuse explicit. The buffer a_buf is L words long and buffers the a array; b_buf is one word long and buffers the b values. These buffers are declared in the program but do not need to exist in the final implementation.

```
int a_buf[L];
int b_buf;
for (i = 0; i < N; ++i ) {
  initialize a_buf;
  for ( j = 0; j < N – L; ++j ) {
    b_buf = 0;
    a_buf[( j + L–1)%L] = a[i ][ j + L – 1];
  for (k = 0; k < L; ++k)
    b_buf + = a_buf[( j + k)%L]
  b[i ][j ] = b_buf;
  }
}
```

Once the copies have been made explicit, analysis methods can be used to determine the lifetimes of values in those buffers.

### 3.3.4 Cache- and Scratch Pad–Oriented Optimizations

*cache hit rate improvement*

Cache-oriented optimizations take advantage of two different cache effects. Clearly, some optimizations are designed to improve cache hit rates by reducing the number of conflicts caused by memory access patterns. By rearranging data so that important elements do not knock each other out of the cache, we can greatly increase performance as well as reduce energy consumption.

*prefetching*

Data can also be rearranged in the cache to take advantage of prefetching. Virtually all caches fetch more than one word at a time. If we can organize data so that a single cache miss pulls in several successive values of interest, then we can greatly reduce the access time for the other elements of the cache line.

*scalar variable placement*

Panda et al. [Pan97] developed algorithms to place data in memory to reduce cache conflicts. Their methodology for scalar variables includes four steps:

1. Build a closeness graph that describes the relationship between accesses.

2. Cluster the variables into cache line-sized units.

3. Build a cluster interference graph that describes how clusters interact in the cache.

4. Use the cluster interference graph to optimize cluster placement.

```
Procedure  AssignClusters
Input: CIG(V,E)—Cluster Interference Graph
Output: Assignment of Clusters to Memory Locations
    Sort the vertices of CIG in descending order of S(u)
    — S(u) is the sum of edge weights incident on vertex u
    Let X be this sorted list of vertices
    while (X ≠ φ) do
      Create new page P in memory
      while (size of page P < k) and (X ≠ φ) do
        u = head of list X
        Assign u to line i of page P, where cost(u, i) is minimum
        over i = 0 ... k − 1
        Delete u from X
      end while
    end while
end Procedure
```

**Figure 3-21**  *An algorithm for assigning clusters of scalar variables to memory to minimize conflicts. From Panda et al. [Pan97] © 1998 ACM Press. Reprinted by permission.*

The closeness graph is built from the access patterns of the variables, and it is a weighted, fully connected undirected graph with one node per variable. The weight of each edge {u, v} is equal to the length of the path between u and v. We then group the nodes of the graph into clusters of size L or less, where L is the number of words in a cache line; they use a greedy heuristic. The cluster interference graph has one node per cluster. The weight of the edge {U, V} is equal to the number of times that clusters U and V are alternately executed. They use the greedy algorithm of Figure 3-21 to place clusters in memory.

*array placement*      Panda et al. [Pan97] use a similar technique to place arrays accessed by inner loops, though the method required to evaluate array conflicts is more complex than the simple test used for scalars. We will concentrate on the direct-mapped cache case here. They first build an interference graph whose nodes are the arrays; the weight of an edge {u, v} is equal to the number of cache conflicts that could arise between the two arrays. To optimize array placement, they need to calculate whether two arrays in the same loop will map into the same cache line. We are given two addresses, $X$ and $Y$. The direct-mapped cache has line size $k$, and a line holds $M$ words. Then $X$ and $Y$ will map onto the same cache line if

$$\left( \left\lfloor \frac{X}{M} \right\rfloor - \left\lfloor \frac{Y}{M} \right\rfloor \right) \bmod k = 0 \quad , \tag{EQ 3-5}$$

which can be rewritten as

$$(nk - 1) < \frac{X - Y}{M} < (nk + 1), \tag{EQ 3-6}$$

where $n$ is an integer.

Figure 3-22 shows the Panda et al. algorithm for assigning addresses to arrays. They use a greedy strategy to move arrays apart to minimize conflicts. The AssignmentCost function uses (EQ 3-6) to test the placement of an array *A* against all other arrays with which it may conflict and return the cost of a particular address assignment.

*combined data and loop transformations*

Kandemir et al. [Kan99a] developed a methodology that combines data and loop transformations to optimize cache performance. They first transform the loop nest such that the destination array (the array on the left side of the assignment) has its innermost index as the only element in one array dimension and that this index is not used in any other dimension. They then align references to the right side matrices to conform to the access pattern for the left side. They search through various transformations on the right side to find the best alternative.

*scratch pads*

Scratch pad memories offer new opportunities for optimization. Data values must be partitioned between the cache and scratch pad. We also have to decide whether to manage the scratch pad contents statically or dynamically.

*scratch pad management*

Panda et al. [Pan00] developed methods for managing scratch pad contents by allocating variables to the scratch pad. They determined that static variables were best managed statically, with allocation decisions made at compile time. They chose to map all scalars to the scratch pad to avoid creating cache conflicts between arrays and scalars.

```
Procedure  AssignArrayAddresses
Input: IG – Interference Graph, k – no. of cache lines
Output: Assignment of addresses to all arrays (nodes in IG)
    Address  A = 0
    Sort nodes in IG in decreasing order of S(u) (sum of incident edge weights)
    Let the list of nodes be: v_0 ... v_{n-1}
    for  i = 0 ... n–1
        Initialize cost c = ∞
        min = 0  — keeps track of cache line with minimum mapping cost
        for j  = 0 ... k − 1
            if AssignmentCost(v_i, A + j) < c then
                c = AssignmentCost(v_i, A + j)
                min = j
            end if
        end for
        Assign address (A + min) to first element of v_i
        A = A + min + size(v_i)  — updating A for next iteration
    end for
end Procedure
```

**Figure 3-22** *Algorithm for assigning addresses to arrays to minimize direct-mapped cache conflicts. From Panda et al. [Pan97] © 1998 ACM Press. Reprinted by permission.*

Arrays can be mapped into either the cache or the scratch pad. If two arrays have nonintersecting lifetimes, then their relative allocation is not important. Arrays with intersecting lifetimes may conflict; analysis is required to determine which ones are mapped into the cache versus the scratch pad. Panda et al. define several metrics to analyze conflicts.

- *VAC(u)*, the **variable access count** of variable *u*, counts the number of times that *u* is accessed during its lifetime.

- *IAC(u)*, the **interference access count** of variable *u*, counts the number of times other variables ($v \neq u$) are accessed during the lifetime of *u*.

- *IF(u)*, the **interference factor** of *u*, is defined as

$$IF(u) = VAC(u) + IAC(u). \qquad \text{(EQ 3-7)}$$

Variables with a high *IF* value are likely to be interfered with in the cache and are good candidates for promotion to the scratch pad.

Panda et al. then use these metrics to define a loop-oriented conflict metric, known as the **loop conflict factor** or *LCF* of a variable *u*.

$$LCF(u) = \sum_{1 \leq i \leq p} \left[ k(u) + \left( \sum_{v} k(v) \right) \right]. \qquad \text{(EQ 3-8)}$$

In this formula, the *k(a)* function denotes the number of accesses to variable *a*. The outer summation is over all *p* loops in which *u* is accessed, and the inner summation is over all *variables* $v \neq u$ accessed in the $i^{th}$ loop.

The **total conflict factor**, *TCF*, for an array *u* is

$$TCF(u) = LCF(u) + IF(u). \qquad \text{(EQ 3-9)}$$

*scratch pad allocation algorithms*

These metrics are used by algorithms to allocate variables between the scratch pad and main memory/cache. We can formulate the problem as follows:

Given a set of arrays, each with a *TCF* value, a size

$$\{A_1, TCF(A_1), S_1\}, ..., \{A_n, TCF(A_n), S_n\}$$

and an SRAM of size *S*

find an optimal subset of arrays *Q* such that $S \geq \sum_{i \in Q} S_i$ and $\sum_{i \in Q} TCF(i)$ is maximized.

This problem is a generalized knapsack problem in that several arrays with non-overlapping lifetimes can intersect in the scratch pad.

Panda et al.'s algorithm starts by clustering together arrays that could share scratch pad space. It then uses an approximation algorithm that first sorts the items by value per weight as given by access density *AD*.

$$AD(c) = \frac{\displaystyle\sum_{v \in c} TCF(v)}{\max\{size(v), v \in c\}}.$$

(EQ 3-10)

Arrays are then greedily selected for allocation to the scratch pad, starting with the array with the highest *AD* value, until the scratch pad is full.

Figure 3-23 shows the allocation algorithm of Panda et al. Scalar variables are allocated to the scratch pad, and arrays that are too large to fit into the scratch pad are allocated to main memory. A compatibility graph is created to determine arrays with compatible lifetimes. Cliques are then allocated, but the algorithm may allocate either a full clique or a proper subset of the clique to the scratch pad. Clique analysis takes $O(n^3)$ time, and the algorithm can iterate *n* times, so the overall complexity of the algorithm is $O(n^4)$.

*scratch pad evaluation*

Figure 3-24 shows the performance of scratch pad allocation algorithms [Pan00] on one benchmark. The experiment compared using on-chip memory only for SRAM, using on-chip memory only for data cache, random allocation into scratch pad that occupies half the available SRAM, and Panda et al.'s allocation algorithm into a scratch pad that occupies half the available SRAM.

## 3.3.5   Main Memory-Oriented Optimizations

An idealized model of a memory chip is functional: present an address to the memory and receive the desired memory location after a fixed delay. However, high-performance memory systems, to provide higher performance and lower energy consumption, break this simple model.

- **Burst access modes** access a sequence of memory locations.

- **Paged memories** take advantage of the properties of memory components to reduce access times.

- **Banked memories** are systems of memory components that allow parallel accesses.

*burst modes*

Burst modes are provided by some memory components as well as memory subsystems such as Rambus. A burst mode access provides a start address and a length; the length may be provided as a sequence of pulses or as a binary count. The memory accesses the sequence of locations starting with the given location. Burst accesses reduce the number of addresses that must be sent to memory. They also take advantage of internal registers to increase the transfer rate.

```
Algorithm Memory Assign
Input: Application Program P with Register-allocated variables marked;
SRAM_Size: Size of Scratch-Pad SRAM
Output: Assignment of arrays to SRAM/DRAM
        AuSpace = SRAM_ Size - - Available SRAM space
        Let U = {array u|u is an array in P}
        - - U is the set of all behavioral arrays in program P
        Let W = φ — W is the  set  of  arrays  assigned to DRAM
        for all variables v
            if v is a scalar variable or constant
                Assign v to SRAM
                AvSpace = AvSpace — size(v)
            else
                if size(v) > SRAM_Size
                    W = W ∪ {v} - - Assign υ to DRAM
                end if
            end if
        end for
        Generate compatibility graph G from life-times of remaining arrays
        U = U-W - - U is the set of all arrays < SRAM size
        while (U = φ)
            for each arrays u ∈ U
                Find largest clique c (u) in G such that u ∈ c(u) and
                size(v) ≤ size (v)∀v ∈ c(u)
```

$$\text{Compute sccess density } AD(u) = \frac{\Sigma v \epsilon c(u) \ TC\delta(u)}{size(u)}$$

```
            end  for
            Assign clique c(i) to SRAM, where AD(i) = max {AD(u)|u ∈ U}
            - - Assign cluster with highest access density to SRAM
            AuSpace  = AuSpace − size(c) - - size(c) = size of largest arrays in c
            X = {v∈ U|size(u) > AuSpace}
            - - X = set of arrays in U larges than AuSpace
            W = W ∪ X - - Arrays in X are mapped to DRAM
            U = U− {v|(v ∈ c)}−X
            - - Remove from U arrays assigned to SRAM and arrays in X
        end while
        Assign arrays in W to DRAM
end Algorithm
```

**Figure 3-23** *An algorithm for scratch pad allocation. From Panda et al. [Pan00] © 1998 ACM Press. Reprinted by permission.*

*paged addressing mechanisms*

Most large memory components support some form of paged addressing. The details may differ from device to device, but the address is split into two sections: page and offset. (These may also be known as *row* and *column*.) The page is presented first, followed by the offset. The page is also stored in a register in the memory component so that it can be used for subsequent accesses. Successive accesses to the same page take much less time than accesses that hop across pages. This is due not only to the time saved by not sending the page number to the component, but also to signal propagation within the memory

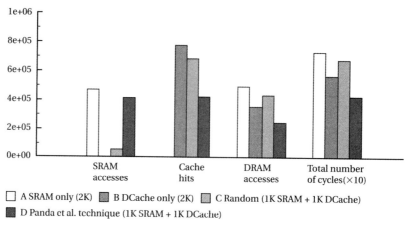

**Figure 3-24** *Performance comparison of scratch pad allocation. From Panda et al. [Pan00] © 2000 ACM Press.*

component. Some paging mechanisms are faster when sequential accesses are referenced. Other schemes merely require that addresses on the same page be accessed.

A compiler may take advantage of paged addressing by proper placement of data and addressing patterns. Scalar data may take advantage of paged addressing by placing successive references in adjacent locations on the same memory page. Array data accesses may also take advantage of locality.

*banked memories*

As illustrated in Figure 3-25, a banked memory is built from several parallel memory components, which may or may not provide paged access. A banked memory may be built from multiple chips; some single-chip memory components provide multiple memory banks. Some of the address bits are decoded outside the memory component to select which chip is being

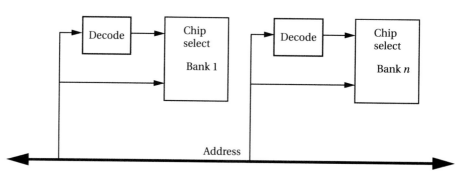

**Figure 3-25** *A banked memory system.*

addressed. Provided that the bus protocol is properly designed, the memory system can start one access in one bank by presenting an address to that bank, then start a second access to a different bank while waiting for the first access to complete.

Panda [Pan99c] designed a custom memory system with multiple memory banks for arrays. Grun et a.l [Gru00] used a timing analyzer to help schedule instructions. They modeled the pipeline and memory to determine the actual delay of a memory access based on the pipeline state.

## 3.4 Program Performance Analysis

Just as we need to know the speed at which hardware modules execute to design a hardware system, we need to analyze the performance of programs to build complex software systems. Unfortunately, software performance analysis is much more difficult than hardware timing analysis. Synchronous hardware design restricts the structure of digital logic so that we can accurately bound delay with reasonable effort. Software designers, in contrast, insist on the full power of Turing machines, which makes it much more difficult to find tight bounds on execution time.

*performance measures*

We generally measure program execution time from program initiation at presentation of some inputs to termination at the delivery of the last outputs. Several different measures of software performance are of interest.

- **Worst-case execution time (WCET)**—the longest execution time for any possible combination of inputs

- **Best-case execution time (BCET)**—the shortest execution time for any possible combination of inputs

- **Average-case execution time** for typical inputs

*uses of average performance*

Average-case performance is used for very different purposes than are worst-case and best-case execution times. Average performance is used to tune software (and perhaps the underlying hardware platform); average performance data is particularly useful when it is recorded not just for the entire program but for program units. Average-case behavior can be used to find hot spots due to poor algorithms, bad coding, poor choice of instructions, or other causes. Average performance is typically evaluated using CPU simulators of the sort we described in Chapter 2.

*uses of WCET and BCET*

Worst-case and best-case execution times, in contrast, are used during schedulability analysis. As we will see in Chapter 4, many scheduling algorithms and analysis methods guarantee schedulability based on knowledge of execution time. Many scheduling algorithms assume that the execution time of a program is constant, which is not realistic given the data-dependent behavior of most interesting programs. WCET is often used as a substitute for exact execution time. However, short execution times can cause scheduling problems that do not occur when all programs run to the worst-case limits, so a more helpful strategy is to measure both worst-case and best-case execution times.

*performance analysis challenges*

We cannot bound execution times through simulation because interesting programs have far too many input combinations to enumerate. We need to analyze the program to determine its timing behavior. When analyzing hardware to determine its maximum clock rate, we rely on the fact that combinational logic is generally acyclic to simplify analysis. When we analyze programs, we must handle arbitrary control flows. As illustrated in Figure 3-26, performance analysis algorithms must handle not only branches but also loops and other types of cyclic control flow.

*performance = paths + timing*

The basic approach to worst-case execution time analysis still followed today was suggested by Shaw [Sha89] and extended by Park and Shaw [Par91]. They broke WCET analysis into two phases.

1. Analyze the program to find the worst-case path through a program. This problem is sometimes called **path analysis**.

2. Measure the execution time along the worst-case path. Let us call this problem **path timing**.

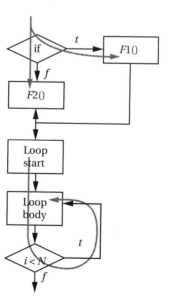

**Figure 3-26** *Execution paths through a program.*

The initial step in this methodology was to efficiently identify the worst-case execution path through the program. Park and Shaw developed a performance model of a 68000 that gave them good results. Unfortunately, modern high-performance microprocessors are much more complex, and the timing of instruction sequences is much more difficult. Research over the past 20 years has improved both the path identification process and the processor performance models.

Path analysis and path timing interact to some extent for complex machines. If the execution time of an instruction depends on the previous instructions, as is the case for both caches and pipelines, then we cannot easily find long paths without a detailed analysis of the timing of path segments. We can handle this by finding candidate long paths with abstract timing models and then refining the analysis using detailed timing models on a smaller set of paths.

### 3.4.1  Performance Models

*performance from instructions*

Determining the performance of a program fragment generally requires reducing high-level language code to instructions. Compilers perform many complex, interacting transformations on high-level language programs that make it difficult to directly determine the execution time of high-level language statements.

*variations in CPU performance*

Given a sequence of instructions and a CPU, we want to determine the WCET of that sequence on the processor. The simplest case would be if all instructions took the same amount of time to execute; we could then simply count instructions and multiply by the execution rate. However, that ideal world has never existed. Even the early computers were designed to take varying amounts of time to execute different instructions; the PDP-8, for example, exhibited large variations between the fastest and slowest instruction. The performance model Park and Shaw [Par91] developed for the 68000, by today's standard, was relatively simple. Although it had a large instruction set, it had only a simple pipeline and no cache. The manufacturer provided a table that gave the execution time of the various opcodes. The execution time for a code fragment could be accurately determined by looking up various instructions' execution times.

Today's processors do not admit this simple approach because the execution time of a processor depends on the processor state in various ways. The pipeline is one important source of variation. The execution time of an instruction depends in part on the behavior of other instructions in the pipeline. Two instructions that compete for the same resource will execute more slowly when executed together than if they were executed at widely separated times. The memory system is an even larger source of variation. Caches can introduce an order of magnitude, or more variation in memory accesses, depending on whether the access is a hit or a miss. Parallel memory systems can add further variation, as can DRAM refreshing, page modes, and other details of the types of memory components used.

Wilhelm [Wil04] used the term **timing accident** to describe the cause for an increase in the instruction time in a program, and **timing penalty** to describe the amount of increase. Timing accident can come from many different mechanisms at any stage in program execution. Wilhelm points out that the interference between these mechanisms makes for nonintuitive results, in which the best case for one part of the system may lead to longer total execution time.

### 3.4.2 Path Analysis

*computability and path analysis*

The goal of abstract program flow analysis is to bound the set of feasible paths. Because path analysis is equivalent to the halting problem, it cannot find the exact set of paths and may include some paths that are not feasible.

Puschner and Koza [Pus89; Pus93] analyzed the execution time of structured programs. They syntactically analyzed the program and assigned an execution time for each element in the parse tree. The execution time of the program was computed as the sum of the execution times of the statements. They added a MAX COUNT construct to their programming language to allow programmers to specify the maximum number of times that a loop will be executed.

*path analysis by ILP*

Today, many WCET methodologies use **integer linear programming (ILP)** to implicitly solve for paths. A set of constraints describes the structure of the program and some aspects of its behavior. Any solver finds the values for variables that identify the longest path through the program; this is done without enumerating all the paths.

Li and Malik [Li97c] modeled a program with a system of constraints: structural constraints describe conditionals and other control flow. Finiteness and start constraints help bound loop iterations; tightening constraints either come from the user or from an analysis of infeasible paths.

Figure 3-31 illustrates the use of structural constraints (see page 193). Each edge in the CDFG is represented by a variable whose value is equal to the number of times the program control flow passes through that edge. Conservation of flow tells us several facts: $i5o$, since the conditional is exited the same number of times it is entered; $i5a1b$ and $o5r1s$ for similar reasons. This implies that $a1b5r1s$. A constraint solver can use all the constraints collected for the program to solve for a bound on the number of times each edge is executed.

Figure 3-27 shows the program flow constraints for a while statement. In this case, we know that $i + b = o + t$. Since C defines for loops in terms of while loops [Ker78], we can use this construct to build for loops as well. User constraints can easily be added to an integer linear program. The user could, for example, bound the number of iterations of a while loop by writing an inequality involving the while loop's $b$ variable.

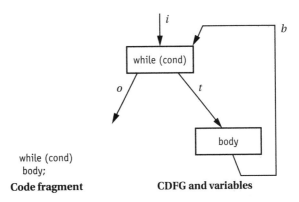

while (cond)
body;

**Code fragment**                    **CDFG and variables**

**Figure 3-27**  *Program flow statements in a while loop.*

The objective function for the integer linear program is to minimize the total flow through the network. Li and Malik [Li97c] used standard solvers to solve these systems of constraints. They evaluated their technique by analyzing several benchmark programs to find their worst-case inputs and related execution time bounds. Figure 3-28 shows the results of their experiments, in which they compared their analysis method to both hand-analyzed WCET bounds and measured execution times of worst-case inputs on an Intel i960 CPU.

*cache behavior and paths*

Li et al. [Li95] added instruction cache behavior into the model. They did this by breaking the program into units of cache line. In the basic model, a block in the CDFG represents straight-line code. The extended model handles direct-mapped instruction caches. Each straight-line code segment is broken into one or more units known as *l-blocks* that correspond to cache lines. Each *l*-block has two execution times, one for a cache hit and one for a cache miss. Two cache lines conflict if the execution of one *l*-block will cause the other *l*-block to be displaced from the cache; two *l*-blocks cannot conflict if they do not map onto the same cache line. A *cache conflict graph* is constructed for every cache line that has two or more conflicting *l*-blocks to keep track of the state of the cache lines.

As shown in Figure 3-29, the graph has a start node $s$ and an end node $e$, as well as a node for every *l*-block mapped into the cache line. The graph has an edge from one node to another if a path exists from the first basic block to the second, and the path does not require passing through other *l*-blocks mapped into the same cache line; in other words, an edge represents a direct conflict caused when one *l*-block knocks another out of the cache. Constraints from the cache conflict graph are added to the solution.

*user constraints*

The programmer may have knowledge of the program's behavior that is difficult for a timing analysis tool to reproduce. Many timing analysis methodologies allow user constraints to be incorporated into their analyses. User constraints can provide tighter bounds, assuming of course that the constraints

| Program | Constraint sets | Estimated bound | | Calculated bound | | Pessimism | |
|---|---|---|---|---|---|---|---|
| | | Lower | Upper | Lower | Upper | Lower | Upper |
| check_data | 4 ⇒ 2 | 35 | 1,193 | 35 | 1,193 | 0.00 | 0.00 |
| circle | 1 | 431 | 15,958 | 431 | 15,726 | 0.00 | 0.01 |
| des | 2 | 73,912 | 672,298 | 75,033 | 667,127 | 0.01 | 0.01 |
| dhry | 8 ⇒ 3 | 314,266 | 1,326,475 | 314,266 | 1,326,475 | 0.00 | 0.00 |
| djpeg | 1 | 12,703,432 | 122,838,368 | 12,925,769 | 98,696,050 | 0.02 | 0.24 |
| fdct | 1 | 5,587 | 16,693 | 5,587 | 16,693 | 0.00 | 0.00 |
| fft | 1 | 1,589,026 | 3,974,624 | 1,593,122 | 3,974,601 | 0.00 | 0.00 |
| line | 1 | 380 | 9,148 | 380 | 9,148 | 0.00 | 0.00 |
| matcnt | 1 | 1,722,105 | 8,172,149 | 1,722,105 | 8,172,149 | 0.00 | 0.00 |
| piksrt | 1 | 236 | 5,862 | 236 | 5,862 | 0.00 | 0.00 |
| sort | 1 | 13,965 | 50,244,928 | 13,965 | 50,244,928 | 0.00 | 0.00 |
| stats | 1 | 1,007,815 | 2,951,746 | 1,007,815 | 2,951,746 | 0.00 | 0.00 |
| whetstone | 1 | 5,634,926 | 14,871,610 | 5,634,926 | 14,871,610 | 0.00 | 0.00 |

**WCET bound vs. calculated bound**

| Program | Estimated bound | | Measured bound | | Pessimism | |
|---|---|---|---|---|---|---|
| | Lower | Upper | Lower | Upper | Lower | Upper |
| check_data | 35 | 1,193 | 35 | 430 | 0.00 | 1.77 |
| circle | 431 | 15,958 | 585 | 14,483 | 0.26 | 0.10 |
| des | 73,912 | 672,298 | 111,468 | 243,676 | 0.34 | 1.76 |
| dhry | 314,266 | 1,326,475 | 575,492 | 575,622 | 0.45 | 1.30 |
| djpeg | 12,703,432 | 122,838,368 | 14,975,268 | 35,636,948 | 0.15 | 2.45 |
| fdct | 5,587 | 16,693 | 7,616 | 9,048 | 0.27 | 0.84 |
| fft | 1,589,026 | 3,974,624 | 1,719,813 | 2,204,472 | 0.08 | 0.80 |
| line | 380 | 9,148 | 929 | 4,836 | 0.59 | 0.89 |
| matcnt | 1,722,105 | 8,172,149 | 2,202,276 | 2,202,698 | 0.22 | 2.71 |
| piksrt | 236 | 5,862 | 337 | 1,705 | 0.30 | 2.44 |
| sort | 13,965 | 50,244,928 | 16,492 | 9,991,172 | 0.15 | 4.03 |
| stats | 1,007,815 | 2,951,746 | 1,158,142 | 1,158,469 | 0.13 | 1.55 |
| whetstone | 5,634,926 | 14,871,610 | 6,935,612 | 6,935,668 | 0.19 | 1.14 |

**WCET bound vs. measured bound**

**Figure 3-28** *Experimental evaluation of the accuracy of -based WCET analysis. From Li et al. [Li97c] © 1997 IEEE Computer Society.*

accurately reflect program behavior. Exactly how these user constraints are incorporated into the analysis depends on the analytical technique used.

### 3.4.3  Path Timing

Several techniques are used to analyze path timing at different levels of abstraction. Abstract interpretation analyzes the behavior of the program in detail to more accurately understand the execution states of the program. Data flow anal-

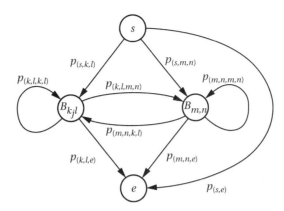

**Figure 3-29** *A cache conflict graph for two cache blocks. From Li et al. [Li95] © 1995 IEEE.*

ysis provides a more detailed view of how the program behaves. The most concrete technique is simulation, which is used to determine the details of how the processor responds to the program.

*loop iterations*     Bounding the number of iterations taken by a loop is particularly important for WCET analysis given that much of the execution time of most programs is spent in loops. Some loops, such as the FIR filter, are easy to analyze.

```
for (i = 0; i < N; i+)
   y [i ] = c [i ] * x [i ];
```

But loops with conditionals create problems.

```
for (i = 0; i < N; i++)
  for ( j = 0; j < M; j ++)
    if (i ! = j )
       c[i ][j ] = a[i ]*b[i ][j ];
    else
       c[i ][j ] = 0;
```

The algorithm of Healy et al. [Hea99a] bound loop iterations in four phases:

1.  It first uses an iterative algorithm to identify branches that affect the number of iterations.

2.  It then identifies the loop iteration on which a loop-dependent branch changes direction.

3.  It determines when the branches found in step 1 are reached.

4.  Finally, it uses these results to calculate the iteration bound.

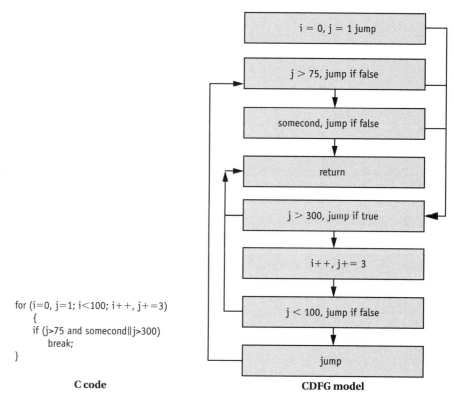

```
for (i=0, j=1; i<100; i++, j+=3)
    {
    if (j>75 and somecond||j>300)
        break;
    }
```

C code                                    CDFG model

**Figure 3-30** *An example of loop iteration bounding. After Healy et al. [Hea99a].*

Figure 3-30 shows an example of loop iteration bounding from Healy et al. The loop can be exited by a complex condition.

In the first step, it identifies the four control flow boxes with jumps as the points at which loop-dependent branches can change direction. It then determines that the first conditional branch, j > 75, occurs on iteration 26 (since *j* is incremented by 3 on each iteration). The condition j > 300 is taken on iteration 101, as is the condition j < 100. This gives a bound on the number of iterations as a minimum of 26 and a maximum of 101.

*parametric*
*timing analysis*
Vivancos et al. [Viv01] proposed a parametric timing analysis method to determine the timing behavior of programs with indefinite loops. They iteratively test the worst-case execution time of the program, starting with zero iterations and increasing the number of iterations by one at each step. Their testing terminates when the WCET stabilizes. Figure 3-31 shows a simple conditional, its associated CDFG, and the flow variables assigned to the edges in the CDFG.

*clustered*
*analysis*
Ermedahl et al. [Erm05] use a clustering technique to determine which parts of a program must be handled as a unit. They annotate the control flow graph of

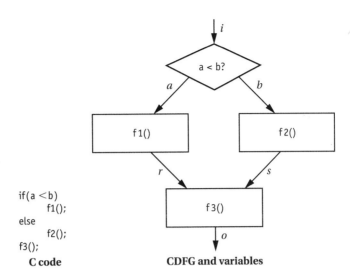

```
if(a <b)
        f1();
else
        f2();
f3();
     C code
```
**CDFG and variables**

**Figure 3-31** *Program flow constraint in an if statement.*

the program with **flow facts**, which include the defining scope, a context speci-
fier, and a constraint expression. The constraints may involve execution count
variables and constants. As illustrated in Figure 3-32, they cluster facts together
to find the maximum scopes over which flow facts apply, such as in nested
loops.

*instruction*
*caching*
Healy et al. [Hea99b] use static cache simulation to categorize each instruction's behavior in the cache. Given the CDFG for the program, they use an iterative algorithm to determine the program lines that may be in the cache during
the entry and exit of each basic block. They categorized the behavior of instructions in the instruction cache. Worst-case categories include the following.

- **Always miss**—Not guaranteed to be in the cache when referenced.

- **Always hit**—Guaranteed to be in the cache when it is referenced.

- **First miss**—Not guaranteed to be in the cache on the first loop iteration but
  guaranteed to be in the cache on subsequent iterations.

- **First hit**—Guaranteed to be in the cache on the first iteration but not guaranteed on subsequent iterations.

Best-case categories include the following.

- **Always miss**—Guaranteed not to be in the cache when first referenced.

- **Always hit**—May be in the cache every time it is referenced.

```
void foo(bool x) {    // scope: m
  ...
  for (i=0 ; i<10 ; i++)    // scope: n, loop bound: 10
    for (j=i ; j<10 ; j++)    // scope: o, loop bound: 10
      {. . . 01 ; . . . }    // code including block 01
  ...
  if ( . . . )
    x = true ;    // block M1
  bar(x) ;
  ...
  for ( . . . )    // scope: r
    {. . .
      bar () ;    // code including
      . . . }    // blocks R1, R2, R3
}
```

**Triangular loop**

**Long reaching dependency**

**Conditional dependency**

```
void bar(bool x) {    // scope: p
  for ( . . . )    // scope: q
    if (x==true)
      Q1 ;    // block Q1, execution
    . .    // implied by M1
}
```

```
void bar () {    // scope: s
  . . .    // code including blocks S1, S2, S3
  for ( . . . )    // scope: t, loop bound: 10
    if (T2) {    // block T2, jalse during last 3 iters
      S4 ;    // block S4, big chunk of work
      break;  }
  . . .    // code including block S5
}
```

**Example code**

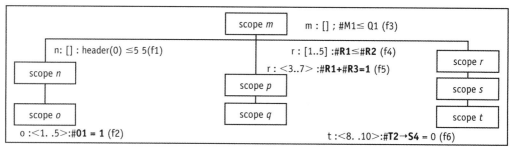

(a) Example scope-hierarchy with associated facts

| Fact | Defining scope | Span def scope | Covered scopes |
|------|---------------|----------------|----------------|
| f1 | n | 1..lb(n) | {n,o} |
| f2 | o | 1..5 | {o} |
| f3 | m | 1..lb(m) | {m,p,q} |
| f4 | r | 1..5 | {r} |
| f5 | r | 3..7 | {r} |
| f6 | o | 8..10 | {o} |

**(b)** Information about facts

| Fact cluster | Defining scope | Span def scope | Covered scopes |
|--------------|---------------|----------------|----------------|
| {f1,f2} | n | 1..lb(n) | {n,o} |
| {f2} | o | 1..5 | {o} |
| {f3} | m | 1..lb(m) | {m,p,q} |
| {f4,f5} | r | 1..7 | {r} |
| {f6} | o | 8..10 | {o} |

**(c)** Information about fact clusters

**Flow facts and clusters**

**Figure 3-32** *Example code (top) and flow facts and clusters (bottom). From Ermedahl et al. [Erm05] © 2005 IEEE.*

- **First miss**—Guaranteed not to be in the cache on the first loop iteration but may be on later iterations.

- **First hit**—Instruction may be in the cache on the first loop iteration but is guaranteed not to be in the cache for later iterations.

To analyze the behavior of the instructions in the pipeline, Healy et al. used a table to describe, for each type of instruction, worst-case and best-case number of cycles required at every stage of the pipeline. They analyzed the iterations in a loop iteration or single invocation of a function, which could consist of multiple basic blocks. Their algorithm for determining the worst-case timing along a path is shown in Figure 3-33.

*abstract interpretation*      **Abstract interpretation** executes a program using symbolic values rather than specific numeric values [The99]. This technique allows us to generalize information about program execution across sets of variable values in a reasonable amount of computation time. Abstract interpretation first determines concrete semantics for a program that describes a particular aspect of the program's behavior, such as cache or pipeline behavior. Based on the concrete semantics, an abstract semantic is built that operates on the program's abstract domain. An element of the abstract domain of the program represents a set of members of the concrete domain. An abstract state represents a set of concrete states; the

```
void Time_Path (struct path_node *path) {
    struct block_node *block;
    struct inst_node *instruction;

    path->wc_pipeline_information  =  NULL.
    FOR each block in path->block_list DO
        FOR each instruction in block->inst_list DO
            IF (Instruction->cat_list->wc_cat == first miss AND
                this instruction has not been encountered already) OR
                (instruction ->cat_list->wc_cat == first hit AND
                this instruction has been encountered already) OR
                instruction->cat_list->wc_cat == miss THEN
                Treat this instruction fetch as a miss in the pipeline.
            ELSE
                Treat this instruction fetch as a hit in the pipeline.
            Concatenate w.c. pipeline information for instruction->inst_type
                with path->wc_pipeline_information.
        END FOR
    END FOR
    path_ptr->wcot = temporal length of path->WC_pipeline_information.
}
```

**Figure 3-33** *Algorithm for worst-case path analysis. From Healy et al. [Hea99b] © 1999 IEEE.*

abstract representation may be conservative in that it includes concrete states that do not actually occur.

The concrete semantics for cache state represent how cache lines map into memory blocks. The abstract cache states map a cache line to a set of cache blocks. Theiling et al. described three types of analysis of this abstract state: **must analysis**, **may analysis**, and **persistence analysis**.

Must analysis looks at the upper bounds of the ages of the memory blocks. When combining two cache states, a memory block stays in the abstract cache only if it is in both predecessors and it receives the larger of their ages. This operation is similar to set intersection.

May analysis looks at the lower bounds on the ages of the memory blocks. A block is in the abstract cache if it is in one predecessor and it receives the youngest of the cache ages. Persistence analysis does not know whether the first access will be a hit or a miss but does guarantee that succeeding accesses will be hits.

*abstract interpretation and ILP*

Wilhelm [Wil04] argues for a modular approach to timing analysis in which abstract interpretation is used to analyze processor behavior, and integer linear programming is used to analyze program path behavior. Abstract interpretation helps to exclude timing accidents that cannot occur and provides the worst-case execution time for basic blocks, within their execution context. ILP determines an upper bound on execution time and the associated path.

*simulation-based timing analysis*

Some aspects of program performance require detailed understanding of the processor state. So long as these effects can be isolated to small segments of the program, simulation is a reasonable and valuable tool for detailed WCET analysis. Engblom and Ermedahl [Eng99a] used simulation to analyze pipeline effects. They break the execution time of a code sequence into the individual execution times plus the timing effects for subsequences. Timing effects capture the interactions between instructions. Engblom and Ermedahl use a cycle-accurate simulator to determine the execution time of a sequence of instructions. They do not use static analysis to determine whether combinations of instructions should have timing effects—a CPU can exhibit a large number of inter-instruction dependencies that could depend on data values and may not be well documented. Instead, Engblom and Ermedahl use the simulator to discover timing effects by executing successively longer code sequences. The length of a sequence that is tested is bounded by the length of time, typically equal to the length of the pipeline, in which the CPU can exhibit inter-instruction pipeline effects.

Healy et al. [Hea99b] use tables of structural and data hazards to analyze pipeline interactions in instruction sequences.

Engblom and Jonsson [Eng02] developed a model for single-issue in-order pipelines. Given a pipeline with $n$ stages, an instruction takes a certain number of clock cycles in each stage, denoted as $r_i^1, \ldots, r_i^n$, depending on the resources it needs. A sequence of $m$ instructions in the pipeline obeys two constraints, as

$$p_i^{j+1} \geq p_i^{j} + r_i^{j},$$
(EQ 3-11)

where $p_i^{j}$ is the time at which instruction $i$ enters pipeline stage $j$; and

$$p_{i+1}^{j} \geq p_i^{j+1},$$
(EQ 3-12)

which constrains the next instruction from entering a stage until the last instruction has finished. Branch instructions generate dependencies between the stage at which the branch is decided and instruction fetching:

$$p_{i+1}^{1} \geq p_i^{j+1}.$$
(EQ 3-13)

Data dependencies generate additional dependencies, as

$$p_i^{j} \geq p_k^{l+1},$$
(EQ 3-14)

in which the data dependency is between instructions $i$ and $k$, and the $k$ instruction must finish stage $l$ before the $i$ instruction can proceed. Longest-path algorithms can be used to solve these systems of constraints.

Engblom and Jonsson used this formulation to determine which types of pipelines have long timing effects. They defined a **crossing critical path** and showed that pipelines with this property do not have long timing effects that increase execution time. They showed that a single in-order pipeline has the crossing critical path property if each constraint introduced by branching and data dependencies either occurs between adjacent instructions or is subsumed by the basic constraints of (EQ 3-11) and (EQ 3-12). Pipelines with forks do not in general exhibit the crossing critical path property, and such pipelines are widely used in high-performance processors. For example, most processors with a separate floating-point pipeline do not have the crossing critical path property.

## 3.5 Models of Computation and Programming

What we think of as high-level programming languages grew out of the Algol movement of the 1960s. A great many higher-level programming languages have been proposed, but programmers still use Algol-style languages. Embedded computing is one area in which higher-level programming languages have been used in practice. Signal-processing languages both increase programmer productivity and give a natural model for algorithm designers who may be uncomfortable with imperative programming. Control-oriented languages have been used to design systems that react to external events. Several trends suggest that higher-level programming languages will continue to be used in embedded systems: embedded computing applications often put a high premium on correctness; software may be developed by algorithm designers who are not comfortable with Algol-style programming languages; and software synthesis methods can leverage the descriptive power of these languages to create efficient implementations.

Many of the languages that we describe here do not use a memory-oriented programming model like that of the Algol-style languages. Abandoning memory-oriented programming provides a much more abstract platform for programmers but requires new compilation techniques. Communication mechanisms become very important when memory is not used as the universal communication mechanism.

*synchronous languages*    Computing systems that transduce or react to inputs are called **reactive systems**. An important category of reactive system languages is **synchronous languages** [Ben91]. These languages are based on a model of computation that bears some similarity to digital hardware semantics. A synchronous language assumes that inputs and their associated outputs happen simultaneously and synchronously. Thus, the system's reaction time to an input is zero. This assumption allows control specifications to be divided into communicating components that communicate with each other to get their work done.

A synchronous language allows a program to be written as several communicating modules, similar to the modules shown later in this chapter in Figure 3-40 (see page 207). The rules of synchronous languages include the following as described in Benveniste and Berry [Ben91].

- A change in state in a module is simultaneous with the receipt of inputs by the module.

- Outputs from a module are simultaneous with the change in state.

- Communication between modules is synchronous and instantaneous.

- The output behavior of the modules is entirely determined by the global interleaving of the two input signals.

Synchronous languages are deterministic. This is an important shift in approach from Hoare-style communications using semaphores. Hoare's semaphores are designed for asynchronously communicating programs. Synchronous languages are used to simplify the specification of control; techniques at lower levels of abstraction can be used to ensure that the implementation sufficiently satisfies the synchronous hypotheses to work properly.

We also discuss languages and scheduling in Section 4.3. That section concentrates on thread-level scheduling and concurrency. The boundary between that section and this one is somewhat blurry and arguably some of the material in one section could be moved to another.

We first talk about languages designed to describe interrupt processing. Next we describe data flow-oriented languages, followed by control-oriented languages. We discuss Java in Section 3.5.4, and we look at heterogeneous models of computation in Section 3.5.5.

### 3.5.1 Interrupt-Oriented Languages

Interrupts are important phenomena in embedded systems because they enable I/O and timing. Interrupt drivers must be correct and are very difficult to debug. Interrupt drivers perform parallel programming operations, since the CPU and the device operate concurrently, but they do so using low-level techniques. Building layers of software to abstract devices would lead to slow drivers that slow down the real-time responsiveness of the rest of the system. Compiling specialized code is an attractive alternative way to create efficient, correct drivers.

*video drivers*
Thibault et al. [Thi99] developed a domain-specific language for video device drivers for X Window servers. Their language is based on an abstract machine that describes video adapters. The abstract machine defines some common operations, data transfers, and control operations. The language allows specification of the particulars of a video adapter—display characteristics such as resolution, ports, registers, fields, parameters, clocks, video card identification, and modes of operation. Thibault et al. found that an existing X server driver written in C consisted of more than 35,000 lines of code and that the driver described in their language was about nine times smaller than the C driver.

*NDL*
Conway and Edwards [Con04] developed NDL as a language for device drivers. NDL allows the state of the I/O device to be declared as part of the program. Memory-mapped I/O locations can be defined and described using the ioport facility, which resembles a C struct. An NDL program also includes a set of state declarations for the device's states. A state has a name and a sequence of actions, which may test or set registers or cause the driver to go into a different state. NDL simplifies device description by allowing one device declaration to inherit the characteristics of another, but NDL is not a fully object-oriented language. An interrupt-handling function is tagged with the Boolean expression that controls its enablement.

The NDL compiler generates drivers in C. The compiler eliminates redundant writes to registers. Many device registers are designed to respond to state changes but not to repeated writes of the same value; NDL refers to these registers as *idempotent*. The compiler also aggregates accesses to bits within a given address. For example, a status may hold several bits with different meanings; rather than accessing the register multiple times, the optimized code accesses it once and manipulates the constituent bits separately.

*methodologies*

Reghr [Reg05] proposed a restricted discipline for interrupt programming. Many interrupts, such as those from timers, are requested by a program. The discipline requires that interrupts remain disabled except between the time they are requested and the time they run. Reghr uses this methodology to implement a testing methodology.

### 3.5.2 Data Flow Languages

The term **data flow** has been used in several different ways in computer systems design. Data flow machines were designed in the 1960s and 1970s as an alternative means of scheduling operations in the CPU. Here, we concentrate on data flow as a model for signal-processing systems.

*synchronous data flow*

We introduced the synchronous data flow (SDF) graph [Lee87] in Section 1.5.3. An SDF models the behavior of signal-processing and periodic systems. It is designed to handle multirate processing, which is common in signal processing. Lee and Messerschmitt use the term *block* to denote a computational unit; in Section 3.5.5, we use the term *actor* for computational units. In the example of Figure 3-34, *a* and *b* are blocks of computation in a directed graph. The *a* block produces data at a rate $r_1$ and *b* consumes data at a rate $r_2$. By default, data passes from source to sink in the graph without delay, but an edge can be annotated with a delay equal to the number of samples stored along the edge.

*schedulability*

To implement an SDF graph on a computer, we need to schedule the operations in the graph. Depending on the platform, different types of schedules may be legal. For a sequential processor, we need a sequential schedule. Lee and Messerschmitt identified the **periodic admissible sequential schedule (PASS)** as an important category of schedule for SDF. We can use matrix algebra to determine the schedulability of an SDF.

Figure 3-35 shows an example SDF graph. We can construct a *topology matrix* to describe the graph: columns represent nodes, rows represent edges, and the weight of an edge corresponds to the amount of data flowing along the given edge from the given node (flow into a node is given negative weight). We can represent the schedule of operations used to implement an SDF as a schedule matrix, as shown in the figure. Each column denotes a timestep in the sched-

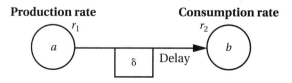

**Figure 3-34** *Elements of a synchronous data flow graph.*

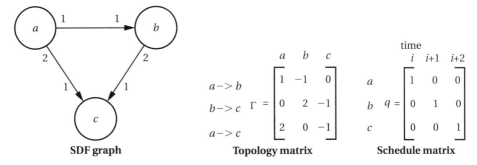

**Figure 3-35** *A synchronous data flow graph, its topology matrix, and a schedule matrix.*

ule; a 1 entry shows that the node represented by that row is active. We can also write the schedule as a string, such as *abc*; we can write subsequences with parentheses and add notations for repetitions, such as *a(2bc)* for *abcbc*.

Lee and Messerschmitt showed that, if the number of blocks in the graph is equal to *s*, then a necessary condition for the existence of a PASS schedule is that the rank of the topology matrix must be equal to $s - 1$. They showed that the buffers required to hold values passed between nodes remain bounded in size if and only if

$$\Gamma q = 0, \qquad\qquad\qquad \text{(EQ 3-15)}$$

where *O* is a matrix of all zero entries. This requires that the rank of $\Gamma$ be less than *s*; other conditions require that the rank be no less than $s - 1$.

Bhattacharyya et al. [Bha95] developed algorithms to schedule SDF graphs to produce compact code. They use the term *iteration* to describe the repeated execution of a data flow node; they use the term *looping* for the program construct used to repeatedly execute the operation.

Given an SDF graph *G*, one subgraph is **subindependent** of another if no samples from the second subgraph are consumed by the first one in the same schedule period in which they are produced. The graph *G* is **loosely interdependent** if it can be partitioned into two subgraphs, one subindependent of the other. A **single-appearance schedule** is a schedule in which each SDF node appears only once. Such a schedule exists for *G* if and only if each strongly connected component of *G* can be partitioned into two subgraphs, one subindependent of the other, and each partition has a single-appearance schedule.

Figure 3-36 shows two examples of how poor decisions about how to cluster operations can destroy a single-appearance schedule. In the top example, we cluster *B* and *C* into a single node. The resulting graph has a subgraph consisting of $\Omega$ and *D* that is tightly interdependent and so has no single-appearance schedule. In the second example, the subgraph *{B,C,D}* is tightly interdependent, but

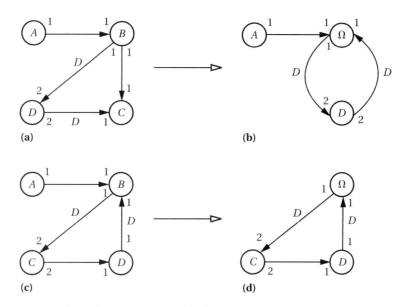

**Figure 3-36** *Clustering and single-appearance schedules. From Bhattacharyya [Bha94a].*

*A* is not in a tightly interdependent subgraph and so could appear only once in a schedule. But if we cluster *A* and *B* together, then we can no longer find a schedule with only one appearance of *A*—the shortest schedule for the new graph is *ABC(2D)AB*.

We can use this recursive property of a single-appearance schedule to schedule an SDF. The scheduling algorithm recursively decomposes a graph into sub-independent pieces to determine its schedule.

*buffer management in SDFs*
Bhattacharyya and Lee [Bha94b] developed scheduling methods that can be used to implement efficient buffering schemes. They use the **common code space set graph** of a schedule, shown in Figure 3-37, to describe the iteration

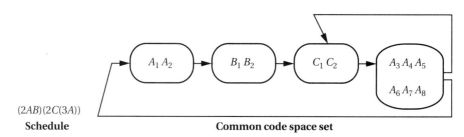

(2*AB*)(2*C*(3*A*))
**Schedule**                    **Common code space set**

**Figure 3-37** *The common code space set graph of an SDF schedule.*

structure of a schedule. The operators in a node of the graph are known as a **common code space set**.

They use the term *static buffer* to describe a buffer in which the $i^{th}$ sample always appears at the same location in the buffer. The state of the buffer in the software implementation is represented in the SDF graph as the state of the arc connecting two nodes—more specifically, the number and order of tokens waiting on that arc to be processed by the arc's sink node. A static buffering scheme simplifies addressing since the code that uses the sample does not have to compute its address. If all the members of a common code space set access a given arc at the same offset, then the arc is statically accessed.

Bhattacharyya and Lee show that a pointer into the buffer must be spilled into memory if and only if there is a cycle in the common code space set graph for which a given operator accesses an arc nonstatically. They analyze the graph using a **first-reaches table**. Its rows and columns are the sets in the common code space set graph. An entry is true if and only if there is a control path that goes from the row set to the column set without passing through another set for the SDF node that corresponds to the column set.

For longer schedules, it may be possible to schedule operations such that some samples are overlaid in buffers. Figure 3-38 shows an example in which the *{B,D}* and *{C,E}* subgraphs operate independently. A schedule that, for example, executed *B* twice and then *D* 20 times would require large buffers. By using a schedule such that a set of 10 samples is produced and then consumed, we can reduce the amount of buffering required as well as share that buffer between the *{B,D}* and *{C,E}* subgraphs.

*LUSTRE*

LUSTRE [Hal91] is a synchronous data flow language. Variables in LUSTRE represent **flows**: a sequence (possibly infinite) of values, all at the same time; a clock that describes the sequence of times of those values. The value of a flow is equal to the $n^{th}$ member of the sequence at time $n$. LUSTRE programs are made of variables formed into expressions. LUSTRE is not an imperative language, so an equation uniquely defines a variable. LUSTRE includes standard mathematical operators and four temporal operators.

- pre(E) provides the previous value of flow *E*.

- E -> F produces a new flow whose first value comes from *E* and whose subsequent values come from *F*.

- E when B creates a flow with a slower clock, taking values from flow E at the times when *B* is true.

- The current operator produces a stream whose clock is interpolated at a faster rate than the stream's original clock.

An implementation of a LUSTRE program must satisfy its data dependencies. It must also be checked to ensure that its formulas constitute valid clock

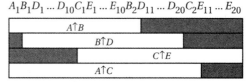

(a) **Schedule:** $AB(10D)C(10E)B(10D)C(10E)$

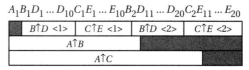

$A_1 B_1 D_1 \dots D_{10} C_1 E_1 \dots E_{10} B_2 D_{11} \dots D_{20} C_2 E_{11} \dots E_{20}$

(b) **Aggregate buffer lifetimes**

$A_1 B_1 D_1 \dots D_{10} C_1 E_1 \dots E_{10} B_2 D_{11} \dots D_{20} C_2 E_{11} \dots E_{20}$

(c) **Buffer period lifetimes**

**Figure 3-38** *Scheduling to overlay samples in buffers. From Bhattacharyya and Lee [Bha94b] © 1994 IEEE.*

operations. Primitive operations must be performed on flows with the same clock. To avoid generating undecidable problems, the LUSTRE compiler checks whether the clocks of the signals can be unified by syntactically substituting clocks in the expressions that generate the flow.

*SIGNAL*    SIGNAL [LeG91] is a synchronous language in which programs are written as equations and block diagrams. SIGNAL and LUSTRE vary somewhat in their view of sequences of values. A **signal** is a sequence of data with an implicit time sequence. A signal may be absent or present at any time; two signals that are both present at some time possess the same clock. SIGNAL includes the standard Boolean and arithmetic operators that do not modify the time indexes of the signals on which they operate. SIGNAL uses the expression y $ i to signify the delay of signal y by $i$ time units.

The expression Y when C produces Y whenever both Y and C are present and C is *true*, nothing otherwise. The expression Y default X merges Y and X: when one of X or Y is available, it produces that signal; when both are available, it delivers Y.

Signals can be composed to create processes with more complex behavior. Systems of equations can be represented in block diagrams. The signals can be analyzed to determine whether their clocking conditions are consistent. A combination of formulas and cyclic graphs are used to check the consistency of clocking.

*compiling*
*distributed*
*implementations*

Caspi et al. [Cas99] developed a compilation method to create a distributed implementation of a synchronous program in a language such as LUSTRE, SIGNAL, or Esterel. Their algorithm starts with an allocation of the program variables to processing elements. It consists of five stages:

1. Replication and localization

2. Insertion of puts

3. Insertion of gets

4. Synchronization of threads

5. Elimination of redundant outputs

The first phase determines which processing elements (PEs) compute values for each variable and output. It uses that information to determine which control and assignment statements must be performed on every PE. Each PE must perform a control action; the PE that owns a variable must perform the assignment to that variable.

Interthread communication is performed by asynchronous message passing. When inserting puts and gets, we want to minimize the number of communication actions. A thread can be represented as a DAG whose leaves are the gotos that end the thread and whose nonleaf nodes are program actions. We can traverse the DAG to insert puts such that any PE that needs a variable will receive the variable before it is needed.

Caspi et al. developed two algorithms. The when-needed algorithm propagates information backward from the leaves; it determines variables that are needed using def-use style analysis and inserts a put for any variables needed just before any write to that variable. The as-soon-as-possible strategy inserts puts just after variables are computed. Similarly, gets can be inserted by analyzing the program DAGs. The gets have to be inserted such that the proper value is received, not a value sent later or earlier.

Threads are synchronized by adding dummy communications to nodes that only produce nodes. This ensures that the producers cannot run arbitrarily far ahead and overflow buffers.

Conditionals can induce redundant outputs when the as-needed communication strategy is used. If a value is sent before a branch and then modified in one of the branches, the value may have to be sent again. Static analysis can eliminate such redundant communication.

*Compaan*

Compaan [Kie02] synthesizes process network models from Matlab descriptions. It first transforms the Matlab program into single-assignment code. It then

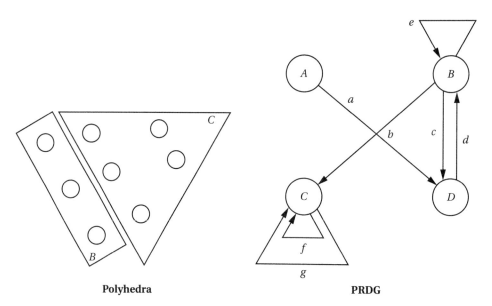

**Figure 3-39** *Polyhedral reduced dependence graphs and polyhedra.*

uses a polyhedral reduced dependence graph (PRDG) to analyze the behavior (see Figure 3-39). As we saw in Section 3.3.1, a polytope models a loop nest, with points in the polytope-modeling nodes in the program's data dependency graph. The *node domain* of the PRDG consists of a set of polytopes, a function, and a set of port domains. Each node in the PRDG represents a polyhedron. A *port domain* is a set of input or output ports. Input ports and output ports correspond to the inputs and outputs, respectively, of the function. An *edge domain* is an ordered pair of node domains that define the edge, along with an ordered pair of port domains. Edges in the PRDG represent the data dependencies between the polyhedra.

The process network model is called the *SBF model*. As with other types of process models, the read ports are guarded by unbounded queues. A set of functions in the model can take tokens from the read ports and generate tokens on the write ports. A controller and the current state of the SBF object determine the exact behavior of these functions.

A PRDG is mapped into the SBF model to create the process network implementation. Each node in the PRDG is mapped onto a single SBF object. Each edge in the PRDG becomes a connection between an output port and an input port on two SBF objects. The controller for each SBF object is constructed based on the lexicographical order defined by the nested-loop program.

### 3.5.3  Control-Oriented Languages

*control and*
*reactive systems*

We introduced control-oriented modeling in Section 1.5.2; this section discusses these languages in more detail. Control-oriented languages are often used to model reactive systems. A reactive system responds to some input. A control system is an example of a reactive system. The behavior of a reactive system depends on its state—that is, its history of inputs—as well as its current inputs.

*control*
*decomposition*

Modularity is an appealing concept in all areas of programming. In traditional programming languages, control is not thought of as highly modular, with the possible exception of subroutines. Structured languages divide control into if statements but do not provide a rich set of mechanisms for combining control. Decomposition of control is somewhat more natural in hardware. Consider the example of Figure 3-40 in which a system is decomposed into a finite-state machine (FSM) and a counter. The FSM typically has more random control. The counter can be thought of as a particular type of control with a very structured state-transition graph. We could build a single equivalent controller by forming the product of the FSM and counter, but that machine would have considerably more states.

One of the important contributions of control-oriented languages for embedded computing is new ways of decomposing and modularizing control. Control is an important part of many embedded systems because so many embedded processors are used in reactive systems. Because a high premium is given to correctness in embedded computing, the field has encouraged the development of new methods to describe and manipulate control.

*event-driven*
*state machines*

**Event-driven state machine** models are widely used. The term is generally used to describe machines that react aperiodically, such as when inputs change value. To some extent, this is simply a matter of interpreting the notion of time in the state machine. A sequence of inputs may be viewed as mapping periodically onto a real-valued timeline or aperiodically. The main descriptive improve-

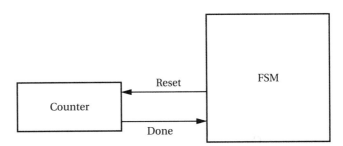

**Figure 3-40**  *A simple example of control decomposition.*

*Statecharts*

ment in event-driven machines is that states do not need self-loops that keep the machine in the same state when an input does not change.

An early, widely known event-driven model is the Statechart [Har87]. The Statechart formalism provides a hierarchy of states using two basic constructs: the *AND* state and the *OR* state. Statecharts are not formally more expressive than standard FSMs—we can convert any Statechart to an FSM—but a Statechart may be exponentially smaller than its FSM equivalent.

Figure 3-41 illustrates the Statechart *OR* state. The *OR* state *S12* combines two substates, *S1* and *S2*. The substates can be entered under a variety of conditions. If the machine receives input *i3* when in any of *S12*'s substates, then state moves to *S3*. Figure 3-42 illustrates the Statechart *AND* state. Input *i1* causes the machine to enter state *SAND*, which has two substate partitions. In one partition, the state can flip between *S1* and *S2*; in the other, it can loop back to *S3*. The machine's state is the cross-product of the substates in the partitions.

Statecharts are an important variation in finite-state machines because they make specifications smaller and easier to understand. Statecharts and their variations have been used in many software projects. For example, the TCAS-II aviation collision-avoidance system was designed using a language created by Leveson et al. [Lev94] that included Statechart-style hierarchical states.

The STATEMATE [Har90] system provides graphical entry for Statechart-style descriptions. STATEMATE captures the system from their views: structural, functional, and behavioral. The structural view of a reactive system is similar to a hardware block diagram. It shows the physical components and the communication paths between them. These diagrams are known as *module*

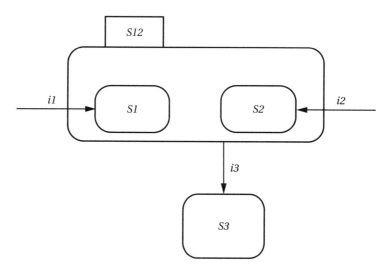

**Figure 3-41** *A Statechart* OR *state.*

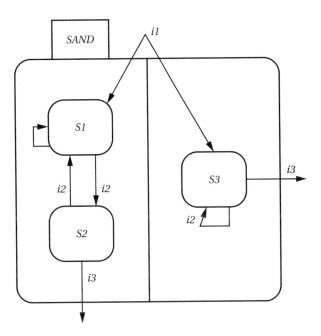

**Figure 3-42** *A Statechart* AND *state.*

*charts* in STATEMATE. Activity charts show the functional view. An activity chart shows data flows in the system. Each block in an activity chart is a function; solid arrows represent data flow, and dashed arrows represent control flow. Statecharts represent the behavioral view of the system. The *AND* and *OR* states of Statecharts provide a novel and useful form of control decomposition.

*Statechart interpretation*

Wasowski [Was03] describes efficient methods for compiling Statechart programs. The program needs to keep track of its current state in the state space defined by the State-chart state. A flat representation of the program could use a bit vector to keep track of the program's activity in each state. Unfortunately, forming the product machine can result in very large code. Wasowski uses a **hierarchy tree** to more compactly represent the state of the program. The levels of the hierarchy tree alternate between *AND* and *OR* states. During execution, the program must check on the ancestor relationship between states, which is equivalent to determining whether a path exists between the two states in the hierarchy tree. A labeling scheme reduces the time required to test ancestry.

*Statechart verification*

Alur and Yannakakis [Alu01] developed verification algorithms for sequential hierarchical state machines. They showed that invariants can be checked more efficiently because component FSMs need to be checked only once, not independently in each context in which they appear. The authors analyzed the reachability of the state-transition graph using a depth-first search algorithm.

*Esterel*

They also gave efficient algorithms for linear-time requirements and branching-time requirements.

Esterel [Bou91] is another synchronous language. In Esterel the term *signal* is used to refer to an event. The await statement in Esterel reacts to inputs—execution stops until the signal given in the statement's argument becomes available. The emit statement sends a signal that is broadcast throughout the system.

Unlike STATEMATE, Esterel combines the structural and behavioral views into a single textual program. Figure 3-43 shows a simple Esterel example from Boussinot and De Simone [Bou91]. The program is divided into three modules: a main module, a counter, and an output module (*emission* is a common French term for *output*). The Counter module updates its count on a click (an external clock signal); it emits its value once every time the value is updated; it also watches a reset signal. The emission module tests the counter value. If the counter signal VAL is zero, it emits a NONE output; if the counter is one, it emits SINGLE; if the counter is greater than one, it emits MANY. The main module for the Mouse causes one counter and one emission to be executed in parallel, as specified by the || operators. It also includes a third process that emits one RST for every five TOP signals received.

*compiling Esterel*

Esterel programs are implemented by compiling them into automatons (either in software or hardware) that implement the control. The first method for compiling Esterel into software was to generate the product machine of the automata in the Esterel description, then generate a program for the product machine. This method ensured that communication between Esterel processes took zero time. But state explosion may result in unacceptably large machines.

An alternate method transforms the Esterel program into combinational logic, then translates those logic formulas into software. This method avoids

```
module Mouse:
input CLICK,TOP;
output NONE, SINGLE, MANY;

signal RST, VAL (integer) in
  loop
    copymodule Counter
  ||
    await 5 TOP;
    emit RST;
  ||
    copymodule Emission
  end
end
```
**Main module**

```
module Counter:
input RST, CLICK;
output VAL(integer);

var v : integer in
  do
    v := 0;
    every immediate CLICK do
      v := v+1;
    watching RST;
    emit VAL(v);
end
```
**Counter module**

```
module Emission:
input VAL(integer);
output  NONE, SINGLE,
MANY;
  await VAL;
  if?VAL = 0 then
    emit NONE
  else
    if ?VAL = 1 then
      emit SINGLE
    else
      emit MANY
  end
end
```
**Output module**

**Figure 3-43** *An example Esterel program Boussinot and De Simone [Bou91] © 1991 IEEE.*

state explosion, but it is limited to Esterel programs that can be captured by such combinational logic—the operations must run in the same order for every state.

Edwards [Edw00] compiled Esterel into C with multiple threads. A **concurrent control flow graph** (CCFG) has four types of nodes: plain, conditional, fork, and join. The implementation of some Esterel statements in CCFGs is straightforward: an emit becomes an assignment, a loop becomes a for loop, a present-then-else statement becomes a conditional. A pause statement in Esterel causes the process to pause, then resume in the next cycle. This can be implemented as setting the next state. An exit statement throws an exception that is caught by a trap. This can be implemented by causing each thread to set an exit level at the end of a cycle.

At the end of a cycle, a thread uses its switch statement to select the state to execute on the next cycle. A fork statement passes control to the labels in the switch. A join statement waits until all the threads branch to it before it continues. The compiler first removes loops by unrolling to prepare for the concurrency-processing step. It then removes concurrency by inserting code to suspend and restart threads, resulting in a CCFG that has no fork or join nodes. The instructions must be scheduled so that all of them run only when their data is ready. The schedule must satisfy the data dependencies in the program. The schedule can be optimized to reduce the number of context switches required in the implementation.

The sequential version of the CCFG is implemented by making copies of the nodes in the original CCFG at the locations prescribed by the schedule and adding edges that provide the required control paths. Figure 3-44 illustrates the process on a simple Esterel program. The dashed arrows in the concurrent graph show how the left thread interrupts the thread on the right. When a node is copied into its scheduled position, any other threads from the same fork are suspended, and the selected node is made to run. Next, arcs are added from the node's potential nodes. Finally, the node becomes a potential node of each of its immediate successors in the concurrent graph. Resuming a thread requires testing the thread's state variable to determine which thread to run next. The final C code is implemented with nested conditionals as shown in the figure.

### 3.5.4 Java

Java is designed to provide a single language that can be used across a wide variety of platforms ranging from servers to mobile devices. Java is defined relative to a **Java Virtual Machine** (**JVM**) that can run on top of the host platform.

*bytecodes*

The intermediate representation for Java is known as **bytecodes**. A Java compiler translates Java source code into bytecodes that can be interpreted by the JVM. A bytecode consists of a one-byte opcode and zero or more operands. Java has a stack-oriented execution model that helps to minimize the number of

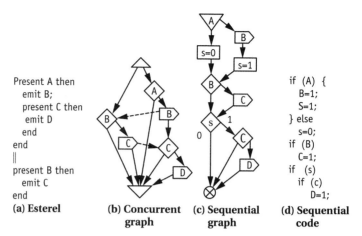

Present A then
    emit B;
    present C then
        emit D
    end
end
||
present B then
    emit C
end

**(a) Esterel**

**(b) Concurrent graph**

**(c) Sequential graph**

```
if (A) {
    B=1;
    S=1;
} else
    s=0;
if (B)
    C=1;
if (s)
    if (c)
        D=1;
```

**(d) Sequential code**

**Figure 3-44** *Compiling an Esterel fragment into sequential code. From [Edw00] © 2000 ACM Press.*

operands. Bytecodes can also be disassembled into symbolic form as shown in Table 3-1.

*compact virtual machines*

The Connected Limited Device Configuration (CLDC) [Sun05] defines a virtual machine and APIs for devices with limited resources. Shaylor et al. [Sha03] describe a JVM implementation based on CLDC.

*just-in-time compilation*

**Just-in-time (JIT)** compilation has become popular with languages such as Java and C#. These languages are often distributed over the network, and the same code must execute on a wide variety of platforms. However, a platform-independent representation that requires some sort of interpretation will not run as fast as native code. A JIT compiler translates the platform-independent code into native instructions on the fly.

*when to use JIT compiler*

The first decision for the JIT designer is when to compile code and when to rely on interpretation. A function that is executed only once may not be worth compiling; a function that is executed many times may well be worth compiling.

| Mnemonic | Bytecode |
|----------|----------|
| istore_0 | 3b |
| iload_0 | 1a |
| goto_7 | a7 ff f9 |

**Table 3-1** *Java mnemonics and bytecodes*

*JIT compilation*

Many functions fall in between these two extremes, and some heuristics must be used to determine when to invoke the JIT compiler.

JIT compilers work on just a single function at a time, which somewhat limits their ability to optimize the program. The JIT compilers must assign registers and issue instructions; they may also try to optimize control flow to some extent.

*memory management*

Java automatically manages the memory allocation for objects and uses garbage collection to recycle the memory used by objects that are no longer needed. Traditional garbage collectors are not designed for real-time or low-power operation. In garbage collection research, the application program that requires garbage collection is often called the **mutator**.

Kim et al. [Kim99] proposed aperiodically scheduling the garbage collector. They ran the garbage collector as the highest-priority task, giving the garbage collector a preset fraction of the total CPU time. They also proposed a modified garbage collection algorithm with hardware support.

Bacon et al. [Bac03a; Bac03b] developed a garbage collector for use in embedded Java systems. Their garbage collector is based on several principles, as follows.

- Memory for objects is allocated using segregated free lists—memory blocks are divided into different free lists based on their size.

- Objects are usually not copied. Some memory managers frequently copy objects to reallocate their memory and defragment the memory system, but Bacon et al. found that fragmentation was relatively rare.

- When a page becomes fragmented, its objects are moved to another page, usually one that is mostly full.

- A forwarding pointer in the head of each object aids the relocation of the object.

- Garbage is collected using an incremental mark-sweep algorithm.

- Large arrays are broken into fixed-size pieces. This both reduces fragmentation and bounds the time required to scan or copy.

These authors also developed a time-based scheduler for the garbage collector that is both efficient and provides more predictable memory management timing. The scheduler interleaves the collector and the mutator, assigning fixed-time quanta to each. The maximum mutator utilization (MMU) is the largest CPU utilization of the mutator over all intervals of width $\Delta t$. Bacon et al. showed that the MMU of their time-based algorithm asymptotically approaches

$$u_T = \frac{Q_T}{Q_T + C_T},$$

(EQ 3-16)

where $Q_T$ is the time quantum for the mutator and $C_T$ is the time quantum for the garbage collector.

The maximum excess space required by their garbage collector is determined by the number of collections required to free an object. The first collection collects an object. If an object is created just after a collection, it will not be discovered until the next collection. If the object needs to be copied, that will take one additional collection.

### 3.5.5   Heterogeneous Models of Computation

Embedded systems must often perform many different types of computation on a data stream. An audio player, for example, must read a file system, parse the audio packet stream, perform lossless decompression, and then run the samples through digital filters to reconstruct the audio. Different styles of programming may be useful for different stages of processing. Even if we use the same language, we must ensure that the programs in the system communicate properly and do not drop data or cause other problems.

*coordination languages*

Lee and Parks [Lee95] developed a formalism for **coordination languages** for signal-processing systems. Their model is based on the **Kahn process network**—a model for parallel computation. In this model, processes communicate via unbounded queues. Each input to a process is guarded by an infinite-capacity FIFO. A channel can carry a sequence or **stream** of values. Processes consume tokens from their input FIFOs; once a token is consumed, it cannot be consumed again. Processes produce new tokens at their outputs.

Because physical signal-processing systems are causal—outputs are caused by inputs in predictable ways—we want to show an equivalent property for these sorts of networks. Kahn process networks, however, do not have an explicit notion of time as a ticking clock; they only view time as ordering. The property related to causality for Kahn process networks is monotonicity. This property can be expressed formally as

$$X \subseteq X' \Rightarrow F(X) \subseteq F(X').$$   (EQ 3-17)

This means that a new input token cannot change previous outputs, only future outputs. Lee and Parks argued that a network of monotonic processes is itself monotonic, which means that we can build complex systems with consistent properties.

*data flow actors*

Lee and Parks showed how to build data flow languages on top of this coordination language model. Processes in data flow systems are often called **actors**. An actor is governed by a set of **firing rules**. Under certain conditions, the actor fires: it consumes some tokens at its inputs and produces other tokens at its outputs. Lee and Parks impose a stricter condition on the behavior of actors than is required by the Kahn model. They require that an actor's outputs be functions of its present input tokens and not of any prior state; they also require that an actor not cause side effects. In addition, they require that the firing rules be applied in a fixed order using only blocking reads from the inputs.

A simple actor model is the digital filter. This actor consumes one token at each input and produces one token at its output. Firing rules can also involve choice. A multiplexer, for example, has two data inputs and a control input. It reads a control input, then reads one of its data inputs based on the control input value. This actor does not always read the same number of tokens from each input.

*Ptolemy*

The Ptolemy II system [Eck03; Pto05] is built around this data flow actor model. Ptolemy allows large heterogeneous systems to be modeled in a variety of styles that are coordinated by the data flow actor model. Its graphical user interface provides a unified system view to the system designer.

An actor can be atomic or composite. Actors are connected into networks through their ports. A top-level composite model is allowed to have no ports. An execution step in Ptolemy II has three phases:

1. The setup phase is divided into preinitialize and initialize subphases. Preinitialization may construct dynamically created actors, determine the width of ports, and so on. Initialization takes care of the actor's internals.

2. The iteration phase is a finite computation of the actors. Each iteration is broken down into prefiring (test the conditions), firing (do the work), and postfiring (update state).

3. The wrapup phase releases resources that were used during execution.

A composite actor may be implemented in one or more domains that can be used to describe the actor at different levels of abstraction. Several domains, such as communicating sequential processes, continuous time, and discrete event, have been implemented in Ptolemy II. The **receiver class** of a domain defines the communication mechanism used in this domain. The order of execution of actors in the domain is defined by the **director class**.

*Metropolis*

Metropolis [Bal05] is a metamodel for embedded system design. Metropolis is designed to capture a wide range of meaning in embedded systems and to support synthesis, simulation, and verification. Metropolis defines three major axes of description.

1. Computation versus communication

2. Functional specification versus implementation platform

3. Function/behavior versus nonfunctional requirements (which Metropolis calls **performance indices**)

The function of the system is described as a set of objects that represent oncurrent sequential programs, which are known as *threads*. The threads communicate through ports defined on the objects; the ports and their connections are defined by a network. As with object-oriented programming languages, objects define methods that can be accessed through the ports.

Constraints on communication or coordination between processes are defined using **linear-time temporal logic**, which is widely used to model and verify concurrent systems. To specify constraints on quantities, Metropolis defines a logic of constraints, which allows the description of several important types of quantities, as follows.

- Rates, of the form $t(e_{i+1}) - t(e_i)\ 5\ P$

- Latencies of the form $t(o_j) - t(i_j) \leq L$

- Jitter of the form $\left| t(o_j) - j \times P \right| \leq J$

- Throughput of the form $t(o_{i+E}) - t(o_i) \leq T$

- Burstiness of the form $t(i_{j+E}) - t(i_j) > T$

The architectural model is fundamentally defined by the services of the architecture and their underlying efficiency; the structural model of the architecture supports these descriptions. The architecture's functionality is defined by a set of services, described by methods. Each service is decomposed into a sequence of events that describes its behavior; the events are then annotated with the costs of the events, such as performance or energy.

Balarin et al. [Bal02] describe simulation algorithms for the Metropolis metamodel. The simulator models threads as **action automata**. An action is the execution of a method call; the action is marked by an event marking the start of the action and another event marking the end of the action. Each action is guarded by blocking events and also releases other actions when it finishes.

*model-integrated development*

Karsai et al. [Kar03] use a methodology called **model-integrated computing** that generates software from **domain-specific modeling languages**. A model may have different elements, depending on the application, but a typical model includes the following several aspects.

- A model of the environment in which the system operates

- A model of the application/algorithms

- A model of the hardware platform

A modeling language includes a collection of concepts, attributes, and composition rules. The concepts may relate to the algorithm or the platform. Attributes may be nonfunctional requirements of the application, performance of components, and so on.

A modeling language is described in a **metamodel**. Figure 3-45 shows a metamodel for a language used to describe hierarchical signal flow graphs.

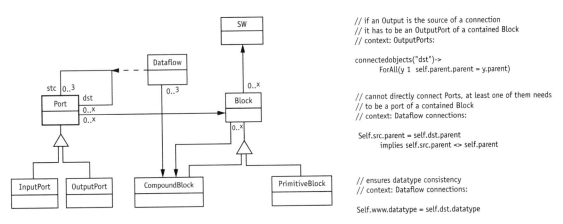

// if an Output is the source of a connection
// it has to be an OutputPort of a contained Block
// context: OutputPorts:

connectedobjects("dst")->
       ForAll(y 1  self.parent.parent = y.parent)

// cannot directly connect Ports, at least one of them needs
// to be a port of a contained Block
// context: Dataflow connections:

Self.src.parent = self.dst.parent
         implies self.src.parent <> self.parent

// ensures datatype consistency
// context: Dataflow connections:

Self.www.datatype = self.dst.datatype

**Figure 3-45** *A metamodel with constraints for hierarchical signal flow graphs. From Karsai et al. [Kar03] © 2003 IEEE.*

Unified Modeling Language (UML) notation describes the language: the top-level construct in the language is SW, which includes models of type Block, and so on. The right side of the figure shows some well-formedness rules described as Object Constraint Language (OCL) expressions.

Karsai et al. argue that embedded systems, because they are complex and must be reliable, should be designed in languages with well-defined semantics, not simply by informal English descriptions. One common method for specifying the semantics of a domain-specific modeling language is *metamodeling*, which writes the semantics in another language with well-defined semantics. Z and Larch are examples of languages used for metamodeling.

An alternative is to specify the mapping of the domain-specific modeling language to another language with well-understood semantics. Metamodels must be checked for consistency. The various components and rules of the meta-model may interact in nonobvious ways that cause the compositions to take on unintended meanings.

A description in a domain-specific modeling language can be turned into an implementation using a generator. Generators need to combine syntax-directed translation with search and optimization. Generators can be created with the help of **metagenerators**. A metagenerator can be constructed around a graph grammar that allows transformations to be concisely described; traversal strategies can be used to help guide the mapping process.

*Simulink*     Simulink is a commercial system for the analysis and design of complex systems. Simulink is built around a simulation engine and also provides model libraries and code-generation facilities. The following example describes the use of Simulink in automobile design.

### Example 3-1

*Steer-by-Wire System Design Using Simulink*

Langenwalter and Erkkinen [Lan04] described how to use Simulink to design an automotive steer-by-wire system. The system uses electronic controls to translate steering column turns to the wheels. Langenwalter and Erkkinen use a model-based design methodology to successively refine the system from concept to verified system.

A behavioral model of the system includes the physical plant—in this case, the car—and a simple model of the control system. This behavioral model can be simulated to determine that the car behaved properly while controlled by the steer-by-wire algorithms. The system can be prototyped on various platforms, depending on the requirements for timing accuracy versus ease of programming: a high-end microprocessor provides a more convenient target, while using the intended target platform provides more details about timing and interfaces.

Detailed software design includes several tasks. The algorithms must be converted to fixed point with sufficient accuracy to retain the control system's characteristics. The functions must be mapped onto processes. And testing and diagnostic hooks must be added to the code. The detailed software can be executed on a model of the car to test it before running the code on the actual platform. This simulation can take into account the multiple processors that will run different pieces of code in the car.

## 3.6   Summary

Embedded software must be designed to meet real-time performance, energy, and size constraints. We can leverage techniques ranging from new, abstract programming languages to back-end compiler algorithms to attain these goals. Emdded software tools tend to be designed differently than general-purpose compilers. A compiler for arbitrary code is designed to give reasonably good results on a wide variety of programs. When we design embedded software, in contrast, we have specific targets in mind for performance, energy, and so on. We can use that information to optimize the software to precisely meet our goals. Nicholas Halbwachs has produced a good tutorial on reactive programming languages titled "Synchronous Programming of Reactive Systems: A Tutorial and Commented Bibliography," which is available at *http://www.citeseer.ist.psu.edu*.

## What We Have Learned

■ A wide range of CPU architectures are used in embedded systems, requiring us to develop a range of compilation methods.

■ Software that hits the memory system must be designed to properly utilize the memory system at all levels of abstraction: buffer management, data scheduling, and data reuse.

■ Accurate worst-case execution time analysis requires both abstract analysis of flow and detailed models of the processor platform.

■ Higher-level programming languages provide abstractions for particular types of computation; the information captured by these languages can be used to analyze and synthesize software.

## Further Reading

Bacon et al. [Bac94] provide an extensive review of loop optimization techniques, ranging from the abstract to very machine-dependent transformations. Darte et al. [Dar98] provide a thorough review of the history and use of loop transformations. Goossens et al. [Goo97] describe compiler techniques for embedded software, including techniques developed for general-purpose machines and those developed especially for ASIPs and DSPs. Several authors have written surveys on memory systems and compilation: Panda et al. [Pan01], Wolf and Kandemir [Wol03], and Kandemir and Dutt [Kan05]. Puschner and Burns [Pus99] provide an excellent survey of the development of worst-case execution time analysis.

## Questions

**Q3-1** Write instruction templates for the following instructions.

a. Add ADD r1, r2, r3

b. Multiply accumulate MAC m1, a1

c. Increment INCR r1

**Q3-2** How do instruction scheduling and register allocation interact? Do general-register architectures (like ARM) simplify those interactions or make them more difficult?

**Q3-3** How would you modify a graph coloring-based algorithm for register allocation to handle a machine that has several different types of registers, with each type able to receive the results of certain types of operations?

**Q3-4**  Compare the pros and cons of greedy and nongreedy algorithms for determining what registers to spill.

**Q3-5**  Is code placement more important for direct-mapped or set-associative caches? Explain.

**Q3-6**  Describe how a procedure call graph might be used to guide code placement.

**Q3-7**  Describe how loop interchange affects each of these.

a. Program performance

b. Program energy consumption

**Q3-8**  Describe how loop fusion affects each of these.

a. Program performance

b. Program energy consumption

**Q3-9**  Which properties help to determine which scalar variables should be placed close together in the cache?

**Q3-10**  Given this loop

```
for (i = 0; i < N; i++)
  for (j = i; j < N; j++){
    a [j ] = b [i ][j ] + c [j ][i ];
    d [j ] = f (c[i ][j ]);
    }
```

What is the loop conflict factor for a[] and for c[]? Assume that all matrices conflict.

**Q3-11**  Identify the longest execution path through this code.

```
for (sx = 0; sx < X; sx++){
  for (sy = 0; sy < Y; sy++) {
    best = 0; bpx = 0; bpy = 0;
    for (i = 0; i < N; i++)
      for (j = 0; j < N; j++) {
        val = iabs(t[i][j] – f[sx + ox][sy + oy]);
        if (val > best) {
          best = val;
          bpx = sx;
          bpy = sy;
        }
      }
  }
}
```

**Q3-12**  Write the constraints that describe the flow through this code fragment.

```
if (a < b) {
  while (c < 50)
    if (b[c] == 0) c = c + 2;
      else c++;
} else {
  for (i = 0; i < 20; i++)
    b[i] = x[i] * y[i];
}
```

**Q3-13**  Derive a set of flow facts for the code in Q3-11.

**Q3-14**  Compare and contrast an object-oriented programming language, such as C++, with a synchronous language.

**Q3-15**  How might you use object-oriented techniques to describe interrupt handlers?

**Q3-16**  Does the SDF graph of Figure 3-35 have a periodic admissible sequential schedule? Explain your answer.

**Q3-17**  What sorts of program transformations can be performed on a polyhedral reduced dependence graph?

**Q3-18**  Use Statechart OR and AND states to describe a device driver that handles a complex device. The handler receives an interrupt; it determines what subdevice generated the interrupt; it tests the state of the subdevice; it then performs the requested operation.

**Q3-19**  How do Kahn process networks differ from SDF graphs?

**Q3-20**  You use domain-specific modeling languages to describe two different types of embedded systems: audio compression and networking. How might the meta-models for these two systems differ? How might they be the same?

## Lab Exercises

**L3-1**  Compare the compiled code for a DSP and a general-register machine. Compare how they use registers and instructions.

**L3-2**  Analyze the cache behavior of a simple program such as a motion estimation algorithm.

**L3-3**  Analyze the worst-case execution time for a radix-16 fast Fourier transform (FFT).

**L3-4** Analyze the worst-case execution time for a block motion estimation algorithm, such as a three-step search.

**L3-5** Pick a sample program and attempt to determine by inspection the worst-case execution path through the program. Compare your result with that of a WCET analysis tool.

**L3-6** Write an Esterel program for an antilock braking system. The antilock brake controller pulses the brakes during a skid.

# 4

# Processes and Operating Systems

- Real-time scheduling
- Scheduling for power/energy
- Performance estimation
- Operating system mechanisms and overhead
- Embedded file systems
- Concurrent system verification

## 4.1 Introduction

Many embedded systems must perform several tasks simultaneously. Real-time operating systems (RTOSs) allow a single CPU to juggle multiple processes. Unlike general-purpose operating systems, RTOSs must adhere to strict timing requirements. They may have to minimize energy consumption while they obey those timing requirements.

We start by describing real-time scheduling methods, including both traditional scheduling algorithms and newer algorithms for more complex sets of conditions. Section 4.3 looks at the relationship between programming languages and scheduling, particularly languages and compilation methods that allow for static scheduling. Section 4.4 considers the implementation of real-time operating systems, including context-switching overhead, power management, and file systems. The chapter concludes in Section 4.5 with a discussion of methodologies for verifying concurrent systems.

## 4.2 Real-Time Process Scheduling

Let us begin with definitions of some common terms. We then review traditional real-time scheduling algorithms. Next, we consider extensions to traditional schedulers for new criteria in Section 4.2.2 and spend Section 4.2.3 concentrating on real-time scheduling for dynamic voltage scaling. We conclude with a discussion of performance estimation for multiple-process systems.

### 4.2.1 Preliminaries

This section surveys algorithms for scheduling processes on real-time systems. Scheduling has been studied in many contexts. Some general scheduling techniques apply to real-time systems; other techniques are designed for the specific characteristics of real-time computer systems.

*processes and scheduling*

One of the most fundamental abstractions in computing is the **process**. A process is a unique execution of a program—it includes the program and all of its state. Operating systems allow several processes to run concurrently on a single CPU by interleaving the processes' executions, using a technique known as **context switching**. The time between successive operating system preemptions for scheduling is known as the **time quantum**. The times when processes execute on the CPU is a **schedule**.

*processes versus tasks*

Several different words are used in the literature for similar concepts, and sometimes the same word is used in different ways. In scheduling, the terms **thread**, **process**, and **task** are all used in various ways. We use the term *thread* to mean a lightweight process that shares an address space with other threads, and the term *process* as a generic term for any execution of a program. We use *task* to mean a collection of processes that must execute together. Tasks are often related by data dependencies. The word *task* is sometimes used to refer to what we call a *process*, but we find it useful to distinguish between a single program and a collection of programs. The processes that make up a task may be called **subtasks**.

*static versus dynamic*

Scheduling algorithms can be divided into two general categories. **Static scheduling algorithms** determine the schedule offline, before the system begins to operate. **Dynamic scheduling algorithms** build the schedule on-the-fly during execution. Many scheduling algorithms are NP-complete. As a result, we must use heuristics to solve them.

*constructive versus iterative improvement*

Static scheduling algorithms are widely used in both hardware and software design. The major types of static schedulers are **constructive** and **iterative improvement**. Constructive schedulers use rules to select the next task in the schedule. Iterative improvement schedulers, in contrast, revisit their decisions to change the schedule.

*priority schedulers*

Dynamic schedulers in real-time systems are generally **priority** schedulers. These schedulers assign priorities (integer or real values), then use those priorities to determine which process to run next.

*real-time versus general-purpose*

Real-time scheduling algorithms are very different from scheduling policies for general-purpose operating systems. General-purpose systems are generally concerned with fairness—they do not want to starve any process of computation time, while still allowing for some processes to execute more frequently than others. Real-time scheduling, in contrast, is concerned with **deadlines**. The penalties for missing a deadline may vary, but all real-time scheduling algorithms are somehow aimed at satisfying deadlines or throughput requirements.

*hard versus soft*

The literature often distinguishes between **hard** and **soft real-time** scheduling. Some people use the term *hard real-time* to mean only safety-critical computations, but we prefer to use it for any computation that fails when a deadline is missed. A laser printer, for example, may print a bad page if it misses a deadline, though this does not (usually) cause people to die. We use *soft real-time* systems to mean any system that prefers to meet deadlines but does not meet catastrophic deadlines if it fails. A user interface on a digital television is an example of a system that meets soft real-time deadlines.

*deadline definitions*

We need to establish a few terms to specify deadlines and describe process behavior. As shown in Figure 4-1, the **deadline** is the time when all computation must finish. In many cases, the process may start executing at the end of the previous deadline, but in some cases, we may want to define a **release time** after the last deadline. The **period** $T_i$ is the interval between successive deadlines. The deadline and start time are both specifications of desired behavior. The **relative deadline** is the difference between the process's release time to the end of its deadline.

We also need to describe the actual execution of the process. The **initiation time** is the time when the process actually starts executing, while the **completion time** is the time when it finishes. The **response time** of a process is the time from its release to the time it completes. As illustrated in Figure 4-1, the process may not execute every time it is initiated. The **execution time** or **CPU time**, which we call $C_i$, is the total amount of time that the process executes; that time is generally independent of the initiation time but often depends on the input data.

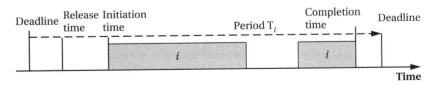

**Figure 4-1** *Deadline-related terminology.*

We often define deadlines for periodic processes, but we may also want to define a deadline for an aperiodic process. Scheduling such a process must take into account the state of the system when the process executes, but the basic definition of a deadline does not change much.

*process specifications*

To define the real-time requirements of a process, we specify its period (and perhaps its start time). When we build tasks out of several processes, we define the deadline for the entire task. Figure 4-2 shows a task with three processes and data dependencies between the processes. The period of the task includes the execution of all the processes in the task. A system may include several tasks, each running at its own rate.

*utilization*

We can observe some basic properties of systems of processes and schedules. Clearly, the total execution time of all the processes must be less than the total available time. Given a set of processes $1...n$, the total execution time required to complete all the processes is

$$C = \sum_{1 \le i \le n} C_i \qquad \text{(EQ 4-1)}$$

If the total time available to execute the processes is $t$, then the **utilization** or **maximum utilization** of the CPU is

$$U = \frac{C}{t}. \qquad \text{(EQ 4-2)}$$

Utilization is often expressed as a percentage. Clearly, the CPU's maximum utilization cannot exceed 100%.

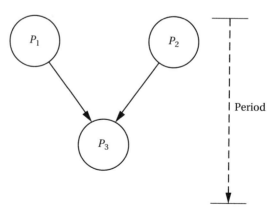

**Figure 4-2** *A task with several processes.*

### 4.2.2    Real-Time Scheduling Algorithms

*static scheduling algorithms*

Static scheduling algorithms have been studied in many different contexts ranging from shop floor scheduling to hardware/software co-design. This section looks at a few static scheduling techniques that can be useful in software design. There is a rather soft line between static scheduling and code synthesis. The last chapter discussed code synthesis techniques that could be viewed as static scheduling algorithms.

*data dependencies and scheduling*

Static schedulers often look at data dependencies between processes. Data dependencies make the scheduling problem much more difficult. Without data dependencies, there is little need to use a static scheduler. Data dependencies are represented by directed edges in a graph whose nodes are the processes. Unweighted directed edges simply specify order. Weighted directed edges specify the minimum time required between the completion of the source node process and the initiation of the sink node process.

We can compute some simple bounds on sets of processes with data dependencies that can be used to guide scheduling algorithms. The **as-soon-as-possible (ASAP)** schedule for a set of processes is constructed by putting each process at its earliest possible time as limited by the data dependencies. In the **as-late-as-possible (ALAP)** schedule, each process takes place at its latest possible time. If a process is at the same position in both the ASAP and ALAP schedules, then it is a **critical** process in the schedule; the set of critical nodes and edges from the source to the sink of the graph is the **critical path**.

*resource dependencies*

In contrast to data dependencies, **resource dependencies** come from the implementation. Two processes that need the same memory location, for example, require the same resource. Resource dependencies can be represented by undirected edges in the process graph. Two processes that need the same resource in general do not have to execute in any particular order, but they cannot execute at the same time. If the processes must access the resource in a particular order, then a data dependency can be used to express that fact.

*implementation*

We can implement static schedulers in several ways. We can interleave code from several programs to create a unified program. We can also build a state machine that uses subroutines or co-routines to call the processes. Neither of these programs use timers, which reduces overhead but also limits the accuracy of program timing. We can also set a timer to the next time a process must run, with the timer under the control of a state machinelike program.

*list scheduler*

A common form of constructive scheduler is the **list scheduler**. As the name implies, this algorithm forms a list of processes to be scheduled, then takes processes at the head of the list to form the schedule. The scheduling heuristic is embodied in the algorithm that determines where in the list a process is placed.

Figure 4-3 shows an example problem for list scheduling. Given two different heuristics for building the lists, we obtain two different schedules. The first

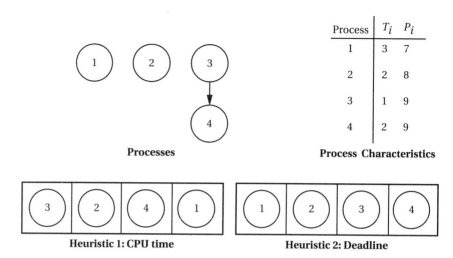

| Process | $T_i$ | $P_i$ |
|---------|-------|-------|
| 1 | 3 | 7 |
| 2 | 2 | 8 |
| 3 | 1 | 9 |
| 4 | 2 | 9 |

**Processes**      **Process Characteristics**

**Heuristic 1: CPU time**      **Heuristic 2: Deadline**

**Figure 4-3** *List scheduling.*

heuristic adds processes to the list in order of CPU time; the process with the smallest CPU time goes first. Note that in this case, two schedules are possible since 2 and 4 take the same amount of CPU time. The second heuristic adds processes in order of their periods, with the shortest period going first. The process orders in these two cases are very different. Which heuristic is best depends on the circumstances and goals of the system.

*interval scheduling*

Chou and Borriello developed an **interval-scheduling** model [Cho95a] and algorithm to statically schedule deadline-driven operations. They represent the processes and their timing constraints as a weighted directed graph. Each node in the graph represents a process; a node is weighted with a [1, $u$] pair that gives the lower and upper bounds on execution time of the node. Each directed edge is weighted with a minimum delay required from the source to the sink process. Each node has an anchor node that serves as the source node.

The interval-scheduling algorithm is a constructive algorithm that can be formulated as a recursive procedure. The algorithm searches each subgraph in topological order of the forward edges in the graph. At each step, it selects a node to be scheduled such that the partial schedule will be valid. This is ensured by requiring both the min-run and max-run are valid. The algorithm is outlined in Figure 4-4 [Cho95a].

Heuristics can be used to select algorithms that satisfy secondary optimization criteria as well as provide correct schedules. Choosing the candidate node with the smallest difference between lower- and upper-bound execution times helps to maximize available slack. Choosing the candidate with the smallest required separation from its parent requires less idle time in the schedule. Choosing the node with the highest indegree helps reduce starvation.

*dynamic and*
*priority-driven*
*scheduling*

Dynamic scheduling algorithms for periodic sets of processes are often cast as priority-driven scheduling. A priority-driven scheduler assigns priorities to each process. It then takes the process with the highest priority as the next process to run.

```
Boolean
ScheduleInterval(extended graph G, anchor a, current vertex c
{
    form G₁=(V[G], E[G], L[G], w[G]);
    if (not SingleSourceLongestPath(G₁, a))
        or (not VerifyUpper (G',a) ) return false;
    C := Candidates(C);
    if (C = ∅ ) return true;
    while  (C ≠ ∅ ) {
      p : = SelectCandidate(C);
      foreach q ∈ C, p ≠ q {
            E[G'] : = E [G'] U (p, q ) with weight  δ₁(p)
      }
      append p to O[G'];
      if (ScheduleInterval(G', a, p)) return true;
      G: = G'; // Undo
    }
        return false;
}
Boolean
VerifyUpper(extended graph G, anchor a)
{
    foreach edge (p,q) ∈ E[G] {
      if ((p, q) are adjacent in O[G] )
            W(p, q ) := L[G](q) − L [G](P)+ δᵥ (p) − δₗ (p);
      else W (p, q) := w(p, q);
    }
    form Gᵥ : = (V[G], E[G], L', W);
    return SingleSourceLongestPath (Gᵥ, a);
}
```

**Figure 4-4**  *The interval-scheduling algorithm. From Chou and Borriello [Cho95a] © 1995 ACM Press.*

*static versus dynamic priorities*

A priority-driven scheduler may use either **static** or **dynamic priorities**. (Note that priority-driven scheduling is dynamic in that the next process to execute is determined at run time, but the scheduler may use statically assigned priorities to determine scheduling.) In a static priority system, the priority of a process does not change during execution. A dynamic priority system, in contrast, changes the priorities of processes on-the-fly.

*Liu and Layland*

In their classic paper, Liu and Layland [Liu73] analyzed examples of both static and dynamic priority scheduling algorithms. Their static priority algorithm was called **rate-monotonic scheduling (RMS)** or **rate-monotonic analysis (RMA)**. Their dynamic priority algorithm was known as **earliest-deadline first (EDF)**. Their analysis made some common assumptions.

- There are no data dependencies between processes.

- Process periods may have arbitrary relationships.

- Context-switching overhead is negligible.

- The release time of each process is at the start of its period.

- Process execution time (C) is fixed.

In our discussion, we will assume that lower-numbered processes have higher priority, with process 1 having the highest priority. (Readers of Liu and Layland's article should note that they use the term *task* for what we refer to as *process*.) The assumptions underlying RMS and EDF mean that a system scheduled using these policies could also be scheduled by a static scheduler. In the absence of newly arriving tasks—in which case we can use RMS or EDF to check whether the task is admissible and determine how to schedule it—RMS and EDF are in part implementation techniques.

Because the deadlines of the processes do not have to be related in any way, many different combinations of deadlines are possible. It is not possible to enumerate all possible deadline sets to evaluate schedulability. Liu and Layland's analysis of rate-monotonic scheduling centered on the **critical instant**. As illustrated in Figure 4-5, the critical instant is the worst-case combination of process executions that will cause the longest delay for the initiation time of a process. Liu and Layland showed that the critical instant for process $i$ occurs when all higher-priority processes are ready to execute—that is, when the deadlines of all higher-priority processes have just expired and new periods have begun. In Figure 4-5 the critical instant for process 4 occurs when processes 1, 2, and 3 become ready; the first three processes must run to completion before process 4 can start executing.

*RMS priority assignment*

Liu and Layland used critical instant analysis to show that process priorities should be assigned in order of period, with the shortest priority process receiving the highest priority. This priority scheme is the motivation for the

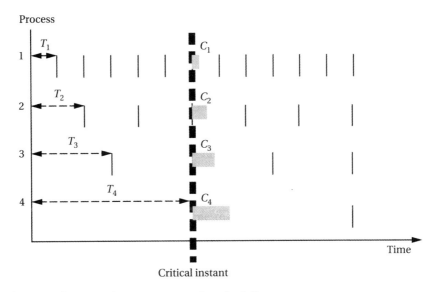

**Figure 4-5** *The critical instant in rate-monotonic scheduling.*

term "rate-monotonic." Their analysis used two processes, 1 and 2, with process 1 having the shorter period. If process 2 is given the higher priority and the resulting system has a feasible schedule, then it must be true that

$$C_1 + C_2 < T_1 . \tag{EQ 4-3}$$

The condition for process 1 to be schedulable is

$$\left\lfloor \frac{T_2}{T_1} \right\rfloor C_1 + C_2 \leq T_2 . \tag{EQ 4-4}$$

Since EQ 4-3 is satisfied when EQ 4-4 is satisfied, then process 1 has a feasible schedule when it has the lower priority and process 2 is feasible. However, the reverse is not true—in some cases, processes 1 and 2 are feasible when process 1 has the higher priority but not if process 2 is given the higher priority. Liu and Layland showed that RMS is a feasible schedule for any set of processes that has a feasible static priority assignment.

*RMS utilization*     Liu and Layland defined process utilization as the sum of the utilizations of the component processes.

$$U = \sum_{1 \leq i \leq m} \frac{C_i}{T_i} \tag{EQ 4-5}$$

They showed that the least upper bound on utilization for a set of $m$ tasks scheduled by RMS is

$$U = m(2^{1/m} - 1) \tag{EQ 4-6}$$

If the periods of the processes are simply related, there may be in fact a schedule that allows the utilization to reach 100%. However, in a wide range of circumstances, the CPU utilization approaches $\ln 2$ for large $m$. This result means that we cannot always use 100% of the CPU if we want to guarantee that all processes will meet their deadlines.

*earliest deadline first*

Liu and Layland also studied earliest-deadline first scheduling, which they called **deadline driven scheduling**. Priorities are assigned to processes based on the time remaining until the process's deadline—the highest-priority process is the one that is closest to reaching its deadline. These priorities are updated at each potential context switch. Liu and Layland showed that if a set of processes can be scheduled by any algorithm, then it can be scheduled by EDF. However, they also showed that in some cases, it is possible for EDF to overflow and not meet the deadlines of all processes.

Liu [Liu00] gave a feasibility condition for the schedulability of a system of processes using EDF. Given a set of $n$ processes, let $D_i$ be the relative deadline of process $i$. Then the process set must satisfy this relation:

$$\sum_{1 \le i \le n} \frac{T_i}{\min(D_i, C_i)} \le 1. \tag{EQ 4-7}$$

Albers and Slomka [Alb05] developed an efficient feasibility test for EDF-scheduled systems.

*least-laxity first scheduling*

A variation of EDF is **least-laxity first (LLF)** scheduling. **Laxity** or **slack** is the difference between the remaining computation time required to finish the process and the time remaining until the deadline. Least-laxity first scheduling assigns the highest priority to the process with the smallest laxity or slack value. LLF differs from EDF in that it takes into account the remaining computation time. EDF gives high priority to a process even if it needs only a fraction of its remaining period to finish its work; LLF, in contrast, gives priority to the process that will have the hardest time finishing by its deadline.

*priority inversion*

The analysis of RMA and EDF assumed that a process could always be preempted, but that is not always true in practical systems. If a process includes a critical section, then it cannot be preempted while it is in the crital section. A critical section is often used to protect the process's access to a shared resource. The critical section causes higher-priority processes to be excluded from executing. This phenomenon is known as **priority inversion**.

An example of priority inversion in a schedule is shown in Figure 4-6. Priority 1 is the highest-priority process; it can preempt process 3 during normal operation. But when process 3 enters a critical section that it shares with process 1,

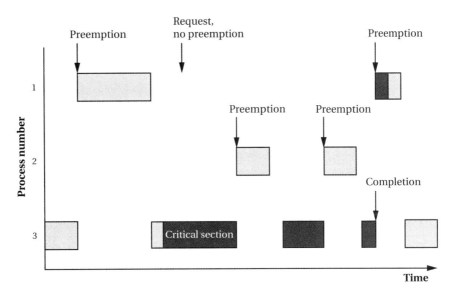

**Figure 4-6** *An example of priority inversion.*

then process 1 cannot preempt 3 until 3 finishes with the critical section. However, process 2, which does not share that critical section, can preempt process 3 as many times as it wants since it has higher priority. Process 2's preemptions can delay process 3 for an arbitrarily long time, even though process 1 has priority over both 1 and 2.

*priority inheritance protocols*

Sha et al. [Sha90] introduced the **priority inheritance protocol** to avoid priority inversion. They credit Lampson and Redell with first recognizing priority inversion in the Mesa operating system [Lam80]. Sha et al. recognized that temporarily changing priorities could help reduce the effects of priority inversion.

Their **basic priority inheritance protocol** causes a process that is inside a critical section to execute at the highest priority of any process that shares that crital section. In the example of Figure 4-6, this means that process 2 cannot interrupt process 3 while 3 is in its critical section. As a result, process 3 finishes more quickly and allows process 1 to run. However, Sha et al. noted that if a process needs several critical sections, it can be blocked sequentially at each of those critical sections by different processes, causing a blocking chain that slows down the higher-priority process. The basic protocol is also vulnerable to deadlocks.

*priority ceiling protocol*

Sha et al. developed the **priority ceiling protocol** to overcome the limitations of the basic protocol. Given a process $i$, we want to schedule the process. In this protocol, each semaphore $S_j$ guarding a critical section is assigned its own priority ceiling $\Pi(S_j)$. As before, the priority ceiling of a semaphore is equal to the priority of the highest-priority process that may use the semaphore.

Given the set of semaphores that are currently locked by processes other than $i$, we call the semaphore in that set with the highest priority ceiling $S^*$. For process $i$ to obtain semaphore $S_j$, it must have a priority higher than $\Pi(S^*)$. While in a critical section, process $i$ inherits the priority of the highest-priority job that may be blocked by process $i$; priorities are inherited transitively.

Sha et al. extended Liu and Layland's analysis of RMS (namely, EQ 4-5) to determine the schedulability of tasks under the priority ceiling protocol. If $B_i$ is the worst-case time that process $i$ can be blocked by lower-priority processes, then

$$\frac{C_1}{T_1} + \frac{C_2}{T_2} + \ldots + \frac{C_i}{T_i} + \frac{B_i}{T_i} \leq i(2^{1/i} - 1). \tag{EQ 4-8}$$

*hot swapping*
Some systems may use several implementations of a process or change the process parameters to cause a large change in the process's execution time. For example, a communication system may change error-correction codes on-the-fly to adapt to changing channel characteristics. When the process execution time changes substantially, we must schedule the system to handle not only the steady-state condition of the new system but also the transient effects caused by the switch. Lee et al. [Lee02a] developed a hot-swapping algorithm that combines offline analysis and online scheduling. In the hot-swapping model, switching a process from one implementation to another invokes an additional computation time that corresponds to the setup time for the new implementation. At design time, they analyze the possible combinations of implementation swaps and build a table to be used by the operating system. At run time, the operating system uses the table to determine how to schedule the transition to the new implementation of the task.

### 4.2.3 Scheduling for Dynamic Voltage Scaling

*scheduling for dynamic voltage scaling*
Many groups have studied how to schedule tasks on processors that implement **dynamic voltage scaling (DVS)**. Yao et al. [Yao95] developed early scheduling algorithms for DVS. They assumed that the processor clock could be varied continuously. They modeled each process $j$ with an arrival time $a_j$, a deadline $b_j$, and a required number of CPU cycles $R_j$. (Execution time depends on the clock frequency as well as the number of clock cycles.) They defined the intensity of an interval $I = [z, z']$ in the schedule as

$$g(I) = \frac{\sum R_j}{z' - z}. \tag{EQ 4-9}$$

The **intensity** of an interval defines a lower bound on the average processing speed required to create a feasible schedule. Yao et al. called the interval that maximizes the intensity to be the **critical interval** (known as $I*$) and the set of processes that run in that interval the **critical group**. They showed that an optimal schedule for the process set is equal to the intensity of the critical interval $g(I*)$. They developed an optimal offline scheduling algorithm that repeatedly identified critical intervals and scheduled the critical group. They also developed an online scheduling heuristic. Their **average rate heuristic** sets the processor speed at

$$s(t) = \sum_j \frac{R_j}{b_j - a_j}. \qquad \text{(EQ 4-10)}$$

The order in which processes are executed is determined using an EDF policy. They showed that the average rate heuristic (AVR) is optimal to within a constant factor of the energy of an optimal schedule. The **slowdown factor** of a process is often called either a or h.

Pillai and Shin [Pil01] proposed testing for the feasibility of EDF or RMS scheduling under voltage scaling by multiplying the maximum utilization by the slowdown factor. They also proposed a cycle-conserving scheduling algorithm that measured the difference between the actual and worst-case execution times of the tasks and scaled the processor frequency to adjust for the unused execution time. They also proposed predicting run times and using that information to scale the processor frequency before the jobs had finished.

*discrete voltages and frequencies*
Yao et al.'s assumption of continuously scalable frequencies is naive. In practice, the processor clock and power supply voltage can be set to a relatively small set of discrete values within the operating envelope of the processor.

Ishihara and Yasuura [Ish98a] proved some useful theorems about DVS with discrete voltages. They used $v_{ideal}$ to refer to the voltage at which the CPU executes a process so that it finishes exactly at the deadline. They showed that if the processor is restricted to a small number of voltage levels, then two voltage levels are sufficient to minimize total energy consumption under a time constraint. This requirement can be formulated as

$$V_1^2 x1 + V_2^2 x2 + V_3^2 x3 \geq V_1^2 y1 + V_2^2 y2 \qquad \text{(EQ 4-11)}$$

subject to the execution time and execution cycles of the two schedules being the same:

$$\frac{x1 V_1}{(V_1 - V_T)^\alpha} + \frac{x2 V_2}{(V_2 - V_T)^\alpha} + \frac{x3 V_3}{(V_3 - V_T)^\alpha} = \frac{y1 V_1}{(V_1 - V_T)^\alpha} + \frac{y2 V_2}{(V_2 - V_T)^\alpha} \qquad \text{(EQ 4-12)}$$

$$x1 + x2 + x3 = y1 + y2. \qquad \text{(EQ 4-13)}$$

The constraints can be satisfied only if $x1 \geq y1$. In this case, we can rewrite the constraints in the following form.

$$V_1^2(x1 - y1) + V_3^2 x3 \geq V_2^2(y2 - x2) \qquad \text{(EQ 4-14)}$$

EQ 4-14 implies that voltage scheduling with the three voltages cannot minimize energy consumption when $v_{ideal}$ is between $V_1$ and $V_2$. Similarly, three voltages cannot minimize energy when $v_{ideal}$ is between $V_2$ and $V_3$. Therefore, two voltage levels minimize energy consumption.

Ishihara and Yasuura also showed that the two voltages to use are immediate neighbors to $v_{ideal}$. Figure 4-7 illustrates the proof. Both the continuous time-energy curve and linear approximations are shown. If, for example, the time constraint falls between $t_2$ and $t_3$, then the $V_2$ to $V_3$ line gives lower energy consumption than the $V_1$ to $V_3$ line.

*slack-based scheduling*

Kim et al. [Kim02] developed an algorithm to use slack times from processes to scale processor voltage. Their algorithm takes advantage of slack from both higher-priority and lower-priority tasks. Their algorithm for determining the available slack is shown in Figure 4-8.

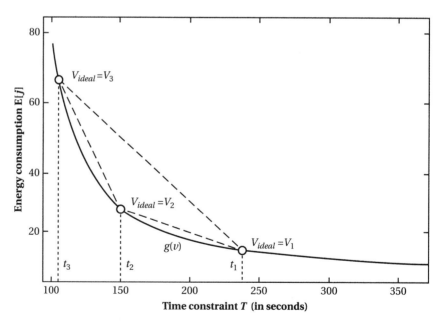

**Figure 4-7** *Voltage scaling-based scheduling with two voltages. From Ishihara and Yasuura [Ish98a] © 1998 IEEE.*

Input : the active task $T_\alpha$, waitQ, readyQ, current time $t_{cur}$;

**Output :** the available execution time $S(T_\alpha)$for $T_\alpha$;

$T_H(T_\alpha, t_{cur})$ = the set of already completed higher-priority task instances;

$T_L(T_\alpha, t_{cur})$ = the set of already completed lower-priority task instances;

$S_H = \sum r_i \in T_H (r_\alpha, t_{cur}) U_i^{rem} + U_\alpha^{rem}$;

$S_L = 0$;

$t_\alpha^h$ = the earliest arrival time of a task instance whose priority is higher than $T_\alpha$;

if $t_{cur} + S_H < t_\alpha^h$ then

   $t_a$ = the worst case completion time of $T_\alpha$ with the clock speed of $\dfrac{W_\alpha^{rem}}{S_H}$

   if there will be no activated task instance (i.e., readyQ = $\varnothing$) at $t_a$ **then**

      let $t'_\alpha = \mathbf{min}(a_i \backslash T_i \in \text{waitQ})$;

      $t_\alpha = \max(t_\alpha, t'_\alpha)$;

      $T_\beta$ = the task instance expected to be scheduled at $t_\alpha$;

      $T'_L(T_\beta, t_{cur})$ = the set of completed task instances whose priorities are
                    higher than or equal to that of $T_\beta$ but less than that of $T_\alpha$;

      $S_L = (U_\beta^{rem} - W_\beta^{rem}) + \sum r_i \in T'_L(T_\beta, t_{cur}) U_i^{rem}$;

      $t_\beta^h$ = the earliest arrival time of task instance whose priority is
          higher than $T_\beta$;

      $S_L = \min(S_L, t_\beta^h - t_\alpha)$;

   end if

$S(T_\alpha) = \min(S_H + U_\alpha^{rem} + S_L, d_\alpha - t_{cur})$;

Output $S(T_\alpha)$;

**Figure 4-8** *An algorithm for estimating slack for dynamic voltage scaling-based scheduling. From Kim et al. [Kim02] © 2002 IEEE Computer Society.*

*checkpoint-driven scheduling*

Azevedo et al. [Aze02] used profile information to guide DVS scheduling. They profiled the program using simulators to determine the program's performance and energy consumption for a variety of inputs. The designer can insert checkpoints at arbitrary places in the program to measure performance and energy. During execution, the program generates an event at each checkpoint. The scheduler can use either average power or a maximum power budget as its objective. To schedule the program, the scheduler considers all the possible events from the current checkpoint to the deadline. It then calculates the optimal frequency based on power and time constraints. Azevedo et al.'s scheduling algorithm is shown in Figure 4-9.

1. At a checkpoint execution, create a new CDB with the active checkpoint transitions.
2. Check type of current node in the HCFG.

    Case 1: Node type is normal (not function call nor loop header).

        I. Estimate the number of cycles C from curr node to all active checkpoint transitions.

           Formula 1:

              $C$ = longest_path(curr node, active checkpoint transition end point)

              Or for inherited time constraints:

              $C$ = longest_path_length(curr node, end node of curr sub-CFG) + extraC,

              Where extraC is obtained by

              extraC = remaining number of iterations * max cycle per iter + inherited max cycle

              (for parent node of type loop header)

              or extraC = inherited max cycle (for parent node of type function)

           Formula 2:

              $C$ = max profiled number of cycles for active checkpoint transition –

                    elapsed number of cycles for active checkpoint transition

        II. Select for each checkpoint transition

           $C = C_{Formula1}$ or $C = C_{Formula2}$ or $C = \min(C_{Formula1}, C_{Formula2})$

        III. Create a new CPDB using C for each active checkpoint transition.

        IV. Invoke DVS algorithm from Section 2 using new CDB and CPDB.

        V. Continue with program execution.

    Case 2: Node is function call or loop header.

        I. Calculate the tightest active checkpoint transition selecting by frequency

           max(longest_path(curr node, active checkpoint transition end point)/time constraint

           Name tightest time constraint as inherited and compute max cycle C:

           $C$ = longest_path(next node, active checkpoint transition end point) – inherited max cycle

        II. Add an end-node to the curr node's sub-CFG with max cycle = C.

        III. Add inherited time constraint to CDB with time = inherited constraint remaining time.

        IV. Continue with program execution.

**Figure 4-9** *A checkpoint-driven DVS scheduling algorithm. From Azevedo et al. [Aze02] © 2002 IEEE Computer Society.*

*leakage
minimization*

    Idle modes save even more processor energy than does voltage scaling; this is particularly true for processors with high leakage rates. However, because entering and leaving an idle mode incurs considerable penalties in both energy and performance, we want to maximize the length of any idle time that is entered and minimize the number of distinct idle times. **Procrastination scheduling** is a family of scheduling algorithms designed to maximize the length of idle periods.

Jejurikar et al. [Jej04] used procrastination scheduling to maximize idle periods. They modeled the power consumption of a processor as three components:

$$P = P_{AC} + P_{DC} + P_{on} \qquad \text{(EQ 4-15)}$$

the dynamic power, the static power consumption, and on-state power. On-state power is consumed by the clock, I/O devices, and other peripheral circuitry. They compute the minimum breakeven time for a shutdown as

$$t_{threshold} = \frac{E_{shutdown}}{P_{idle}} . \qquad \text{(EQ 4-16)}$$

Given a set of processes, they use EDF scheduling with the deadline equal to the period and a known worst-case execution time. When a new task arrives, they do not wake up the processor immediately; instead, they wait for a procrastination timer to expire before waking up the processor and starting the highest-priority task (using the EDF policy). The procrastination interval of a process is $Z_i$. They showed that the procrastination algorithm guarantees all process deadlines if the procrastination interval satisfies

$$\frac{Z_i}{T_i} + \sum_{1 \le k \le i} \frac{C_k}{T_k \eta_k} \le 1 \qquad \text{(EQ 4-17)}$$

for all $i \in 1....n$ and for all $k < i$, $Z_k \le Z_i$. They showed that their policy provided a 5% energy gain over DVS and a 20% again over non-DVS scheduling.

### 4.2.4  Performance Estimation

The assumption that the computation time of a process is fixed is not very realistic. Not only do data-dependent paths in the program cause execution time to vary, but the cache causes large variations in run time. We can, however, model the cache to estimate its effects on programs.

*multitasking and caches*

We are particularly interested in the effects of multiple tasks on the cache. Kirk and Strosnider [Kir90] proposed a segmented, locked cache. A program could lock a range of lines in the cache so that no other program could modify those cache locations. This would allow the program to keep certain parts of itself in the cache after a preemption. However, it reduces the cache size not only for the program with the lock but also for the other programs in the system.

*program placement for caches*

Mueller [Mue95] used software methods to partition the cache for use by multiple processes. His method used the compiler to split the code into portions of equal size, based on the size of the instruction cache partition. Each partition ends in an unconditional jump. Similarly, the method splits data into smaller

*simplified
process caching
models*

units. In some cases, splitting large data structures like arrays may require transformations on the parts of the program that manipulate the data structure. Local data is split into partitions by manipulating the stack pointer. Statically linked libraries can be transformed to create fixed-size partitions, but dynamically linked libraries are problematic.

Li and Wolf [Li97b] developed a model for multitasking in caches. They characterized a program as occupying a set of lines in the cache. Each program was modeled with a two-state machine: one state represents the program in the cache, while the other state models the program outside of the cache. The total state of the cache is given by the union of all the models for the programs that use the cache. Li and Wolf modeled the performance of a program by two major numbers: the worst-case execution time when the program is not in the cache and the average-case execution time when the program is in the cache. (For synthesis purposes, they also used a best-case time assuming that there were no cache misses, but it was used only to bound possible schedules.)

Given the cache state model and the performance characteristics of each process, they could construct an abstract schedule that approximated the execution time of the multitasking system. They tested the accuracy of this model by comparing it to detailed simulations of the programs, using interleaved sections of the code of the various processes. Figure 4-10 shows the results of simulation that compared the execution times predicted by the two-state model with simulation instruction traces for the interleaved processes using QPT and Dinero [Li98b].

*caches and
scheduling*

Kastner and Thesing [Kas98] developed a scheduling algorithm that takes cache behavior into account. Their analysis handled associative caches. They determined which memory lines must be in the cache at a given point in the program. Their scheduling algorithm checks the cache state at scheduling decision points to more accurately estimate execution time.

*multitasking and
scratch pads*

When several programs execute on the CPU, all the programs compete for the scratch pad, much as they compete for the cache. However, because the

| Example | Number of tasks | Schedule length WCET/Number of task instances | Simulated execution time | Trace length | Average error (percent) | Standard deviation (percent) |
|---|---|---|---|---|---|---|
| Image Processing | 7 | 1,814,375/32 | 1,679,822 | 1,078,139 | 7.6 | 2.3 |
| Array | 3 | 3,843,337/11 | 3,656,839 | 3,071,293 | 4.7 | 1.2 |

**Figure 4-10** *Experimental validation of two-state cache model. From Li [Li98b].*

scratch pad is managed in software, the allocation algorithm must take multitasking into account. Panda et al. propose dividing the scratch pad into segments and assigning each task its own segment. This approach reduces run-time overhead for scratch pad management but results in underutilization of part of the scratch pad. When the programs are prioritized, they weight the total conflict fetch (TCF) by the task priority (see Section 3.3.4), with higher-priority tasks given more weight. (Note that this is the inverse of the convention in real-time systems, in which the highest priority task is given a priority of 1.)

## 4.3 Languages and Scheduling

We can use programming languages to capture information about tasks and interprocess communication. Because a programming language may restrict the things that tasks can do, it can make possible some types of scheduling that would otherwise not be possible. This section looks at languages that provide task-level models for system activity.

*CFSMs*

The **codesign finite state machine (CFSM)** [Bal96] is a control model explicitly designed to be implemented as combinations of hardware and software. As with traditional automata, a CFSM is defined by input and output events, possible valuations for those input and output events, initial values for some output events, and a transition relation. A CFSM repeatedly executes a four-phase cycle:

1. Idle

2. Detect input events

3. Go to new state based on current state and inputs

4. Emit outputs

CFSMs are modeled by automata with one-input buffers for each input and one-input buffers for each output.

Chiodo et al. [Chi95] developed a compiler for control FSMs that could be used to compile Esterel. Their compiler first generated an **s-graph** that represents the transition function of the CFSM. The s-graph is a form of control data flow graph (CDFG) that has four types of nodes: *begin*, *end*, *test*, and *assign*. *Begin* and *end* are the source and sink nodes, respectively. An *assign* node is labeled with a variable assignment. A *test* node has two children, one for the true condition and one for the false condition.

The s-graph is generated using Shannon decomposition to analyze the s-graph and minimize the size of the s-graph. Because the s-graph represents the

CFSM's transition function, it represents one execution of a task; the repetition of the task is performed by the operating system. This means that shortest-path and longest-path algorithms can be used to estimate the performance of the software. Code size can be estimated from table lookup or by generating and analyzing assembly code. Most of the optimizations are performed on the s-graph, which is ultimately turned into C code: a *test* node becomes an if and two gotos; an *assign* node becomes a C assignment.

*Petri net*
*fragments*

Lin and Zhu [Lin98; Zhu99] developed an algorithm for statically scheduling processes using Petri nets. Given a Petri net model for a program, they find maximal acyclic fragments of the program, then schedule the operations in each fragment. They define an **expansion** of a Petri net model as an acyclic Petri net in which every transition has at least one input or output place, at least one place that has no input transitions, and at least one place that has no output transitions. A **maximal expansion** is defined relative to an initial marking $m$ of the net and is transitively closed: for each transition, or place in the expansion, all preceding places and transitions reachable from $m$ are also in the maximal expansion. A marking $m_c$ is said to be a cut-off marking if it is reachable from $m$ and no transitions are enabled to fire. Figure 4-11 shows a Petri net, its maximal expansion, and two different cut-off markings.

Code is generated from a maximally expanded fragment by pre-ordering the operations in the segment. A pre-ordering assigns times to operations in the graph that satisfy the precedence constraints defined in the Petri net fragment. A control flow graph is generated for the fragment that satisfies the pre-ordering. This can be used to generate a C implementation.

*software thread*
*integration*

**Software thread integration** (**STI**) [Dea04] schedules multiple threads such that they can be implemented in a single program. Software thread integration starts with a set of threads, some of which may have real-time deadlines. The result is a single program that interleaves the execution of the threads, guaranteeing real-time responsiveness for all threads.

On the left in Figure 4-12, a **primary thread** has real-time requirements; the thread without real-time requirements is known as the **secondary thread**. Software thread integration copies portions of the primary thread into the secondary thread so that the primary thread executes correctly and meets its deadlines. The integrated threads do not need any context-switching mechanism, reducing execution time. The major cost of this technique is that several copies of parts of the primary thread may need to be inserted in to the secondary thread to ensure that the primary thread executes correctly.

Each thread is represented by a **control dependence graph** (**CDG**) [Fer87] that has a node for each basic block/conditional test and an edge for each control decision. Figure 4-13 shows a program's CDFG and the CDG derived from it. Note that block *B6* is at the top level of the CDG because it is always executed. The CDG is a levelized form of the control flow, with a new level of graph for each level of nested conditional.

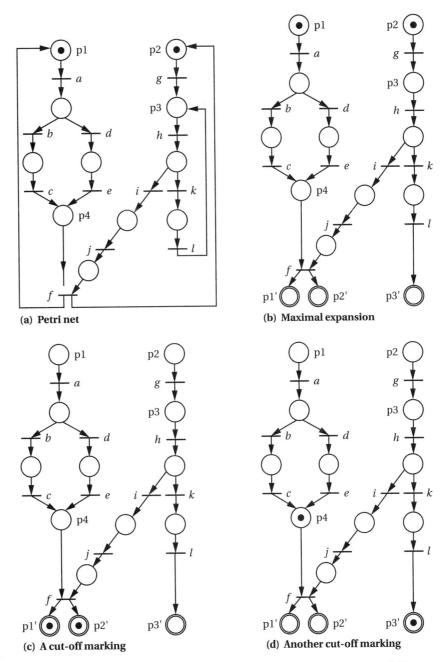

**Figure 4-11** *Maximal expansions and cut-off markings of Petri nets. From Lin and Zhu*
*[Lin98] © 1998 IEEE Computer Society.*

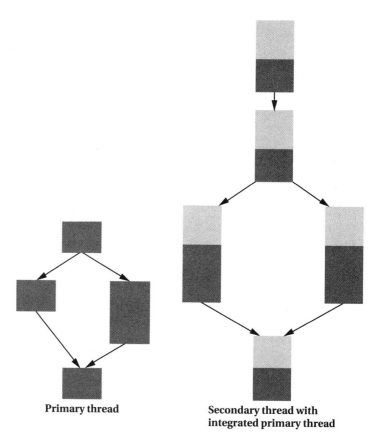

**Primary thread**

**Secondary thread with
integrated primary thread**

**Figure 4-12** *Integrating threads together into a single executable.*

Software thread integration requires execution time information about each node in the control dependence graph; that information may come from WCET analysis or from programmer annotations. Each CDG is annotated with the execution times for each block. In addition to execution times, the primary threads require timing constraints. Each block in a primary thread is assigned a latest start time and finish time.

Because the secondary thread has no timing constraints, code from the primary thread can be inserted at arbitrary locations. The basic scheduling algorithm greedily assigns primary thread blocks to positions within the secondary thread. A primary thread block is scheduled in the first interval between two blocks that satisfy its start time requirement. The algorithm may descend into a control node of the secondary thread if no unconditional block provides an acceptable start time and a conditional node is in the desired time window. When code is inserted into a conditional subtree of the CDG, the scheduler must

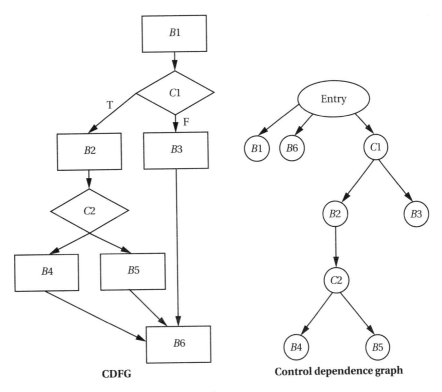

**Figure 4-13** *An example control dependence graph.*

make copies of the selected primary thread node in all conditional branches of that node; this results in the code explosion mentioned previously.

If a node's execution time is too large, program transformations can break it into several smaller nodes. For example, loop peeling can remove one iteration of a loop, breaking the loop into two nodes. Loop splitting breaks a loop into two loops whose iterations together cover the required iteration space.

*Giotto*

Giotto [Hen03] is a language for describing concurrent systems. A Giotto task is a sequential program that can be implemented in a standard programming language. A task has a set of input and output ports; a port is generally used for point-to-point communication. Primary inputs and outputs of the system are known as **sensor ports** and **actuator ports**, respectively. Execution is organized into **modes**—a mode is a repeated invocation of a sequence of tasks in a fixed order. The mode is specified by a period, mode ports, task invocations, actuator updates, and mode switches. A single invocation of a mode is known as a **round**.

Figure 4-14 shows an example mode specification. The mode has two input ports, $i_1$ and $i_2$, and one output port $x_1$. It also has a mode port $o_1$. A mode port's

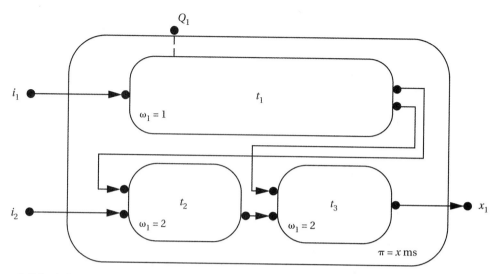

**Figure 4-14** *A Giotto mode with three tasks.*

value remains constant while the mode remains active. Any output of the mode is also considered to be a mode port and must be initialized upon entering the mode. The mode specifies its period $\pi$. Each task has its own invocation rate v, which is equal to the number of times during the period the task is invoked. In the figure, $t_1$ is invoked once per cycle while $t_2$ and $t_3$ are invoked twice. A port's value changes at the period rate, so a task may see the same value on a port during several invocations in a period.

A **mode switch** is specified by several elements. The **switch frequency** is an $\omega$ value that represents the frequency at which mode switches are evaluated. The **driver** supplies a value to a port; the port is guarded by an **exit condition** that determines whether the mode will switch. Upon a switch, the **target mode** starts to execute.

An execution cycle in Giotto consists of nine steps:

1. Task output and internal ports are updated.

2. Actuator ports are updated.

3. Sensor ports are updated.

4. Modes are updated, possibly selecting some target modes.

5. Mode ports are updated.

6. The mode time is updated so that mode switches jump to a time that is as close as possible to the end of the round at the target mode as closely as is possible.

7. Task input ports are updated.

8. The set of active tasks is updated.

9. The time clock is updated.

Giotto allows separate specification of implementation information. The platform specification defines a hardware platform using techniques like those used in hardware/software co-design; we discuss these models in Section 7.4.2. The jitter tolerance defines how much task timing can vary. A variety of scheduling and allocation algorithms can be used to implement the Giotto program onto the platform. Giotto provides an annotation mechanism that can be used to supply hints for synthesis.

*SHIM*        SHIM [Edw05] is a programming model that connects sequential processes through fixed communication channels. The processes communicate with rendezvous-style communication, which does not use buffers. (Buffers can be added on top of the basic communication mechanism.) The model is deterministic because each communication channel has only one reader and only one writer. SHIM specifications can be implemented as single-threaded programs using the scheduler of Lin and Zhu or other algorithms.

## 4.4  Operating System Design

*general-purpose versus real-time*   The most fundamental difference between a general-purpose operating system and a real-time operating system is the goal of its scheduler. A general-purpose operating system is interested in fairness and wants to avoid starving processes from lack of CPU access. A real-time operating system, in contrast, is concerned with meeting deadlines.

However, real-time operating systems for embedded systems are often called upon to provide many of the features that are provided by general-purpose operating systems. Embedded systems often maintain file systems, communicate over TCP/IP, run a large suite of programs, provide memory management, and handle accounts. And, of course, general-purpose operating systems like Linux can be adapted to use in real-time systems.

Early real-time operating systems, such as the Hunter/Ready OS of the 1980s, were very small. Mach [Tok90] was one of the early attempts to build real-time properties into an operating system that ran on a full-scale CPU and provided modern services. Since then, real-time operating systems that provide a rich feature set have become more common, ranging from POSIX to various commercial RTOSs.

Section 4.4.1 looks at memory management in embedded operating systems. Section 4.4.2 describes the structure of an RTOS. Section 4.4.3 considers overheads in RTOS operation. Section 4.4.4 briefly looks at support mechanisms for real-time scheduling. In Section 4.4.5, we learn how to implement interprocess communication. Section 4.4.6 considers power management, and Section 4.4.7 studies embedded file systems.

## 4.4.1 Memory Management in Embedded Operating Systems

Memory management is more often associated with general-purpose than real-time operating systems, but as we have noted, RTOSs are often called upon to perform general-purpose tasks. An RTOS may provide memory management for several reasons.

- Memory mapping hardware can protect the memory spaces of the processes when outside programs are run on the embedded system.

- Memory management can allow a program to use a large virtual address space.

The next example describes the memory management structure of Windows CE.

---

### Example 4-1

*Memory Management in Windows CE*

Windows CE [Bol03] is designed as a real-time, full-featured operating system for lightweight consumer devices. Windows desktop applications cannot run on Windows CE directly, but the operating system is designed to simplify porting Windows applications to Windows CE.

Windows CE supports virtual memory; the paging memory can be supplied by a flash memory as well as more traditional devices such as disks. The operating system supports a flat 32-bit virtual address space. The bottom 2 GB of the address space is for user processes, while the top 2 GB is for the kernel. The kernel address space is statically mapped into the address space.

The user address space is dynamically mapped. It is divided into 64 slots of 32 MB each. Slot 0 holds the currently running processes. Slots 1–33 are the processes, with slot 1 holding the Dynamically Linked Libraries (DLLs). This means that only 32 processes can run at any one time. Slots 33–62 are for memory mapped files, operating system objects, and so on. The last slot holds resource mappings.

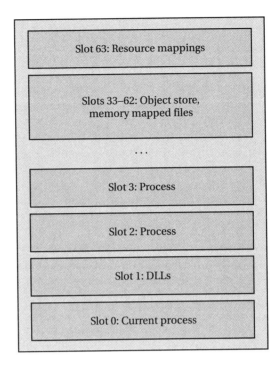

Each process slot is divided into several sections. The bottom 64KB is used as a guard section. The user code grows from the bottom up. The memory required for DLLs that are called by the process grows from the top of the memory space down.

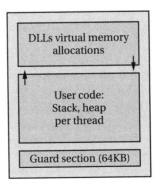

## 4.4.2   Structure of a Real-Time Operating System

*interrupts and*
*scheduling*

The two key elements of a real-time operating system are the interrupt-handling mechanism and the scheduler. These two elements determine the real-time behavior of the RTOS. Our discussion of scheduling in Section 4.2 ignored interrupts, but in fact interrupts must be carefully handled to avoid destroying the real-time properties of the operating system.

The interrupt system provides its own priorities for the interrupt handlers. The interrupt handlers can be seen as a distinct set of processes that are separate from the operating system's regular processes. The interrupt system priorities are determined by hardware. Furthermore, all interrupt handlers have priority over the operating system processes, since an interrupt will be automatically fielded unless the interrupts are masked. As a result, an RTOS must be carefully architected so that interrupts do not subvert the operating system's scheduler.

*ISRs and ISTs*

A key rule-of-thumb for the design of responsive operating systems is that we want to spend as little time as possible in the interrupt handlers that are dispatched by the hardware interrupt system. However, many realistic devices need a significant amount of computation to be done somewhere. As a result, device-oriented processing is often divided into two sections: the **interrupt service routine (ISR)** and the **interrupt service thread (IST)**. The ISR is dispatched by the hardware interrupt system, while the IST is a user-mode process. The ISR performs the minimum work necessary to field the interrupt; it then passes on data to the IST that can finish the task.

The next example describes scheduling and interrupts in Windows CE.

---

## Example 4-2

*Scheduling and Interrupts in Windows CE*

Windows CE divides interrupt handling into an ISR and an IST [Bol03]. It provides two types of ISRs. A static ISR is built into the kernel, which also provides the ISR's stack. Static ISRs provide one-way communication to their IST. An installable ISR can be dynamically loaded into the kernel. Installable ISRs can use shared memory to communicate. They are processed in the order in which they were installed.

An interrupt is processed over several stages. Interrupt latency can be attributed to several factors. The main components of ISR latency are the time required to turn off interrupts and the time required to vector the interrupt, save registers, and so on. Both of these factors depend on the CPU platform. The main components of IST latency are the ISR latency, the time spent in the kernel (*kcall*), and the thread-scheduling time.

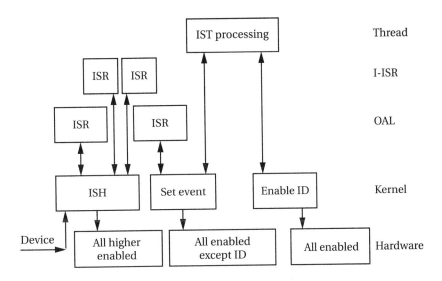

The Windows CE scheduler provides two types of preemptive multitasking. In a more general-purpose style of scheduling, a thread runs until the end of the time quantum. In a more real-time style, a thread runs until a higher-priority thread is ready to run. The OS provides 256 total priorities. Within a priority level, threads run in round-robin mode. Windows CE provides a priority inheritance protocol. The system timer normally uses a 1 ms tick.

### 4.4.3  Operating System Overhead

Most scheduling analyses assume that context-switching time is negligible. This assumption is reasonable when the context-switching time is small compared to the execution time of the process. However, for very short processes or at very high utilizations, context switching can take up a significant fraction of the available CPU time.

*OS simulation*    The effects of context-switching overhead can be studied using simulators. Some RTOSs, such as VxWorks, provide simulators that accurately model the CPU time for interrupts, operating system calls, and so forth. These simulators can be fed with traces and provide timing diagrams that show not only the total execution time but the actions performed by the CPU over time. Simulators can be very helpful when one is debugging a real-time system.

*overhead study*    Rhodes and Wolf [Rho99] studied the effects of context-switching overhead using simulation. They studied a two-processor system with a bus, but these results suggest the situation in a single-processor system. They generated 100 random task graphs and generated schedules for each. They varied two design parameters: the time of the interrupt service time and the context-switching time. They also adjusted the deadlines of the tasks to provide varying amounts of slack: no slack, 10% slack, 20% slack, and 40% slack. The results are shown in Figure 4-15. In each plot, the system rapidly changes from highly schedulable in the region with small interrupt service and context-switching times, to unschedulable in the region with large interrupt service and context-switching times. Interrupt and context-switching overheads can be traded off.

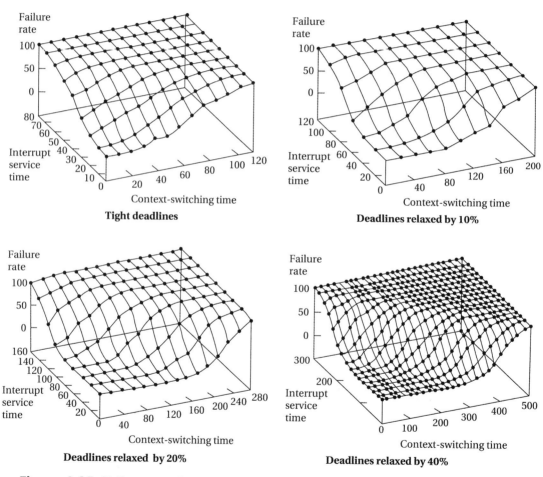

**Figure 4-15** *Failure rate of schedules as a function of interrupt and computation time. From Rhodes and Wolf [Rho99] © 1999 IEEE Computer Society.*

### 4.4.4  Support for Scheduling

*RTU*

Adomat et al. [Ado96] developed an accelerator for real-time scheduling known as RTU. (They described it as a co-processor, but it is not controlled by the CPU instruction issue mechanism.) Their accelerator could support up to three processors. The system bus was arbitrated in round-robin fashion to ensure that events could be handled in a bounded amount of time. The RTU evaluated process readiness and priorities using hardware to determine which process should run next on each CPU.

*Spring scheduler*

Burleson et al. [Bur99] designed a scheduling accelerator for Spring. Although they refer to their unit as a co-processor, it is a memory-mapped device attached to the CPU bus. The system is designed to support dynamically appearing tasks. Once a task is given a guarantee for completion by a deadline, that guarantee will not be violated, but later tasks may not be able to gain admission to the system due to the commitments made to earlier tasks. Their scheduling algorithm constructs a schedule by adding one process at a time to the partial schedule. If the new task makes the schedule infeasible, then the scheduler backtracks and tries to add a different task to the partial schedule.

The architecture of their accelerator is shown in Figure 4-16. First, the earliest possible start times for the processors are generated. Based on those values, a heuristic scheduling function is evaluated (they considered several different scheduling heuristics); based on the heuristic function evaluated, if the partial schedule is feasible, then a task is added to the queue of processes.

*RTM*

Kohout et al. [Koh03] developed a real-time task manager, RTM, to support scheduling and time and event management in real-time operating systems.

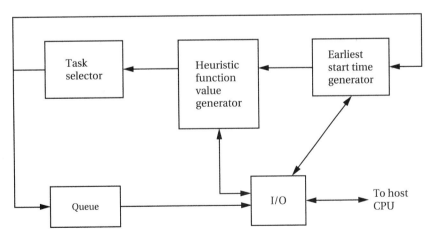

**Figure 4-16** *Architecture of the Spring scheduling accelerator [Bur99].*

RTM is a peripheral device with a memory-mapped interface. The device contains a number of records for processes (64 records in their design). Each record includes:

- Status bits that describe the state of the record, such as whether the process is ready to run.

- Priority of the process.

- Process ID.

- A delay field that tells how long after the start of the period the delay task is to run.

The fields are evaluated using a tree of ready test cells. Each cell takes as input the priorities and ready bits of two processes; the cell emits the priority and ready bit for the higher-priority process. The delay through this tree network scales well, allowing a large number of processes to be evaluated quickly in hardware.

### 4.4.5 Interprocess Communication Mechanisms

**Interprocess communication** (**IPC**) mechanisms are used as abstract devices by programs, but they may be implemented in any of several ways in the operating system. The mechanism used to implement interprocess communication can affect performance and energy consumption.

*IPC in general-purpose systems*
General-purpose operating systems use interprocess communication to move large quantities of data. IPC transfers may be heavily buffered to improve overall system performance at the expense of transaction latency. While real-time systems may also have to push large amounts of data through the system, they must also be optimized to meet real-time requirements.

*mailboxes*
**Mailboxes** can be used for small data transfers. A mailbox allows only one writer but many readers. While mailboxes can be implemented in software, they are frequently implemented as hardware units. A hardware mailbox has a fixed number of registers or locations, so it cannot hold arbitrarily large communications. Because the mailbox can have only one writer, it is not subject to contention. The TI OMAP system, for example, provides four mailboxes for its two processors. Each CPU owns two of the mailboxes for writing.

*streaming and large transfers*
Streaming data is one category of large data transfer common to embedded systems. Other less periodic transfers may also move large amounts of data. Specialized memories may be used to hold such data. Because many data transfers in embedded systems are producer-consumer—that is, one writer and one or more readers—a specialized buffer can provide more predictable access.

### 4.4.6   Power Management

As we have seen, hardware may provide a variety of mechanisms to manage power, including sleep modes and clock rate control. Methods that reconfigure system state to optimize power consumption are known as **dynamic power management**. These mechanisms are typically managed by the operating system, which provides a software interface to the system tasks. The operating system views its own power states as a resource to be managed along with other resources. Centralizing the control of the power management mechanisms in the operating system allows the OS to ensure that all necessary components are notified of any change to the power management state.

The Advanced Configuration and Power Interface (ACPI) [Int96] is widely used in PCs to manage power modes. ACPI does not specify particular power management mechanisms; instead, it defines levels of power management as global power states.

- G3 is the mechanical off state.

- G2 is the soft off state, which requires the operating system to be rebooted when leaving the state for a higher level of system readiness.

- G1 is the sleeping state, in which the system appears to be off.

- G0 is the working state, in which the system is on.

- A Legacy state denotes non-ACPI power modes.

Benini et al. [Ben99] built stochastic models of system behavior for power management. They model both the system and workload as Markov chains. A service requester models the workload as a sequence of service requests. A service provider is a Markov chain whose probabilities are controlled by commands from the power manager. The power manager maps combinations of service request and service provider states into power management actions. A set of cost metrics is used during system optimization. They showed that finding a minimum-power policy that meets the given performance constraints can be cast as a linear program.

### 4.4.7   File Systems in Embedded Devices

Modern embedded systems must support sophisticated file systems. To some extent, limitations on power consumption and code size cause embedded file systems to be designed differently than workstation-oriented file systems. But the most important difference is caused by the fact that flash memory is often used as the storage component for **embedded file systems**.

*embedded file
systems*

Embedded file systems are used in many types of embedded computing systems. Music players catalog large quantities of music and other information (such as playlists); music players may use flash, magnetic disc, or CDs for storage. Digital cameras also provide mass storage for images and other information. Embedded file systems may vary along several dimensions.

- **Compatibility**—Some embedded systems do not directly expose their file systems to other computers, and so the file system may use any internal structures. Other devices, particularly those with removable media, may see their file storage mounted on other types of computers and so must be compatible with those systems.

- **Writeability**—Some devices, like CD players, need only read files. Others, like digital cameras, must be able to write files as well.

Compatibility is an important issue in some types of consumer devices. CD/MP3 players, which play compressed MP3 files as well as audio CDs, offer a good example of the complexity entailed by compatibility. CDs with MP3s evolved out of the PC community without any established standards. As a result, the CDs could be written by a variety of computer types. Furthermore, discs may be created with many different directory structures. As a result, the CD/MP3 player must implement a complex file system even though the device only reads discs.

*flash-based file
challenges*

Flash-based memory introduces new challenges, even beyond the ability to write files as well as read them. The first major difference is that flash cannot be written word-by-word as with RAM. Flash memory must first be erased in large blocks and then written. Flash memory blocks may be as large as 64 KB in size, which is considerably larger than even a typical magnetic disc sector. Erasing the block also takes much longer than a read. The second major difference is that a program/erase cycle entails significant wear on the device. The voltages applied during a program/erase cycle stress the delicate oxides in the memory and eventually cause the memory cell to fail. Today's flash memories can withstand a million program/erase cycles, but careless design of the file system can cause far more writes than are necessary, reducing the lifetime of the memory device.

*NAND versus
NOR flash*

The two major technologies for flash memory are NAND and NOR flash, with different circuit structures for their respective memory elements. NOR flash can be read using a procedure similar to that used for RAM. NAND memories are accessed as block devices. NAND memory blocks may fail during use, or the device may arrive from the manufacturer with bad blocks. NAND flash is also more prone to transient read errors. As a result, many developers develop different file system implementations for NAND-based and NOR-based flash memory.

*wear leveling*    Because flash memory wears out much more quickly with writes than other types of permanent storage, flash memory systems use **wear-leveling** techniques to maximize the lifetime of the flash memory. Wear-leveling methods distribute writes around the memory to avoid using one block excessively. However, one Achilles heel of flash-based memory systems is the file allocation table. Whenever a file is created, destroyed, or changed in size, the file allocation table must be updated. The file allocation table can therefore wear out much more quickly than the remainder of the flash memory. This is one reason that many device manufacturers recommend formatting or bulk erasing flash memory rather than deleting individual files—bulk erasure performs many fewer program/erase cycles than file-by-file deletion.

*virtual mapping*    Figure 4-17 shows the organization of a virtual mapping-based flash memory system [Ban95]. The virtual mapping system handles wear leveling and other operations particular to flash memory-based file systems. The file system sees the memory as a linear array of bytes, addressed with virtual addresses. The virtual mapping system uses a virtual memory mapping table to translate these virtual addresses into physical addresses in the flash memory. The virtual mapping table may be stored entirely in the flash, or it may be cached in RAM in the host processor. The virtual mapping system can handle several tasks.

- Manage the scheduling of block program/erase operations.

- Consolidate data, moving some data in a block to a new location to make an entire block empty so that the block can be erased and reused.

- Identify bad blocks of memory, much as a magnetic disc controller substitutes good sectors for bad sectors.

- Occasionally move infrequently modified data to a new location to equalize wear levels across the memory.

*log-structured file systems*    Some embedded file systems use techniques developed for general-purpose computers to make file systems more resistant to corruption. A **log-structured file system** [Ros92] does not store the current version of the file directory.

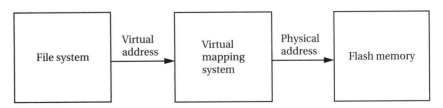

**Figure 4-17** *Organization of a virtual mapping-based flash memory system.*

Instead, it stores a log of the changes to the file. Log structuring is also known as **journaling**.

The Journaling Flash File System (JFFS) [Axi05] is designed to maintain its consistency in the face of sudden power losses. JFFS is designed to provide flash file systems for Linux-based systems; it fits under the Linux Virtual File System but does not use the file system's buffer cache. It is designed to minimize the number of times that the flash memory must be erased. The flash memory is organized as a queue; new data is written at the tail of the flash queue and old data, known as "dirt," is marked as such where it appears in the queue.

Yet Another Flash Filing System (YAFFS) [Ale05] is a log-structured file system for NAND flash memories. YAFFS is also designed to work with the Linux Virtual File System. File data is stored in chunks the same size of flash pages. Each flash page includes a file ID and chunk number.

*block-device emulation*   Some flash file systems emulate the block-structured file systems used in PCs. FTL-LITE [Int98] is an embedded version of the FTL file system. It provides a file allocation table for compatibility with DOS. FTL-LITE does support wear-leveling and reclamation.

The next example describes a flash-based file system.

## Example 4-3

*Intel Flash File System*

The Intel Flash File System [Int04] is designed to be a POSIX-aware file system for flash memory devices. The file system is organized into the following layers:

- OS wrapper layer provides a basic interface to the operating system.
- File system layer manages the basic file system information.
- Data object layer breaks objects into fragments.
- Basic allocation layer allocates space.
- Flash interface layer implements flash reads and writes in terms of low-level functions.
- Low-level layer provides basic flash operations and handles interrupts and timing.

A flash write operation is performed in several steps. The file system layer looks up the file information to determine its present location and size. New data is written into unused locations. The basic write operations take a substantial amount of time, so they are handled with interrupts. The file system must also update the file system tables to remember the state of the file.

A flash read operation is somewhat simpler. Once the file system layer determines the address to be read, it breaks the read request into a series of data object reads. The reads are translated into low-level read commands on the flash. Unlike writes, reads happen at high speed.

---

## 4.5 Verification

Operating systems allow concurrent execution of processes. Concurrent execution is much harder to design and implement than sequential code. Concurrently executing processes are also harder to debug. As a result, formal methods have been developed to analyze and verify concurrent systems.

The document *Software Considerations for Airborne Systems and Equipment Certification* [RTC92] defines standards for the certification of airborne software.

*models of programs*

While we need to verify code, we often work on more abstract **models** of concurrent systems. One reason to verify models is to verify the design before we spend time on a detailed implementation. Some implementations may also be complex enough that we need to construct a model to efficiently verify some properties.

*properties*

Formal methods are most useful when we can specify general properties to be checked. A simple example of an important property of a concurrent system is **liveness**. The state machine of Figure 4-18 represents the behavior of a process. State *S3* can be entered, but there is no way to exit that state. As a result, once the process enters that state it stays there. A state machine may also cycle through a sequence of states indefinitely without ever leaving those states.

*deadlock*

An important property of communicating processes is **deadlock**. Two processes can deadlock when each needs a signal or resource from the other but never receives it. Consider the example in Figure 4-19. The two machines communicate over two signals *x* and *y*. When *M1* is in state *S1* and *M2* is in state *T1*, they each provide inputs to the other to make *M1* go to state *S3* and *M2* to state *T2*. Once in these states, the machines cannot provide to the other machine the inputs required to exit those states.

*property specification*

Designers may want to specify their own properties to be checked. One way to write properties is with **temporal logic**. Several types of temporal logic have been formulated; these logics allow one to write formulas that involve time. Time is generally viewed as discrete in temporal logics; the system goes through a sequence of states, with each state identified with a particular time. A **linear-time temporal logic** models time as one evolving sequence of states. A **branching-**

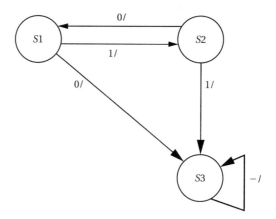

**Figure 4-18** *A state machine that may not remain live.*

**time temporal logic**, in contrast, allows for two or more discrete states to evolve from a given time/state.

Temporal logic formulas may be quantified over time. For example, we can quantify an expression as always happening:

$$[]f(x) \qquad \qquad \text{(EQ 4-18)}$$

in which case *f(x)* must be true at every time.

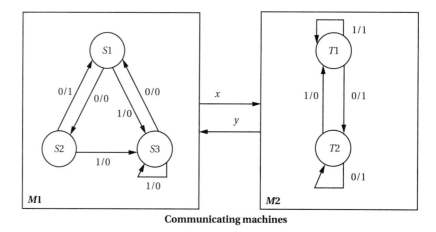

**Figure 4-19** *An example of deadlock in communicating machines.*

*product*
*machines*

    As with synchronous languages, we can analyze networks of communicating processes by generating product machines of the component processes. The system behavior is described by the product machine; it tells us how the components will interact.

    However, the product of even relatively small processes can produce a large product machine that cannot be reasonably searched. To effectively analyze large systems, we need to use the following specialized techniques.

- We can generate the product machine incrementally without generating the entire machine at once.

- We can implicitly search the product machine without explicitly generating it.

*debugging*

    Simply knowing that a desired property is not satisfied is not sufficient. We need to debug the system—understand what caused the problem. Simulation can be used in conjunction with automated proofs to provide useful debugging information to designers. Once the system identifies a property that must be debugged, it can then generate a trace of the system behavior that involves the property—for example, the deadlock in Figure 4-19. The designer can use the trace to figure out what is wrong with the specification and how to fix it.

    The next example describes a well-known model checker.

---

## Example 4-4

*The SPIN Model Checker*

    SPIN [Hol97] is a model checker for distributed software systems. It accepts descriptions written in the PROMELA language, and it also allows correctness claims to be specified in linear temporal logic. SPIN includes a variety of tools.

    SPIN represents systems as Buchi automata, which are defined over infinite input sequences. A Buchi automaton accepts an input sequence by passing through an accepting state or set of accepting states an infinite number of times. SPIN formulates its tests to look for negative properties—if a property is not satisfied, then the corresponding machine is of zero size, making the test more efficient.

    SPIN uses a variety of techniques to efficiently build automata and determine their properties. It uses nested depth-first search to walk through automata using efficient bitmap representations. It also builds reduced automata that implicitly represent a set of paths without enumerating all the possible paths. In addition, it uses a variety of methods to manage memory.

    An example of a scheduling problem for a client/server system is shown on the following page.

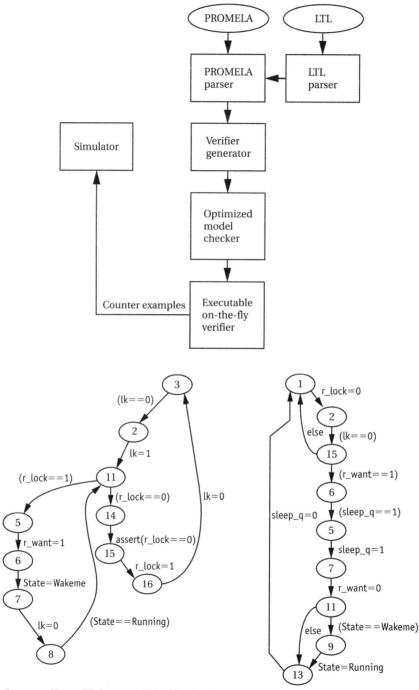

*Source*: From Holzmann [Hol97] © 1997 IEEE.

The following table presents a trace of an error condition in this specification, along with some handwritten comments. The error is caused by a race condition that allows a client to go to sleep forever.

| Client process | Server process | Line number | Local states | Comments |
|---|---|---|---|---|
| [r_lock = 1] | | 22 | 16,15 | Consume resource |
| [lk = 0] | | 23 | 3,15 | Release the lock |
| [lk==0] | | 10 | 2,15 | Test the lock |
| [lk = 1] | | 10 | 11,15 | Set the lock |
| [r_lock==1] | | 12 | 5,15 | Resource not available |
| [r_want = 1] | | 13 | 6,15 | Set want flag |
| | [r_want==1] | 33 | 6,6 | Server checks the flag |
| | [sleep_q==0] | 35 | 6,5 | Wait lock on sleep_q |
| | [sleep_q = 1] | 35 | 6,7 | Set it |
| | [r_want = 0] | 37 | 6,11 | Resets the flag |
| | [else] | 44 | 6,13 | No process sleeping! |
| | [sleep_q = 0] | 46 | 6,1 | Release the lock |
| | [r_lock = 0] | 30 | 6,2 | Provide new resource |
| [State = Wakeme] | | 14 | 7,2 | Client goes to sleep! |
| [lk = 0] | | 15 | 8,2 | Release the lock |
| | [lk==0] | 31 | 8,15 | Server checks the lock |
| | [else] | 47 | 8,1 | No flag is set |
| Nonprogress cycle | [r_lock = 0] | 30 | 8,2 | The server repeats this |
| | [lk==0] | 31 | 8,15 | forever, while the client |
| | [else] | 47 | 8,1 | remains suspended |

*Source:* From Holzmann [Hol97] © 1997 IEEE.

## 4.6 Summary

We execute multiple processes on a single CPU to save hardware and, to some extent, to save energy. The cost of multitasking is that we have to be careful to share the CPU so that we meet all our real-time deadlines. A large body of literature has been written on real-time scheduling, taking into account various conditions on execution and assumptions. Real-time operating systems must be designed to efficiently implement basic operations such as scheduling, interrupt handling, and interprocess communication.

### What We Have Learned

- Several scheduling protocols can be used to guarantee basic real-time behavior. However, we may not be able to use 100% of the CPU if we want to guarantee meeting all deadlines.

- Scheduling for dynamic voltage scaling tries to stretch the execution time of processes to just meet their deadline in order to take advantage of the lower operating voltages allowed by slower execution.

- Context switching and interrupt overhead may be important in heavily utilized systems.

- File systems implemented in flash memory must use specialized techniques to avoid wearing out the flash memory.

- Concurrent system verification builds and searches state machine models to determine whether desired properties are satisfied.

### Further Reading

Liu [Liu00] gives an excellent, in-depth account of real-time scheduling. Davidson et al. [Dav81] describe a variety of scheduling algorithms as part of their study of microcode compaction algorithms.

### Questions

**Q4-1** Prove Theorem 1 of Liu and Layland: *A critical instant for any process occurs whenever the process is requested simultaneously with requests for all higher-priority processes.*

**Q4-2** You are designing an embedded system using a 500 MHz CPU. If you want scheduling preemption to take no more than 1% of a 1 ms time quantum, how many instructions can you execute during a scheduling interrupt? What factors come into play?

**Q4-3** You are scheduling three tasks:

■ *P1* has a period of 10 ms and a CPU time of 1 ms.

■ *P2* has a period of 20 ms and a CPU time of 1 ms.

■ *P3* has a period of 25 ms and a CPU time of 3 ms.

**Q4-4** Compare the first 100 ms of execution time of these three processes under round-robin, RMS, and EDF scheduling policies. Find, for each process, its worst-case response time. Find the total CPU utilization.

**Q4-5** Write pseudocode to implement the priority ceiling protocol.

**Q4-6** When scheduling with dynamic voltage scaling, should the time quantum change with the processor frequency? Explain.

**Q4-7** Write pseudocode for a DVS scheduler that operates at two voltage levels.

**Q4-8** You are given a CPU with a direct-mapped cache. The machine is word-addressable, and each instruction is one word long. The cache has 256 lines of 4 instructions each. You want to apply the software cache-partitioning technique of Mueller to a program with 5,000 instructions. How many partitions would the program have, and what range of addresses would they occupy?

**Q4-9** Write pseudocode to generate the transition function of a CFSM from its state transition graph.

**Q4-10** Can we predict the size of a software thread integration implementation from the control dependence graph for the threads? Explain.

**Q4-11** How does memory management affect real-time scheduling?

**Q4-12** Why is a log-structured file system useful for flash memory?

**Q4-13** Are task graphs or BFSMs more useful as specifications for SPIN-style verification? Explain.

## Lab Exercises

**L4-1** Measure the context-switching time of an operating system.

**L4-2** Measure how accurately an RTOS can generate a square wave.

**L4-3** Measure how variations in execution time of a set of processes affect the response time of the processes.

**L4-4** Evaluate one or more DVS scheduling algorithms under a load.

**L4-5** Design a wear-leveling algorithm for a flash file system.

# 5

# Multiprocessor Architectures

- Why we design embedded multiprocessors
- Architectures for embedded multiprocessing
- Interconnection networks for embedded multiprocessors
- Memory systems for embedded multiprocessors
- Physically distributed multiprocessors
- Design methodologies for embedded multiprocessors

## 5.1 Introduction

This chapters studies embedded multiprocessors in detail. Multiprocessing is very common in embedded computing systems because it allows us to meet our performance, cost, and energy/power consumption goals. Embedded multiprocessors are often heterogeneous multiprocessors, made up of several types of processors. These multiprocessors run sophisticated software that must be carefully designed to obtain the most out of the multiprocessor.

A multiprocessor is made of multiple **processing elements** (**PEs**). As shown in Figure 5-1, a multiprocessor consists of three major subsystems:

1. Processing elements that operate on data.

2. Memory blocks that hold data values.

3. Interconnection networks between the processing elements and memory.

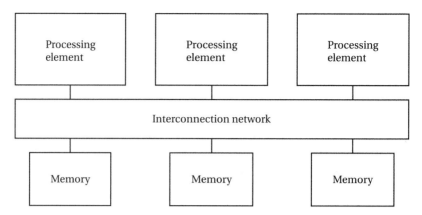

**Figure 5-1** *A generic multiprocessor.*

In any multiprocessor design, we have to decide how many processing elements to use, how much memory and how to divide it up, and how rich the interconnections between the PEs and memory should be.

However, when designing an embedded multiprocessor, the choices are more varied and complex than for the typical multiprocessor. Servers typically use symmetric multiprocessors built of identical processing elements and uniform memory. This simplifies programming the machine. But embedded system designers are often willing to trade off some programming complexity for cost/performance/energy/power, which provides some additional variables.

■ We can vary the types of processing elements. Not all the PEs have to be the same type. We can use several different types of CPUs; we can also use PEs that are not programmable and perform only a single function.

■ We can use memory blocks of different sizes, and we do not have to require that every processing element access all the memory. Using private memories or memories that are shared by only a few PEs allows us to improve the performance of that memory for the units that use it.

■ We can use specialized interconnection networks that provide only certain connections.

Embedded multiprocessors certainly make use of SIMD parallelism techniques, but MIMD architectures are the dominant mode of parallel machines in embedded computing. As we will see in this chapter, embedded multiprocessors tend to be even more varied than scientific multiprocessors. While scientific parallel computers tend to use several copies of the same type of processing element, embedded multiprocessors often use several different types of processing elements.

We also consider physically distributed multiprocessors in this chapter. These systems use networks to connect physically separate processing elements to provide real-time control and other functions.

Section 5.2 looks at why we need to use multiprocessors in embedded applications. Section 5.3 introduces basic design techniques for multiprocessors. Section 5.4 studies example embedded multiprocessors. In Section 5.5, we briefly consider the selection of processing elements for embedded multiprocessors. Section 5.6 describes interconnection networks for multiprocessors, including networks-on-chips. In Section 5.7, we discuss memory systems for embedded multiprocessors. Section 5.8 looks at networks for physically distributed multiprocessors. Finally, in Section 5.9, we take an in-depth look at design methodologies for embedded multiprocessors, based on our study of embedded multiprocessors themselves.

## 5.2 Why Embedded Multiprocessors?

Multiprocessors are commonly used to build scientific and business servers, so why do we need them in an embedded computing system? Although embedded computers may appear small and innocuous, many of them must support huge amounts of computation. The best way to meet those demands is by using multiprocessors. This is particularly true when we must meet real-time constraints and are concerned with power consumption.

Embedded multiprocessors face many more constraints than do scientific processors. Both want to deliver high performance, but embedded systems must do several things in addition, including the following.

*requirements on embedded systems*

- They must provide real-time performance. Many features of scientific multiprocessors are designed to improve average performance at the expense of predictability. Real-time processes may not work reliably in the face of features such as snooping caches. A combination of hardware and software techniques must be used to provide predictable performance.

- They must often run at low energy or power levels. Not all embedded systems are power-limited, but energy and power is one of the defining themes of embedded computing. Low power reduces heating problems and system cost, while lower energy consumption increases battery life. Scientific and general-purpose computing systems are much less sensitive to power and energy consumption.

- Embedded computers must be cost-effective. Embedded computers must provide high performance without using excessive amounts of hardware to do so.

*design techniques*

The rigorous demands of embedded computing push us toward several design techniques.

- Heterogeneous multiprocessors are often more energy-efficient and cost-effective than symmetric multiprocessors.

- Heterogeneous memory systems improve real-time performance.

- Networks-on-chips support heterogeneous architectures.

We consider the motivation for these techniques in detail in this section.

## 5.2.1 Requirements on Embedded Systems

*high-performance embedded computing*

Let us first look at the computational requirements of applications that use embedded computers. The next two examples consider cell phones and video cameras.

---

## Example 5-1

*Computation in Cellular Telephones*

A cellular telephone must perform a variety of functions that are basic to telephony.

- Compute and check error-correction codes

- Perform voice compression and decompression

- Respond to the protocol that governs communication with the cellular network

Furthermore, modern cell phones must perform a variety of other functions that are either required by regulations or demanded by the marketplace.

- Cell phones in the United States must keep track of their position in case the user must be located for emergency services. A Global Positioning System (GPS) is often used to find the phone's position.

- Many cell phones play MP3 audio. They may also use MIDI or other methods to play music for ring tones.

- High-end cell phones provide cameras for still pictures and video.

- Cell phones may download application code from the network.

## Example 5-2

*Computation in Video Cameras*

Video compression requires a great deal of computation, even for small images. Most video compression systems combine three basic methods to compress video.

- Lossless compression is used to reduce the size of the representation of the video data stream.

- The discrete cosine transform (DCT) is used to help quantize the images and reduce the size of the video stream by lossy encoding.

- Motion estimation and compensation allow the contents of one frame to be described in terms of motion from another frame.

Of these three, motion estimation is the most computationally intensive task. Even an efficient motion estimation algorithm must perform a $16 \times 16$ correlation at several points in the video frame, and it must be done for the entire frame. For example, a QCIF frame, commonly used in cell phones, is $176 \times 144$ pixels in size. That frame is divided into $11 \times 9$ of these $16 \times 16$ macroblocks for motion estimation. If we perform only seven correlations per macroblock, then we must perform $11 \times 9 \times 16 \times 16 = 25,344$ pixel comparisons, and all the calculations must be done on almost every frame, at a rate of 15 or 30 frames per second.

The DCT operator is also computationally intense. Even efficient algorithms require a large number of multiplications to perform the $8 \times 8$ DCT that is commonly used in video and image compression. For example, the Feig and Winograd algorithm [Fei92] uses 94 multiplications and 454 additions to perform an $8 \times 8$ two-dimension DCT. This amounts to 148,896 multiplications per frame for a size frame with 1,584 blocks.

### 5.2.2 Performance and Energy

Many embedded applications need lots of raw processing performance, as we saw in the last section. But speed is not enough—those computations must also be performed efficiently.

Austin et al. [Aus04] posed the embedded system performance problem as *mobile supercomputing*. Today's PDA/cell phones already perform a great deal of computation, but consider extending that device to perform functions that traditionally have required large processors:

- Speech recognition

- Video compression and recognition

- High-resolution graphics

- High-bandwidth wireless communication

Austin et al. estimate that a mobile supercomputing workload would require about 10,000 SPECint of performance, about 16 times that provided by a 2 GHz Intel Pentium 4 processor.

In the mobile environment, all this computation must be performed at very low energy. Battery power is growing at only about 5% per year; given that

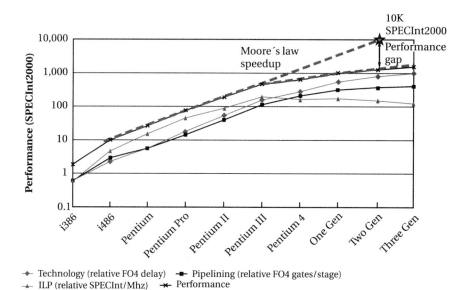

**Figure 5-2** *Performance trends for desktop processors. From Austin et al. [Aus04] © 2004 IEEE Computer Society Press.*

today's highest-performance batteries have an energy density close to that of dynamite, we may be close to the amount of energy that people are willing to carry with them. Mudge et al. [Mud04] estimate that to power the mobile supercomputer by a circa 2006 battery for five days, with it being used 20% of the time, it must consume no more than 75 milliwatts (mW).

Unfortunately, general-purpose processors do not meet those trends. Figure 5-2 shows the trends in performance for desktop processors. Moore's Law dictates that chip sizes double every 18 months, which allows the circuits to run faster. If we could make use of all the potential increase in speed, we could meet the 10,000 SPECint performance target. But trends show that we are not keeping up with performance. The figure shows the performance of several commercial processors and predicted trends. Unfortunately, the traditional optimizations—pipelining, instruction-level parallelism—that have helped CPU designers capture Moore's Law–related performance improvements are becoming less and less effective.

Figure 5-3 shows that power consumption is getting worse. We need to reduce the energy consumption of the processor to use it as a mobile supercomputer, but desktop processors consume more power with every generation.

Breaking away from these trends requires taking advantage of the characteristics of the problem: adding units that are tuned to the core operations that we need to perform and eliminating hardware that does not directly contribute to performance for this equation. By designing hardware that more efficiently meets its performance goals, we reduce the system's power consumption.

One key advantage that embedded system architects can leverage is task-level parallelism. Many embedded applications neatly divide into several tasks

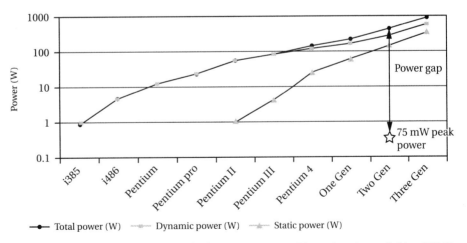

**Figure 5-3** *Power consumption trends for desktop processors. From Austin et al. [Aus04] © 2004 IEEE Computer Society Press.*

or phases that communicate with each other, which is a natural and easily exploitable source of parallelism. Desktop processors rely on instruction-level parallelism to improve performance, but only a limited amount of instruction-level parallelism is available in most programs. We can build custom multiprocessor architectures that reflect the task-level parallelism available in our application and meet performance targets at much lower cost and with much less energy.

### 5.2.3 Specialization and Multiprocessors

It is the combination of high performance, low power, and real time that drives us to use multiprocessors. And these requirements lead us further toward **heterogeneous multiprocessors**, which starkly contrast with the symmetric multiprocessors used for scientific computation.

*multiprocessing versus uniprocessing*

Even if we build a multiprocessor out of several copies of the same type of CPU, we may end up with a more efficient system than if we used a uniprocessor. The manufacturing cost of a microprocessor is a nonlinear function of clock speed—customers pay considerably more for modest increases in clock speed. Splitting the system functions over several processors can be cheaper.

*real time and multiprocessing*

Real-time requirements also lead us to multiprocessing. When we put several real-time processes on the same CPU, they compete for cycles. As discussed in Chapter 4, it is not always possible to guarantee that we can use 100% of the CPU if we want to meet our real-time deadlines. Furthermore, we must pay for those reserved cycles at the nonlinear rate of higher clock speed.

*multiprocessing and accelerators*

The next step beyond symmetric multiprocessors is heterogeneous multiprocessors. We can specialize all aspects of the multiprocessor: the processing elements, the memory, and the interconnection network. Specializations understandably lead to lower power consumption; perhaps less intuitively, they can also improve real-time behavior.

*specialization*

The following parts of embedded systems lend themselves to specialized implementations.

- Some operations, particularly those defined by standards, are not likely to change. The $8 \times 8$ DCT, for example, has become widely used well beyond its original function in JPEG. Given the frequency and variety of its uses, it is worthwhile to optimize not just the DCT, but in particular its $8 \times 8$ form.

- Some functions require operations that do not map well onto a CPU's data operations. The mismatch may be due to several reasons. For instance, bit-level operations are difficult to perform efficiently on some CPUs; the operations may require too many registers, or there may be advantages to controlling the precision of the arithmetic. We can design either a specialized CPU or a special-purpose hardware unit to perform these functions.

■ Highly responsive input and output operations may be best performed by an accelerator with an attached I/O unit. If data must be read, processed, and written to meet a very tight deadline—for example, in engine control—a dedicated hardware unit may be more efficient than a CPU.

*cost versus power*

Heterogeneity reduces power consumption because it removes unnecessary hardware. The additional hardware required to generalize functions adds to both dynamic and static power dissipation. Excessive specialization can add so much communication cost that the energy gain from specialization is lost, but specializing the right functions can lead to significant energy savings.

*real-time performance*

In addition to reducing costs, using multiple CPUs can help with real-time performance. We can often meet deadlines and be responsive to interaction much more easily when we put those time-critical processes on separate CPUs. Specialized memory systems and interconnects also help make the response time of a process more predictable.

### 5.2.4  Flexibility and Efficiency

*use hardware and software*

We also have to consider why we need programmable processors. Some digital systems in fact rely on networks of interconnected hardwired units—data paths, state machines, and so on—to perform their functions. But many embedded systems perform complex functions that would be too difficult to implement entirely in hardware. This is particularly true of standards-based systems. As we saw in Section 1.4.3, standards bodies typically generate reference implementations in standard programming languages. Translating all the standards to hardware may be too time-consuming and expensive.

Furthermore, multiple standards encourage software implementation. A consumer audio device, for example, must be able to play audio data in many different formats: MP3, Dolby Digital, Ogg Vorbis, and so on. These standards perform some similar operations but cannot be easily collapsed into a few key hardware units. Given the hundreds of thousands of lines of code that must be implemented, processors running software, perhaps aided by a few key hardware units, are the only reasonable design choices.

## 5.3  Multiprocessor Design Techniques

Before we go into the details of embedded multiprocessors themselves, this section briefly looks at the techniques used to design embedded multiprocessors. We first consider design methodologies, then multiprocessor simulation methods. In Section 5.9, we discuss embedded multiprocessor design methodologies in detail, based on our study of the multiprocessors themselves.

### 5.3.1 Multiprocessor Design Methodologies

The design of embedded multiprocessors is data-driven and relies on analyzing programs. We call these programs the **workload**, in contrast to the term *benchmark* commonly used in computer architecture. Because embedded systems operate under real-time constraints and overall throughput, we often use a sample set of applications to evaluate overall system performance. These programs may not be the exact code run on the final system, and the final system may have many modes, but using workloads is still useful and important. Benchmarks are generally treated as independent entities, while embedded multiprocessor design

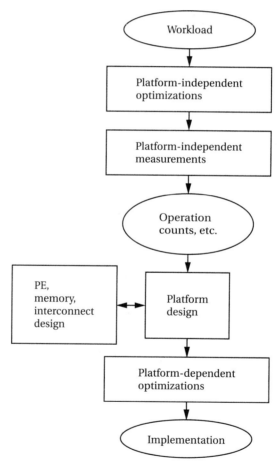

**Figure 5-4** *Multiprocessor-based embedded system design methodology.*

requires evaluating the interaction between programs. The workload, in fact, includes data inputs as well as the programs themselves.

Figure 5-4 shows a simple methodology for designing an embedded system based on a multiprocessor. This workflow includes both the design of the hardware platform and the software that runs on the platform.

Before the workload is used to evaluate the architecture, it generally must be put into good shape with **platform-independent optimizations**. Many programs are not written with embedded platform restrictions, real-time performance, or low power in mind. Using programs designed to work in non-real-time mode with unlimited main memory can often lead to bad architectural decisions.

Once we have the workload programs in shape, we can perform simple experiments before defining an architecture to obtain **platform-independent measurements**. Simple measurements, such as dynamic instruction count and data access patterns, provide valuable information about the nature of the workload.

Using these platform-independent metrics, we can identify an initial **candidate architecture**. If the platform relies on static allocation, we may need to map the workload programs onto the platform. We then measure **platform-dependent characteristics**. Based on those characteristics, we evaluate the architecture, using both numerical measures and judgment. If the platform is satisfactory, we are finished. If not, we modify the platform and make a new round of measurements. Along the way, we need to design the components of the multiprocessor: the processing elements, the memory system, and the interconnects.

Once we are satisfied with the platform, we can map the software onto the platform. During that process, we may be aided by libraries of code as well as compilers. Most of the optimizations performed at this phase should be platform-specific. We must allocate operations to processing elements, data to memories, and communications to links. We also have to determine when things happen.

## 5.3.2 Multiprocessor Modeling and Simulation

We discussed CPU simulation in Section 2.8. In this section, we describe how to extend instruction-level simulation to multiprocessors.

*modeling approaches*

Cai and Gajski [Cai03] defined a hierarchy of modeling methods for digital systems and compared their characteristics. Their categorization is summarized in Figure 5-5. They define six levels of models.

1. **Implementation model**—Corresponds directly to hardware. It captures both computation and communication to cycle accuracy.

2. **Cycle-accurate computation model**—Captures accurate computation times but only approximate communication times.

3. **Time-accurate communication model**—Captures communication to cycle accuracy but captures computation times only approximately.

4. **Bus-transaction model**—Models the basic function of a bus arbitration scheme but is not a cycle-accurate model of the bus.

5. **PE-assembly model**—Represents the system as processing elements communicating through channels. Communication is untimed, while PE execution is approximately timed.

6. **Specification model**—Primarily a functional model without any implementation details.

*communicating simulators*

Most multiprocessor simulators are systems of communicating simulators. The component simulators represent CPUs, memory elements, and routing networks. The multiprocessor simulator itself negotiates communication between those component simulators.

*simulation as parallel computing*

We can use the techniques of parallel computing to build the multiprocessor simulator. Each component simulator is a process, both in the simulation metaphor and literally as a process running on the host CPU's operating system. The

| | Communication time | Computation time | Communication scheme | PE interface |
|---|---|---|---|---|
| Spec | No | No | Variable | No PEs |
| Component assembly | No | Approximate | Variable channel | Abstract |
| Bus arbitration | Approximate | Approximate | Abstract bus channel | Abstract |
| Bus functional | Cycle accurate | Approximate | Protocol bus channel | Abstract |
| Cycle accurate | Approximate | Cycle accurate | Abstract bus channel | Pin accurate |
| Implementation | Cycle accurate | Cycle accurate | Wires | Pin accurate |

**Figure 5-5** *Multiprocessor-based embedded system design methodology. From Cai and Gajski [Cai03].*

operating system provides the abstraction necessary for multiprocessing; each simulator has its own state, just as each PE in the implementation has its own state. The simulator uses the host computer's communication mechanisms—semaphores, shared memory, and so on—to manage the communication between the component simulators.

Consider the simulation of a write from a processing element to a memory element (ME). The PE and ME are each component simulators that run as processes on the host CPU. The write operation requires a message from the PE simulator to the ME simulator. The data in this message includes the write address and the data to be written. The PE simulator generates a message to the multiprocessor simulator including this data. The multiprocessor simulator must route that message by determining which simulation process is responsible for the address of the write operation. After performing the required mapping, it sends a message to the memory element simulator asking it to perform the write.

*heterogeneous simulators*

Traditional multiprocessor simulators are designed for fairly symmetric multiprocessors; they generally assume that all the processing elements are of the same type. Embedded multiprocessors, on the other hand, generally use several different types of PEs. This is not a major stumbling block; however, a simulator designed for symmetric multiprocessors may take some programming shortcuts by assuming that all PEs are the same type.

*SystemC*

SystemC (*http://www.systemc.org*) is a widely used framework for transaction-level design of heterogeneous multiprocessors. It is designed to facilitate the simulation of heterogeneous architectures built from combinations of hard-wired blocks and programmable processors. SystemC, which is built on top of C++, defines a set of classes used to describe the system being simulated. A simulation manager guides the execution of the simulator.

## 5.4 Multiprocessor Architectures

Because many embedded systems are very cost-sensitive, these heterogeneous multiprocessors are often fabricated on a single chip. A **system-on-chip (SoC)** is a complete digital system built on a single chip. Systems-on-chips do not have to include embedded processors, but they often do. An SoC that is also a multiprocessor is known as a **multiprocessor system-on-chip (MPSoC)**. MPSoCs are often heterogeneous processors in order to squeeze the maximum amount of performance out of the chip—by tailoring the architecture to the application, we can eliminate unnecessary elements and use the room for components that more directly contribute to performance or reduce energy/power consumption.

The next two examples look at multiprocessors designed for cell phones and multimedia applications.

## Example 5-3

*Qualcomm MSM5100*

The Qualcomm MSM5100 [But02] is designed to provide the baseband (i.e., non-radio-frequency) functions for third-generation (3G) CDMA cell phones. This chip must provide many diverse functions for the cell phone. First, it must provide the baseband functions for several different communication standards.

- CDMA IS-2000 for CDMA cellular telephony
- IS-95 CDMA standard
- AMPS analog cell phone standard
- GPS for position information
- Bluetooth for personal area networking

The chip must also support several other functions.

- MP3 music playback
- Compact Media Extension (CMX) for multimedia (image and sound) presentations
- MMC mass storage controller

Here is a block diagram from Butler et al. of the chip.

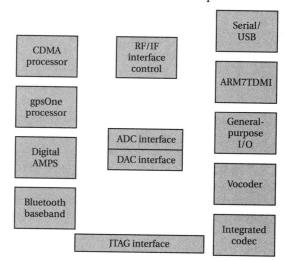

*Source:*
After Butler et al. [But02].

The MSM5100 uses many small processors to provide the necessary functions. Dedicated processors help preserve real-time performance since many of the functions must be performed simultaneously. The ARM7 processor can be used for MP3 decoding as well as other code execution. Many other functions have their own processors: voice coding, data coding, Bluetooth, AMPS, GPS, and CDMA all have separate dedicated processors.

## Example 5-4

*Philips Nexperia*

The Philips Nexperia [Dut01] is a multiprocessor system-on-chip designed for digital video and television applications. It has been used to build set-top boxes (i.e., the interface between a cable TV or satellite network and the subscriber's television), personal video recording, and high-speed Internet access. The Viper chip is the first implementation of the Nexperia architecture; it was designed to be able to decode HDTV at a resolution of $1,920 \times 1,080$ interlaced pixels. It is a sophisticated heterogeneous multiprocessor that combines two powerful CPUs with a variety of specialized function units to meet the intensive processing requirements of video at the low cost point required to compete in the set-top box market.

Here is the block diagram of the Viper Nexperia:

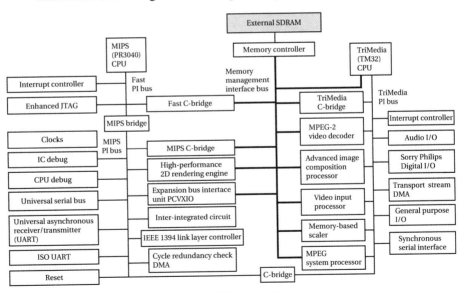

C-bridge   Crossover bridge    PI   Peripheral interconnect    XIO   Extended I/O
DMA   Direct memory access    PCI   Peripheral component interconnect    ISO   International Organization for Standardization

*Source:* From Dutta et al. [Dut01] © 2001 IEEE.

The architecture includes two processors and four busses. One processor is a MIPS PR3940 RISC CPU; the other is a Trimedia TM32 VLIW processor. The MIPS processor runs the real-time operating system, communicates with the network, and so on. The Trimedia processor concentrates on media operations such as video decoding.

Because video requires so much memory, the Viper includes a synchronous DRAM interface for bulk storage. One bus connects the SDRAM's on-chip memory controller to the other parts of the system. The Trimedia processor has its own bus. The MIPS processor is directly connected to a fast bus, and a bridge connects the fast MIPS bus to a slower MIPS bus for the lower-speed peripherals. Other bridges connect the memory bus to the MIPS and Trimedia busses and the Trimedia bus to the MIPS low-speed bus.

The Viper includes a wide variety of I/O devices, including the following.

- A USB host controller

- Three UARTs

- Two $I^2C$ interfaces

- A serial interface for a soft modem

- Two $I^2S$ and one SPDIF digital audio interfaces

- General-purpose I/O pins

It also includes quite a few special-purpose function units and accelerators designed for media applications.

- An image composition engine that composes images, such as picture-in-picture or menu information, from main memory

- A scaler unit that can be used to rescale video and graphics

- An MPEG-2 video decoder

- Two video input processors that can be used to receive the NTSC and PAL broadcast standards

- A drawing engine that can perform a variety of 2D graphics functions

- Three transport stream processors for parsing MPEG-2 inputs

These special-purpose units off-load some work from the CPUs and enable the chip to perform the required work with much less silicon than would be needed if done with general-purpose CPUs.

The next example describes a more symmetric embedded multiprocessor. Then, Example 5-6 describes the two platforms for mobile multimedia.

## Example 5-5

*Lucent Daytona Multiprocessor*

The Lucent Daytona multiprocessor [Ack00] is a MIMD multiprocessor for signal-processing applications. It is designed for base stations for wireless communications and other environments where high performance is required to process multiple parallel channels. The basic architecture of Daytona looks like this:

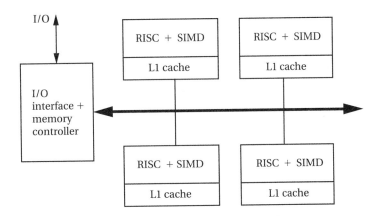

Each processing element is a high-performance CPU. The PE is based on a SPARC V8, a 32-bit RISC processor. It has been enhanced with some DSP-oriented instructions for $16 \times 32$ multiplication, division steps, conditional call, and so on. It includes a touch instruction to explicitly prefetch data and a force instruction to force write-back of cached data. The processing element also includes a 64-bit vector co-processor known as the **reduced precision vector unit** or RVU. The RVU includes a $16 \times 64$-bit register file for vector data. The register file has five ports for parallel accesses. Its peak performance is 2,400 mega-operations per second.

The Daytona designers decided to use smaller caches on the chip to dedicate more transistors to other functions. To make the limited amount of cache more useful, they created a reconfigurable level 1 cache. Each PE has 8 KB of cache that is divided into 16 banks. Each bank can be independently configured as instruction cache, data cache, or scratch pad memory. This allows the cache to be changed in size as well as the set associativity of the cache to be changed.

The PEs are connected by the Daytona bus, a high-speed split transaction bus. Every bus transaction carries a transaction ID that is used to match up the various parts of the split transaction. A read is performed in two steps. First, the address is sent in a four-cycle bus operation:

1. Arbitrate for the address bus.

2. Send the transaction data, including transaction ID, direction, address, size, and priority.

3. Decode the transaction and determine the response.

4. Respond with either *retry*, *acknowledge*, *memory inhibit* (for data modified in the cache), or *shared*.

Second, the data is returned in a three-cycle bus operation:

1. Arbitrate for the data bus.

2. Send the transaction ID.

3. Send the data.

---

## Example 5-6

*STMicroelectronics Nomadik Multiprocessor*

Nomadik [STM04] is designed for mobile multimedia systems such as cell phones, PDAs, and car entertainment systems. It uses an ARM926 as a host processor and programmable accelerators to efficiently implement a variety of tasks: location determination, video, audio, 2D and 3D graphics, personal and wide area networking, and security.

The following figure shows the system architecture. The system components are interconnected with a multilayer AMBA crossbar interconnect. The ARM core includes Jazelle Java acceleration.

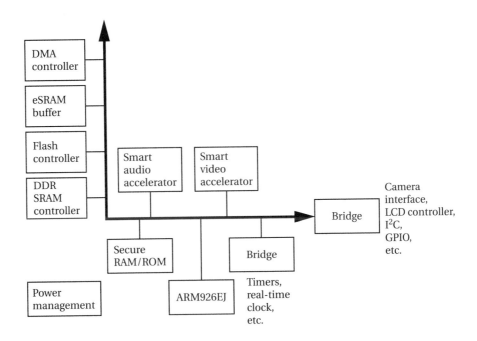

The accelerators are built around the MMDSP+ core, which executes one instruction per cycle and supports 16- and 24-bit fixed-point and 32-bit floating-point data.

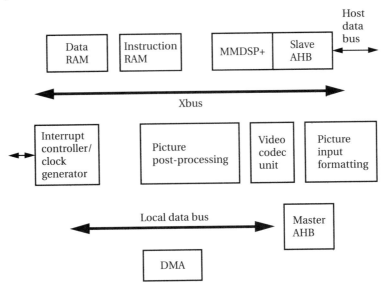

The video accelerator is designed to encode or decode MPEG-4 video at VGA resolution (i.e., $640 \times 480$) at 24 frames/sec or CIF resolution ($352 \times 288$) at 30 frames/sec and 384 Kbps. It includes an MMDSP as well as several video accelerators.

As shown in the following figure, the audio accelerator is designed to support a wide range of audio codecs.

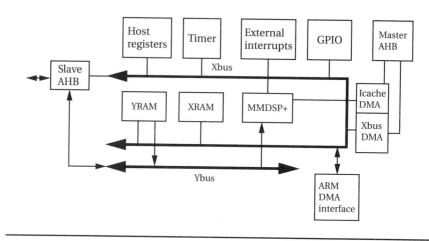

## Example 5-7

*TI OMAP Multiprocessor*

The Texas Instruments OMAP family of multiprocessors was designed for mobile multimedia applications: camera phones, portable imaging devices, and so forth. The OMAP standard conforms to the OMAPI standard, a standard that defines hardware and software interfaces for multimedia multiprocessors. OMAPI does not define a particular multiprocessor configuration. Some members of the TI OMAP family are, in fact, uniprocessors, but the most interesting OMAPs for our purposes are heterogeneous multiprocessors. They include a RISC processor—an ARM9—along with a DSP—a TI C55x. A shared memory interface allows the two processors to communicate efficiently.

The following figure shows the overall structure of the OMAP hardware/software architecture. The DSP/BIOS bridge is the abstraction for the multiprocessor communication interface. The system is organized so that the ARM provides high-level control of the DSP's real-time functions. This frees the DSP from the lower-rate control tasks while it performs high-rate signal processing. The DSP manager server, which runs on the C55x, provides services to the corresponding DSP manager on the ARM9.

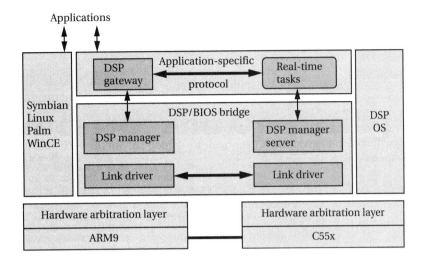

The following block diagram here shows the OMAP 5912 [Tex05], one of the members of the OMAP family. The memory interface traffic controller mediates the shared memory traffic. Note that a frame buffer for video is a separate block of memory, distinct from the main data and program memory; it is managed by the memory interface traffic controller. (The frame buffer is contained on-chip while the flash memory and SDRAM are off-chip.)

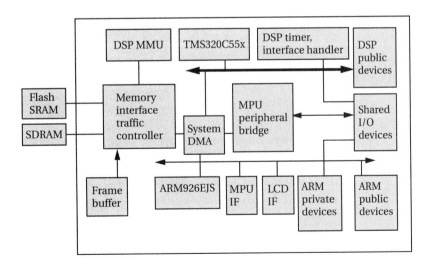

OMAP provides four mailboxes in hardware for multiprocessor communication. Two are writable by the ARM9 and readable by either processor; two are writable by the C55x and readable by either.

Each processor has some dedicated I/O devices. They also share some devices through the MPU peripheral bridge. Only those devices likely to be used by both the ARM9 and the C55x are put on the peripheral bridge bus.

## 5.5 Processing Elements

The processing elements in a multiprocessor perform the basic computations of the system. A PE may run only one process, or it may be shared among several processes. A scientific processor typically uses the same type of CPU for all its PEs to simplify programming. But an embedded processor can use a wide variety of PEs, including hardwired, single-function blocks of logic.

We have to answer these two major questions about the processing elements when designing an embedded multiprocessor.

1. How many processing elements do we need?

2. What types of processor should we use for each PE?

These questions are somewhat related: if we use a specialized processing element that runs a part of the system's function at a particularly high speed, we may be able to use fewer processing elements than if we relied on some other type of PE. But it is often useful to try to separate the two questions as much as possible.

A good design methodology uses the application as a guide.

1. Analyze each application to determine the performance and/or power requirements of each process in the application.

2. Choose a processor type for each process, usually from a set of candidate processor types.

3. Determine which processes can share a CPU to determine the required number of PEs.

We can use all the techniques described in Chapter 2 to select and refine CPUs for inclusion in the multiprocessor. Software performance analysis can be used to determine how fast a process will run on a particular type of CPU. We can use standard CPUs or configurable processors.

## 5.6  Interconnection Networks

The interconnection network used to connect the processing elements and memory is a key component of a complex multiprocessor. The bandwidth of the network is a key factor in performance; the network design also plays a critical role in power consumption.

*terms*

We should establish some terminology for networks. We use the term **client** to refer to a sender or receiver connected to a network. A **port** is a connection to a network on a client. A **link** is a connection between two clients. You may see the terms **half-duplex** and **full-duplex**; a full-duplex connection can simultaneously transmit data in both directions, while a half-duplex connection can transmit in only one direction at a time.

*topology*

Interconnection networks are generally classified by their **topology**—the organization of the links. Network topology helps determine many properties of the network, but topology is only a means toward the end of analyzing the performance, power consumption, and cost of the interconnections.

*network metrics*

We can use several important attributes of networks at different levels of abstraction to evaluate and compare them during design.

- **Throughput**—We are often concerned with the maximum available throughput from one node to another. We may also be concerned with the variations in data rates over time and the effect of those variations on network behavior.

- **Latency**—We are often interested in the amount of time it takes a packet to travel from a source to a destination. If the latency may vary, such as in networks with routing nodes, we are interested in the best-case and worst-case latency.

- **Energy consumption**—We are concerned with the amount of energy required to send a bit through the network; is a typical measure.

- **Area**—The on-chips that are consumed by the network determine its manufacturing cost; the network can also tell us something about power consumption. We can measure it in two ways: (1) silicon area of the transistors and (2) metal area of the wires. Given that wires are a large part of the overall network, metal area is an important cost metric that also tells about the network capacitance and dynamic energy consumption.

An important category of application-level characteristics relates to continuous or streaming data. Many embedded applications require data to be delivered regularly and reliably, as embodied by quality-of-service (QoS). We touch on some QoS characteristics in this section and consider the topic in detail in Section 6.4.3.

Some design decisions for a network are specific to the implementation technology: on-chip or off-chip. But some aspects of networking can be understood for all types of networks.

This section describes both network topology and network characteristics. We start developing some basic models of network elements. Section 5.6.2 considers network topologies. Section 5.6.3 introduces routing and flow control. Section 5.6.4 surveys networks-on-chips for multiprocessor systems-on-chips.

## 5.6.1 Models

To evaluate a network, we will build a simple model of a network link that encapsulates some of the costs of the network. The link model makes it a little easier to evaluate the cost of a network as a function of the size of the network.

Figure 5-6 shows a generic model of a network link. The model consists of three main parts: the **source**, **line**, and **termination**. The source sends information to the termination point using the line. The source and termination each include transistors and logic; the line may contain repeaters but no logic. The source and termination may contain registers but no multipacket buffers.

We can measure several network characteristics directly on the link:

■ Because there are no collisions on the link, we can measure throughput $T$ and latency $D$ directly.

■ Link transmission energy consumption $E_b$ is the energy required to send one bit. We typically use circuit models to determine this value. In many cases, the link transmission energy is dominated by the line's capacitance.

■ We can use the physical length of the link $L$ to compare networks. Longer links generally require longer transmission times and consume more energy. We can also measure total area of the link $A$ as the combination of the areas of the source, termination, and line.

The next example describes a serial port for multichip DSP multiprocessors.

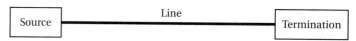

**Figure 5-6** *A generic network link model.*

## Example 5-8

*Texas Instruments McBSP*

The McBSP [Tex05] is a high-speed serial interface designed to allow several TI DSPs to connect to a multiprocessor. The DSP talks to its McBSP units through the 32-bit peripheral bus. Data transmission is full duplex, with a DR pin for data receive and a DX pin for data send. Clocking and frame synchronization is sent via five extra pins.

Communication uses double-buffered data registers to maximize data throughput. McBSP is designed to directly interface to a variety of standard networks, such as T1/E1 framers, IIS, and SPI devices. A device can transmit and receive up to 128 channels. The interface can perform μ-law and A-law companding on-the-fly.

---

*traffic models*

The traffic model characterizes the behavior of the traffic over the network. We need to understand not only the overall rate of traffic, but how the data traffic varies over time.

The Poisson model has been widely used to model traffic in telecommunication networks and other systems in which we are interested in the number of events that occur in a unit of time. Phone calls are independent events—the time of one phone call does not typically depend on the time at which another phone call occurs. The Poisson distribution is well suited to describe this type of traffic.

If μ is the average number of occurrences of an event in a given interval, then the probability that a Poisson random variable $X$ in some value $x$ is given by

$$P(X = x) = \frac{\mu^x e^{-\mu}}{(x)!}, x = 0, 1, \ldots \qquad \text{(EQ 5-1)}$$

It can be shown that the expected value and variance of the Poisson distribution are

$$E(x) = \mu, Var(x) = \mu. \qquad \text{(EQ 5-2)}$$

Once we know the average rate at which events occur, such as the rate at which phone calls occur, we can use that value of μ in the Poisson distribution formula.

The next example illustrates the use of the Poisson distribution in traffic modeling.

## Example 5-9

*Poisson Model for Network Traffic*

Let us assume that a processing element in a multiprocessor emits a datum once every microsecond on average. Then

$$E(x) = \mu = 1 \text{ event / } \mu\text{sec.}$$

If we want to know the probability that 4 will be emitted in a microsecond, we set $x = 4$:

$$P(x = 4) = \frac{1^4 e^{-1}}{4!} = 0.015.$$

*streaming*   At the other extreme we have streaming data that is produced periodically. We generally characterize data streams by the rate at which data are produced and the number of bits per datum. Streaming data is generally characterized by its rate $\sigma$ and burstiness $\rho$.

### 5.6.2   Network Topologies

Many different network structures have been developed and analyzed. This section compares and contrasts a few types of networks to gain a basic understanding of the range of available networking options.

*bus*   The simplest interconnection network is the **bus**. A bus is a common connection between a set of senders and receivers. Because the bus shares a single set of wires between all the clients, it is relatively small compared to other networks. However, we pay for small size with lower performance and sometimes with energy consumption as well.

Let us estimate the performance of the bus by assuming that the bus is operated by a master clock. In a simple bus that transfers one word per bus transaction, we can model the bus throughput as

$$T_1 = P\left(\frac{1}{1 + C}\right) \text{words/sec},  \tag{EQ 5-3}$$

where $C$ is the number of clock cycles required for transaction overhead (addressing, etc.) and $P$ is the bus's clock period. If the bus supports block transfers, then the throughput for block transactions of $n$ word blocks is

$$T_b = P\left(\frac{n}{n + C}\right) \text{words/sec}.  \tag{EQ 5-4}$$

To model the energy consumption of the bus, let us concentrate on dynamic energy consumption. Dynamic energy consumption is determined by the capacitance that must be driven. The capacitance of a bus comes from two sources: the bus wires and the loads at the clients. If the bus has a large number of clients, the clients' capacitance can be a significant fraction of the total capacitance of the bus.

Why might a bus consume more energy than another network? The reason is that the bus wires must connect all the clients; the bus must stretch between the most distant pair of clients. This means that any bus transaction must drive the longest possible interconnection in the system. Other networks, such as the crossbar that we discuss next, are physically larger than a bus with the same number of clients, but the worst-case load that a client must drive in a crossbar can be significantly smaller.

Why not use a bus for a multiprocessor? In fact, many multiprocessors, both scientific and embedded, have been built with busses. However, it is difficult to build a useful multiprocessor with more than a handful of processing elements. Because busses are shared, they are easily saturated with traffic. When the bus saturates, all the processing elements slow down to wait for the bus.

*crossbar*        At the other extreme is the crossbar. A crossbar is a fully connected network; it provides a path from every input port to every output port. Figure 5-7 shows a $4 \times 4$ crossbar. The network gets its name from the structure of the wires in the network. Each input and each output has a wire; at the intersection between any input and output wire is a programming point. When the programming point is activated, a connection is made between the input and output associated with the horizontal and vertical wires.

Because of this rich structure, the crossbar not only provides full connectivity between any input and any output, it also provides full connectivity to any combination of outputs. We can broadcast from an input to all outputs. We can also

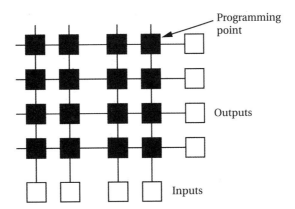

**Figure 5-7** *A crossbar.*

**multicast** an input to several selected outputs. Because of the rich connectivity, we can multicast in any combination of nodes.

The downside of a crossbar is its size. If the crossbar has n inputs and n outputs, then its area is proportional to $n^2$. Because the wires and programming points are fairly small, we can in fact afford crossbars for moderate numbers of inputs and outputs. For example, an $8 \times 8$ crossbar would be quite reasonable on a modern VLSI chip, assuming that the words transferred through the crossbar are not excessively wide. However, a $10,000 \times 10,000$ crossbar of even one-bit wide words would not be reasonable.

When we cannot afford the number of inputs for the area of the crossbar, we can use a buffered crossbar. As shown in Figure 5-8, we can add queues to the inputs of the crossbar with each queue fed by several sources of traffic. Those traffic sources share the crossbar input. We also need a queue controller that decides which packet will enter the queue next (assuming that we can add only one packet at a time to the queue) and what to do when the queue is full.

As shown in Figure 5-9, we can also add buffers to the switching points within the crossbar. This configuration increases the physical size of the crossbar but allows great flexibility in scheduling transfers.

*Clos network*
The Clos network [Clo53] is designed to provide some advantages of a crossbar at less cost. The Clos network is formed by interconnecting smaller crossbars into multiple stages. A Clos network is nonblocking for point-to-point connections, just like a crossbar. However, it is blocking for multicast connections. The number of inputs in a Clos network grows more slowly than the crossbar, so it is considerably smaller than a full crossbar for larger networks.

*mesh networks*
As shown in Figure 5-10, a **mesh** is a network in which every node is connected to all of its neighbors. We can build meshes in different dimensions, including dimensions larger than three. A mesh network is scalable in that a network of

**Figure 5-8** *An input buffered crossbar.*

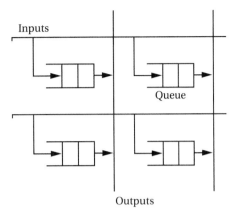

**Figure 5-9** *An internally buffered crossbar.*

dimension $n + 1$ includes subnetworks that are meshes of dimension $n$. A mesh network balances connectivity with link cost. All links are fairly short, but a mesh provides a rich set of connections and multiple paths for data. The RAW machine [Tay04] is an example of a 2D mesh-connected processor.

The shortest path between two nodes in a mesh network is equal to its Manhattan distance, which in general is the sum of the differences between the indexes of the source and destination nodes.

*application-
specific
networks*

Several application-specific networks have been developed for embedded multiprocessors. An application-specific network is not any particular type of topology; rather, it is a topology matched to the characteristics of the application. Application-specific networks can be considerably cheaper and consume less energy than a regular network of equal overall performance. Because most embedded applications perform several different tasks simultaneously, different

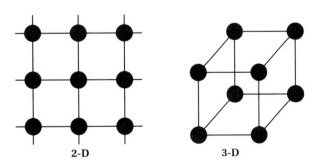

2-D            3-D

**Figure 5-10** *Two- and three-dimensional meshes.*

parts of the architecture require different amounts of network bandwidth to support their operations. By putting bandwidth where it is needed and reducing the capability of less-important nodes, we can make the network more efficient without sacrificing performance for that application.

### 5.6.3 Routing and Flow Control

The way in which packets are sent on the network is an important factor influencing both the cost and performance of the network [Ni93]. Packet flow is determined by two aspects of the network design.

1. **Routing**—Determines the paths that packets follow as they travel from source to destination.

2. **Flow control**—The way that links and buffers are allocated as packets move through the network.

*routing*     Routing algorithms can take a number of different forms. A route may be determined either deterministically or adaptively: deterministic routing is determined solely by a static characteristic of the system, such as the source and destination addresses of the data; adaptive routing adjusts the route based on current network conditions. Routing may be performed using connections or in connectionless form. Connection-oriented routing can be used to provide quality-of-service. Some routing algorithms may drop packets occasionally, such as when buffers along the route are full; other algorithms guarantee packet delivery.

**Wormhole routing** is widely used in interconnection networks for multiprocessors [Dal90]. A packet is split into several **flits** (short for *flow control digits*). The header flit determines the route that the remaining flits in the packet will follow. If the header flit is blocked, it blocks until the channel is ready. The trailing flits are stored in flit buffers along the route. **Virtual cut-through** routing is similar to wormhole routing, but it ensures that the entire path is available before starting transmission. **Store-and-forward** routing stores the packet at intermediate points in the network.

*flow control*     Dally [Dal92] used **virtual channel flow control** to help allocate network resources. A virtual channel includes a flit buffer and associated state information. Virtual channels allow flits in different virtual channels to be treated differently, improving the utilization of communication resources.

### 5.6.4 Networks-on-Chips

**Networks-on-chips (NoCs)** are the interconnection networks for single-chip multiprocessors. As VLSI technology has advanced to the point where we can design true single-chip multiprocessors, many groups have developed on-chip networks. Pande et al. [Pan05] survey design methodologies for NoCs. They identify traffic pattern/network analysis, performance analysis, switch node design, topology design, and network topology as key issues. This section looks at several example networks. We discuss protocol stacks for networks-on-chips in Chapter 6.

*Nostrum*      The Nostrum network [Kum02; Pam03] is a mesh-structured network. As shown in Figure 5-11, each switch connects to its four nearest neighbors using two unidirectional links, plus a link to the processor or memory at that point in

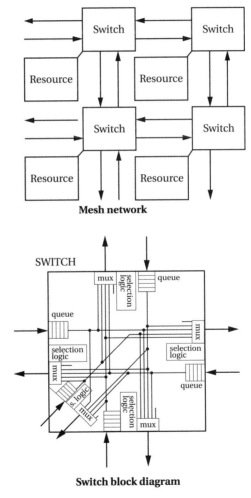

**Mesh network**

**Switch block diagram**

**Figure 5-11** *Organization of the Nostrum network. From Kumar et al. [Kum02] © 2002 IEEE Computer Society.*

the mesh. Processors or memories are known as **resources**. In a 60 nm CMOS technology, a single chip could have room for a $10 \times 10$ mesh of resources and network. Each network link would have 256 data bits plus control and signaling wires. Each switch has a queue at each of its inputs; selection logic at the outputs determines the order in which packets are sent on the output links.

*SPIN*

The SPIN network [Gue00] was designed as a scalable network for a variety of systems-on-chips. The topology used for the SPIN network is a fat-tree [Lei85]. This network is designed to route messages in a treelike style, moving up the tree and then back down, but it is designed to provide more bandwidth at the higher levels than a standard tree. A block diagram of a 16-terminal fat-tree network is shown in Figure 5-12.

The leaf nodes are, in this case, the processing and memory elements. When one PE wants to send a message to another, the message goes up the tree until a common ancestor node is reached, then it proceeds back down the network. Unlike a tree, more links and bandwidth are available at the higher tree levels, reducing contention.

One advantage of the fat-tree network is that all the routing nodes use the same routing function. This allows the same routing node design to be used throughout the network. The SPIN network uses two 32-bit data paths, one for each direction, to provide full-duplex links. The routers are free to choose any of the several equivalent paths that may be available to them.

A packet consists of sequences of 32-bit words. The packet header fits into a single word. Packets can contain an arbitrary number of words. The trailer word, which includes a checksum, is marked by a dedicated control line. The routing scheme uses credit-based flow control. The source checks for buffer overflows at the target end using a counter. The receiver acknowledges every datum consumed using a dedicated feedback wire. The network is implemented using input queues and partial crossbars, as shown in Figure 5-13.

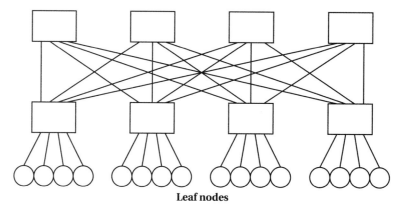

**Leaf nodes**

**Figure 5-12** *Fat-tree structure of the SPIN network.*

*energy modeling*     Ye et al. [Ye03] developed an energy model for networks-on-chips. They assumed that the energy per packet was independent of the data or address of the packet. They used a histogram to capture the distribution of path lengths for flit transmissions. They modeled the energy consumption of a given class of packet as

$$E_{packet} = \sum_{1 \le h \le M} h \times N(h) \times L \times E_{flit},$$     (EQ 5-5)

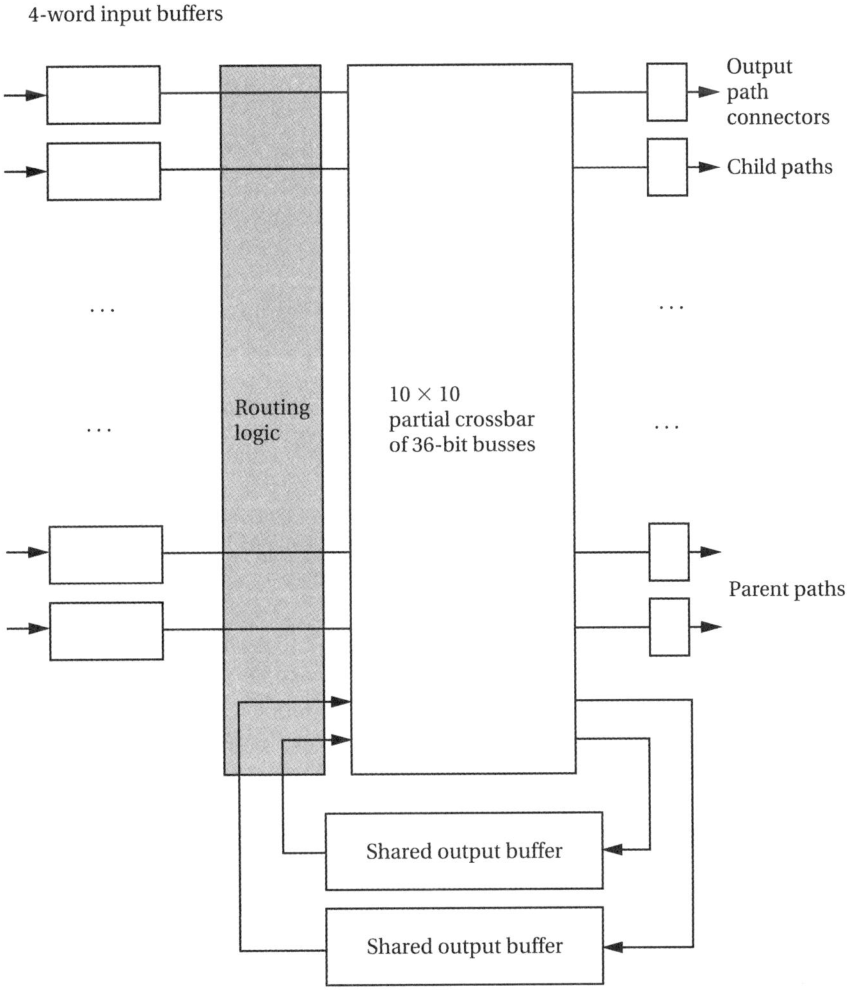

4-word input buffers

**Figure 5-13** *Input queues and partial crossbars in SPIN. From Guerrier and Greiner [Gre00] © 2000 ACM Press. Reprinted by permission.*

where $M$ is the maximum number of hops possible in the network, $h$ is the number of hops, $N(h)$ is the value of the $h^{th}$ histogram bucket, $L$ is the number of flits per packet, and $E_{flit}$ is the energy per flit.

*Slim-spider*

The Slim-spider network [Lee05] uses a hierarchical star topology. The global network was organized as a star, each node of which was a smaller star. Lee et al. used serial connections to reduce, the cost of the switching nodes. Their analysis showed that star networks occupy less area than mesh networks and consume comparable amounts of power for small networks with nine or fewer clusters.

*networks-on-chip design*

Several groups have developed design methodologies for networks-on-chips. Because we are designing a multiprocessor for a particular application area, it makes sense to customize the architecture to the characteristics of those applications. The design of application-specific NoCs requires considering both top-down information from the application and bottom-up information about the capabilities of the implementation technology.

*QoS-sensitive design*

Goossens et al. [Goo05] developed a methodology for network-on-chip design. This methodology is intended to design networks for QoS-intense applications such as multimedia. The methodology is based on several principles.

1. It uses QoS to characterize resource usage.

2. It uses calibration to estimate the characteristics of unpredictable resources.

3. It uses resource management to allocate shared resources.

4. It uses guaranteed services to allocate resources to users.

The design methodology is shown in Figure 5-14.

After the application's requirements have been characterized, the performance required from the network is determined. The network topology is determined next, and the network is configured with its processing and memory elements. The network is simulated to evaluate its actual performance. The network may be modified based on these performance results.

*OCCN*

According to Coppola et al., OCCN [Cop04] is a methodology and tool set for on-chip communication systems. OCCN models intermodule communication using three layers.

1. **NoC communication layer**—Implements the lower levels of the OSI stack. It is described in SystemC using the sc_channel class.

2. **Adaptation layer**—Uses hardware and software to implement middle layers of the OSI stack and is modeled in SystemC using the sc_port object.

3. **Application layer**—Implements the OSI application layer and is built on top of the communication API.

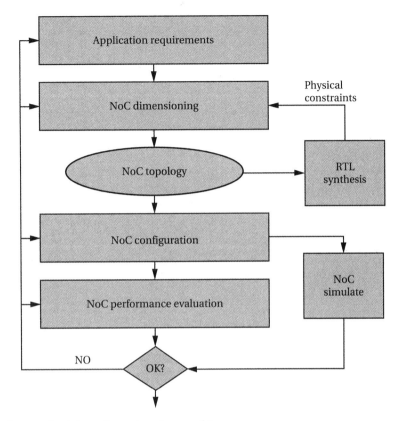

**Figure 5-14** *Design methodology for networks-on-chips.*

A **protocol data unit** defines the minimum messaging unit. The MasterPort/SlavePort API creates a message-passing interface with point-to-point and multipoint communication primitives. A simulation package automates the collection of instantaneous and long-duration statistics about network behavior.

*QNoC*  QNoC [Bol04] is designed to support quality-of-service operations and to be tuned for the application at hand. The basic network is a two-dimensional mesh. Packets are routed using wormhole routing. A fixed *x-y* routing algorithm determines the path taken by the flits. The network supports four different types of service. Each level of service has its own buffers. A next-buffer-state table records the number of slots available at each output port for each service class in the next input port's buffers. An output port schedules flit transmissions based on the number of slots available in the next stage's buffers, the service levels of the pending flits, and the round-robin ordering of the flits within a service level.

The generic network is customized to create an application-specific network. Simulation studies determine the traffic characteristics of the application. Simulations show both the overall traffic levels and the amount of traffic within each service class. Next, a floor plan is constructed for the system. Given a placement of processing elements and allocation of traffic to network links, the structure can be optimized. Some links can be eliminated based on early results of the floor-planning exercise. After the routing algorithm has been selected, link bandwidth can be optimized by changing the number of wires in each link. Buffers and routers can be sized appropriately after studying the results of link bandwidth optimization.

*xpipes and NetChip*

xpipes [Oss03] and NetChip [Jal04; Mur04] are a set of IP-generation tools that generate network-on-chip implementations. xpipes is a library of soft IP macros for network switches and links; NetChip generates custom NoC designs using xpipes' components. The links are pipelined, and the number of pipeline stages can be selected based on the desired system throughput. A retransmission scheme is used for link-level error control, based on the condition of the packet CRC code.

*H.264 design*

Xu et al. [Xu06] compared general-purpose and application-specific networks for an H.264 decoder. Figure 5-15 shows a block diagram of the video decoder and a mapping to a multiprocessor architecture. The H.264 decoder was simulated to create traces for communication between processing elements. Several networks were developed to support this allocation to PEs. A RAW-style mesh network was used as one candidate. Several heterogeneous architectures

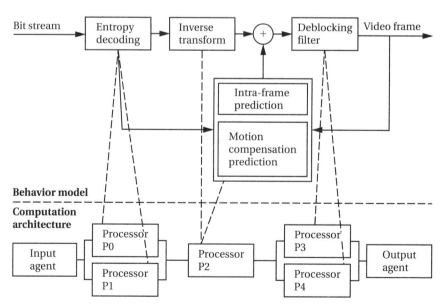

**Figure 5-15** *Mapping of H.264 decoder to a multiprocessor architecture. From Xu et al. [Xu06] © 2006 ACM Press. Reprinted by permission.*

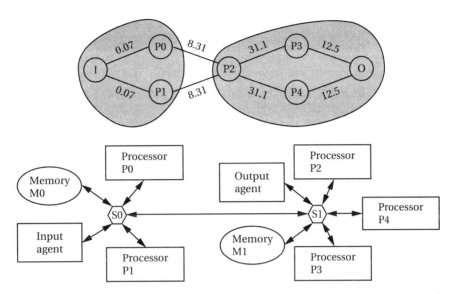

**Figure 5-16** *Process partitioning and multiprocessor architecture for H.264. From Xu et al. [Xu06] © 2006 ACM Press. Reprinted by permission.*

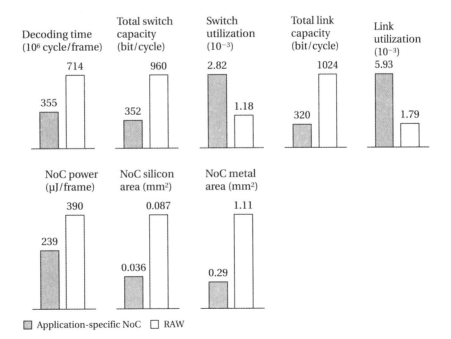

**Figure 5-17** *Comparison of network implementations for H.264 decoder. From Xu et al. [Xu06] © 2006 ACM Press. Reprinted by permission.*

were also tried; most of these networks used several switches that organized the PEs into clusters. The best heterogeneous architecture is shown in Figure 5-16.

The processors, memories, and networks were floor-planned to estimate wire lengths and other physical costs. OPNET was used to simulate the networks. Figure 5-17 summarizes the results of this comparison between RAW and the best application-specific network. The application-specific network gave higher performance and required less energy per frame.

The next example describes a commercial network-on-chip.

## Example 5-10

*Sonics SiliconBackplane III*

SiliconBackplane III [Son02] is designed for the nonblocking, streaming communications required for multimedia applications. It provides a raw data bandwidth of 4.8 GBps at 300 MHz. Bursting facilities can be used to implement streaming multimedia communications. The network can be configured at runtime to multicast data.

## 5.7  Memory Systems

The memory system is a traditional bottleneck in computing. Not only are memories slower than processors, but processor clock rates are increasing much faster than memory cycle times. We start with a look at parallel memory systems in scientific multiprocessors. We then consider models for memory and motivations for heterogeneous memory systems. Then we look at what sorts of consistency mechanisms are needed in embedded multiprocessors.

### 5.7.1  Traditional Parallel Memory Systems

Scientific processors traditionally use parallel, homogeneous memory systems to increase system performance. Multiple memory banks allow several memory accesses to occur simultaneously.

*multiple memory banks*

Figure 5-18 shows the structure of a multiple-bank memory system, which consists of several memory banks. Each bank is separately addressable. (The address and data lines are shown as busses; those connections have to be

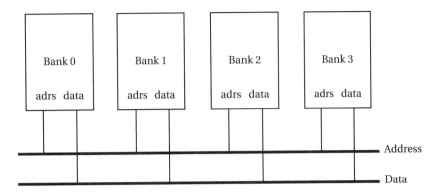

**Figure 5-18** *Structure of a multiple-bank memory system.*

designed with a protocol that allows multiple simultaneous accesses.) If, for example, a read is performed on bank 0, a write could be simultaneously performed on bank 1.

*peak access rate*    If the memory system has *n* banks, then *n* accesses can be performed in parallel. This is known as the **peak access rate**. If the memory locations and access patterns are laid out properly, we may be able to achieve this peak rate for some part of a program. If, for example, we access the banks in the order 0, 1, 2, 3, 0, 1, 2, 3, ... , then we will be able to keep all the banks busy all the time.

*average access rate*    However, in realistic systems we cannot keep the memory busy all of the time. A simple statistical model lets us estimate performance of a random-access program. Let us assume that the program accesses a certain number of sequential locations, then moves to some other location. We will call $\lambda$ the probability of a nonsequential memory access (a branch in code to be a non-consecutive data location). Then the probability of a string of *k* sequential accesses is

$$p(k) = \lambda(1-\lambda)^{k-1}. \qquad \text{(EQ 5-6)}$$

The mean length of a sequential access sequence is

$$L_b = \sum_{1 \leq k \ \leq \infty} kp(k)$$
$$= \frac{1-(1-\lambda)^m}{\lambda} \qquad \text{(EQ 5-7)}$$

We can use program statistics to estimate the average probability of non-sequential accesses, design the memory system accordingly, and then use software techniques to maximize the length of access sequences wherever possible.

## 5.7.2 Models for Memory

As we design memory systems, we need to model memory components and systems in order to make design decisions. A simple model of memory components for parallel memory design would include three major parameters of a memory component of a given size.

1. **Area**—The physical size of the logical component. This is most important in chip design, but it also relates to cost in board design.

2. **Performance**—The access time of the component. There may be more than one parameter, with variations for read and write times, page mode accesses, and so on.

3. **Energy**—The energy required per access. If performance is characterized by multiple modes, energy consumption will exhibit similar modes.

We can use the memory component models discussed in Section 2.6.1 to describe memory components for multiprocessor design. We can make some general observations about memory components that can be important in embedded memory system design.

- **Delay is a nonlinear function of memory size.** If we use a memory block that has twice as many words, an access to that memory will take more than twice as long. Bit line delays will dominate the access time, and the delay through that wire is a nonlinear function of the length of the wire.

- **Delay and energy is a nonlinear function of the number of ports**. When we want to access a memory from multiple processing elements, it is tempting to use a multiport SRAM memory. This memory design puts a multiplexer in each memory cell to allow simultaneous accesses from several ports. (Each access must be to a different location, of course.) The details of this circuit design cause the memory delay to be a nonlinear function of the number of ports.

Dutta et al. [Dut98] developed a methodology for the design of parallel memory systems. As shown in Figure 5-19, the methodology uses both top-down and bottom-up information. The number of processing elements and the clock cycle are determined from the application and area/delay information about the memory modules. The clock rate determines the maximum size of memory module that can be used. This information in turn determines the number of ports on the network. Various topologies can be considered that fit these parameters. The networks are evaluated using scheduling information as well as circuit delay information. Dutta et al. showed that different network topologies may be best for different values for the number of PEs or memory cycle time.

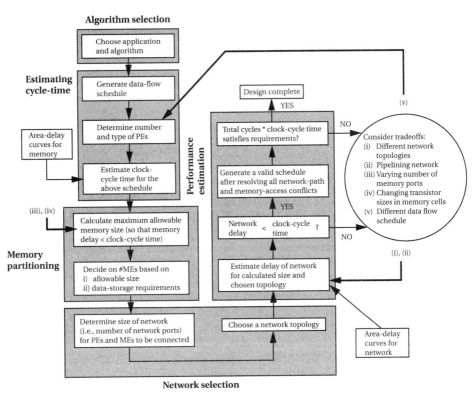

**Figure 5-19** *A methodology for parallel memory system design. From Dutta et al. [Dut98] ©*
*1998 IEEE.*

### 5.7.3  Heterogeneous Memory Systems

Embedded systems can make use of multiple-bank memory systems, but they
also make use of more heterogeneous memory architectures. They do so to
improve the real-time performance and lower the power consumption of the
memory system.

*real-time*
*performance*
Why do heterogeneous memory systems improve real-time performance?
Putting all of our data into a single large pool of common memory makes life
easier if we are only concerned with functionality but causes problems if we are
concerned with real-time responsiveness. If we share a memory component
across several processing elements, those PEs will contend for the memory. PEs
will in general have to wait for another PE to finish an access; in most applications, we cannot predict exactly when these conflicts will occur. If we have a
block of memory that has to be accessed to meet real-time deadlines and that
memory is accessed by only one PE, we can guarantee avoiding conflicts if we

*power consumption*

build a specialized memory for that PE. If a block of real-time sensitive memory has to be accessed by more than one PE, we can still improve real-time performance by connecting that memory to only the PEs that need it.

Heterogeneous memories also help reduce power consumption. The energy required to perform a memory access depends in part on the size of the memory block being accessed. A heterogeneous memory may be able to use smaller memory blocks, reducing the access time. Energy per access also depends on the number of ports on the memory block. By reducing the number of units that can access a given part of memory, the heterogeneous memory system can reduce the energy required to access that part of the memory space.

The next example looks at a heterogeneous memory system designed for real-time performance.

---

## Example 5-11

*HP DesignJet Printer*

The HP DesignJet [Boe02; Meb92] is a large-format inkjet plotter used for drafting. The plotter accepts drawings in a **page description language** format, either HP-GL2 or PostScript, and produces plots up to 36 inches wide. The printer accepts roll paper and can generate very long plots.

To create a plot, the plotter must convert the page description language version of the page into pixels. Because it can create very large plots, it does not generate the entire plot before starting to plot. It instead rasterizes a **swath** of the plot. As it prints one swath, it rasterizes another swath.

The plotter uses several programmable processors and ASICs (shown below).

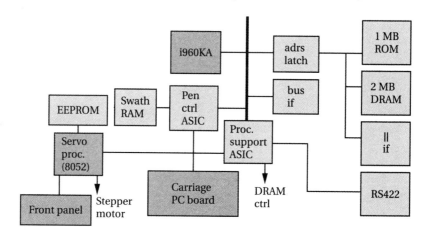

*Source:* After Mebane et al. [Meb92].

The i960 is a 32-bit microprocessor that performs a variety of functions, including rasterizing the page description language version of the plot into pixels. The pen control ASIC feeds pixel values to the inkjet heads. The i960 and the pen control ASIC communicate through the swath RAM, which is not on the i960's main bus. Because the swath RAM feeds the inkjet pens as they move across the page, its access times must be very reliable. If the swath were stored in a memory on the i960's bus, it would be subject to a variety of influences from both the CPU and the I/O devices. Using a separate memory causes the memory's access time to be very reliable, thus eliminating further buffering closer to the pens.

---

*power/energy*

How do heterogeneous memory systems lower power/energy consumption? Once again, connecting memory only to the components that really need it reduces the consumption of power/energy. A more general memory system has more and longer wires that increase memory power consumption. We described a model for memory components in Section 2.6.1. We can extend that system to cover system-level interconnects. The dynamic power consumption of a memory transaction is determined by the memory modules, the switching blocks in the interconnection network, and the wires connecting them.

$$E_M = \sum_{i \in modules} E_{i, module} + \sum_{j \in switch} E_{j, switch} + \sum_{k \in wires} E_{k, wire}. \quad \text{(EQ 5-8)}$$

The power consumption of the wire depends on its length and its buffering. However, the wire may be longer than the shortest path between the memory access source and destination. A memory module or control block may have to drive a bus or other long wire that has many signal sinks. The excess capacitive loading caused by multisource, multisink memory systems is a major source of power consumption.

## 5.7.4  Consistent Parallel Memory Systems

We have to deal with several problems in parallel memory systems that we do not need to worry about as much in uniprocessors. (Some of these effects are also induced in uniprocessors by I/O devices that act as processing elements.) The basic effects are common to all multiprocessors, but our solutions to them may vary in some cases when we build embedded multiprocessors.

*shared variables*

We have to worry about whether two processors see the same state of a shared variable. If reads and writes of two processors are interleaved, then one processor may write the variable after another one has written it, causing that processor to erroneously assume the value of the variable. We use critical sections, guarded by semaphores, to ensure that critical operations occur in the right order. We can also use atomic test-and-set operations (often called **spin locks**) to guard small pieces of memory.

Akgul and Mooney [Akg02] proposed an SoC lock cache to provide locking mechanisms for systems-on-chips. The SoC lock cache can be viewed as a piece of IP that can be dropped into a multiprocessor design. Their lock cache provides busy–wait mechanisms to access variables for short amounts of time (less than 1,000 cycles) and block synchronization mechanisms to access data structures that must be manipulated for long periods. The lock cache implements key operations in hardware and leaves part of the lock implementation to software in order to make the system more flexible. The lock cache also keeps track of which PE request locks so that it can implement fairness algorithms.

*cache consistency*

We also need to worry about cache consistency. The problem is illustrated in Figure 5-20. If two processors access the same memory location, then each may have a copy of the location in its own cache. If one processing element writes that location, then the other will not immediately see the change and will make an incorrect computation.

*snooping caches*

The solution to this problem, commonly used in scientific multiprocessors, is a **snooping cache**. This type of cache contains extra logic that watches the multiprocessor interconnect for memory transactions. When it sees a write to a location that it currently contains, it invalidates that location. The normal cache mechanisms will then make sure the location is read again before it is used. Stenstrom [Ste90] surveyed cache coherence mechanisms.

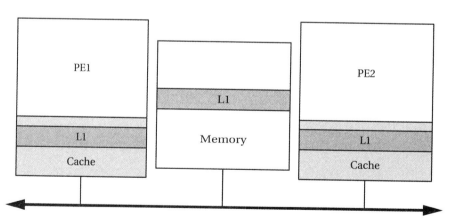

**Figure 5-20** *Cache consistency in multiprocessors.*

A variety of software-based cache coherence methods have been proposed. Tartalja and Milutinovic [Tar97] provide a classification of software-based cache coherence methods. Moshovos et al. [Mos01] used a small cachelike memory to reduce the energy consumption of snooping memory systems. A **JETTY** sits between the bus and the level 2 cache of each processor. When a location is requested, the JETTY may respond with a guarantee that no copies exist in its L2 cache, in which case the cache itself does not need to be queried. If the JETTY cannot guarantee that the cache does not hold the location, then the system proceeds with a cache inquiry.

*memory consistency in embedded processors*

Memory consistency is an important problem in many embedded systems. We can use snooping caches to solve such problems. However, we may not need to use snooping caches to enforce memory consistency throughout the memory space. Scientific processors often run the same application code on several processors, and more than one processor may need to access the same data in a parallel algorithm. However, embedded applications typically exhibit task-level parallelism, which means that different processors are running different programs that operate on different data. If two processors know they will never use a particular location in common, the hardware does not need to protect it. And a great deal of shared memory in task-parallel systems is used for producer–consumer data, in which there is only one writer. Often, we can build simple mechanisms to protect producer–consumer transactions for data buffers.

The next example describes an embedded multiprocessor with configurable cache consistency mechanisms.

## Example 5-12

*ARM MPCore Multiprocessor*

The ARM MPCore multiprocessor is built from ARM11 processors. The MPCore can be composed of up to four processors, each with instructions and data caches that can range from 16 KB to 64 KB.

The block diagram shows the MPCore as a traditional symmetric multiprocessor: identical CPUs connected by a snooping cache to a shared memory. However, the memory system can be configured to support asymmetric as well as symmetric processing. The multiprocessor's memory can be divided into regions, with some regions working as shared memory and others as private memory. This allows the processors to be used as a combination of symmetric and asymmetric multiprocessors.

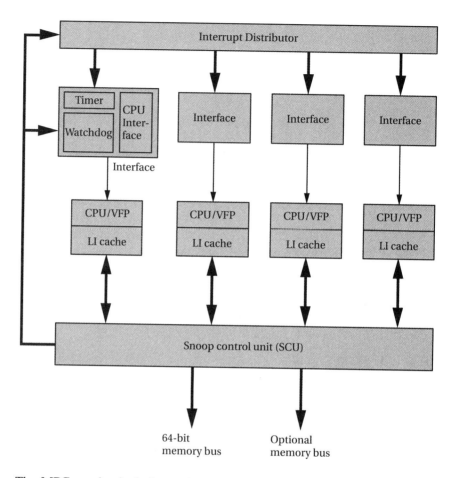

The MPCore also includes an interrupt distributor that allocates interrupts among the processors. Interrupt handling is not a major concern of traditional scientific multiprocessors.

## 5.8 Physically Distributed Systems and Networks

This section describes **networks** that can be used to build physically distributed embedded systems for cars, airplanes, and so on. These systems are more loosely coupled than multiprocessors—they generally do not use shared memory. The application is distributed over the processing elements, and some of the work is performed at each node in the network. Of course, the distributed system must provide guaranteed real-time behavior.

There are several reasons to build network-based embedded systems. When the processing tasks are physically distributed, it may be necessary to put some of the computing power near where the events occur. Consider, for example, an automobile: the short time delays required for tasks, such as engine control, generally mean that at least parts of the task are performed physically close to the engine. Data reduction is another important reason for distributed processing. It may be possible to perform some initial signal processing on captured data to reduce its volume—for example, detecting a certain type of event in a sampled data stream. Reducing the data on a separate processor may significantly reduce the load on the processor that makes use of that data.

Modularity is another motivation for network-based design. For instance, when a large system is assembled out of existing components, those components can use a network port as a clean interface that does not interfere with the internal operation of the component in ways that using the microprocessor bus would. A distributed system can also be easier to debug—the microprocessors in one part of the network can be used to probe components in another part of the network. Finally, in some cases, networks are used to build fault tolerance into systems. Distributed embedded system design is another example of hardware/software co-design, since we must design the network topology as well as the software running on the network nodes.

We first discuss time-triggered architecture, an important class of real-time distributed networks. We then look at FlexRay, a relatively new network for vehicles. We close with a brief description of networks for aircraft.

## 5.8.1 Time-Triggered Architecture

**Time-triggered architecture** (TTA) [Kop97; Kop03] is a distributed architecture for real-time control. It is designed to be sufficiently reliable for safety-critical systems and to be accurate enough to control high-rate physical processes.

*real-world time*  TTA is different from many traditional computer science notions of distributed computing in that it has a notion of real time. Many distributed computing algorithms are primarily concerned with maintaining a proper partial order of events. However, when controlling physical systems, we have to worry about the real-time behavior of the system to be sure that we react within the physical system's time constants. In this section, we refer to the *clock* as a *real-time clock*, not the pulse generator that controls the sequential execution of the digital logic in the system.

TTA represents time using a timestamp based on the Global Positioning System (GPS). An instant is represented as a 64-bit value, with the three lower bytes containing fractions of a second and the five upper bytes containing

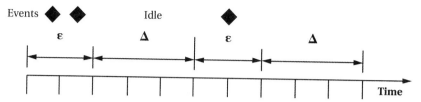

**Figure 5-21** *A sparse model of time.*

whole seconds. The zero time value is set at the start of the GPS epoch, which is 0:00:00 Coordinated Universal Time on January 6, 1980.

*sparse time model*

Physical systems operate under continuous time, while computers generally operate under a discrete time model. We need a model of time that allows the two to reliably interact. The time-triggered architecture models time sparsely as shown in Figure 5-21. Time alternates between active periods, denoted by ε, and idle periods, denoted by Δ. Events can occur during ε intervals but not during Δ intervals. The duration of these intervals is chosen to be larger than the precision of the clock.

The sparse time model ensures that events will not be reordered due to small variations in the clock between nodes. In a dense timing model, an arriving

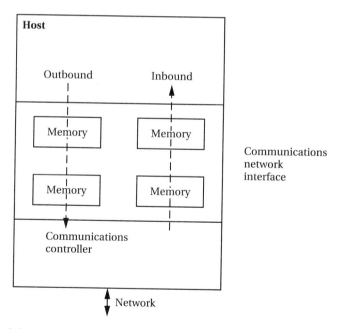

**Figure 5-22** *The role of the communications network interface in TTA.*

event may be timestamped with two different times due to variations in the clock value at different nodes. Because the sparse model has a coarser-grained view of real-world events than it does of the clock synchronization within the system, it will not inadvertently reorder events.

*communication
interface*

The **communications network interface** (**CNI**) helps maintain the consistent view of time. As shown in Figure 5-22, the CNI sits between the **communications controller**, which provides the low-level interface to the network, and the **host node** (the TTA term for a processing element in the network). The CNI enforces a unidirectional flow of data. Each CNI provides two channels, one inbound and one outbound, each of which operates in only one direction. Buffering ensures that tasks on the host are not delayed by unpredictable communication delays.

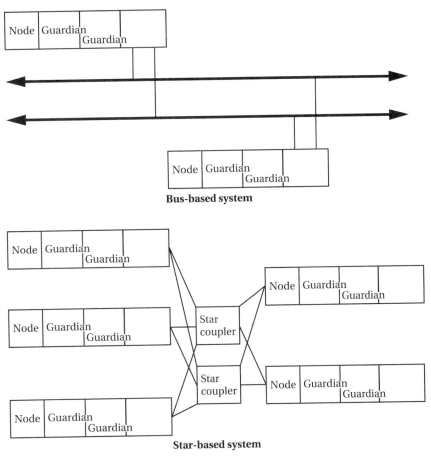

**Figure 5-23**  *Time-triggered architecture topologies.*

*interconnection topologies*

The time-triggered architecture can be implemented on two styles of interconnect: bus and star. As shown in Figure 5-23, a bus-based system uses replicated busses; these busses are passive to avoid components that may fail. Each physical node includes a node and two guardians as well as a bus transceiver. The guardians monitor the transmissions of the node and cut off a transmission that they regard to be outside the node's proper time slot. A star configuration, also shown in Figure 5-23, is more expensive but generally more reliable.

*cliques*

Fault-tolerant systems identify failures by internal inconsistencies. When different nodes in the system have a different view of the system state, then improper and potentially harmful actions can be taken by the nodes. TTA uses a **clique avoidance algorithm** to identify faulty nodes when its protocols find that the system state is inconsistent. Once the faulty node or nodes have been found, the action to be taken to recover from the fault is determined by the application.

### 5.8.2 FlexRay

**FlexRay** (*http://www.flexray.com*) is a second-generation standard for automotive networks. It is designed to provide higher bandwidth as well as more abstract services than are provided by CAN. It is based on some of the principles of the time-triggered network discussed in Section 5.8.1.

*block diagram*

Figure 5-24 shows a block diagram of a generic FlexRay system [Fle05]. The host runs applications. It talks to both communication controllers, which provide higher-level functions, and the low-level bus drivers.

*bus guardians*

A node that watches the operation of a network and takes action when it sees erroneous behavior is known as a **bus guardian** (whether the network is actually a bus or not). FlexRay uses bus guardians to check for errors on active stars.

*FlexRay timing*

Because FlexRay is designed for real-time control, it provides network-scheduling phases that guarantee real-time performance. This mode is known as the **static phase** because the scheduling of frames is chosen statically. It also provides a mode, known as **dynamic phase**, for non-time-critical and aperiodic data that will not interfere with the static mode. The transmissions in the static phase have guaranteed bandwidth, and dynamic phase messages cannot interfere with the static phase. This method creates a **temporal firewall** between time-sensitive and non-time-sensitive transmissions.

Figure 5-25 illustrates the hierarchy of timing structures used by FlexRay. Larger timing phases are built up from smaller timing elements. Starting from the lowest level of the hierarchy.

- A **microtick** is derived from the node's own internal clock or timer, not from the global FlexRay clock.

- A **macrotick**, in contrast, is derived from a clusterwide synchronized clock. A macrotick always includes an integral number of microticks, but different macroticks can contain different numbers of microticks to correct for differ-

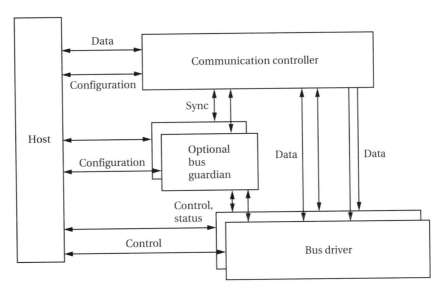

**Figure 5-24** *FlexRay block diagram.*

ences between the nodes' local clocks. The boundaries between some macroticks are designated as **action points**, which form the boundaries for static and dynamic segments.

■ The **arbitration grid** determines the boundaries between messages within a static or dynamic segment. An arbitraiton algorithm determines which nodes are allowed to transmit in the slots determined by the action points.

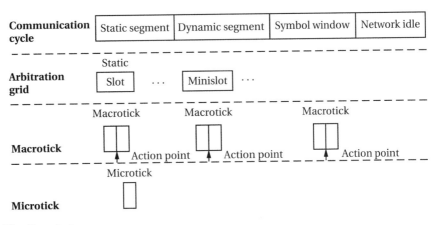

**Figure 5-25** *FlexRay timing.*

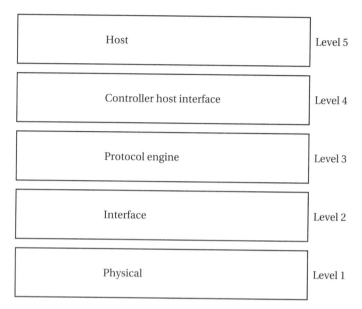

**Figure 5-26** *Levels of abstraction in FlexRay.*

■ A **communication cycle** includes four basic elements: a static segment, a dynamic segment, a symbol window, and network idle time. A symbol window is a single unarbitrated time slot for application use. The idle time allows for timing corrections and housekeeping functions at the nodes.

*FlexRay network stack*

As shown in Figure 5-26, FlexRay is organized around five levels of abstraction.

1. **Physical level**—Defines the structure of connections.

2. **Interface level**—Defines the physical connections.

3. **Protocol engine**—Defines frame formats and communication modes and services such as messages and synchronization.

4. **Controller host interface**—Provides information on status, configuration, messages, and control for the host layer.

5. **Host layer**—Provides applications.

*active stars*

As shown in Figure 5-27, FlexRay is not organized around a bus [Fle05]. It instead uses a star topology known as an **active star** because the router node is active. The maximum delay between two nodes in an active star is 250 ns. As a

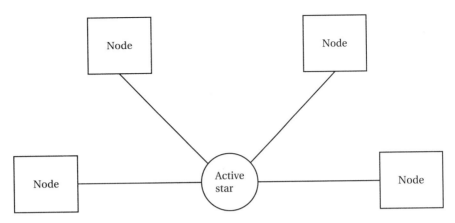

**Figure 5-27** *Active star networks.*

result, the active star does not store the complete message before forwarding it to the destination.

*redundant active stars*      A node may be connected to more than one star to provide redundant connections in case one active star fails. In Figure 5-28, some of the nodes are connected to both stars A and B, while other nodes are connected to only one of the stars.

*physical layer*      FlexRay transmits bits over links using differential non-return-to-zero (NRZ) coding as shown in Figure 5-29. A low-power idle phase operates at zero volts. The idle phase transmits a mid-range voltage, and bits are modulated around that value. The links transmit at 10 Mbps, independent of the length of

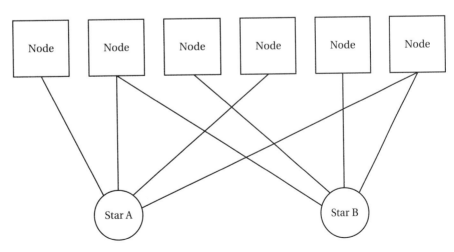

**Figure 5-28** *Redundant active stars.*

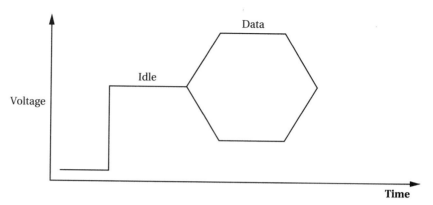

**Figure 5-29** *FlexRay data transmission.*

the link. FlexRay does not arbitrate on bits, so link length is not limited by arbitration contention.

Figure 5-30 shows the encoding of static frames, the basic frame type. Data is sent as bytes. TSS stands for **transmission start sequence**, which is low for 5 to 15 bits. FSS—**frame start sequence**—is one high bit. BSS stands for **byte start sequence**, and FES stands for **frame end sequence**, which is a LO followed by a HI. Dynamic frames, which we describe later in this section, add a **dynamic trailing sequence field**.

*frame fields*

Figure 5-31 shows the following format of a FlexRay frame.

- **Frame ID**—Identifies the frame's slot. Its value is in the range 0 . . . 2,047.

- **Payload length**—Gives the number of 16-bit words in the payload section. All messages in the static section of a communication cycle must use the same length payload.

- **Header CRC**—Provides error correction.

- **Cycle count**—Enumerates the protocol cycles. This information is used within the protocol engines to guide clock synchronization.

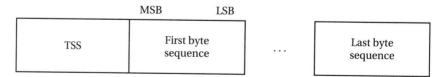

**Figure 5-30** *FlexRay frame encoding.*

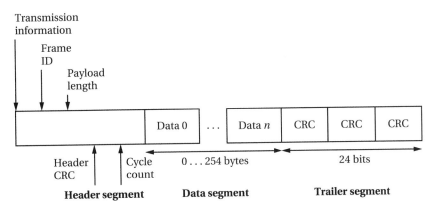

**Figure 5-31** *Format of a FlexRay frame.*

- **Data field**—Provides payload from 0 to 254 bytes in size. As mentioned previously, all packets in the static segment must provide the same length of data payload.
- **Trailer CRC**—Provides additional error correction.

*static segments*  The static segment is the basic timing structure for time-critical messages. Figure 5-32 shows the organization of a FlexRay static segment. The static segment is scheduled using a time-division multiple-access discipline—this allows

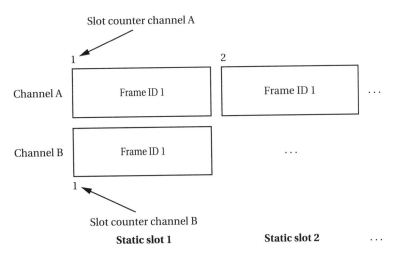

**Figure 5-32** *A FlexRay static segment.*

the system to ensure a guaranteed amount of bandwidth for messages. The TDMA discipline divides the static segment into slots of fixed and equal length. All the slots are used in every segment in the same order. The number of slots in the static segment is configurable in the range 0 . . . 1,023.

The static segment is split across two channels. Synchronization frames are provided on both channels. Messages can be sent on either one or both channels; less critical nodes may be designed to connect to only one channel. The slots are occupied by messages with ascending frame ID numbers. The slot numbers are not used for timing but instead are used by software to identify messages. (The message ID in the payload area can also be used to identify messages.)

*dynamic segments*
The dynamic segments provide bandwidth for asynchronous, unpredictable communication. The slots in the dynamic segment are arbitrated using a deterministic mechanism. Figure 5-33 shows the organization of a dynamic segment. The dynamic segment has two channels, each of which can have its own message queue.

Figure 5-34 illustrates the timing of a dynamic segment. Messages can be sent at minislot boundaries. If no message is sent for a minislot, it elapses as a short idle message. If a message is sent, it occupies a longer interval than a minislot. As a result, transmitters must watch for messages to determine whether each minislot was occupied.

The frame ID is used to number slots. The first dynamic frame's number is one higher than the last static segment's number. Messages are sent in order of frame ID, with the lowest number first. The frame ID number acts as the message priority. Each frame ID number can send only one message per dynamic segment. If there are too many messages in the queue to be sent in a single dynamic segment, those messages are carried over to the next dynamic segment.

*system startup*
A network with complex timing, such as a FlexRay, must be started properly. FlexRay starts with a wake-up procedure that turns on the nodes. It then per-

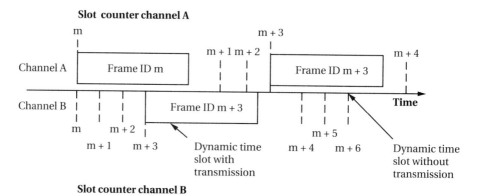

**Figure 5-33** *Structure of a FlexRay dynamic segment.*

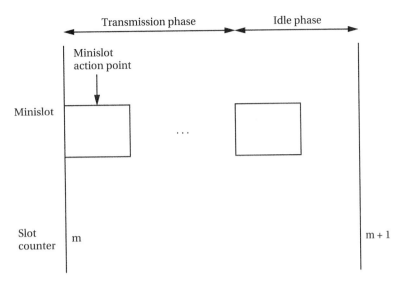

**Figure 5-34** *FlexRay dynamic segment timing.*

forms a **coldstart** that initiates the TDMA process. At least two nodes in the system must be designated as capable of performing a coldstart. The network sends a wake-up pattern on one channel to alert the nodes to wake up. The wake-up procedure has been designed to easily detect collisions between nodes that may wake up and try to transmit simultaneously.

*timekeeping*  A TDMA network like FlexRay needs a global time source to synchronize messages. The global time is synthesized by the **clock synchronization process** (**CSP**) from the nodes' clocks using distributed timekeeping algorithms. The global time is used to determine the boundaries of macroticks, which are the basic timekeeping unit. Macroticks are managed by the **macrotick generation process**, which applies the clock and any updates provided by the CSP. Figure 5-35 illustrates the FlexRay clock synchronization process. The CSP periodically measures clocks, then applies a correction.

*bus guardians*  The bus guardians' role is to prevent nodes from transmitting outside their schedules. FlexRay does not require a system to have a bus guardian, but it should be included in any safety-critical system. The bus guardian sends an *enable* signal to every node in the system that it guards. It can stop the node from transmitting by removing the *enable* signal. The bus guardian uses its own clock to watch the bus operation. If it sees a message coming at the wrong time, it removes the enable signal from the node that is sending the message.

*controller host interface*  The controller host interface (CHI) provides services to the host. Some services are required while others are optional. These services, which are provided in hardware, include status (macroticks, etc.); control (interrupt service, startup, etc.); message data (buffering, etc.); and configuration (node and cluster).

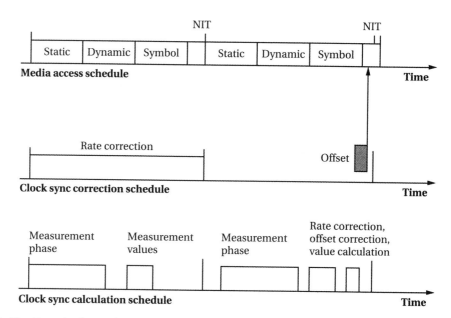

**Figure 5-35** *FlexRay clock synchronization procedure.*

### 5.8.3 Aircraft Networks

*avionics*

Aircraft design is similar in some respects to automobile design, but with more stringent requirements. Airplanes are more sensitive to weight than cars. Aircraft have more complex controls because they must be flown in three dimensions. Finally, most aspects of aircraft design, operation, and maintenance are regulated.

Aircraft electronics can be divided into roughly three categories: **instrumentation**, **navigation/communication**, and **control**. Instruments, such as the altimeter or artificial horizon, use mechanical, pneumatic, or hydraulic methods to sense aircraft characteristics. The primary role of electronics is to sense these systems and to display the results or send them to other systems. Navigation and communication rely on radios. Aircraft use several different types of radios because regulations mandate that certain activities be performed with specific types of radios. Communication can be by voice or data. Navigation makes use of several techniques; moving maps that integrate navigation data onto a map display are common even in general aviation aircraft. Digital electronics can be used both to control the radios, such as set frequencies, and to present the output of these radios. Control systems operate the engines and flight control surfaces (e.g., aileron, elevator, rudder).

*aircraft network categories*

Because of these varied uses, modern commercial aircraft use several different types of networks:

- **Control networks**—These networks must perform hard real-time tasks for instrumentation and control. They generally operate in TDMA mode.

- **Management networks**—These networks control noncritical devices. They can use nonguaranteed modes, such as Ethernet, to improve average performance and limit weight.

- **Passenger networks**—Some airplanes now offer Internet service to passengers through wired or wireless connections. Internet traffic is routed through a satellite link. These networks make use of existing standards and are separated from the aircraft's operating networks by firewalls.

*aircraft network standards*

A number of standards for aircraft data networks have been developed. Several of these standards have been developed by Aircraft Radio, Inc. (ARINC), which was chartered by the U.S. Congress to coordinate radio communications for U.S. airlines. Standards include: ARINC 429, ARINC 629, CDSB, ARINC 573 for flight data recorders, and ARINC 708 for weather radar data.

*ARINC 664*

ARINC 664 [Air04] is a new specification for aircraft networks, particularly those used by scheduled airlines. ARINC 664 is based on the Ethernet standard, which provides higher bandwidth than previous aircraft data networks and allows aircraft manufacturers to use off-the-shelf network components. However, the basic Ethernet is used with protocols and architectures that provide the real-time performance and reliability required by aircraft.

ARINC 664 divides the aircraft network into four domains, with firewalls between them.

1. The flight deck network provides deterministic behavior for real-time control.

2. A separate network supports equipment supplied by outside vendors (original equipment manufacturers or OEMs). This layer also provides temporal determinism, but not the same level of controlled latency as in the flight deck subnetwork.

3. An airline systems' subnetwork supports secondary operations, such as in-flight entertainment.

4. The passenger subnetwork provides Internet access to travelers.

## 5.9 Multiprocessor Design Methodologies and Algorithms

This section looks at design methodologies and tools for multiprocessors, primarily for systems-on-chips. A system-on-chip is composed of many predesigned hardware and software modules. Additional hardware and software modules must be synthesized or modified to create interfaces between those existing components. The management of module interfaces is a key problem in the design of heterogeneous embedded multiprocessors.

A common approach to design reuse is to standardize around a few key components and their interfaces. For example, several methodologies have been built around standardized busses. The ARM AMBA bus, the IBM CoreConnect bus, and the Sonics Silicon Backplane are well-known busses used to build systems-on-chips. Alternatively, standards and tools can be built around processor interfaces. The Virtual Socket Interface Alliance (VSIA) defines a virtual component interface and a functional interface. CoWare N2C and Cadence VCC both provide tools for system-on-chip integration methodologies.

*core-based strategy*

One example of a core-based approach is based on the IBM CoreConnect bus [Ber01]. As shown in Figure 5-36, CoreConnect provides three types of busses:

1. A high-speed processor local bus (PLB).

2. An on-chip peripheral bus (OPB).

3. A device control register (DCR) bus for configuration and status information.

The IBM Coral tool automates many tasks required to compose a system-on-chip for CoreConnect-based architectures. **Virtual components** are used to describe a class of real components. For example, a PowerPC virtual component describes general properties of all PowerPCs. Virtual components provide virtual interfaces that can be specialized during instantiation. Figure 5-37 shows the classification hierarchy for virtual cores and pins.

Coral synthesizes glue logic between components. Some of the interface logic is supplied directly by the core. Other logic for simple Boolean functions is automatically generated as required. When third-party cores that were not designed for this methodology need to be integrated into the design, they may be described with wrappers. The synthesis process is illustrated in Figure 5-38.

An interconnection engine generates the netlist while performing a number of checks and determining how to instantiate the virtual components and pins. The properties of virtual components and pins are described as Boolean functions. Boolean decision diagrams (BDDs) can be used to efficiently compare and manipulate these descriptions.

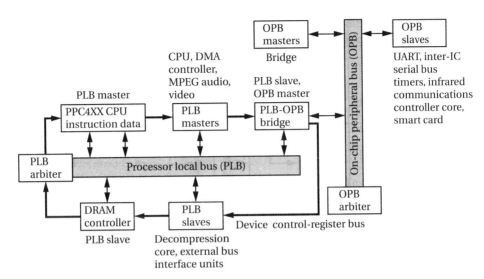

**Figure 5-36** *A SoC template using the IBM CoreConnect bus architecture. From Bergamaschi et al. [Ber01] © 2001 IEEE Computer Society.*

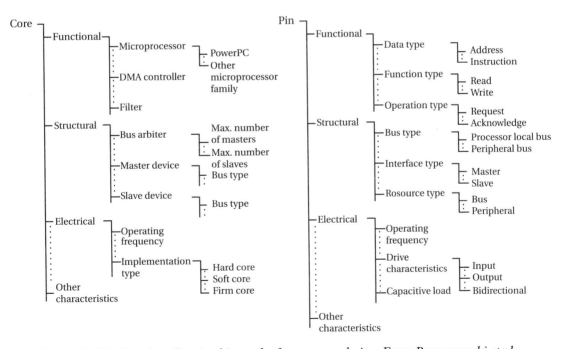

**Figure 5-37** *The classification hierarchy for cores and pins. From Bergamaschi et al. [Ber01] © 2001 IEEE Computer Society.*

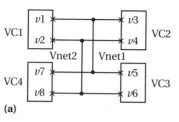

**(a)**

Virtual pin v1 maps to real pin r1(0:0),   output
                        real pin r2(0:15),   input, CONNECTION_LOGIC = CONCAT
Virtual pin v2 maps to real pin r3(0:15),   output
                        real pin r4(0:0),   output, PRIORITY = 2
Virtual pin v3 maps to real pin r5(0:0),   input, CONNECTION_LOGIC = XOR
                        real pin r6(0:3),   output
Virtual pin v4 maps to real pin r7(0:7),   input
                        real pin r8(0:0),   output, PRIORITY = 0
Virtual pin v5 maps to real pin r9(5:11),   output
                        real pin r10(0:0),   output
Virtual pin v6 maps to real pin r11(0:3),   input, CONNECTION_LOGIC = CONCAT
Virtual pin v7 maps to real pin r12(4:0),   output
                        real pin r13(0:0),   output
Virtual pin v8 maps to real pin r14(0:0),   output, PRIORITY = 1

**(b)**

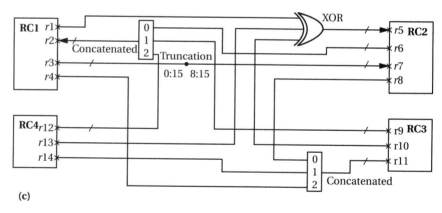

**(c)**

**Figure 5-38** *Virtual-to-real synthesis with interface logic insertion—virtual design (a) through virtual-to-real interface mappings (b) to real design (c). From Bergamaschi et al. [Ber01] © 2000 IEEE Computer Society.*

*wrappers*          Cesario and Jerraya [Ces05] developed a design methodology, based on **wrappers**, that treats both hardware and software as components. As shown in Figure 5-39, a wrapper is a design unit that interfaces a module to another module. A wrapper can be hardware or software and may include both. The wrapper performs only low-level adaptations, such as protocol transformation.

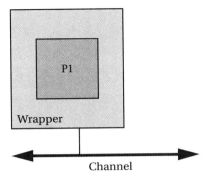

**Figure 5-39** *Components and wrappers.*

Heterogeneous multiprocessor introduce several types of problems:

■ Many chips have multiple communication networks to match the network to the processing needs. Synchronizing communication across network boundaries is more difficult than communicating within a network.

■ Specialized hardware is often needed to accelerate interprocess communication and free the CPU for more interesting computations.

■ The communication primitives should be at a higher level of abstraction than shared memory.

When a dedicated CPU is added to the system, its software must be adapted in several ways:

1. The software must be updated to support the platform's communication primitives.

2. Optimized implementations of the host processor's communication functions must be provided for interprocessor communication.

3. Synchronization functions must be provided.

*system-level design flow*

Figure 5-40 shows the system-level design flow. An abstract platform is created from a combination of system requirements, models of the software, and models of the hardware components. This abstract platform is analyzed to determine the application's performance and power/energy consumption. Based on the results of this analysis, software is allocated and scheduled onto the platform. The result is a golden abstract architecture that can be used to build the implementation.

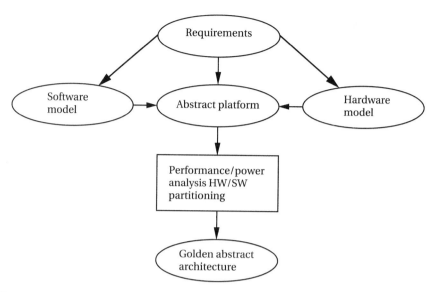

**Figure 5-40** *System-level design flow.*

*abstract architecture template*

Figure 5-41 shows the form of an abstract architecture template, which has three major elements.

1. Software tasks are described by their data and scheduling dependencies; they interface to an API.

2. Hardware components consist of a core and an interface.

3. The hardware/software integration is modeled by the communication network that connects the CPUs that run the software and the hardware IP cores.

*hardware and software abstractions*

Figure 5-42 shows the abstractions that interface hardware and software components to the communications network. On the hardware side, a wrapper that translates signals and protocols is sufficient. On the software side, a number of layers are required, as follows.

■ The application libraries provide application-specific functions.

■ The operating system and communication system, along with its API, provide scheduling and resource management.

■ The hardware abstraction layer and its API provide low-level functions like clock and interrupts.

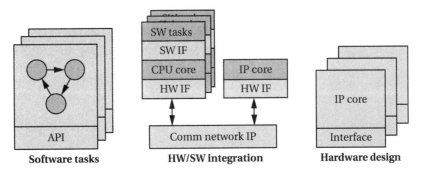

**Figure 5-41** *Abstract architecture template.*

- The CPU executes all these levels of software.

- The CPU wrapper translates signal levels and protocols between the CPU and the communication network.

A wrapper-oriented design methodology presents several challenges. First, the methodology must be supported by tools that automatically generate the

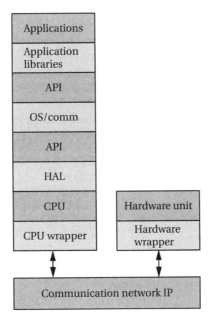

**Figure 5-42** *Hardware and software abstraction layers. From Cesario and Jerraya [Ces05] © 2004 Morgan Kaufmann.*

wrappers and deploy them within the architecture. Wrapper design is tedious and error prone when left to humans. The wrapper generators must be able to build wrappers for several different types of protocols since realistic chips will use several types of interconnect. Furthermore, some wrappers may have to interface two different protocols. The wrapper generator must generate both hardware and software elements. Finally, wrappers must be designed to support mixed-level co-simulation.

*register-transfer implementation*

Given a golden architecture model, we still need to generate the complete register–transfer design of the hardware as well as the final software wrappers. The register–transfer design enumerates all the required components and connects them together. One of the major steps in register-transfer generation is the creation of the memory subsystem. This subsystem may include both connections between internal memory blocks and interfaces to the interconnection network.

## 5.10  Summary

Multiprocessors are at least as important in embedded computing as they are in scientific computing. Multiprocessors are critical to the delivery of real-time computation; they can also be more energy efficient than uniprocessors. Heterogeneous multiprocessors are widely used in embedded applications.

We can adapt all the major components of the multiprocessor to optimization and customization. Care must be taken, of course, not to eliminate necessary flexibility from the architecture, but customization can yield major benefits in cost and power consumption.

A variety of methodologies and tools are available to help design application-specific multiprocessors. The techniques of hardware/software co-design can be used to help tune the multiprocessor architecture to the application.

### What We Have Learned

- A multiprocessor is composed of processing elements and memory elements with an interconnection network.

- Embedded multiprocessors must provide real-time performance and be energy efficient.

- Multiprocessor simulators are built by connecting several uniprocessor simulators, each running as a separate process. Multiprocessors can be simulated at different levels of abstraction.

- Memory systems can be customized to improve real-time performance and reduce energy consumption by isolating parts of the memory from unnecessary accesses.

- The interconnection network can be organized around many different topologies, including both regular and irregular organizations.

- Physically distributed multiprocessors require a reliable time base to be able to reliably perform real-time tasks.

- Design methodologies for embedded multiprocessors must be able to integrate hardware and software from multiple suppliers.

## Further Reading

Dally and Towles [Dal04] and Duato et al. [Dua02] study interconnection networks for multiprocessors. The volume edited by Jantsch and Tenhunen [Jan03] concentrates on networks-on-chips. Bjerregaard and Mahadevan [Bje06] provide a comprehensive review of networks-on-chips. De Micheli et al. [DeM01] collected a number of papers on hardware/software co-design. The volume edited by Jerraya and Wolf [Jer05] contains contributed chapters on multiprocessor systems-on-chips, including network-on-chip design. Kopetz [Kop97] provides a thorough introduction to the design of distributed embedded systems. Peterson and Davie [Pet03] and Stallings [Sta97; Sta04] provide a good introduction to data networking. Helfrick [Hel04] discusses avionics, including aircraft networks. For those interested in the principles of instrument flight, Dogan [Dog99] provides an excellent introduction.

## Questions

**Q5-1** How much harder is it to create a workload for a multiprocessor than it is to design a benchmark for a CPU?

**Q5-2** Estimate the computational workload for a mobile supercomputer. Define a set of tasks and estimate the number of operations per second required for those tasks. Also estimate the amount of memory required to perform those tasks.

**Q5-3** Compare and contrast bus-based multiprocessors versus multiprocessors with more general interconnect structures.

**Q5-4** How would you determine whether an embedded multiprocessor should use more than one type of processing element?

**Q5-5** How would you determine whether a hardwired unit makes sense as a processing element?

**Q5-6**   Compare and contrast a multiprocessor built from a set of identical CPUs versus a multiprocessor with one master CPU of one type and a set of slave CPUs, each of a different type.

**Q5-7**   What types of specialized processing elements might be useful in a cell phone?

**Q5-8**   Given a multiprocessor with $n$ processing elements, how do the worst-case and average path length grow as a function of $n$ for a mesh network? For a tree network?

**Q5-9**   What factors influence the choice of network topology? What factors influence the choice of flow control?

**Q5-10**   Why are packets divided into flits?

**Q5-11**   What characteristics must a memory unit have to support real-time operation?

**Q5-12**   How do we determine the relative size of the active period and idle period required to ensure proper operation of a TTA network?

**Q5-13**   How do faults in processing elements create inconsistencies in the network? How might those inconsistencies be detected by the network?

**Q5-14**   How do the requirements of aircraft and automobile networks differ? How are they similar?

**Q5-15**   Describe a FlexRay bus at the following OSI-compliant levels of detail.

a. Physical

b. Data link

c. Network

d. Transport

**Q5-16**   How could you use a broadcast network like Ethernet for hard real-time control? What assumptions would you have to make? What control mechanisms would need to be added to the network?

**Q5-17**   What sorts of variations might we expect to see in the characteristics of IP components used to build an embedded multiprocessor?

## Lab Exercises

**L5-1**   Simulate several networks using randomly generated Poisson traffic. Compare a bus, a $4 \times 4$ crossbar, and a two-dimensional mesh.

**L5-2**   Develop a program that can connect two different simulators that simulate different instruction set processors.

**L5-3**  Study buffer traffic in an application such as MPEG-2. Determine the average and worst-case buffer sizes required by simulating the application.

**L5-4**  Build a time base for a TTA-style network. The time base provides the same time to all global nodes.

**L5-5**  Build an experimental setup that allows you to monitor messages on an embedded network. Inject errors into the components and try to identify the problem using network information.

**L5-6**  Measure energy for a single instruction versus transmission of a single packet for a sensor network node.

**L5-7**  Identify the IP blocks required to build a complete embedded multiprocessor for an application of your choice.

*Chapter*

# 6

# Multiprocessor Software

- Performance analysis of multiprocessor software
- Middleware and software services
- Design verification of multiprocessor software

## 6.1 Introduction

While real-time operating systems provide apparent concurrency on a single processor, multiprocessor platforms provide true concurrency. The concurrency and performance provided by multiprocessors can be very powerful but also harder to analyze and debug.

The next section briefly reviews what is unique about multiprocessor software as compared to both uniprocessor embedded systems and general-purpose systems. Section 6.3 studies scheduling and performance analysis of multiple tasks running on a multiprocessor. Section 6.4 considers middleware and software stacks as well as design techniques for them. Section 6.5 looks at design verification of multiprocessor systems.

## 6.2 What Is Different about Embedded Multiprocessor Software?

As we move up to software running on embedded multiprocessors, we face two types of differences.

- How is embedded multiprocessor software different from traditional, general-purpose multiprocessor software? We can borrow many techniques

**337**

from general-purpose computing, but some of the challenges in embedded computing systems are unique and require new methods.

■ How is the software in a multiprocessor different from that in a uniprocessor-based system? On the one hand, we would hope that we could port an embedded application from a uniprocessor to a multiprocessor with a minimum of effort, *if* we use the proper abstractions to design the software. But there are some important, fundamental differences.

*heterogeneous processors*

The first pervasive difference is that, as we saw in Chapter 5, embedded multiprocessors are often heterogeneous, with multiple types of processing elements, specialized memory systems, and irregular communication systems. Heterogeneous multiprocessors are less common in general-purpose computing; they also make life considerably more challenging than in the embedded uniprocessor world. Heterogeneity presents several types of problems.

■ Getting software from several types of processors to work together can present challenges. Endianness is one common compatibility problem; library compatibility is another.

■ The development environments for heterogeneous multiprocessors are often loosely coupled. Programmers may have a hard time learning all the tools for all the component processors. It may be hard to debug problems that span multiple CPU types.

■ Different processors may offer different types of resources and interfaces to those resources. Not only does this complicate programming but it also makes it harder to decide certain things at runtime.

*variability*

Another important difference is that delays are much harder to predict in multiprocessors. Delay variations come from several sources: the true concurrency provided by multiprocessors, the larger size of multiprocessors, CPU hetero-geneity, and the structure and the use of the memory system. Larger delays and variances in delays result in many problems, including:

■ Delay variations help expose timing-sensitive bugs that can be hard to test for and even harder to fix. A methodology that avoids timing bugs is the best way to solve concurrency-related timing problems.

■ Variations in computation time make it hard to efficiently use system resources and require more decisions to be made at runtime.

■ Large delays for memory accesses makes it harder to execute code that performs data-dependent operations.

Scheduling a multiprocessor is substantially more difficult than scheduling a uniprocessor. Optimum scheduling algorithms do not exist for most realistic multiprocessor configurations, so heuristics must be used. Equally important, the information that one processor needs to make good scheduling decisions often resides far away on another processor.

Part of the reason that multiprocessor scheduling is hard is that communication is no longer free. Even direct signaling on a wire can take several clock cycles and the memory system may take tens of clock cycles to respond to a request for a location in a remote memory. Because information about the state of other processors takes too long to get, scheduling decisions must be made without full information about the state of those processors. Long delays also cause problems for the software processes that execute on top of the operating system.

Of course, low energy and power consumption are important in multiprocessors, just as in uniprocessors. The solutions to all the challenges of embedded multiprocessor software must be found so that energy-efficient techniques can be used.

*resource allocation*

Many of these problems boil down to resource allocation. Resources must be allocated dynamically to ensure that they are used efficiently. Just knowing which resources are available in a multiprocessor is hard enough. Determining on-the-fly which resources are available in a multiprocessor is hard too. Figuring out how to use those resources to satisfy requests is even harder. As discussed in Section 6.4, middleware takes up the task of managing system resources across the multiprocessor.

## 6.3  Real-Time Multiprocessor Operating Systems

This section looks at multiprocessors real-time operating systems (RTOSs) in general and multiprocessor scheduling in particular. Section 6.3.1 briefly looks at the organization of multiprocessor operating systems. Section 6.3.2 studies scheduling analysis and algorithms for multiprocessors. Section 6.3.3 considers scheduling in the face of dynamically created tasks.

### 6.3.1  Role of the Operating System

An embedded multiprocessor may or may not have a true multiprocessor operating system. In many cases, the various processors run their own operating systems, which communicate to coordinate their activities. In other cases, a more tightly integrated operating system runs across several processing elements (PEs).

*master/slave*

A simple form of multiprocessor operating system is organized with a master and one or more slaves. The **master PE** processor determines the schedules for itself and all the slave processors. Each **slave PE** simply runs the processes assigned to it by the master. This organization scheme is conceptually simple and easy to implement. All the information that is needed for scheduling is kept by the master processor. However, this scheme is better suited to homogeneous processors that have pools of identical processors.

*PE kernel*

Figure 6-1 shows the organization of a multiprocessor operating system in relation to the underlying hardware. Each processor has its own kernel, known as the **PE kernel**. The kernels are responsible for managing purely local resources, such as devices that are not visible to other processors, and implementing the decisions on global resources. The PE kernel selects the processes to run next and switches contexts as necessary.

But the PE kernel may not decide entirely on its own which process runs next. It may receive instructions from a kernel running on another processing element. The kernel that operates as the master gathers information from the slave PEs. Based on the current state of the slaves and the processes that want to run on the slaves, the master PE kernel then issues commands to the slaves about their schedules. The master PE can also run its own jobs.

*limited scheduling information*

One challenge in designing distributed schedulers is that communication is not free and any processor that makes scheduling decisions about other PEs usually will have incomplete information about the state of that PE. When a kernel schedules its own processor, it can easily check on the state of that processor.

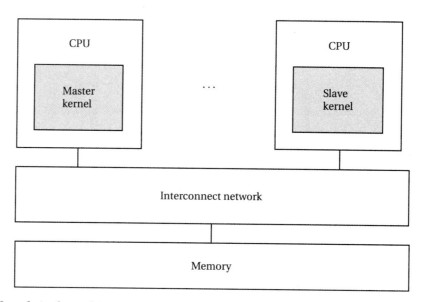

**Figure 6-1** *Kernels in the multiprocessor.*

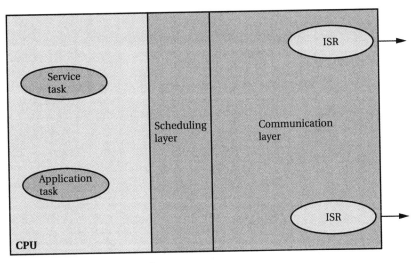

**Figure 6-2** *Custom multiprocessor scheduler and communication.*

When a kernel must perform a remote read to check the state of another processor, the amount of information the kernel requests needs to be carefully budgeted.

*scheduling and communication*   Vercauteren et al. [Ver96] developed a kernel architecture for custom heterogeneous processors. As shown in Figure 6-2, the kernel architecture includes two layers: a scheduling layer and a communication layer. The basic communication operations are implemented by interrupt service routines (ISRs), while the communication layer provides more abstract communication operations. The communication layer provides two types of communication services. The kernel channel is used only for kernel-to-kernel communication—it has high priority and is optimized for performance. The data channel is used by applications and is more general purpose.

The following example looks at the operating systems on the TI OMAP.

---

## Example 6-1

*Operating Systems and Communication in the TI OMAP*

As we saw in Chapter 5, the OMAPI standard defines some core capabilities for multimedia systems. One of the things that OMAPI does not define is the operating systems used in the multiprocessor. The TI OMAP family implements the OMAPI architecture. The following figure shows the lower layers of the TI OMAP, including the hardware and operating systems.

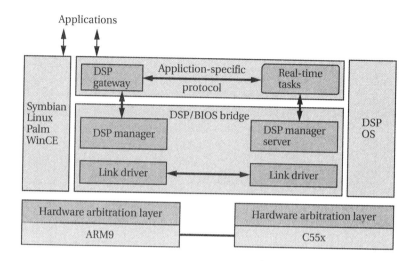

Not only does the OMAPI standard not define an operating system, but the OMAP multiprocessor also does not run a single unified operating system. Each processor runs an existing OS that was already developed for that processor. On the DSP side, the C55x runs the existing C55 operating system. The ARM can run any of several well-known OSs.

The main unifying structure in OMAP is the DSPBridge, which allows the DSP and RISC processor to communicate. The bridge includes a set of hardware primitives that are abstracted by a layer of software. The bridge is organized as a master/slave system in which the ARM is the master and the C55x is the slave. This fits the nature of most multimedia applications, where the DSP is used to efficiently implement certain key functions while the RISC processor runs the higher levels of the application. The DSPBridge API implements several functions: it initiates and controls DSP tasks, exchanges messages with the DSP, streams data to and from the DSP, and checks the status of the DSP.

The OMAP hardware provides several mailbox primitives—separate addressable memories that can be accessed by both. In the OMAP 5912, two of the mailboxes can be written only by the C55x but read by both it and the ARM, while two can be written only by the ARM and read by both processors.

## 6.3.2  Multiprocessor Scheduling

In general, multiprocessor scheduling is NP-complete [Gar79]. That is, if we want to minimize total execution time on an arbitrary processor, we have no

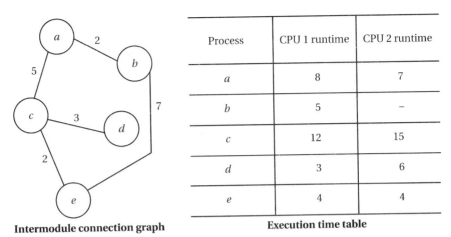

| Process | CPU 1 runtime | CPU 2 runtime |
|---------|---------------|---------------|
| a | 8 | 7 |
| b | 5 | – |
| c | 12 | 15 |
| d | 3 | 6 |
| e | 4 | 4 |

Intermodule connection graph                     Execution time table

**Figure 6-3**  *Models for Stone's multiprocessor scheduling algorithm. After Stone [Sto77].*

known way to find the shortest schedule in polynomial time. Of course, many NP-complete problems have useful approximations and heuristics. By taking advantage of what we know about the multiprocessor structure, by limiting the combinations of process executions that we consider, or by other simplifications, we can create a number of simplified but useful multiprocessor scheduling problems. For example, two-processor multiprocessors can be scheduled optimally under some conditions.

*network flow*

One of the first multiprocessor algorithms was developed by Stone [Sto77]. Although he referred to the problem as a scheduling one, it is more accurately referred to as an allocation problem, since it selected the CPUs on which to execute processes but only implicitly the times at which they executed. He solved the problem using network flow algorithms. Stone's model considered a network of heterogeneous processors. He found an exact solution to the two-processor scheduling problem and heuristics to solve schedules for systems with arbitrary numbers of processors.

As shown in Figure 6-3, the problem is scheduled in two parts. An **intermodule connection graph** describes the time cost of communicating between two processes that are assigned to different processors; communication between processes on the same processor has zero cost. The execution time table specifies the execution time of each process on each processor; it is possible that not all processes will be able to run on both processors.

The minimum running time balances the communication cost and the execution cost. Stone formulates the scheduling problem as one of finding a cutset of a modified version of the intermodule connection graph.

- Two additional nodes are added to represent the two processors. One such node is the source of the graph (representing CPU 1) and the other is the sink (representing CPU 2).

- Edges are added from each non-sink node to the source and the sink. The weight of an edge to the source is equal to the cost of executing that node's module on CPU 2 (the sink); the weight of an edge to the sink is equal to the cost of executing that node's module on CPU 1 (the source).

The cutset divides the intermodule connection graph into two sets, with the nodes in each set being assigned to the same processor. The weight of a cutset is the cost of an assignment of the nodes to the two processors as given by the cutset. To find the allocation that minimizes the total execution time, we solve a maximum flow problem on the graph.

Stone extended the problem to *n* processors by generalizing the notion of a cutset. The generalized cutset divides the graph into *n* disjoint subsets such that no proper subset of a cutset is also a cutset. He generalized the node to include *n* types of distinguished nodes rather than just the source and sink. His heuristic for solving this problem iteratively used several two-processor assignments to find the *n*-processor assignment.

*Why static tasks?*

Many embedded systems statically allocate processes to processing elements. We can efficiently find bounds on the execution time of the processes in these multiprocessor systems. We will assume that there is a set of processes with data dependencies between them; in general, they can form one or more subtasks. We will also assume that each CPU schedules processes using rate-monotonic scheduling. Although we can easily figure out the schedule if we don't have data dependencies, the combination of data dependencies and rate-monotonic scheduling makes the problem more challenging, although tractable.

*minimizing buffer sizes*

Bhattacharyya et al. [Bha97] developed methods to efficiently schedule synchronous data flow graphs on multiprocessors. Figure 6-4 shows an SDF graph with the nodes assigned to processing elements in a multiprocessor. We are primarily interested in the communication between PEs, since we can schedule each SDF on a processor using other methods that produce a sequential schedule. We model the system using an **interprocessor communication modeling (IPC) graph**, also shown in the figure. The IPC graph has the same nodes as the SDF graph. The IPC graph has all the edges of the SDF graph plus additional edges. We add edges to the IPC graph to model the sequential schedule on each PE; these edges are shown by the dashed line in the figure.

The edges in the allocated SDF graph that cross processor boundaries are known in the IPC graph as **IPC edges** because they define interprocessor communication. Any communication across an IPC edge must use an interprocess communication mechanism to cross the boundary between the processors.

We can determine whether communication across each IPC edge is bounded; edges not in a strongly **connected component** (SCC) are not bounded. When

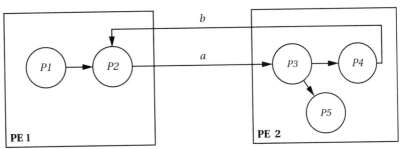

**SDF graph and processor allocation**

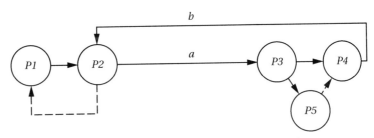

**Interprocessor communication modeling graph**

**Figure 6-4** *Models for multiprocessor communication.*

implementing interprocess communication on an unbounded edge, we can use a protocol that ensures that the number of tokens crossing the edge does not exceed a predetermined buffer size. We can implement interprocess communication on bounded edges by using a simpler protocol.

The IPC graph may have some redundant edges. An edge *e* is redundant if there is another path from *source(e)* to *sink(e)* that has a longer delay than the delay along *e*. The redundant edges do not have to be removed in any particular order to ensure that we remove the maximum number of redundant edges.

The asymptotic iteration period *T* for a strongly connected IPC graph *G* is

$$T = \sum_{cycle\, C \in G} \frac{\sum_{v \in C} t(v)}{delay(C)},$$
(EQ 6-1)

where *C* is a cycle through the graph, *t(v)* is the execution time of a node *v*, and *delay(C)* is the sum of the delays around the path *C*. *T* is also known as the **cycle mean**. The maximum cycle mean of an IPC graph, $\lambda_{max}$, is the largest cycle mean for any SCC in the graph. A cycle whose cycle mean is equal to the maximum is known as a **critical cycle**.

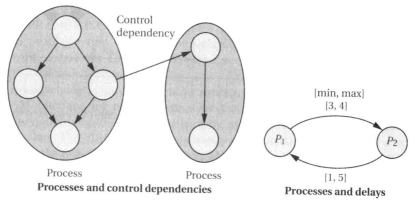

**Figure 6-5** *RATAN process model.*

We can construct a strongly connected synchronization graph by adding edges between strongly connected components. We add edges that chain together source SCCs, edges that chain together sink SCCs, and an edge that connects the overall sink of the graph to the source. (A strongly connected component is a **source SCC** if any edge whose sink is in the strongly connected component also has its source in the strongly connected component. A **sink SCC** is such that any edge whose source is in the SCC also has its sink in the SCC.)

We need to add delays to the edges, corresponding to buffer memory, that ensure the system will not deadlock and that we can minimize the sum of the buffer bounds over all the IPC edges. We can use the added edges to help us determine these delays—the added edges can be divided into disjoint sets that help organize the graph. Delay can be added optimally if the graph has one source SCC and one sink SCC, and it is heuristic if the graph's structure is more complex. We can determine the minimum delay on each edge that ensures that the graph's cycle mean is not exceeded.

Mathur et al. [Mat98] developed the RATAN tool for analyzing the rates of multiple-tasking systems. As shown in Figure 6-5, a process consists of a single-threaded CDFG-style model. Data dependencies may extend from a node within one process to a node within another process. When we look only at the processes themselves, and the edges between them, a control edge is labeled with [min,max] delays measured from the activation signal for the process to the start of execution. Those bounds are specifications on the allowable delay; our goal is to find execution rates for the processes that satisfy these bounds. A process starts to execute after all of its enable signals have become ready.

If we denote the delay of an edge $i \rightarrow j$ in the graph as $d_{ij}$, then the delay of a cycle $C$ in the process graph is given by

$$d(C) = \sum_{(i,j) \in C} \delta_{ij}.$$ 

(EQ 6-2)

The mean delay of the cycle is given by

$$\frac{d(C)}{|C|},$$   (EQ 6-3)

where $|C|$ is the number of edges in $C$. The maximum mean cycle delay is known as $\lambda$. In a strongly connected graph, all nodes execute at the same rate, namely $\lambda$.

We call $[r_l(X), r_u(X)]$ the lower and upper bounds on the rate of a subgraph $X$. If we have two maximal SCC of the graph, $P$ and $C$, and the graph has edges from $P$ to $C$, then $P$ is a producer and $C$ is a consumer; therefore the actual rate interval for the consumer $C$ is

$$[\min\{r_l(P), r_l(P)\}, \min\{r_u(P), r_u(C)\}].$$   (EQ 6-4)

*data dependencies and scheduling*

The problems created by data dependencies are illustrated in Figure 6-6. Here, two subtasks are divided among three processors. Take, for example, processing element $M_1$. This CPU runs two processes that will clearly affect each other's schedules. But the completion times of the processes on $M_1$ also depends on the behavior of the processes on all the other PEs in the system. Data dependencies link $P_1$ and $P_2$, which adds $M_2$ to the set of interrelated PEs. The data dependency between $P_3$ and $P_4$ also adds $M_3$ to the system.

Getting a process to run faster doesn't always help. Consider Figure 6-7; in this example, changing the computation time of process $P_x$ changes the response time of $P_3$ even though they run on different processors. The data dependencies

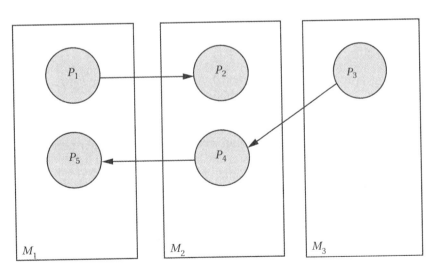

**Figure 6-6** *Preemption and scheduling.*

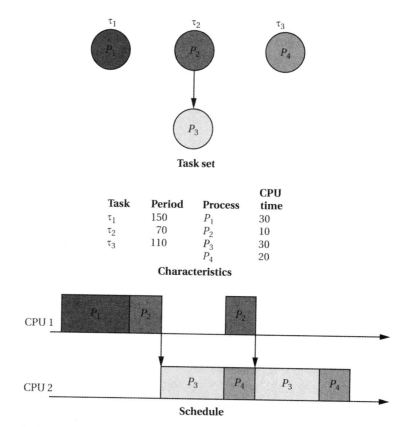

| Task | Period | Process | CPU time |
|------|--------|---------|----------|
| $\tau_1$ | 150 | $P_1$ | 30 |
| $\tau_2$ | 70 | $P_2$ | 10 |
| $\tau_3$ | 110 | $P_3$ | 30 |
| | | $P_4$ | 20 |

**Characteristics**

**Figure 6-7** *Period shifting. From Yen and Wolf [Yen98] © 1998 IEEE.*

cause the shortened computation time of $P_x$, resulting in process $P_2$ running sooner and preempting $P_3$.

*unrolled schedules*

Ramamritham [Ram90b] proposed scheduling over an unrolled schedule. He noted that the maximum interval that must be considered for a set of processes is the **least common multiple** (LCM) of their periods; in a longer schedule, the order of processes must necessarily repeat itself. He then constructed a schedule using the LCM interval.

*response time theorem*

To develop bounds on the CPUs in the system, we can make use of a theorem from Lehoczy et al. [Leh89]. They bounded the response times for a set of independent (no data dependencies) processes running on a single CPU. The processes are $\{P_1, P_2, ...\}$, with $P_1$ being the highest-priority process. The minimum period of the $i^{th}$ process is $p_i$ and its worst-case execution time is $c_i$. The worst-case response time of $P_i$ is $w_i$, which can be computed as the smallest non-negative root of

$$x = g(x) = c_i + \sum_{j=1}^{i-1} \lceil x/p_j \rceil. \tag{EQ 6-5}$$

The $c_i$ term gives the computation time for the process. The $x/p_j$ terms give the fraction of the period of each process that delays the execution of the $i^{th}$ process. We cannot solve this equation directly but can use numerical methods to solve it. We can use the worst-case response times of the various processes to help us solve the system schedule. But this formula is not sufficient because it does not take into account the data dependencies either between the CPUs or within a CPU. To handle those data dependencies, we need to use a more complex graph algorithm.

*static scheduling algorithm*

Yen and Wolf [Yen98] developed an algorithm that handles multiple CPUs and data dependencies. This algorithm models the processes to be run as a task graph that can have one or more subtasks. Each process in the task graph is given bounds for its computation time $[c_i^{lower}, c_i^{upper}]$. This is more general than a single, fixed computation time, but it does assume that we can strictly bound the computation time of a process. Each subtask has a period that is also modeled as an interval $[p_i^{lower}, p_i^{upper}]$. The architecture of the platform is modeled as a processor graph. The allocation of each process in the task graph to a processing element is given in Figure 6-8.

The algorithm finds bounds on the start and the finish times of the processes. Given a process $P_i$, the start time is bounded by earliest[$P_i$, request] and latest[$P_i$, request]; the end time is bounded by earliest[$P_i$, finish] and latest[$P_i$, finish].

*delay estimation algorithm*

The following code summarizes the delay estimation algorithm. The maxsep[] data structure holds the earliest[] and latest[] bounds for each process; it starts out with infinite (unbounded) times for the processes. This performance analysis algorithm iteratively tightens these bounds until they stop changing (or until a predetermined iteration limit is reached).

```
maxsep.lower = maxsep.upper = infinity;
step = 0; /* keep track of number of iterations */
do {
    /* use longest path algorithm to find the request and finish times */
    foreach P_i { EarliestTimes(G_i); LatestTimes(G_i);
    /* handle max constraints */
    foreach P_i { MaxSeparations (G_i);
    step++;
} while (maxsep has changed and step < limit);
```

At each iteration, the algorithm performs two types of operations. The EarliestTimes()/LatestTimes() procedures analyzes data dependencies using a

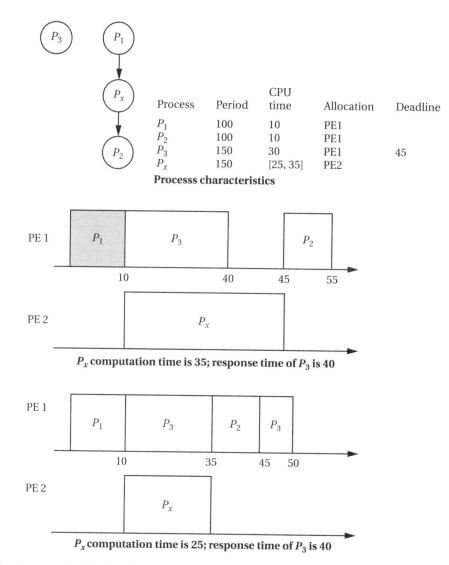

**Figure 6-8** *An example of reduced computation time leading to longer response times. From Yen and Wolf [Yen98].*

modified longest-path algorithm. The MaxSeparations() procedure uses a modified max-constraint algorithm to look for combinations of process executions that cannot occur. Each of these procedures is applied separately to each subtask $P_i$ in the task graph, but the procedures look at the execution times of all the other subtasks while updating $P_i$.

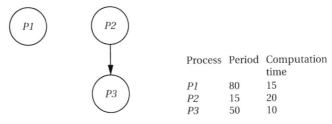

| Process | Period | Computation time |
|---------|--------|------------------|
| P1 | 80 | 15 |
| P2 | 15 | 20 |
| P3 | 50 | 10 |

**Figure 6-9** *An example of phase adjustment and separation analysis. From Yen and Wolf [Yen98] © 1998 IEEE*

To understand why we need these two steps, consider the example of Figure 6-9. A naive analysis might lead one to conclude that the total time required to finish both tasks is 80. But two conditions cause it to be shorter. First, *P1* cannot preempt both *P2* and *P3* in a single execution of the task. Second, *P2* cannot preempt *P3* since *P2* must finish before *P3* can start. Therefore, the worst-case delay to execute both tasks is only 45.

*phase constraints*

We will use phase constraints to summarize the relationships between a process that is preempted and the process that preempts one. The algorithm uses two types of phases.

- The **request phase** $\phi_{ij}^r$, which we will call phase[i,j,r] in the code, describes the smallest interval between the execution of $P_i$ on one iteration and the succeeding iteration of $P_j$.

- The **finishing phase** $\phi_{ij}^f$, which we will call phase[i,j,f] in the code, describes the smallest interval between the finishing time of one iteration of $P_i$ and the first request time of the next iteration of $P_j$.

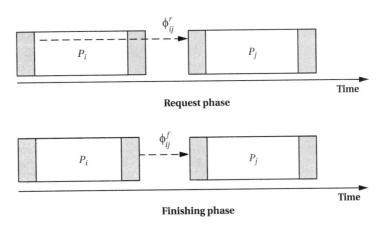

**Figure 6-10** *Request and finishing phases.*

These definitions are illustrated in Figure 6-10. The gray boxes at the ends of the boxes represent the min/max timing bounds.

Data dependencies are one form of constraint on the relative execution times of processes. LatestTimes() and EarliestTimes() are modified longest-path algorithms that determine the timing and slack of the processes based on their data dependencies. Pseudocode for LatestTimes() is shown in the following block of code from [Yen98]; it is similar in form to the EarliestTimes() procedure.

```
LatestTimes(G) {
    /* initialize */
    foreach (process P_i) {
        latest[P_i,request] = 0;
        foreach (process P_j) phase[i,j,r] = 0;
    }
    foreach (process P_i in topological order) {
        w_i = worst-case response time of P_i with phase adjustment phase[i,j,r];
        foreach (process P_j such that priority(P_j) > priority(P_i)) {
            latest{P_i,finish] = latest[P_i,request]+w_i
            calculate phase[i,j,f] relative to latest[P_i,finish] for each j;
            foreach (immediate successor P_k of P_i) {
                delta = latest[P_k,request] 2 latest[P_i,finish];
                if (latest[P_k,request] < latest[P_i,finish])
                    latest[P_k,request] = latest[P_i,finish]
                update phase[k,j,r] for each process P_j according to
                    phase[i,j,f] and delta;
            }
        }
    }
}
```

The algorithm walks through the graphs in the order in which they appear in the task graph. The worst-case response time $w_i$ is computed using EQ 6-6, with the modification that the term inside the summation takes into account the request phase:

$$x = g(x) = c_i + c\sum_{j=1}^{i-1}\left\lceil (x - \phi_{ij}^r)/p_j \right\rceil. \tag{EQ 6-6}$$

After we have computed $w_i$, we then compute the phases relative to latest[$P_i$, finish]. There are two cases to consider, $P_j$ preempts $P_i$ and $P_j$ does not preempt $P_i$. Updating the request phases requires looking ahead one iteration, examining the successor $P_k$s of $P_i$. If $\delta > 0$, then there is slack between the latest finish time of

$P_i$ and the latest request time of $P_k$. If $\delta > 0$, then the request phase $\phi_{ij}^r$ must be updated. We then update

$$\phi_{kj}^r = \min\left(\phi_{kj}^r, \phi_{ij}^f\right).$$

These relationships are illustrated in Figure 6-11.

The MaxSeparations() procedure uses combinations of processes that cannot interfere to tighten the bounds on execution time. It uses the results of the phase analysis performed in LatestTimes() and EarliestTimes() to check the separations of phases of processes, taking preemption into account.

Max constraints model the relationship between a process and its predators: the initiation time of a process is the max of the finish times of its predecessors. Max constraints are harder to solve than the linear constraints imposed by data dependencies. We can use a modified version of an algorithm developed by McMillan and Dill [McM92] to solve these constraints.

*event-oriented analysis*
An alternative approach to performance analysis, SymTA/S, is based on **events** [Hen05]. The inputs and outputs to the system and between the processing elements are modeled as events. Unlike rate-monotonic analysis, which assumes one event per period, the SymTA/S model allows a more complex description of when events can and must occur. SymTA/S starts with a description of the system, including the tasks and their mapping to processing elements, as well as the set of input events. It produces the output events and, as a side effect, the internal events as well. SymTA/S does not, strictly speaking, provide a schedule for the processes, but it does provide tight bounds on when processes can be scheduled to assure that they meet the input requirements.

*event model*
An event is an atomic action. We can describe several categories of events, depending on their timing behavior. A **simple event model** is defined by a period **P**. These events happen strictly periodically. A **jitter event model** has a period and jitter *(P,J)*. These events occur at roughly the described period, but

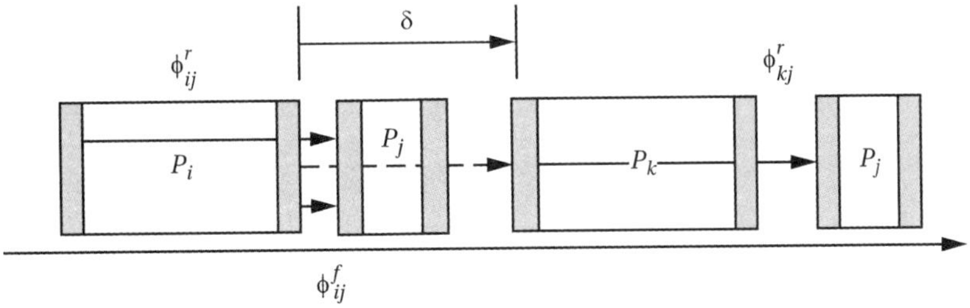

**Figure 6-11** *Relationships related to phases.*

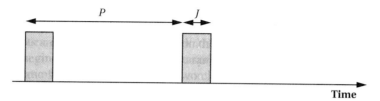

**Figure 6-12** *A jitter event model.*

they can appear within the jitter interval as shown in Figure 6-12. An **event function model** allows us to vary the number of events in an interval. The number of events in an interval $\Delta t$ ranges between $\eta^l(\Delta t)$ and $\eta^u(\Delta t)$.

An event function counts the number of events in an interval, so it is a piecewise constant function with unit steps—each step adds one more event to the system. We can also define a periodic with jitter event model as

$$\eta^l_{P+J} = \max\left(0, \left\lfloor \frac{\Delta t - J}{P} \right\rfloor\right),$$
(EQ 6-7)

$$\eta^u_{P+J} = \left\lceil \frac{\Delta t + J}{P} \right\rceil.$$
(EQ 6-8)

We can also define a **minimum distance function** $\delta^{min}(N)$ and **maximum distance function** $\delta^{max}(N)$, which define the minimum and maximum distance between $N$ = two or more events. We can describe **sporadic events** as periodic event streams with the lower bound on the number of events per unit time as zero.

*output event*
*timing*

As illustrated in Figure 6-13, processing elements consume input events and emit output events. SymTA/S concentrates on modeling the timing, not the functionality, between these inputs and outputs. Because these event models are relatively simple, we can easily calculate the timing of an output event given the input event. A strictly periodic input event produces a strictly periodic output

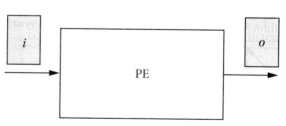

**Figure 6-13** *Input events produce output events.*

event. In the case of an event with jitter, we just add the response time jitter (that is, the difference between minimum and maximum response times) to the input jitter in order to find the output event's jitter:

$$d(J_{out} = J_{in} + (t_{resp,max} - t_{resp,min})) . \qquad \text{(EQ 6-9)}$$

*system timing analysis*

We need to be able to analyze the timing of a system of processing elements by computing the relationships between the outputs of one processing element and the input of another. Analysis starts with the definitions of the input events, which are given by the designer; analysis determines the events at the system outputs and along the way generates the internal events between the processing elements.

As illustrated in Figure 6-14, some systems may be unanalyzable because they have cyclic scheduling dependencies. The figure shows two input events but each processing element (*R1* and *R2*) has a task with a missing input. These PEs communicate, but we need to know the timing of *R2* to calculate the output of *R1* (which feeds *R2*), while we need to know the timing of *R1* to calculate the output of *R2* (which feeds *R1*). These dependencies between events makes it impossible to start and finish the analysis.

*task activation*

Events activate tasks; we can define combinations of events that are required to activate a task. An AND activation requires all of a set of events to activate; an OR activation requires any of a set of events to activate. We do not allow NOT activations because those would turn off events and make analysis intractable.

*AND activation*

As shown in Figure 6-15, an AND activation task takes events at its inputs and fires when all its inputs are available. Each input is buffered with a queue since events may not all arrive at the same time. However, to ensure that the buffers are of finite size, we require that all the inputs to an AND-activation task

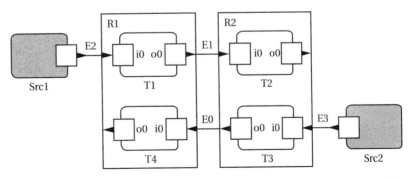

**Figure 6-14** *A cyclic scheduling dependency. From Henia et al. [Hen05] © 2005 IEEE.*

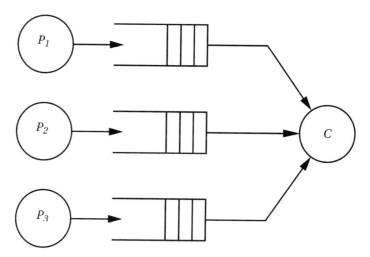

**Figure 6-15** *An AND-activation task.*

have the same arrival rate. The activation jitter of the AND-activation task is determined by the largest jitter of any of the inputs:

$$J_{AND} = \max_i(J_i). \qquad \text{(EQ 6-10)}$$

*OR-activation*

An OR-activated task does not require input buffers since any input event is immediately consumed. However, analysis of OR-activated tasks is more complex than that of AND-activated tasks precisely because OR-activated tasks are more easily activated. Figure 6-16 illustrates a pair of input events and their resulting OR activations. One input stream has $P_1 = 4, J_1 = 2$ while the other has $P_2 = 3, J_2 = 2$.

Although each input event stream can be characterized by this event model, the OR-activation stream cannot. The OR combination of these input event streams has an irregular pattern that does not fit any of our analyzable event models. We must therefore use an approximation of the activation stream as shown in part (d) Figure 6-16, using a periodic with jitter model.

*OR activation period*

The period of an OR-activation is determined by unrolling the schedule to find the hyperperiod. We find the least-common multiple of the input event periods and divide that by the sum of all the input events over that hyperperiod (assuming no jitter). This can be written as

$$P_{OR} = \frac{LCM(P_i)}{\displaystyle\sum_{i=1}^{n} \frac{LCM(P_i)}{P_i}} = \frac{1}{\displaystyle\sum_{i=1}^{n} \frac{1}{P_i}}. \qquad \text{(EQ 6-11)}$$

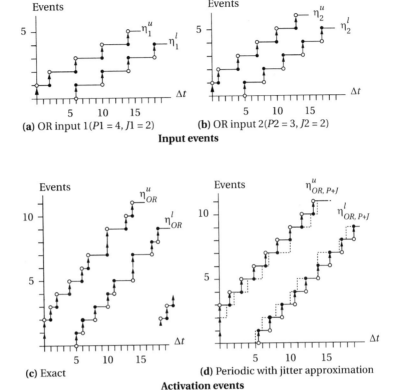

**Figure 6-16** *OR activations and approximations. From Henia et al. [Hena05] © IEEE.*

*OR activation jitter*

The OR-activation jitter needs to be approximated, as shown in Figure 6-16. We want to find the smallest jitter that satisfies these inequalities:

$$\left\lceil \frac{\Delta t + J_{OR}}{P_{OR}} \right\rceil \geq \sum_{i=1}^{n} \left\lceil \frac{\Delta t + J_i}{P_i} \right\rceil \qquad \text{(EQ 6-12)}$$

$$max\left(0, \left\lfloor \frac{\Delta t - J_{OR}}{P_{OR}} \right\rfloor\right) \geq \sum_{i=1}^{n} max\left(0, \left\lfloor \frac{\Delta t - J_i}{P_i} \right\rfloor\right). \qquad \text{(EQ 6-13)}$$

We can evaluate (EQ 6-12) piecewise in order to bound the OR-activation jitter. Each piece can be written as:

$$\left\lceil \frac{\Delta t + J_{OR,j}}{P_{OR}} \right\rceil \geq k_j, \Delta t_j \leq \Delta t \leq \Delta t_{j+1}, \tag{EQ 6-14}$$

where $k_j$ is a natural number. The ceiling function monotonically increases in $\Delta t$, so we need to evaluate it only for the smallest value of $\Delta t$, which approaches $\Delta t_j$. This gives

$$J_{OR,j} \geq (k_j - 1)P_{OR} - \Delta t_j. \tag{EQ 6-15}$$

*cyclic task dependencies*

Tasks can be connected in cycles—either primitive cycles where the output of a task feeds its own input, or long cycles in which a series of tasks folds back on to itself. AND activation is the natural mode for tasks in cycles. However, an AND-activated task has a larger jitter at its output than at its input in our basic analysis. This would mean that cycles of tasks could never be stable. To analyze tasks, we cut the cycle, analyze the open-loop system, and check the results in the closed-loop context.

*contextual analysis*

The basic event models do not describe correlation between events. In realistic systems, events can be correlated in a way that allows us to usefully narrow the range of feasible schedules. Correlations often come from **context-dependent behavior**, which can come from either of two sources: different types of events and internal modes in the tasks. We can use these behaviors to define correlations within a single stream known as **intra-event stream context**. We can also find **inter-event stream contexts** that allow us to find relationships, such as offsets, between events in two different streams.

*distributed software synthesis*

Kang et al. [Kan99b] developed a tool suite to synthesize distributed implementations of signal processing algorithms. Their methodology is shown in Figure 6-17. The designer provides the task graph, the hardware platform architecture, and design constraints such as deadlines. The designer also provides statistical information about process behavior in the form of probability distribution functions.

During synthesis, each subgraph of the task graph is treated as an independent **channel**. Processes in the subgraph are executed quasicyclically. Time is divided into quanta and each process is assigned a time budget and a position in the schedule known as an **interval**. Processes may use additional time quanta if the load is low enough that extra quanta are available.

The **load threshold estimator** determines the schedule for processes. It figures out the throughput required for each channel, allocates processes to processing elements to balance load, and schedules the intervals to minimize latency. Because load is modeled statistically, iterative algorithms must be used to allocate processes. To analyze a channel, the estimator breaks it into chains, analyzes each chain separately, then combines the estimates into an overall estimate for the complete channel. Because the load may vary, system behavior is validated through simulation.

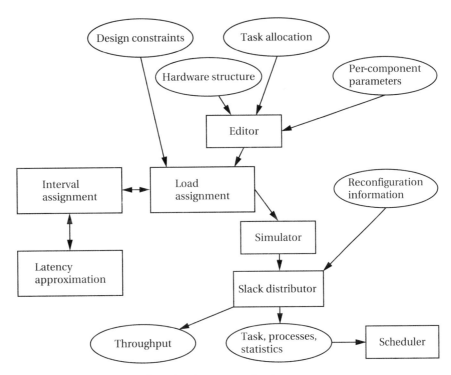

**Figure 6-17** *A methodology for distributed software synthesis.*

### 6.3.3  Scheduling with Dynamic Tasks

*dynamic tasks*

When tasks arrive at the system dynamically, we cannot guarantee that we will be able to meet the required demand. Unless the source of the tasks limits itself, it may generate more task requests than the system can allow. A system that takes dynamically-allocated tasks must figure out on-the-fly whether it can accept a task and, in the case of a multiprocessor, which processing element should handle the task. This decision needs to be accomplished quickly. If task allocation is performed by a node that performs other tasks, scheduling overhead eats into the available CPU time for useful work. Even if task allocation is performed by a dedicated processor, longer decision times delay the task from starting execution, giving it less time to complete before its deadline.

General-purpose multiprocessors commonly receive dynamic tasks from users. The multiprocessor operating system allocates tasks to processors based on system loads. However, general-purpose multiprocessors are often homogeneous, which simplifies many scheduling decisions. Embedded multiprocessors are often heterogeneous. As a result, not all tasks may run on all nodes. Although this simplifies some scheduling decisions—a task that runs on only one node must run on that node—it complicates other matters. If a processing element can run a combination of general-purpose tasks and specialized tasks, then it may accept general-purpose tasks before it knows that it will be required to run a specialized task. The operating system can either reserve the processing element for specialized tasks, thus wasting computational capability, or it must be able to move tasks on-the-fly to make room for the specialized task.

*dynamic task scheduling*

Ramaritham et al. [Ram90a] developed a **myopic algorithm** for dynamic scheduling of real-time tasks. Their algorithm performs a heuristic search to find a good schedule for a newly arrived task. They assume that the tasks are nonperiodic and executed nonpreemptively; they also assume that there are no data dependencies between tasks. Each task is characterized by its arrival time $T_A$, its deadline time $T_D$, worst-case processing time $T_P$, and resource requirements $\{T_R\}$.

*search metrics*

The factor that chooses which process to schedule next during a search can be encapsulated as a decision function $H$. Possible decision functions include shortest deadline first, shortest processing time first, minimum earliest start time first, or minimum laxity first.

search algorithms for scheduling

The search algorithm constructs partial schedules during its search, starting from a set of tasks $P = \{p_i\}$ that need to be scheduled. It adds tasks to the schedule to create more complete schedules. It may also backtrack, removing tasks from the partial schedule to try another solution. At each point in the search, a task is taken from $P$ and added to the partial schedule $S$; we call the depleted task set $P$ and the remaining tasks $P_R$. A partial schedule is **strongly feasible** if the partial schedule itself is feasible and every possible next choice for a task to execute also creates a feasible partial schedule.

The myopic algorithm considers only a subset of the remaining tasks during search. It keeps $P_R$ sorted by deadlines and takes only the first $k$ tasks in the set. It then evaluates $H$ for these $k$ tasks and chooses the best task to add to the partial schedule. If $k$ is small relative to the total number of tasks, then this process is approximately linear in the total number of tasks.

*load balancing*

**Load balancing** is a form of dynamic task allocation in which the tasks come from internal sources. A processing element may decide to shift one of its tasks somewhere else in the system for any of several reasons: it inaccurately estimated its ability to finish all its tasks; it wants to improve cache behavior or some other performance metric; or it needs to accept a task that can only run on a subset of the available PEs.

To balance processor loads, we must be able to stop a task running on one PE, save its state, and restore that state on the new processing element—a procedure often called **task** or **process migration**. This task may be straightforward or difficult depending on the situation.

■ **Homogeneous multiprocessor with shared memory**—In this case, we can copy the task's activation record from the old PE to the new PE and restart the PE.

■ **Heterogeneous multiprocessor with shared memory**—We have to assume that we have versions of the code available that will run on both new and old PEs. In this case, we cannot simply copy the activation record from one type of processor to another type. In certain cases, there may be a straightforward transformation between the activation record information of the two PEs. In general, we must use specialized code in the processes that will save the task state in memory so that we do not need to explicitly transfer the activation record.

■ **Multiprocessor with nonshared memory**—If the PEs do not execute tasks in a shared memory area, we must copy all of the program data (and possibly code) from the old PE to the new one. This is generally expensive and it is unlikely that tasks can be usefully migrated without shared memory.

*load-balancing algorithm*

Shin and Chang [Shi89] developed a load-balancing algorithm for real-time multiprocessors. Each processing element in the system maintains a **buddy list** of nodes with which it can share tasks; the buddies may be determined, for example, by the communication cost between the processors. To make scheduling decisions quickly, processing elements send information about their state to the PEs on their buddy list. Each PE may be in one of three states: underloaded, medium loaded, or fully loaded. When a PE changes state, it sends an update to all its buddies.

Each PE further organizes the buddy list into a **preferred list**, which is ordered by the communication distance of the processing element. When a PE wants to move a task to another node, it requests help from the first underloaded PE on its preferred list. By properly constructing the preferred PE lists, the system can ensure that each processing element is at the head of no more than one other PE. This reduces the chance that a PE will be overwhelmed by multiple task migration requests.

## 6.4 Services and Middleware for Embedded Multiprocessors

This section considers the services provided by an embedded multiprocessor. Such services can be provided by the operating system or by other software packages, but the services are used to build applications. Services may include

*What is middleware?*

relatively low-level operations, I/O device handling, interprocessor communication, and scheduling. It may also provide higher-level services.

Many services are provided by **middleware**—a term coined for general-purpose systems to describe software that provides services for applications in distributed systems and multiprocessors. Middleware is not the application itself, nor does it describe primitive services provided by the operating system. Middleware may provide fairly generic data services, such as data transport among processors that may have different endianness or other data formatting issues. Middleware can also provide application-specific services.

Middleware is used in embedded systems for several purposes.

■ It provides basic services that allow applications to be developed more quickly. Those services may be tied to a particular processing element or an I/O device. Alternatively, they may provide higher-level communication services.

■ It simplifies porting applications from one embedded platform to another. Middleware standards are particularly useful since the application itself can be moved to any platform that supports the middleware.

■ It ensures that key functions are implemented efficiently and correctly. Rather than rely on users to directly implement all functions, a vendor may provide middleware that showcases the features of the platform.

*Middleware and resource allocation*

One of the key differences between middleware and software libraries is that middleware manages resources dynamically. In a uniprocessor, the operating system manages the resources on the processor (for example, the CPU itself, the devices, etc.) and software libraries perform computational tasks based on those allocations. In a distributed system or multiprocessor, middleware allocates system resources, giving requests to the operating systems on the individual processors to implement those decisions.

One reason that resources need to be allocated at runtime, not just statically by designer decisions, is that the tasks performed by the system vary over time. If we statically allocate resources, we end up with a drastically overdesigned system that is not only very expensive but burns much more power. Dynamic allocation lets us make more efficient use of resources (and hopefully manage cases in which we do not have enough resources to properly handle all the current requests). Embedded systems increasingly employ middleware because they must perform a complex set of tasks whose resource requirements cannot be easily evaluated statically.

*embedded versus general-purpose stacks*

A key trade-off is generality versus efficiency. General-purpose computing systems are built with software stacks that provide useful abstractions at different levels of granularity. Those stacks are often deep and provide a rich set of functions. The constraints on embedded computing systems—power/energy consumption, memory space, and real-time performance—often dictate that we design software stacks more carefully.

Embedded system designers have experimented with a variety of middleware architectures. Some systems make liberal use of general standards: Internet Protocol (IP), CORBA, and so on. Other systems define their own services and support. The extent to which standard services versus custom services are used to build middleware is a key design decision for embedded multiprocessors and distributed systems.

The next section looks at middleware based on standards; Section 6.4.2 looks at middleware for systems-on-chips. Section 6.4.3 concentrates on quality-of-service (QoS), an important type of service in many embedded systems.

### 6.4.1 Standards-Based Services

A number of middleware systems have been built using various combinations of standard services; the Internet Protocol is one that's often used. CORBA has also been used as a model for distributed embedded services.

The **Common Object Request Broker Architecture** (**CORBA**) [Obj06] is widely used as an architecture for middleware services. It is not itself a specific protocol; rather it is a metamodel that describes object-oriented services. CORBA services are provided by **objects** that combine functional interfaces as well as data. An interface to an object is defined in an **interactive data language** (**IDL**). The IDL specification is language-independent and can be implemented in many different programming languages. This means that the application and the object need not be implemented in the same programming language. IDL is not a complete programming language; its main job is to define interfaces. Both objects and the variables carried by objects have types.

*object request broker*

As shown in Figure 6-18, an **object request broker** (**ORB**) connects a client to an object that provides a service. Each object instance has a unique **object reference**. The client and object need not reside on the same machine; a request to a remote machine can invoke multiple ORBs. The stub on the client-side provides the interface for the client while the skeleton is the interface to the object. The object logically appears to be a single entity, but the server may keep a **thread pool** running to implement object calls for a variety of clients. Because the client and the object use the same protocol, as defined by the IDL, the object can provide a consistent service independent of the processing element on which it is implemented.

*implementation issues*

CORBA hides a number of implementation details from the application programmer. A CORBA implementation provides load balancing, fault tolerance, and a variety of other capabilities that make the service usable and scalable.

*RT-CORBA*

**RT-CORBA** [Sch00] is a part of the CORBA specification that describes CORBA mechanisms for real-time systems. RT-CORBA is designed for fixed-priority systems, and it allows priorities to be defined in either CORBA or native

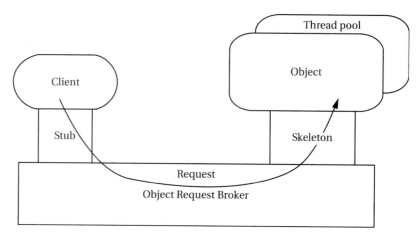

**Figure 6-18** *A request to a CORBA object.*

types. A priority model describes the priority system being used; it may be either server-declared or come from the client. The server may also declare priority transforms that can transform the priority based on system state.

A **thread pool** model helps the server control the real-time responsiveness of the object implementations. The threads in the pool may be divided into **lanes**, with each lane given priority characteristics. Thread pools with lanes allow the server to manage responsiveness across multiple services.

RT-CORBA allows clients to explicitly bind themselves to server services. Standard CORBA provides only implicit binding, which simplifies programming but may introduce unacceptable and variable latency for real-time services.

Wolfe et al. [Wol99] developed the Dynamic Real-Time CORBA system to support real-time requests. A **real-time daemon** implements the dynamic aspects of the real-time services. Clients specify constraints during execution using a type of method known as **timed distributed method invocation** (**TDMI**). These constraints can describe deadline and importance. The method invocation is handled by the runtime daemon, which stores this information in a data structure managed by the daemon.

Server objects and other entities can examine these characteristics. The kernel also provides a **global time service** that can be used by system objects to determine their time relative to deadlines. A **latency service** can be used with objects to determine the times required for communication. It can provide estimated latencies, measured latencies, or analytical latencies. These bounds can be used to help determine schedules and more. A **priority service** records the priorities for system objects.

*ARMADA*

A **real-time event service** exchanges named events. The priorities of events are determined by the priorities of the producers and consumers. The deadline for an event may be either relative to the global clock or relative to an event. The event service is implemented using IP multicasting. The real-time daemon listens to a specified multicast group for events and sends multicast messages to generate events. Each event has a unique identification number.

ARMADA [Abd99] is a middleware system for fault tolerance and quality-of-service. It is organized into three major areas: real-time communications, middleware for group communication and fault tolerance, and dependability tools.

The ARMADA group identifies three major requirements for QoS-oriented communication. First, different connections should be isolated such that errors or malicious behavior on one channel does not starve another channel. Second, service requests should be allowed to differentiate themselves from each other based on urgency. Third, the system should degrade gracefully when overloaded.

The communication guarantees are abstracted by a **clip**, which is an object that guarantees to have delivered a certain number of packets by a certain time. Each clip has a deadline that specifies the maximum response time for the communication system. The real-time channels that provide these services provide an interface similar to a UNIX socket. The **Real-Time Connection Ordination Protocol** manages requests to create and destroy connections. A clip is created for each end of the channel. Each clip includes a message queue at the interface to the objects, a communication handler that schedules operations, and a packet queue at the interface to the channel. The communications handler is scheduled using an EDF policy.

ARMADA supports a group multicast service that distributes timed atomic messages. An admission control service and group membership service manage the configuration and operation of the service. The client-side watches the system state and sends messages to the server to update its copy of the state.

A **real-time primary-backup** service allows state to be replicated in order to manage fault tolerance. The service provides two types of consistency: external consistency with copies of the system kept on servers and internal consistency between different objects in the system. The backup service is built on top of the UDP protocol for IP.

The ARMADA project developed a message-level fault injection tool for analysis of reliability properties. A fault injection layer is inserted between the communication system and the protocol to be tested. The fault injection layer can inject new messages, filter messages, or delay messages.

The next example briefly describes the MPI communication middleware system.

**Example 6-2**

*MPI*

MPI (MultiProcessor Interface) is a specification for a middleware interface for multiprocessor communication. (MPICH is one well-known implementation of MPI.) It was designed to make it easier to develop and port scientific computing applications on homogeneous processors. It is starting to see some use in embedded computing systems.

MPI provides a rich set of communication services based on a few communication primitives. MPI does not itself define the setup of the parallel system: the number of nodes, mapping of processes or data to nodes, and so on. That setup is provided before the MPI activities start.

A minimal MPI program looks something like this:

```
MPI_Init(&argc,&argv); /* initialize*/
MPI_Comm_rank(MPI_COMM_WORLD,&r); /* get the index of this node */
MPI_Comm_size(MPI_COMM_WORLD,&s); /* get the total number of nodes */
MPI_Finalize(); /* clean up */
```

This program simply sets up the system, gets the name (rank) of this node, the total system size, and then leaves MPI. The values of r and s were initialized before MPI started. A program can be written so that the number of nodes and the assignment of a program to a node can change dramatically without rewriting the program.

The basic MPI communication functions are MPI_Send() and MPI_Recv(). These provide point-to-point, blocking communication. MPI allows these routines to include a data type so that the application can easily distinguish several types of data.

MPI allows the program to create groups of processes. Groups can be defined either by name or by topology. The groups can then perform multicast and broadcast.

The MPI standard is large—it includes about 160 functions. However, a minimal MPI system can be provided with only six functions: MPI_Init(), MPI_Comm_rank(), MPI_Comm_size(), MPI_Send(), MPI_Recv(), and MPI_Finalize(). The other functions are implemented in terms of these primitives.

## 6.4.2 System-on-Chip Services

The advent of systems-on-chips (SoC) has resulted in a new generation of custom middleware that relies less on standard services and models. SoC middle-

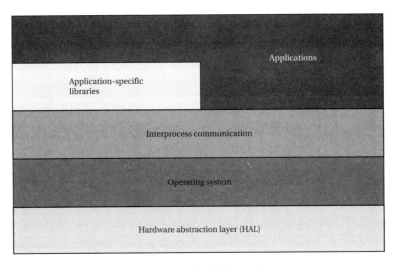

**Figure 6-19** *A software stack and services in an embedded multiprocessor.*

ware has been designed from scratch for several reasons. First, these systems are often power or energy constrained and any services must be implemented very efficiently. Second, although the SoC may be committed with outside standard services, they are not constrained to use standards within the chip. Third, today's SoCs are composed of a relatively small number of processors. The 50-processor systems of tomorrow may in fact make more use of industry standard services, but today's systems-on-chips often use customized middleware.

Figure 6-19 shows a typical software stack for an embedded SoC multiprocessor. This stack has several elements:

- The **hardware abstraction layer** (HAL) provides a uniform abstraction for devices and other hardware primitives. The HAL abstracts the rest of the software from both the devices themselves and from certain elements of the processor.

- The **real-time operating system** controls basic system resources such as process scheduling and memory.

- The **interprocess communication** layer provides abstract communication services. It may, for example, use one function for communication between processes whether they are on the same or different PE.

- The **application-specific libraries** provide utilities for computation or communication specific to the application.

The application code uses these layers to provide the end service or function.

*MultiFlex*
Paulin et al. [Pau02a; Pau06] developed the MultiFlex programming environment to support multiple programming models that are supported by hardware accelerators. MultiFlex supports both **distributed system object component** (**DSOC**) and **symmetric multiprocessing** (**SMP**) models. Each is supported by a high-level programming interface. Figure 6-20 shows the MultiFlex architecture and its DSOC and SMP subsystems. Different parts of the system are mapped onto different parts of the architecture: control functions can run on top of an OS on the host processor; some high-performance functions, such as video, can run on accelerators; some parallelizable operations can go on a hardware multithreaded set of processors; and some operations can go into DSPs. The DSOC and SMP units in the architecture manage communication between the various subsystems.

The DSOC model is based on a parallel communicating object model from client to server. It uses a message-passing engine for interprocess communication. When passing a message, a wrapper on the client-side must **marshal** the data required for the call. Marshaling may require massaging data types, moving data to a more accessible location, and so on. On the server-side, another wrapper unmarshals the data to make it usable to the client.

The object request broker coordinates object communication. It must be able to handle many parallel objects that execute in parallel. A server farm holds the resources to execute a large number of object requests. The ORB matches a client request to an available server. The client stalls until the request is satisfied. The server takes a request and looks up appropriate object servers in a table, then

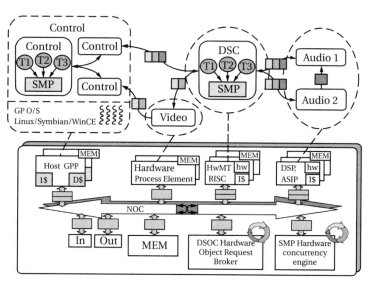

**Figure 6-20** *Object broker and SMP concurrency engine in MultiFlex. From Paulin et al. [Pau06] © 2006 IEEE.*

returns the results when they are available. Paulin et al. [Pau06] report that 300 MHz RISC processors can perform about 35 million object calls per second.

The SMP model is implemented using a software on top of a hardware concurrency engine. The engine appears as a memory-mapped device with a set of memory-mapped addresses for each concurrency object. A protected region for an object can be entered by writing the appropriate address within that object's address region.

*ENSEMBLE*

ENSEMBLE [Cad01] is a library for large data transfers that allows overlapping computation and communication. The library is designed for use with an annotated form of Java that allows array accesses and data dependencies to be analyzed for single program, multiple data execution. The library provides send and receive functions, including specialized versions for contiguous buffers. The emb_fence() function handles the pending sends and receives. Data transfers are handled by the DMA system, allowing the programs to execute concurrently with transfers.

The next example describes the middleware for the TI OMAP.

## Example 6-3

*Middleware and Services Architecture of the TI OMAP*

The figure shows the layers of software in an OMAP-based system. The DSP provides a software interface to its functions. The C55x supports a standard, known as eXpressDSP, for describing algorithms. This standard hides some of the memory and interfacing requirements of algorithms from application code.

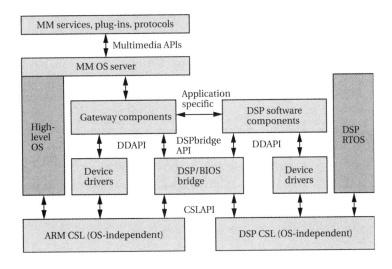

The DSP resource manager provides the basic API for the DSP functions. It controls tasks, data streams between the DSP and CPU, and memory allocation. It also keeps track of resources such as CPU time, CPU utilization, and memory.

---

The DSPBridge in the OMAP is an architecture-specific interface. It provides abstract communication but only in the special case of a master CPU and a slave DSP. This is a prime example of a tailored middleware service.

*Nostrum stack*

The Nostrum network-on-chip (NoC) is supported by a communications protocol stack [Mil04]. The basic service provided by the system is to accept a packet with a **destination process identifier** and to deliver it to its destination. The system requires three compulsory layers: the physical layer is the network-on-chip; the data link layer handles synchronization, error correction, and flow control; and the network layer handles routing and the mapping of logical addresses to destination process IDs. The network layer provides both datagram and virtual circuit services.

*network-on-chip services*

Sgroi et al. [Sgr01] based their on-chip networking design methodology on the Metropolis methodology. They successively refine the protocol stack by adding adaptators. Adaptors can perform a variety of transformations: **behavior adapters** allow components with different models of computation or protocols to communicate; **channel adapters** adapt for discrepancies between the desired characteristics of a channel, such as reliability or performance, and the characteristics of the chosen physical channel.

*power management*

Benini and De Micheli [Ben01b] developed a methodology for power management of networks-on-chips. They advocate a micronetwork stack with three major levels: the physical layer; an architecture and control layer that consists of the OSI data link, network, and transport layers; and a software layer that consists of handle systems and applications. At the data link layer, the proper choice of error-correction codes and retransmission schemes is key. The media access control algorithm also has a strong influence on power consumption. At the transport layer, services may be either connection-oriented or connectionless. Flow control also has a strong influence on energy consumption.

## 6.4.3 Quality-of-Service

**Quality-of-service (QoS)** for processes means that a process will be reliably scheduled periodically with a given amount of computation time. Scheduling techniques, such as RMS, inherently provide process-level QoS; if we use some other scheduling methods or mix scheduling policies, we must ensure that the processes that need quality-of-service obtain the level of service they need.

*QoS model*

Quality-of-service can be modeled using three basic concepts. First, a **contract** specifies the resources that will be provided. The client may propose a set of terms, such as the amount of bandwidth and rate of missed packets, but the server may counterpropose a different set of terms based on its available resources. A **protocol** manages the establishment of the contract and its implementation. Third, a **scheduler** implements the terms of the contract, setting the sizes of buffers, managing bandwidth, and so on.

*QoS and resources*

Assuming that we run a QoS-friendly scheduling policy, such as RMS, we must also ensure that the QoS processes obtain the resources they need to meet their deadlines. QoS methods have been widely studied in networking and operating systems. Resource management algorithms that make decisions on-the-fly simply to avoid deadlock or minimize local scheduling delay are not sufficient to guarantee that the QoS-oriented processes get their resources on time. Periodic reservation methods can help ensure that resources are available when they are required.

*approaches*

As with all middleware, we can use standards to design QoS services or to design custom systems. Early approaches concentrated on standards. The advent of systems-on-chips, and in particular networks-on-chips, has led to a new wave of custom QoS designs.

*multiparadigm scheduling*

Gill et al. [Gil03] used a scheduling framework that could mix and match different scheduling policies. Their Kokyu framework allows the combination of static priority scheduling, dynamic priority scheduling, and hybrid algorithms. Figure 6-21 shows how their scheduling system fits into the service stack. They measured system behavior using three policies: rate-monotonic scheduling, least-laxity first, and a combination of RMS and least-laxity first. They found that the different policies had somewhat different characteristics and that systems that can switch between scheduling policies can provide higher levels of service.

*fine-grained scheduling*

Combaz et al. [Com05] developed a methodology for generating QoS software that can handle both critical and best-effort communication. They use control-theoretic methods to determine a schedule and use code synthesis to create statically scheduled code to implement the schedule. As shown in Figure 6-22, the system being controlled (the **plant**) is under the control of a combination of a quality manager and a scheduler. The controller generates schedules for a given level of quality and evaluates the feasibility of those schedules to choose which schedule to execute. Given an execution time for the code required to implement the QoS action, the controller determines the feasibility of the schedule relative to the deadlines. Different choices for quality result in different schedules. Schedules are generated and selected using an online incremental algorithm.

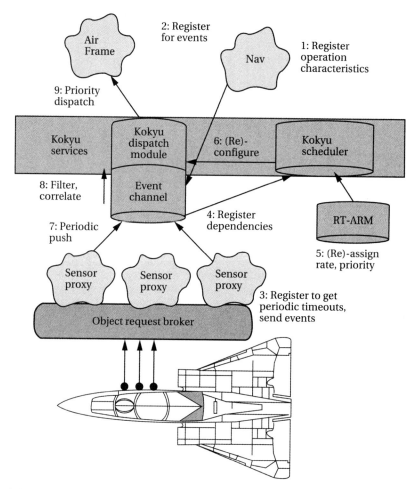

**Figure 6-21** *Middleware organization for multiparadigm scheduling. From Gill et al. [Gil03] © 2003 IEEE.*

*constraint modeling*

Ahluwalia et al. [Ahl05] developed a framework for modeling reactive systems and monitoring those properties using Real-Time CORBA. They developed an architecture definition language for interaction services. A UML description of the model is shown in Figure 6-23 with the parts of the model specific to interactions shown within the dotted line. The InteractionElement type specifies an interaction, which can be atomic or composite. A set of operators allow interaction elements to be combined and define the way in which deadlines

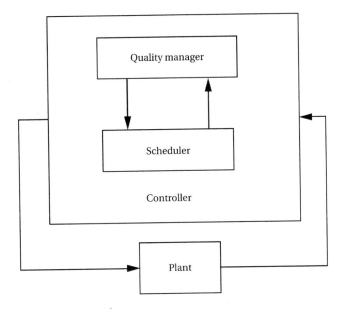

**Figure 6-22** *QoS management as control.*

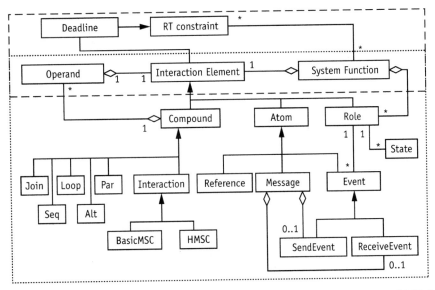

**Figure 6-23** *Interaction domain and system services model. From Ahluwalia et al. [Ah05] © 2005 ACM Press.*

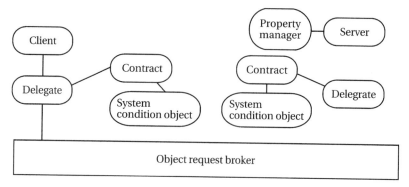

**Figure 6-24** *QuO objects for quality-of-service management.*

*CORBA and QoS*

for the combination are created from the operand interactions. Operators include seq, par, alt, loop, and join. The code generated from these specifications includes monitors that check system operation against specified deadlines.

Krishnamurthy et al. [Kri01] developed methods for CORBA-based QoS. The QuO model, shown in Figure 6-24, uses a variety of mechanisms to manage quality-of-service. **Contract objects** encapsulate the agreement between the client and the system about the level of service to be provided; a **quality description language** is used to describe these contracts. **Delegate objects** act as local proxies for remote objects. System condition objects act as the interface to the parts of the underlying system that control and measure quality-of-service. **Property managers** handle the implementation of QoS characteristics for the server. The object request broker must also be modified to handle the QoS characteristics of the underlying service. Code generators create the various objects required to implement these functions.

*notification service*

A **notification service** provides a publish/subscribe system to propagate events. Gore et al. [Gor01] developed a CORBA notification service that supports QoS services. Their system deals with structured events that include a domain, type and event name, QoS characteristics for the event, and a set of data. The system specification describes several QoS properties.

- **Reliability**—If reliability is specified and supported, the notification service must reconnect and deliver events after a crash.

- **Priority**—It relates to other users of this channel.

- **Expiration time**—The time range in which an event is valid.

- **Earliest deliveries time**—The first time at which an event can be delivered.

- **Maximum events per consumer**—The number of events queued in the channel.

- **Order policy**—The order in which events are buffered for delivery.

- **Discard policy**—A policy for discarding events when queues fill up.

A channel has suppliers and consumers of events. A supplier or consumer can use push style or pull style. Proxy components exist for the producer and consumer sides of push and pull services. The event channel works with supplier and consumer administrator components to manage QoS.

*QoS and NoCs*

Networks-on-chips must provide quality-of-service functions to support multimedia and other rate-sensitive applications. Because NoCs generally do not run the Internet Protocol, they often take advantage of their physical layer to efficiently provide QoS.

*GMRS*

The GMRS system [Hua99] provides QoS services in a heterogeneous multiprocessor. They use the **ripple scheduling** methodology to negotiate resources. They build a scheduling spanning tree that models the resources along the path required for a QoS-governed communication. A negotiation and adaptation protocol uses the tree to allocate the resources required to satisfy the QoS request. The protocol first checks the path to ensure that the required resources are available. It then propagates a commit signal to gather the resources or an abort signal if so required.

*QNoC*

The QNoC network-on-chip [Bol04] provides four levels of service. Signaling is used for urgent, short messages and is given the highest priority. Real-time service guarantees bandwidth and latency for connection. Read/write service is similar to a microprocessor bus operaiton and is used for memory and register access. Block-transfer service is used for long transfers, similar to DMA in microprocessor systems.

*looped containers*

Millberg et al. [Mil04b] used **looped containers** to provide QoS in the Nostrum network-on-chip. To maintain a spot in the network for the packets required by the connection, they return messages from receiver back to sender after they are used. At the sender, a packet is loaded with its data and sent into the network. After reaching the destination, its data is unloaded and the packet is sent back to its source. When it arrives, it can be loaded with new data again. Each processing element runs a distributed system resource manager to handle requests. These agents can negotiate with each other to check resources. The resource management agents may rely on agents that represent the CPU, the network, or other resources on a PE. The structure of their physical network ensures that certain combinations of packets will not interfere with each other. Noninterference plus looped containers allow Nostrum to provide several QoS channels in the network.

# Design Verification

This section briefly considers system verification of multiprocessor software. Verifying software is always a challenge, but verifying multiprocessor software is harder than verifying uniprocessor software for several reasons:

- The data of interest may be harder to observe and/or control.

- It may be harder to drive certain parts of the system into desired states.

- Timing effects are much harder to generate and test.

Software need not be entirely debugged on the target platform. Some aspects of the software may be properly addressed on other types of machines. However, after any porting, the designer must carefully verify the correctness of any port-specific characteristics. In addition, some hidden platform assumptions may not have been tested on the debugging platform and it may take a large number of tests to expose them on the target.

Because embedded systems must meet performance, power/energy, and size constraints, we want to evaluate the software not just for correctness but also for these nonfunctional attributes. We can use multiprocessor simulators, such as cycle-accurate ones, to obtain detailed information about performance and energy consumption.

The next two examples describes a simulator for embedded multiprocessors.

---

### Example 6-4

*The VastSystems CoMET Simulator*

The CoMET simulator [Hel99] is designed to simulate systems of embedded processors. The processor model used in CoMET is known as the virtual processor model (VPN). Part of the VPN is built from the application code; this custom model reflects the behavior of the code that can be determined statically. The other part of the VPN includes parts of the processor that must be modeled dynamically: I/O, cache, and so on. This combination of static and dynamic modeling allows the VPN to run at very high speeds. The simulation framework includes a backplane that connects the various virtual processor models as well as to hardware models.

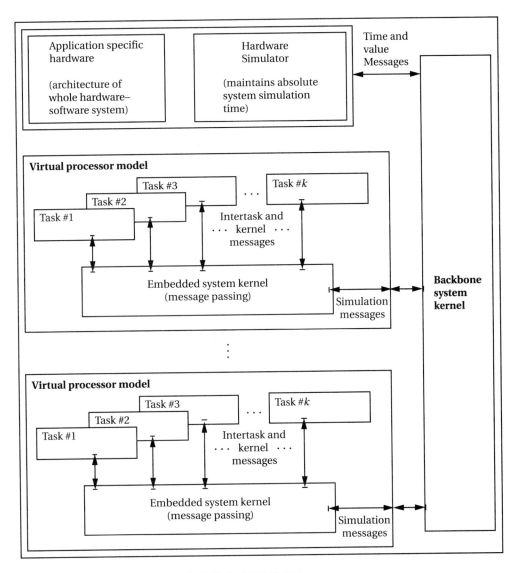

*Source:* From Hellestrand (Hel1999) © 1999 IEEE.

The backbone system allows several different types of simulators to be combined for cycle-accurate simulation.

**Example 6-5**

*The MESH Simulator*

MESH [Pau02b] is a heterogeneous systems simulator that bridges logical and physical time. An event is a pair of a tag and a value. The tag denotes time; but time may not necessarily be wall clock time. The behavior of a thread is given by an ordered set of events. Depending on the level of detail at which the system is modeled, the events may be mapped onto physical time or onto logical sequences. In simple cases, a simulation of the logical simulation can be transformed into a simulation in physical time simply by adding time steps in the logical sequence. However, in many cases, the mapping from logical to physical behavior is not so simple. MESH models more complex relationships between logical and physical time using **macro events** and **micro events**. Each macro event contains a sequence of micro events, thus establishing the correspondence between the two notions of time.

## 6.6 Summary

Many of the techniques developed for uniprocessor operating systems apply to multiprocessors as well. However, multiprocessors are inherently harder because they provide true concurrency, not just apparent concurrency. It is harder to determine how fast multiprocessor software will run, but it is possible to make accurate estimates. Software stacks help abstract the underlying platform, but one must be careful not to make the software layers too inefficient.

### What We Have Learned

- Embedded multiprocessor software must meet timing, energy, and size constraints. It must do so while executing on a heterogeneous platform.

- Several methods are available to estimate the real-time performance of multiple processes running on multiprocessors.

- Software stacks and middleware help designers develop efficient, portable embedded software, with middleware managing resources in the system.

- Middleware can be designed around standards or it can be customized to the hardware platform.

■ Design verification should consider timing and performance as well as functionality.

## Further Reading

The book *Multiprocessor Systems-on-Chips* [Jer05] provides several chapters on multiprocessor software and application development. The Object Management Group (OMG)—*http://www.omg.com*—promulgates standards for UML and CORBA.

## Questions

**Q6-1** What sorts of resources need to be managed on an embedded multiprocessor?

**Q6-2** What are the advantages and disadvantages of a master/slave RTOS?

**Q6-3** You are given a set of processes that may be implemented on two different CPUs:

| Process | CPU 1 runtime | CPU 2 runtime |
|---------|---------------|---------------|
| P1 | 2 | 3 |
| P2 | 12 | 9 |
| P3 | 7 | – |
| P4 | – | 5 |
| P5 | 5 | 6 |

a. Draw the intermodule connection graph for this system.

b. Find the allocation of processes to CPUs that minimizes total execution time.

**Q6-4** Construct a schedule for three processes running on two processing elements: *P1*'s execution time is 3 and its deadline is 7. *P2*'s execution time is 19 and its deadline is 25. *P3*'s execution time is 7 and its deadline is 14.

**Q6-5** Plot the schedule for three processes running on two processors, varying execution time with deadlines remaining constant. *P1*'s deadline is 9, its execution time varies from 3 to 5. *P2*'s deadline is 12, its execution time varies from 4 to 7. *P3*'s deadline is 24, its execution time varies from 5 to 12. Show which regions of the scheduling space are feasible.

**Q6-6** Construct an example in which a set of processes is schedulable when they all run to their worst-case execution time (WCET) but miss a deadline when one process runs more quickly than its WCET. Consider a multiprocessor with two processing elements and an application with two tasks.

**Q6-7** You are given a set of processes allocated to one of three different processors:

| Process | Runtime | Deadline | Allocation |
|---------|---------|----------|------------|
| P1 | 2 | 10 | PE 1 |
| P2 | 4 | 20 | PE 2 |
| P3 | 9 | 60 | PE 2 |
| P4 | 4 | 40 | PE 3 |
| P5 | 3 | 30 | PE 3 |
| P6 | 2 | 15 | PE 1 |

a. Write the data dependencies and max constraints for this set of processes.

b. Perform one iteration of LatestTimes and determine the latest request and finish times for each process.

**Q6-8** You are given two events with jitter: one with a period of 1 ms and a jitter of 0.1 ms; one with a period of 3 ms and a jitter of 0.15 ms. Model the jitter of the OR activation of these two events.

**Q6-9** In the graph of Figure 6-3, let the delay $a = 4$ and $b = 5$. The computation times of the nodes are:

| Process | CPU time |
|---------|----------|
| P1 | 2 |
| P2 | 3 |
| P3 | 4 |
| P4 | 2 |
| P5 | 3 |

a. Identify all the strongly connected components in the graph.

b. Find the asymptotic iteration period for each strongly connected component.

**Q6-10** Compare and contrast the use of the Internet Protocol versus custom communication protocols to build middleware for real-time communication.

**Q6-11** Define some useful properties of a QoS contract.

**Q6-12** Compare and contrast the use of thread-level control versus software thread integration for QoS communication.

## Lab Exercises

**L6-1** Simulate the performance of a set of processes running on a multiprocessor. Vary the multiprocessor architecture and see how performance varies.

**L6-2** First estimate, then measure, the interprocessor communication time for a heterogeneous multiprocessor.

**L6-3** Design and implement a simple object request broker. A message from a client object to a server object should take at least one parameter.

# Hardware and Software Co-design

- Platforms for hardware/software co-design

- Hardware/software partitioning

- Hardware/software co-synthesis onto different types of platforms

- Hardware/software co-simulation

## 7.1 Introduction

Embedded computing systems must meet tight cost, power consumption, and performance constraints. If one design requirement dominated, life would be much easier for embedded system designers—they could use fairly standard architectures with easy programming models. But because the three constraints must be met simultaneously, embedded system designers have to mold hardware and software architectures to fit the needs of applications. Specialized hardware helps to meet performance requirements for lower energy consumption and at less cost than would be possible from a general-purpose system.

As we have seen, embedded computing systems are often heterogeneous multiprocessors with multiple CPUs and hardwired processing elements (PEs). In co-design, the hardwired PEs are generally called **accelerators**. In contrast, a co-processor is controlled by the execution unit of a CPU.

*application-specific systems*

Hardware/software co-design is a collection of techniques that designers use to help them create efficient application-specific systems. If you don't know anything about the characteristics of the application, then it is difficult to know how to tune the system's design. But if you do know the application, as the designer, not only can you add features to the hardware and software that make it run faster using less power, but you also can *remove* hardware and software *co-design as a methodology*

elements that do not help with the application at hand. Removing excess components is often as important as adding new features.

As the name implies, hardware/software co-design means jointly designing hardware and software architectures to meet performance, cost, and energy goals. Co-design is a radically different methodology than the layered abstractions used in general-purpose computing. Because co-design tries to optimize many different parts of the system at the same time, it makes extensive use of tools for both design analysis and optimization.

Increasingly, hardware/software co-design is being used to design non-embedded systems as well. For example, servers can be improved with specialized implementations of some of the functions on their software stack. Co-design can be applied to Web hosting just as easily as it can be applied to multimedia.

First we take a brief look at some hardware platforms that can be used as targets for hardware/software co-design, then Section 7.3 looks at performance analysis. Section 7.4 is a large section that surveys the state-of-the-art in hardware/software co-synthesis. Finally, Section 7.5 looks at hardware/software co-simulation.

## 7.2  Design Platforms

Hardware/software co-design can be used either to design systems from scratch or to create systems to be implemented on an existing platform. The CPU+ accelerator architecture is one common co-design platform. A variety of different CPUs can be used to host the accelerator. The accelerator can implement many different functions; furthermore, it can be implemented using any of several logic technologies. These choices influence design time, power consumption, and other important characteristics of the system.

*types of platforms*

The co-design platform could be implemented in any of several very different design technologies.

■ A PC-based system with the accelerator housed on a board plugged into the PC bus. The plug-in board can use a custom chip or a field programmable gate array (FPGA) to implement the accelerator. This sort of system is relatively bulky and is most often used for development or very low-volume applications.

■ A custom-printed circuit board, using either an FPGA or a custom integrated circuit for the accelerator. The custom board requires more design work than a PC-based system but results in a lower-cost, lower-power system.

- A platform FPGA that includes a CPU and an FPGA fabric on a single chip. These chips are more expensive than custom chips but provide a single-chip implementation with one or more CPUs and a great deal of custom logic.

- A custom integrated circuit, for which the accelerator implements a function in less area and with lower power consumption. Many embedded systems-on-chips (SoC) make use of accelerators for particular functions.

*accelerators*  The combination of a CPU plus one or more accelerators is the simplest form of heterogeneous platform; hardware/software partitioning targets such platforms. The CPU is often called the **host**. The CPU talks to the accelerator through data and control registers in it. These registers allow the CPU to monitor the accelerator's operation and to give it commands.

The CPU and accelerator can also communicate via shared memory. If the accelerator needs to operate on a large volume of data, it is usually more efficient to leave the data in memory and to have the accelerator read and write memory directly rather than to have the CPU shuttle data from memory to accelerator registers and back. The CPU and accelerator synchronize their actions.

*heterogeneous multiprocessors*  More general platforms are also possible. We can use several CPUs, in contrast to the single processor attached to the accelerators. We can generalize the system interconnect from a bus to more general structures. Plus, we can create a more complex memory system that provides different types of access to diffe-rent parts of the system. Co-designing such types of systems is more difficult, particularly when we do not make assumptions about the structure of the platform.

Examples 7-1, 7-2, and 7-3 describe several different co-design platforms that use FPGAs in different ways.

---

## Example 7-1

*The Xiilnx Virtex-4 FX Platform FPGA Family*

The Xilinx Virtex-4 family [Xil05] is a platform FPGA that comes in several different configurations. The higher-end FX family includes one or two PowerPC processors, multiple Ethernet MACs, block RAM, and large arrays of reconfigurable logic.

The PowerPC is a high-performance 32-bit RISC machine with a five-stage pipeline, 32 general-purpose registers, and separate instruction and data caches. The FPGA fabric is built on configurable logic blocks (CLBs) that use lookup tables and a variety of other logic.

The largest Virtex-4 provides up to 200,000 logic cells. The CLBs can be used to implement high-speed adders. A separate set of blocks includes $18 \times 18$ multipliers, an adder, and a 48-bit accumulator for DSP operations. The chip includes a number of RAM blocks that can be configured to a variety of depth and width configurations.

The PowerPC and FPGA fabric can be tightly integrated. The FPGA fabric can be used to build bus-based devices. An auxiliary processor unit allows custom PowerPC instructions to be implemented in the FPGA fabric. In addition, processor cores can also be implemented in the FPGA fabric to build heterogeneous multiprocessors. Xilinx provides the MicroBlaze processor core and other cores can be used as well.

## Example 7-2

*The ARM Integrator Logic Module*

The ARM Integrator is a series of evaluation boards for the ARM processor. The Integrator Logic Module [ARM00] is an FPGA accelerator board that plugs into the ARM Integrator motherboard. The logic module provides a Xilinx FPGA for reconfigurable logic. The FPGA interfaces to the ARM AMBA bus. The logic module board does not contain its own SRAM—the FPGA can use the AMBA bus to connect to the SRAM and I/O devices contained on other boards.

## Example 7-3

*The Annapolis Micro Systems WILDSTAR II Pro*

The WILDSTAR II Pro (*http://www.annapmicro.com*) is a PCI bus card that provides FPGA logic on the bus of a PC or other PCI device. The card hosts one or two Virtex II Pro FPGAs that can connect directly to the PCI bus. It also hosts up to 96 MB of SRAM and 256 MB of SDRAM. The card is organized as shown in the figure. A development environment simplifies system design for the board.

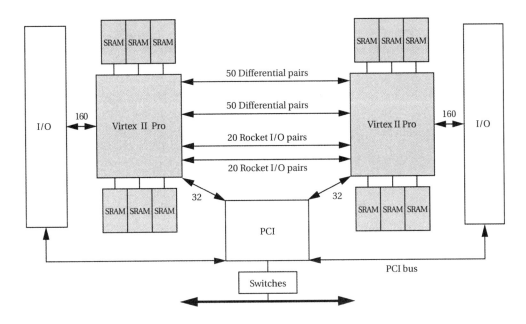

*Source:* After WILDSTAR II Pro data sheet.

# 7.3    Performance Analysis

During co-synthesis, we need to evaluate the hardware being designed. **High-level synthesis** was developed to raise the level of abstraction for hardware designers, but it is also useful as an estimation tool for co-synthesis. This section surveys some high-level synthesis algorithms to provide a better understanding of the costs of hardware and fast algorithms for area and performance estimation. We also look at techniques specifically developed to estimate the costs of accelerators in heterogeneous multiprocessors.

## 7.3.1    High-Level Synthesis

*goals of high-level synthesis*

High-level synthesis starts from a **behavioral** description of hardware and creates a register-transfer design. High-level synthesis schedules and allocates the operations in the behavior as well as maps those operations into component libraries.

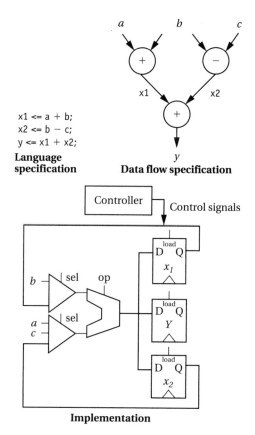

x1 <= a + b;
x2 <= b − c;
y <= x1 + x2;
**Language specification**

**Data flow specification**

**Implementation**

**Figure 7-1** *An example of behavior specification and register–transfer implementation.*

*data flow graph, data dependency, variable function unit*

Figure 7-1 shows a simple example of a high-level specification and one possible register–transfer implementation. The data dependency edges carry **variable** values from one operation or from the primary inputs to another.

The register–transfer implementation shows which steps need to be taken to turn the high-level specification, whether it is given as text or a data flow graph, into a register–transfer implementation:

- Operations have been scheduled to occur on a particular clock cycle.

- Variables have been assigned to registers.

- Operations have been assigned to **function units.**

- Some connections have been multiplexed to save wires.

*control step,*
*time step*

In this case, it has been assumed that we can execute only one operation per clock cycle. A clock cycle is often called a **control step** or **time step** in high-level synthesis. We use a coarser model of time for high-level synthesis than is used in logic synthesis. Because we are farther from the implementation, delays cannot be predicted as accurately, so detailed timing models are not of much use in high-level synthesis. Abstracting time to the clock period or some fraction of it makes the combinatorics of scheduling tractable.

Allocating variables to registers must be done with care. Two variables can share a register if their values are not required at the same time—for example, if one input value is used only early in a sequence of calculations and another variable is defined only late in the sequence. But if the two variables are needed simultaneously they must be allocated to separate registers.

Sharing either registers or function units requires adding multiplexers to the design. For example, if two additions in the data flow graph are allocated to the same adder unit in the implementation, we use multiplexers to feed the proper operands to the adder. The multiplexers are controlled by a control FSM, which supplies the select signals to the muxes. (In most cases, we don't need demultiplexers at the outputs of shared units because the hardware is generally designed to ignore values that aren't used on any given clock cycle.) Multiplexers add three types of cost to the implementation:

1. Delay, which may stretch the system clock cycle.

2. Logic, which consumes area on the chip.

3. Wiring, which is required to reach the multiplexer, also requires area.

*technology*
*library*

Sharing hardware isn't always a win. For example, in some technologies, adders are sufficiently small that you gain in both area and delay by never sharing an adder. Some of the information required to make good implementation decisions must come from a **technology library**, which gives the area and delay costs of some components. Other information, such as wiring cost estimates, can be made algorithmically. The ability of a program to accurately measure implementation costs for a large number of candidate implementations is one of the strengths of high-level synthesis algorithms.

*scheduling*
*terminology*
*FCFS*
*scheduling*

When searching for a good schedule, the as-soon-as-possible (ASAP) and as-late-as-possible (ALAP) ones are useful bounds on schedule length.

A very simple heuristic that can handle constraints is **first-come-first-served (FCFS)** scheduling. FCFS walks through the data flow graph from its sources to its sinks. As soon as it encounters a new node, it tries to schedule that operation in the current clock schedule; if all the resources are occupied, it starts another control step and schedules the operation there. FCFS schedules generally handle the nodes from source to sink, but nodes that appear at the same

*critical-path scheduling*

*list scheduling*

*force-directed scheduling*

depth in the graph can be scheduled in arbitrary order. The quality of the schedule, as measured by its length, can change greatly depending on exactly which order the nodes at a given depth are considered.

FCFS, because it chooses nodes at equal depth arbitrarily, may delay a critical operation. An obvious improvement is a **critical-path scheduling** algorithm, which schedules operations on the critical path first.

List scheduling is an effective heuristic that tries to improve on critical-path scheduling by providing a more balanced consideration of off-critical-path nodes. Rather than treat all nodes that are off the critical path as equally unimportant, **list scheduling** estimates how close a node is to being critical by measuring $D$, the **number of descendants** the node has in the data flow graph. A node with few descendants is less likely to become critical than another node at the same depth that has more descendants.

List scheduling also traverses the data flow graph from sources to sinks, but when it has several nodes at the same depth vying for attention, it always chooses the node with the most descendants. In our simple timing model, where all nodes take the same amount of time, a critical node will always have more descendants than any noncritical node. The heuristic takes its name from the list of nodes currently waiting to be scheduled.

**Force-directed scheduling** [Pau89] is a well-known scheduling algorithm that tries to minimize hardware cost to meet a particular performance goal by balancing the use of function units across cycles. The algorithm selects one operation to schedule using **forces** (see Figure 7-2). It then assigns a control step to that operation. Once an operation has been scheduled, it does not move, so the algorithm's outer loop executes once for each operation in the data flow graph.

To compute the forces on the operators, we first need to find the distributions of various operations in the data flow graph, as represented by a **distribution graph**. The ASAP and ALAP schedules tells us the range of control steps at which each operation can be scheduled. We assume that each operation has a uniform probability of being assigned to any feasible control step. A distribution graph shows the expected value of the number of operators of a given type being assigned to each control step, as shown in Figure 7-3. The distribution graph gives us a probabilistic view of the number of function units of a given type (adder in this case) that will be required at each control step. In this example, there are three additions, but they cannot all occur on the same cycle.

If we compute the ASAP and ALAP schedules, we find that $+_1$ must occur in the first control step, $+_3$ in the last, and $+_2$ addition can occur in either of the first two control steps. The distribution graph $DG_+(t)$ shows the expected number of additions as a function of control step; the expected value at each control step is computed by assuming that each operation is equally probable at every legal control step.

We build a distribution for each type of function unit that we will allocate. The total number of function units required for the data path is the maximum

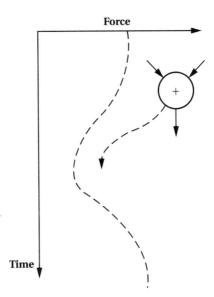

**Figure 7-2** *How forces guide operator scheduling.*

number needed for any control step, so minimizing hardware requirements requires choosing a schedule that balances the need for a given function unit over the entire schedule length. The distribution graphs are updated each time an operation is scheduled—when an operation is assigned to a control step, its

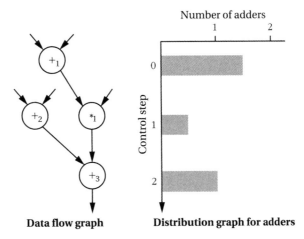

**Figure 7-3** *Example distribution graph for force-directed scheduling.*

probability at that control step becomes 1 and at any other control step 0. As the shape of the distribution graph for a function unit changes, force-directed scheduling tries to select control steps for the remaining operations, which keeps the operator distribution balanced.

Force-directed scheduling calculates forces like those exerted by springs to help balance the utilization of operators. The spring forces are a linear function of displacement, as given by Hooke's Law:

$$F(x) = kx, \qquad \text{(EQ 7-1)}$$

where $x$ is the displacement and $k$ is the spring constant, which represents the spring's stiffness. When computing forces on the operator we are trying to schedule, we first choose a **candidate schedule time** for the operator, then compute the forces to evaluate the effects of that scheduling choice on the allocation.

There are two types of forces applied by and on operators: **self forces** and **predecessor/successor forces**. **Self forces** are designed to equalize the utilization of function units across all control steps. Since we are selecting a schedule for one operation at a time, we need to take into account how fixing that operation in time will affect other operations, either by pulling forward earlier operations or pushing back succeeding ones. When we choose a candidate time for the operator being scheduled, restrictions are placed on the feasible ranges of its immediate predecessors and successors. (In fact, the effects of a scheduling choice can ripple through the whole data flow graph, but this approximation ignores effects at a distance.)

The **predecessor/successor forces**, $P_o(t)$ and $X_o(t)$, are these imposed on predecessor/successor operations. The scheduling choice is evaluated based on the total forces in the system exerted by this scheduling choice: the self forces, the predecessor forces, and the successor forces are all added together. That is, the predecessor and successor operators do not directly exert forces on the operator being scheduled, but the forces exerted on them by that scheduling choice help determine the quality of the allocation. At each step, we choose the operation with the lowest total force to schedule and place it at the control step at which it feels the lowest total force.

*path-based scheduling*

**Path-based scheduling** [Cam91] is another well-known scheduling algorithm for high-level synthesis. Unlike the previous methods, path-based scheduling is designed to minimize the number of control states required in the implementation's controller, given constraints on data path resources. The algorithm schedules each path independently, using an algorithm that guarantees the minimum number of control states on each path. The algorithm then optimally combines the path schedules into a system schedule. The schedule for each path is found using minimum clique covering; this step is known by the name **as-fast-as-possible (AFAP)** scheduling.

### 7.3.2  Accelerator Estimation

Estimating the hardware costs of an accelerator in a heterogeneous multiprocessor requires balancing accuracy and efficiency. Estimates must be good enough to avoid misguiding the overall synthesis process. However, the estimates must be generated quickly enough that co-synthesis can explore a large number of candidate designs. Estimation methods for co-synthesis generally avoid very detailed estimates of physical characteristics, such as might be generated by placement and routing. Instead, they rely on scheduling and allocation to measure execution time and hardware size.

*estimation by numerical methods*

Hermann et al. [Her94] used numerical methods to estimate accelerator costs in COSYMA. They pointed out that as additional layers of a loop nest are peeled off for implementation in the accelerator, the cost of the modified accelerator is not equal to the sum of the cost of the new and additional pieces. For example, if a function is described in three blocks, then eight terms may be necessary to describe the cost of the accelerator that implements all three blocks. They used numerical techniques to estimate accelerator costs as new blocks were added to the accelerator.

*AFAP-based estimation*

Henkel and Ernst [Hen95; Hen01] developed an algorithm to quickly and accurately estimate accelerator performance and cost given a CDFG. They use path-based scheduling to estimate the length of the schedule and the resources required to be allocated. To reduce the runtime of the AFAP and overlapping steps of path-based scheduling, they decompose the CDFG and schedule each subgraph independently; this technique is known as **path-based estimation**. These author use three rules to guide the selection of cut points.

First, they cut at nodes with a smaller iteration count, since any penalty incurred by cutting the graph will be multiplied by the number of tritons. Second, they cut at nodes where many paths join, usually generated by the end of a scope in the language. Third, they try to cut the graph into roughly equal-size pieces. The total number of cuts it is possible to make can be controlled by the designer. Their estimation algorithm, including profiling, generating, and converting the CDFG; cutting the CDFG; and superposing the schedules is shown in Figure 7-4.

*incremental estimation*

Vahid and Gajski [Vah95] developed an algorithm for fast incremental estimation of data path and controller costs. They model hardware cost as a sum

$$C_H = k_{FU}S_{FU} + k_{SU}S_{SU} + k_M S_M + k_{SR}S_{SR} + k_C S_C + k_W S_W, \qquad \text{(EQ 7-2)}$$

where $S_x$ is the size of a given type of hardware element and $k_x$ is the size-to-cost ratio of that type. In this formula:

- *FU* is function units.

- *SU* is storage units.

- *M* is multiplexers.

- *SR* is state registers.

- *C* is control logic.

- *W* is wiring.

```
path_based_estim_tech()
{
    CP := {};

    collect_profiling_data{CDFG};
    DAG := convert_to_DAG{CDFG};
    #paths := compute_num_of_paths{DAG};

    if {#paths < max_paths } {
        CP := compute_cutpoints{DAG};
        DAG := split_DAG{DAG, CP};
    }

    for each dag; ∈ DAG {
        P := calculate_all_paths{dagᵢ};
        CS := {};
        for each p ∈ P {
            CS := CS   do_AFAP_schedule{p};
        }
        Aupurpose_all_schedules {P, CS};
    }
}
                    □
compute_cutpoints{DAG}
{
    CP_list_intialize{};
    for each vᵢ ∈ V { /* apply rule 2 */
        if { fulfills_rule2(vᵢ)} {
            CP_list_insert{∈ᵢ};
        }
    }

    sort_by_profiling{CP_list}; /* apply rule 1 */

    #cut_pts := input{};
    if {len{CP_list} < #cut_pts} {
        if { ambiguous_cut{CP_list, #cut_pts} }
            CP_list := apply_rule 3{CP_list, #cut_pts};
        }
    }
    return{CP_list}:
}
```

**Figure 7-4** *An algorithm for path-based estimation. From Henkel and Ernst [Hen01] © 2001 IEEE.*

They compute these from more direct parameters such as the number of states in the controller, the sources of operands for operations, and so on.

Vahid and Gajski preprocess the design to compute a variety of information for each procedure in the program.

- A set of data path inputs and a set of data path outputs.

- The set of function and storage units. Each unit is described by its size and the number of control lines it accepts.

- A set of functional objects is described by the number of possible control states for the object and the destinations to which the object may write. Each destination is itself described with an identifier, the number of states for which the destination is active for this object, and the sources that the object can assign to this destination.

A tabular form of this information is shown in Figure 7-5. This information can be used to compute some intermediate values as shown in Figure 7-6. These values in turn can be used to determine the parameters in (EQ 7-2).

Vahid and Gajski use an update algorithm given a change to the hardware configuration. Given a design object, they first add the object to the design if it

| Functional object | States | Destination | Sources | Active states |
|---|---|---|---|---|
| Procedure 1 | 5 | A | C<br>Adder 1 | 3 |
| | | Comparator 1 | A<br>D | 1 |
| | | Adder 1 | C<br>D<br>E | 2 |
| | | Storage 1 | Comparator 1 | 1 |
| Procedure 2 | 2 | A | Adder 1 | 1 |
| | | Adder 1 | F<br>D | 1 |
| | | B | 'O' | 1 |

**Figure 7-5** *Preprocessed information used for cost estimation. From Vahid and Gajski [Vah95] © 1995 IEEE.*

| Destination | Sources | Contrib. fct. objs. | Component required | Size | Control lines | Active states |
|---|---|---|---|---|---|---|
| A | C | Procedure1 | 8-bit 2x1 mux | 200 | 1 | 3 |
|  | adder1 | Procedure1 |  |  |  |  |
| comparator1 | A | Procedure1 | 8-bit compare | 300 | 0 | 1 |
|  | D | Procedure1 |  |  |  |  |
| adder1 | C | Procedure1 | 8-bit 2x1 mux | 200 | 1 | 2 |
|  | D | Procedure1 | 8-bit adder | 400 | 0 | 2 |
|  | E | Procedure1 |  |  |  |  |
| storage1 | comparator1 | Procedure1 | 1-bit register | 75 | 1 | 1 |

wires          srcs_list                     units          size_list     ctrl     active_list

Hwsize ( wires, srcs_list, units, size_list, ctrl, active_list, states )

Hwsize (    8,    srcs_list,    5,    size_list,    3,    active_list,    5  )   (from PP)

**Figure 7-6**  *Tabular representation of hardware resources. From Vahid and Gajski [Vah95] © 1995 IEEE.*

does not yet exist. They then update multiplexer sources and sizes and update control line active states for this destination. Finally, they update the number of controller states. Their update algorithm executes in constant time if the number of destinations per object is approximately constant.

## 7.4  Hardware/Software Co-synthesis Algorithms

*co-synthesis activities*

When designing a distributed embedded system, developers need to deal with several design problems:

■ We must *schedule* operations in time, including communication on the network and computations on the processing elements. Clearly, the scheduling of operations on the PEs and the communications between the processing element are linked. If one PE finishes its computations too late, it may interfere with another communication on the network as it tries to send its result to the processing elements that needs it. This is bad for both the processing elements that needs the result and the other PEs whose communication is interfered with.

■ We must *allocate* computations to the processing elements. The allocation of computations to the PEs determines which communications are required—if a value computed on one PE is needed on another, it must be transmitted over the network.

■ We must *partition* the functional description into computational units. Partitioning in this sense is different from hardware/software partitioning, in which we divide a function between the CPU and the accelerator. The granularity with which we describe the function to be implemented affects our choice of search algorithm and our methods for performance and energy analysis.

■ We also need to *map* processing elements and communication links onto specific components. Some algorithms allocate functions to abstract PEs and links that do not model the behavior of a particular component in detail. This allows the synthesis algorithm to explore a larger design space using simple estimates. Mapping selects specific components that can be associated with more precise cost, performance, and power models.

*optimization criteria*

Co-synthesis designs systems to satisfy objective functions and meet constraints. The traditional co-synthesis problem is to minimize hardware cost while satisfying deadlines. Power consumption was added to objective functions as low-power design became more important. Several groups have developed algorithms that try to satisfy multiple objective functions simultaneously; we will look at those techniques in Section 7.4.5.

In the first two sections, we consider design representations. Section 7.4.1 surveys methods used to specify the programs that describe the desired system behavior; Section 7.4.2 looks at ways to describe the characteristics of the hardware. Section 7.4.3 considers techniques to synthesize based on a hardware architecture template. Section 7.4.4 looks at co-synthesis algorithms that generate arbitrary hardware topologies without the use of templates. In Section 7.4.5, we study multi-objective algorithms for co-synthesis, and Section 7.4.6 considers co-synthesis for control and I/O systems. Section 7.4.7 looks at some co-synthesis techniques designed for memory-intense systems; it concludes with a discussion of co-synthesis algorithms for reconfigurable systems in Section 7.4.8.

## 7.4.1 Program Representations

Co-synthesis algorithms generally expect system functionality to be specified in one of two forms: a sequential/parallel program or a task graph.

*program representations*

Programs provide operator-level detail of a program's execution. Most programming languages are also sequential, meaning that synthesis must analyze the available parallelism in a program. Some co-synthesis systems accept fairly straightforward subsets of languages such as C. Others add constructs that allow the designer to specify operations that can be performed in parallel or must be performed in a particular order; an example is the HardwareC language used by Vulcan [Gup93]. The system of Eles et al. [Ele96] takes VHDL programs as behavioral specifications; they use VHDL processes to capture coarse-grained concurrency and use VHDL operations to describe interprocess communication.

*task graphs*    Task graphs, as we saw in Section 6.3.2, have been used for many years to specify concurrent software. Task graphs are generally not described at the operator level, so provide a coarser-grained description of the functionality. They naturally describe the parallelism available in a system at that coarser level.

Task graph variants that allow conditional execution of processes have been developed. For example, Eles et al. [Ele98] used a conditional task graph model. Some edges in their task graph model are designated as conditional; one is labeled with the condition, called a **guard**, that determines whether that edge is traversed. A node that is the source of conditional edges is called a **disjunction node** and a node that is the sink of conditional edges is a **conjunction node**. They require that for any nodes $i$ and $j$, where $j$ is not a conjunction node, there can be an edge $i \rightarrow j$ only if it is the case that the guard for $i$ is true, impling that the guard for $j$ is true. The control dependence graph (CDG) introduced in Section 4.3 can be used to analyze the conditions under which a node will be executed.

*TGFF*    Task Graphs for Free (TGFF) [Dic98c] (*http://www.zhyang.ece.northwestern.edu/tgff*) is a Web tool that generates pseudorandom task graphs. The user can control the range of deadlines, graph connectivity parameters, and laxity.

*UNITY*    A very different specification was used by Barros et al. [Bar94], who used the UNITY language [Cha88] to specify system behavior. UNITY was designed as an abstract language for parallel programming. The assignment portion of a UNITY program specifies the desired computations. It consists of a set of assignments that may be performed either synchronously or asynchronously on a statement-by-statement basis. Execution starts from an initial condition, statements are fairly executed, and execution continues until the program reaches a fixed point at which the program's state does not change.

## 7.4.2  Platform Representations

In addition to representing the program to be implemented, we must also represent the hardware platform being designed. Because a platform is being created and is not given, our representation of the platform itself must be flexible. We need to describe components of the platform so that those components can be combined into a complete platform.

*technology*
*tables*    Some of the information about the platform is closely linked to the representation of the program. For example, processor performance is usually not cap-

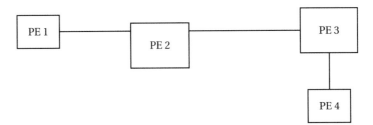

**Figure 7-7** *A multiprocessor connectivity graph.*

tured abstractly; instead, we generally capture the speed at which various pieces of the program execute on different types of PEs. One data structure that is used with some variation in many systems is the **technology table** (see Figure 7-7). This table gives the execution time of each process for each type of processing element. (Some processes may not run on some types of PEs, particularly if the element is not programmable.) A co-synthesis program can easily look up the execution time for a process once it knows the type of PE to which the process has been allocated.

The performance of a point-to-point communication link is generally easier to characterize since transmission time is independent of the data being sent. In these cases we can characterize the link with a data rate.

In general, a multidimensional table could have several entries for each row/column pair.

- The **CPU time entry** shows the computation time required for a process.

- The **communication time entry** gives the time required to send data across a link; the amount of data is specified by the source–destination pair.

- The **cost entry** gives the manufacturing cost of a processing element or communication link.

- The **power entry** gives the power consumption of a PE or communication link; this entry can be further subdivided into static and dynamic power components.

*a co-synthesis platform as graph*

We also need to represent the multiprocessor's structure, which in general changes during co-synthesis. A graph is often used, as shown in Figure 7-8, with nodes for the PEs and edges for the communication links. Complex communication structures, such as multistage networks, are generally not directly represented in the platform description. Instead, the structure of the links shows possible connections that can be implemented using different physical layers. The platform model also does not usually include the location of the memories within the communication topology.

|  | PE 1 | PE 2 | PE 3 |
|---|---|---|---|
| P1 | 5 | – | 14 |
| P2 | 4 | 4 | 5 |
| P3 | 7 | 9 | 6 |

**Figure 7-8** *A process-to-PE technology table.*

### 7.4.3 Template-Driven Synthesis Algorithms

Most early co-synthesis algorithms, and many co-synthesis algorithms in general, generate hardware architectures based on an **architectural template**. The most common architectural template is a bus-based system, with either a single or multiple CPU and one or more accelerators. Co-synthesis that maps the design onto this bus-based template is generally known as **hardware/software partitioning** because the bus defines a boundary between two partitions, making it possible to apply traditional graph partitioning algorithms to co-synthesis.

*hardware/ software partitioning assumptions*

The template provided by the CPU/bus/accelerator configuration is a powerful element of the hardware/software co-synthesis methodology. The template provides some important knowledge that restricts the design space and helps to decouple some operations:

- **The type of CPU is known.** Once we know the CPU type, we can estimate software performance much more accurately. We can also generate a great deal of performance data in advance since knowledge of the CPU type greatly limits the amount of data that we need to generate

- **The number of processing elements is known.** We can more easily build performance models because we know the interconnection topology.

- **Only one processing element can multi-task.** Performance analysis is more complicated when several processing elements can switch between tasks.

When we move to more general architectures, co-synthesis algorithms become considerably more complex. As we will see, different algorithm designers have made different choices about simplifying assumptions and strategies to break the problem into manageable pieces.

*a couple partitioning systems*

Two early hardware/software partitioning systems exemplify different approaches to co-synthesis. COSYMA [Ern93] started with all functions on the CPU and moved some functions to the accelerator to improve performance; Vulcan [Gup93] started with all functions in the accelerator and moved some functions to the CPU to reduce cost. Comparing these two systems gives us a good understanding of the major hardware/software partitioning problems.

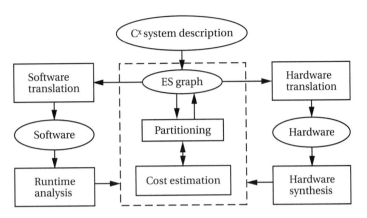

**Figure 7-9** *The COSYMA System.*

*COSYMA*        The block diagram of the COSYMA system is shown in Figure 7-9. The application is described in $C^X$, which extends C with some task constructs and timing constraints. That description is compiled into an intermediate form called an ES graph. The ES graph represents the control and data flow in the program in a way that can be rewritten either as a hardware description or an executable C program. (COSYMA also includes a simulator for ES graphs.) The ES graph is composed of basic scheduling blocks (BSBs) that are the primary units of co-synthesis. COSYMA uses simulated annealing to search the design space to determine which BSBs should be implemented on the accelerator.

*Vulcan*        The Vulcan system started with its own programming language extension known as HardwareC. Vulcan was designed to synthesize multiple tasks running at different rates, so HardwareC allows the description of timing and rate constraints. Input and output operations are nondeterministic operations that do not take a predictable amount of time. The HardwareC description is automatically broken into tasks by Vulcan by splitting the description at the nondeterministic operation points.

Vulcan schedules and allocates threads using iterative improvement. The initial solution puts all threads in the accelerator, which is a high-performance but also high-cost solution. Vulcan iteratively moves threads to the CPU, testing whether the implementation still meets its performance goals after the move. Once a thread is successfully moved, its successors become the next candidates for movement.

Vulcan estimates performance and cost on the CPU by directly analyzing the threads. The latency of each thread has been predetermined; the thread reaction rate is given. Vulcan computes the processor utilization and bus utilization for each allocation. Vulcan estimates hardware size based on the costs of the operators in the function.

*a binary constraint search*

Because the space of feasible designs is large, co-synthesis algorithms rely on efficient search. Vahid et al. [Vah94] developed a binary constraint search algorithm. The algorithm minimizes the size of the required hardware in a hardware/software partitioned system to meet the performance constraint.

Vahid et al. formulate their objective function so as to meet a performance goal and to have hardware area no larger than a specified bound:

$$0 = k_{perf} \sum_{1 \le j \le m} V_{perf}(C_j) + k_{area} V_{area}(W).$$   (EQ 7-3)

In this objective function, $V_{perf}(C_j)$ is the amount by which performance constraint $j$ is violated, and $V_{perf}(W)$ is the amount by which the hardware area exceeds the prescribed hardware size bound $W$.

This objective function is zero when both the performance and area bounds are satisfied. If solutions are arranged on a line, then all solutions to the right of a certain point will be zero; these are satisfying implementations. All the nonsatisfying solutions will be to the left of that boundary. The goal of a search algorithm is to find the boundary between the zero and non-zero objective function regions.

The search algorithm is shown in Figure 7-10. It collects hardware (H) and software (S) elements of the system during the search procedure. PartAlg() generates new solutions to probe different regions of the objective function. The hardware/software partition at the boundary between a zero and non-zero objective function is returned as {Hzero,Szero}.

*CoWare*

The CoWare system [Ver96] supports the design of heterogeneous embedded systems. The system behavior is described as communicating processes. A model can be encapsulated so that existing design tools, such as compilers and simulators, can be reused. The system description is refined over several steps to create an implementation.

```
low =0; high = AIIHWSize;
while (low < high) {
    mid = (low + high + 1)/2;
    {Hprime,Sprime} = PartAlg(H,S,constraints,mid,cost());
    if (cost(Hprime,Sprime,constraints,mid) == 0) {
        high = mid-1;
        {Hzero, Szero} = {Hprime,Sprime};
    }
    else
        low = mid;
}
return {Hzero,Szero};
```

**Figure 7-10**  *Hardware/software partitioning by binary search [Vah94].*

A process specifies the behavior of part of the system. *Processes* can be described in several different host languages such as C or VHDL, and they can be defined hierarchically by composing them from other processes. A *thread* is a single flow of control in a process; a process can have several threads. A **slave thread** is associated with a slave port. **time-loop thread** is not associated with a port and is repeatedly executed. Objects communicate through *ports*; like processes, ports can be described hierarchically. A *protocol* defines the communication syntax and semantics. Protocols can also be described hierarchically.

Co-synthesis implements communicating processes, some of which execute in software on a CPU while others are implemented as hardware attached to the CPU. A library describes the CPU and its interface. On the hardware and software sides of the interface, concurrent processes are combined using inlining into a product process. On the software side, device drivers need to be added to the specified functionality.

*simulated annealing versus tabu search*    Eles et al. [Ele96] compared simulated annealing and tabu search for co-synthesis. Their simulated annealing algorithm has three major parameters: initial temperature *TI*, temperature length *TL*, and cooling ratio α. Their simple move procedure randomly selects a node to be moved from one partition to the other. Their improved move procedure randomly selects a node to be moved and also moves directly connected nodes whose movement would improve the objective function.

Tabu search uses two data structures, **short-term memory** and **long-term memory**. Short-term memory holds some information on recent search moves. Long-term memory holds information about moves over a longer time period. For each node, it holds the number of iterations it has been in during each partition; this information can be used to determine the priority with which it should be moved.

Eles et al. uses an extended form of VHDL to describe the system to be designed; they use VHDL primitives for interprocess communication. They analyze the code to identify processes, loops, and statement blocks. They both statically analyze the code and profile the code during execution. Their co-synthesis system uses an objective function:

$$C = Q_1 \sum_{(i,j) \in \text{cut}} W1_{ij}^E + Q_2 \frac{\sum_{i \in HW} \frac{\sum_{\exists i,j} W2_{ij}^E}{W1_i^N}}{N_H} + Q_3 \left[ \frac{\sum_{i \in HW} W2_i^N}{N_H} + \frac{\sum_{i \in SW} W2_i^N}{N_S} \right].$$

(EQ 7-4)

In this formula, $Q_1$, $Q_2$, and $Q_3$ are weights. *HW* and *SW* represent the hardware and software partitions, while $N_H$ and $N_S$ represent the number of nodes in those sets, respectively. $W1_{ij}^E$ denotes the total amount of data transferred between processes $i$ and $j$. $W2_{ij}^E$ counts the total number of interactions between the two processes, with each interaction counting as one event. $W1_i^N$ is the total number of operations performed by process $i$. We define

$$W2_i^N = M^{CL}K_i^{CL} + M^U K_i^U + M^P K_i^P - M^{SO}K_i^{SO}, \qquad \text{(EQ 7-5)}$$

where the *M*s are weights and the *K*s represent measures of the processes.

$K_i^{CL}$ is the **relative computational load** of process $i$, which is the total number of operations performed by a block of statements in the program divided by the total number of operations in the complete program. $K_i^U$ is the ratio of the number of different types of operations in the process divided by the total number of operations, which is a measure of the uniformity of the computation. $K_i^P$ is the ratio of the number of operations in the process to the length of the computation path, which measures potential parallelism. $K_i^{SO}$ is the ratio of the number of software-style operations (floating-point, recursive subroutine calls, pointer operations, and so on) to the total number of operations.

Eles et al. concluded that simulated annealing and tabu search provided similar quality results but that tabu search ran about 20 times faster. However, tabu search algorithms took considerably longer to develop. They also compared these algorithms to Kernighan–Lin style partitioning; they found that for equal-quality solutions, both simulated annealing and tabu search ran faster than Kernighan–Lin on large problems.

*LYCOS*

The LYCOS co-synthesis system [Mad97] works from a single design representation that can be derived from multiple languages and feed multiple tools.

*Quenya design representation*

LYCOS represents designs internally as CDFGs, using a format known as Quenya, and it can translate subsets of both C and VHDL into its internal representation. Quenya's execution semantics are based on colored Petri nets. Tokens arrive at nodes along input edges; the nodes can remove tokens from their inputs and place tokens on their outputs based on firing rules. Figure 7-11 shows the model for an if-then-else statement. The right block evaluates the condition and sends a token along the *b* edges. If *b* is true, then the s1 block is executed, else the s2 block is executed.

Figure 7-12 shows the model for a while statement. Procedures are translated into separate graphs, which call nodes denoting calls to the procedure body and an edge for each input or output parameter. Shared variables are represented by import/export nodes to sample the value of a shared variable and wait nodes for synchronization.

*profiling and design estimation*

LYCOS uses profiling tools to estimate performance. The Quenya model is translated to C++ and executed for profiling. Hardware models are constructed in the Architectural Construction Environment (ACE), which is used to estimate area and performance.

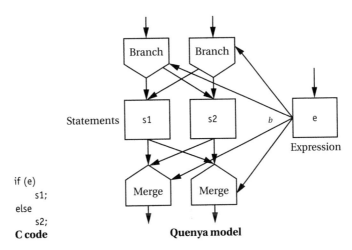

if (e)
    s1;
else
    s2;
**C code**

**Figure 7-11** *A Quenya model for an if-then-else statement. After Madsen et al. [Mad97].*

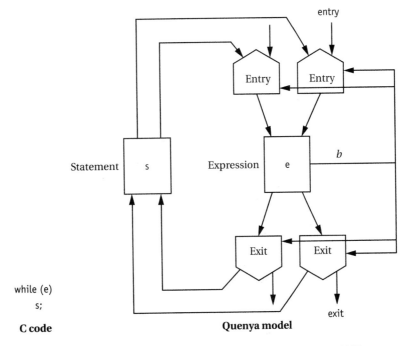

while (e)
    s;
**C code**

**Figure 7-12** *A Quenya model for a while statement. After Madsen et al. [Mad97].*

LYCOS breaks the functional model into **basic scheduling blocks (BSBs)**. BSBs for hardware and software do not execute concurrently. A sequence of BSBs $\langle B_i, \ldots, B_j \rangle$ is denoted by $S_{i,j}$. The read and write sets for the sequence are denoted by $r_{i,j}$ and $w_{i,j}$. The speedup given by moving a BSB sequence to hardware is computed using

$$S_{i,j} = \sum_{i \leq k \leq j} pc(B_k)(t_{s,k} - t_{h,k}) - \left( \sum ac(v) t_{s \rightarrow h} + \sum ac(v) t_{h \rightarrow s} \right)$$

(EQ 7-6)

In this formula, $pc(B)$ is the number of times that a BSB is executed in a profiling run and $ac(v)$ is the number of times that a variable is accessed in a profiling run. $dt_{s \rightarrow h}$ represents the software-to-hardware communication time, and $t_{h \rightarrow s}$ represents the hardware-to-software communication time. The area penalty for moving a BSB sequence to hardware is the sum of the hardware areas of the individual BSBs.

LYCOS evaluates sequences of BSBs and tries to find a combination of nonoverlapping ones that give the largest possible speedup and that fit within the available area. A sequence has some BSBs mapped to hardware and others mapped to software. With proper construction of a table, this problem can be formulated as a dynamic program. The table is organized into groups such that all members of a group have the same BSB as the last member of that sequence. Each entry gives the area and speedup for an entry. Once some BSBs are chosen for the solution, other sequences that are chosen cannot include those BSBs, since they have already been allocated. The table allows sequences that end at certain BSBs to be easily found during search.

Xie and Wolf [Xie00] used high-level synthesis to more accurately estimate performance and area of accelerators during co-synthesis. They targeted a bus-based architecture with multiple CPUs and multiple accelerators. After finding an initial feasible solution, they first iteratively reduced the number of accelerators and the cost of CPUs; they then reduced accelerator cost using more accurate analysis; finally, they allocated and scheduled tasks and data transfers. When choosing whether to allocate a task to an accelerator or to a CPU, they used two heuristics. First, if the speed difference between the CPU and accelerator implementation was small, they chose the task as a candidate for software implementation. They also chose tasks that were not on the critical path as candidates for software implementation.

The accelerator cost-reduction phase looks at two metrics of the schedule. **Global slack** is the slack between the deadline and the completion of the tasks; **local slack** is the slack between the accelerator's completion time and the start time of its successor tasks. This phase relies on the use of a high-level synthesis tool that, given the number of cycles an accelerator has to implement, can generate a register–transfer implementation that meets that performance goal and is also area efficient.

This phase first tries to replace each accelerator with the smallest possible implementation of that accelerator. If the schedule is still feasible, they keep that allocation, else they replace it with the accelerator's fastest implementation. They next calculate the global slack and use it to determine the amount by which accelerators can be slowed down. Each accelerator that uses its fastest implementation is slowed down by the sum of the global and local slacks; other accelerators are slowed down by the local slack. High-level synthesis is used to generate the implementation that meets this time bound; from the synthesis result, the accelerator's area can be accurately estimated. For each accelerator, the minimum-cost implementation at the chosen speed is selected.

*static and dynamic scheduling*

The Serra system [Moo00] combines static and dynamic scheduling of tasks. Static scheduling, which is handled by a hardware executive manager, is efficient for low-level tasks. Dynamic scheduling, which is handled by a preemptive static priority scheduler, handles variations in execution time and event arrival time. Serra targets an architecture with a single CPU and multiple accelerators. Serra represents the task set as a forest of DAGs. Each task graph has a **never set** that specifies tasks that cannot execute at the same time. The never set makes scheduling NP-complete; Serra finds a schedule using a dynamic programming-style heuristic. The scheduler works from the end of the schedule backward, finding a good schedule given the tasks already scheduled.

### 7.4.4 Co-synthesis of General Multiprocessors

In this section, we reconsider hardware/software co-design for more general multiprocessor architectures. Many useful systems can be designed by hardware/software partitioning algorithms based on the CPU+ accelerator template. Hardware/software partitioning can also be used to design PEs that are part of larger multiprocessors. But if we want to design a complete application-specific multiprocessor system, we need to use more general co-synthesis algorithms that do not rely on the CPU+ accelerator template.

*the Gordian knot of co-synthesis*

In the most general case, all these tasks are related. Different partitions of functionality into processes clearly changes scheduling and allocation. Even if we chose a partitioning of functions, scheduling, allocating, and binding are closely related. We want to choose the processing element for a process—both the general allocation and the binding to a specific type—based on the overall system schedule and when that process has to finish. But we can't determine the schedule and the completion time of a process until we at least choose an allocation and most likely a binding. This is the Gordian knot that co-synthesis designers must face—the set of intertwined problems that must somehow be unraveled.

*GCLP algorithm*          Kalavade and Lee [Kal97] developed the **Global Criticality/Local Phase (GCLP)** algorithm to synthesize complex embedded system design. Their algorithm performs the hardware/software partitioning-style task of determining whether a task should be implemented in hardware or software and the schedule of the tasks in the system; it also allows for several different hardware and/or software implementations of a given task and selects the best implementation for the system. The application is specified as a directed acyclic graph.

The target architecture includes a CPU and a custom data path. The hardware is limited to a maximum size and the software is limited to a maximum memory size. The various hardware and software implementations of the task are precharacterized. Each node in the task graph has a hardware implementation curve and a software implementation curve that describe hardware and software implementation costs, respectively, for various bins that represent different implementations.

Their GCLP algorithm adaptively changes the objective at each step to try to optimize the design. It looks at two factors: the global criticality and the local phase. The *global criticality* is a global scheduling measure. It computes the fraction of as-yet unmapped nodes that would have to be moved from software to hardware implementations in order to meet the schedule's deadline. The global criticality is averaged over all the unmapped nodes in each step.

The *local phase* computation improves hardware/software mapping. Heuristics are used to determine whether a node is best implemented in hardware or software; bit manipulations have a bias toward hardware implementation and extensive memory operations have a bias toward software. These heuristics are termed **repelling forces**—for example, bit manipulations repel a node away from software implementation. The algorithm uses several repeller properties, each with its own repeller value. The sum of all the repeller properties for a node gives its repeller measure.

The algorithm computes **extremity measures** to help optimize mappings. A software extremity node has a long runtime but has a small hardware area cost. Similarly, a hardware extremity node has a large area cost but a small software execution time.

The co-synthesis algorithm iteratively maps nodes in the task graph. After selecting a node to map, it classifies a node as a repeller, an extremity, or a normal node.

*SpecSyn*          SpecSyn [Gon97b; Gaj98] is designed to support a **specify–explore–refine** methodology. As shown in Figure 7-13, SpecSyn transforms functional specifications into an intermediate form known as SLIF. A variety of tools can then work on the design. A refiner generates software and hardware descriptions. SpecSyn represents designs using a program-state machine model, which uses a Statechart-like description that allows complex sequential programs at the leaf states. The SLIF representation is annotated with attributes such as area, profiling information, number of bits per transfer, and so on.

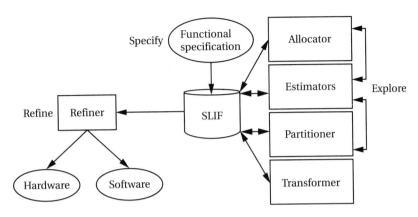

**Figure 7-13** *The SpecSyn system [Gaj98].*

*allocation, partitioning, and refinement*

The allocation phase can allocate standard or custom processors, memories, or busses. Partitioning assigns operations in the functional specification to allocated hardware units. During partitioning, performance is estimated using parameters such as bus frequency, bit width of transformations, and profiling values. Hardware size is estimated using estimates for the processing elements, busses, and so on, while software size is estimated by compiling code into generic three-operand instructions, then estimating code size for a specific processor by multiplying generic code size by a processor-code size coefficient.

A refined design adds detail but is simulatable and synthesizable, so its components can be used for further verification and synthesis. A variety of refinements can be performed, including:

- **Control-related refinement**—This preserves the execution order of a specification when a behavior is split among several behaviors during partitioning. Signals, either unidirectional or handshaking, must be added to ensure that the two modules perform their respective operations in the proper order.

- **Data-related refinement**—This updates the values of variables that are shared by several behaviors. For example, as shown in Figure 7-14, a bus protocol can be used to send a value from one processor to another.

- **Architecture-related refinements**—These add behaviors that resolve conflicts and allow data transfer to happen smoothly. For example, a bus arbiter can be inserted when several behaviors may use the bus at the same time. Bus interfaces are inserted when message-passing is used for data communication.

*iterative improvement*

Wolf [Wol97b] developed a co-synthesis algorithm that performed scheduling, allocating, and binding for architectures with arbitrary topologies. The

```
behavior B is sequential
    variable x ...

    B1: (x > 1, B2);
    B2: (x > 5, B3);

    behaviour B1 is
        . . .
    end;

    behaviour B2 is
        . . .
    end;

    behavior B3 is
        . . .
    end;
end;
```

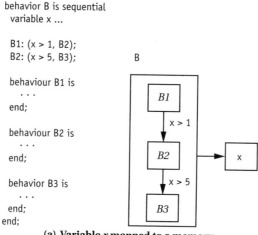

(a) **Variable *x* mapped to a memory**

Component

```
B
    variable tmp ...

    B1: (tmp > 1, B2);
    B2: (tmp > 5, B3);

    behavior B1 is
        . . .
        MST_receive(bus,x_addr,tmp);
    end;

    behavior B2 is
        . . .
        MST_receive(bus,x_addr,tmp);
    end;

    behavior B3 is
        . . .
    end;
```

Memory

```
    variable x ...

    loop
        wait until bus_start =1;
        if bus_start = 1 and bus_rd = 1 and bus_addr = x_addr
            then SLV_send(bus, x);
        if bus_start = 1 and bus_wr = 1 and bus_addr = x_addr
            then SLV_receive(bus, x);
    end loop;
```

Bus

(b) **Data access implemented by bus protocols**

**Figure 7-14** *Data refinement in SpecSyn. From Gong et al. [Gon97b] © 1997 ACM Press.*

application is described as a task graph with multiple tasks. The set of processing elements that can be used in the design is described in a technology table that gives, for each PE and each process, the execution time of that process on each PE as well as the total cost of the processing elements. No initial template for the architecture is given. Synthesis proceeds through several steps.

1. An initial processor allocation and binding is constructed by selecting for each process the fastest PE for that process in the technology table. If the system cannot be scheduled in this allocation, then there is no feasible solution. The initial schedule tells the algorithm the rates at which processing elements must communicate with each other.

2. Processes are reallocated to reduce PE cost. This step is performed iteratively by first pairwise merging processes to try to eliminate PEs, then moving processes to balance the load. These operations are repeated until the total cost of the hardware stops going down. At the end of this step, we have a good approximation of the number and types of PEs required.

3. Processes are reallocated again to minimize inter-PE communication. This step allows us to minimize communication bandwidth, which is an important aspect of design cost. At the end of this step, we have completely determined the number and types of PEs in the architecture.

4. We then allocate communication channels as required to support the inter-PE communication.

5. Finally, we allocate input/output devices, as required, to support the I/O operations required by the processes.

*high-level synthesis for estimates*

Xie and Wolf [Xie00] coupled hardware/software co-synthesis to a high-level synthesis engine that used integer programming, rather than heuristic graph algorithms, to schedule and allocate hardware. This engine was fast enough to be used as a subroutine during co-synthesis. They developed a performance analysis tool based on the high-level synthesis. At the start of synthesis, they constructed an initial solution with every task on the fastest PE, then iteratively improved the design.

The first phase performed tried to move tasks from the accelerator to CPUs and also to reduce the cost of CPUs; these procedures analyze slack to find good candidates for movement. The second phase reduces the cost of the accelerator. The system calculates slacks in the system schedule and assigns them to various accelerators; it uses the performance analysis tool to determine whether each accelerator can be slowed down by the prescribed amount and the area of the modified accelerator.

*large task graphs*

Large sets of tasks present additional problems for co-synthesis. Dave et al. [Dav99a] developed the COSYN system to synthesize heterogeneous distributed embedded systems from large task graphs. COSYN allows task graphs to be formulated using repeated tasks: a prototype task is defined and then copied many times. Communication systems often have many copies of identical tasks—each task represents a call. This technique is also useful in other types of large real-time systems.

*COSYN problem formulation*

COSYN task graphs are directed sets of processes. Each task graph has an earliest start time, period, and deadline. The implementation is built from PEs and communication links. Several tables and vectors define the tasks and their underlying hardware.

- A technology table defines the execution time of each process on each feasible PE.

- A **communication vector** is defined for each edge in the task graph; the value of the $i^{th}$ entry defines the time required to transmit the data sent from source to sink over the $i^{th}$ type of communication link.

- A **preference vector** is indexed by the processing element number; the $i^{th}$ value is 0 if the process itself cannot be mapped onto the $i^{th}$ PE and 1 if it can be.

- An **exclusion vector** is indexed by process number; the $i^{th}$ value is 0 if the two processes cannot be mapped onto the same processing element, $i^{th}$ PE, and 1 if they can co-exist on the same processor.

- An **average power vector** for each process defines the average power consumption of the task on each type of PE.

- A **memory vector** for each process consists of three scalar values: program storage, data storage, and stack storage. There is one memory vector for each task.

- The preemption overhead time is specified for each processor.

- The set of processes allocated to the same PE is called a **cluster**.

*handling large task sets*

COSYN will adjust the periods of tasks by a small amount (3% by default) to reduce the length of the hyperperiod. The number of executions of the task in the hyperperiod causes problems: each execution must be checked. By adjusting the period of a task that has many copies in the hyperperiod, COSYN can reduce the number of times it must consider that task in the hyperperiod. COSYN uses this value to rank tasks for period adjustment. Threshold reduction stops when the number of total executions of a task in the hyperperiod fall below a threshold.

COSYN also uses an **association graph** to manage the representation of multiple executions of a task in the hyperperiod. If all tasks have deadlines shorter than their periods, then the association graph need only be one-dimensional; its entries include the PE to which the task is allocated and its priority, deadline, best-case projected finish time, and worst-case projected finish time. If a task's deadline can extend beyond its period, then the association graph must be two-dimensional because there may be more than one instance of the task executing at a time. The second dimension indexes over the simultaneously executing copies of the task.

*COSYN*
*synthesis*

The COSYN synthesis algorithm is summarized in Figure 7-15. COSYN performs three major phases: (1) It clusters tasks to reduce the search space for allocation; (2) it allocates tasks to processing elements; and (3) the tasks and processes are scheduled.

COSYN forms clusters to reduce the combined communication costs of a set of processes that is on the critical path. This is done by putting the set of processes on the same PE. It first assigns a preliminary priority to each task based on its deadline. It then uses a greedy algorithm to cluster processes: It starts with the highest-priority task, puts it in a cluster, and walks through the fan-in of the task to find further tasks for the cluster. To avoid overly unbalanced loads on the PEs, a threshold limits the maximum size of a cluster.

After clusters are formed, they are allocated, with allocation decisions driven by the dollar cost of the allocation. Clusters are allocated in order of priority, starting with the highest-priority clusters. COSYN checks for the compatibility of connections between PEs during allocation.

After allocation, the processes are scheduled using priorities. COSYN concentrates on scheduling the first copy of each task. The association array is used to update the start and finish times of the remaining copies of the task; other copies need to be explicitly scheduled only when an execution slot is taken by a higher-priority task.

COSYN allows the supply voltages of parts to be mixed so that some non-critical sections of the design can be run at lower power levels. It checks the compatibility of connections between components at different supply voltages.

```
assign priorities by deadline;
form association array;
form clusters of processes;
initialize architecture to empty;
allocate clusters;
foreach unallocated cluster Ci {
    form allocation array for Ci;
    foreach allocation in allocation array{
        schedule allocated clusters;
        evaluate completion time, energy, power.
        if deadline is met in best case then {
            save current architecture;
            break;
            }
        else save best allocation;
        tag cluster Ci as allocated;
        }
    }
}
```

**Figure 7-15** *The COSYN synthesis algorithm. From Dave and Jha [Dav99b] © 1999 IEEE.*

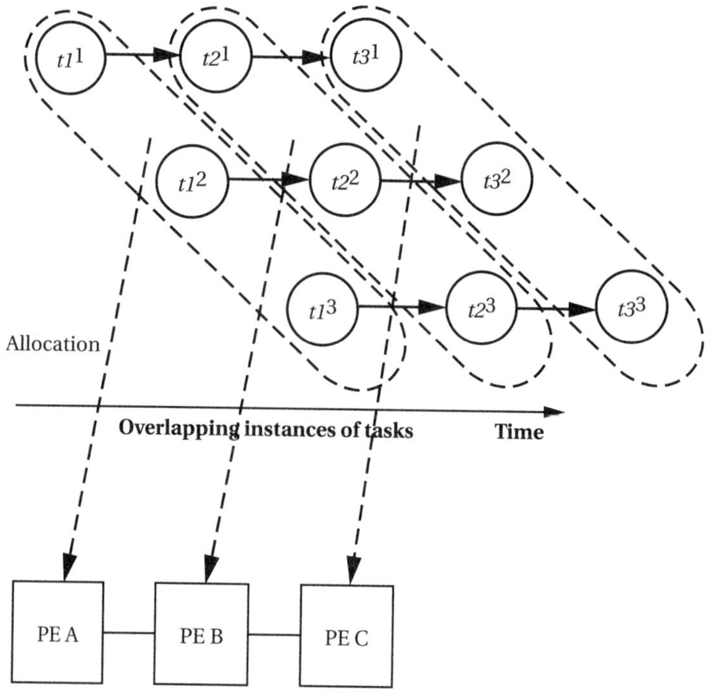

**Figure 7-16** *Allocating concurrent task instances for pipelining.*

COSYN evaluates the feasible allocations by comparing the sum of their worst-case finish times. It chooses the solution with the largest total worst-case finish times for the processes, since the longest finish times are usually associated with the lowest-cost hardware.

COSYN tries to allocate concurrent instances of tasks to allow pipelining. As shown in Figure 7-16, several instances of a task may execute concurrently; the instances of each process in the task are identified by a superscript. If we allocate $t1$ to PE A, $t2$ to PE B, and $t3$ to PE C, then we pass data from process to process in the task at low cost and pipeline the execution of the task instances.

*hierarchical co-synthesis*

Dave and Jha [Dav98] also developed methods for hierarchical co-synthesis. As shown in Figure 7-17, their COHRA system both accepts hierarchical task graphs and produces hierarchically organized hardware architectures. A hierarchical task is a node in the task graph that contains its own task graph. A hierarchical hardware architecture is built from several layers of PEs that are composed in an approximate tree structure, though some non-tree edges are possible.

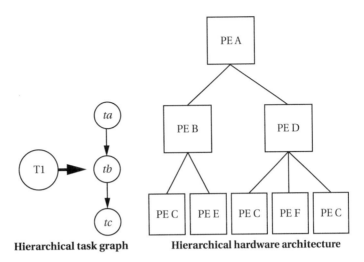

**Figure 7-17** *Hierarchical specifications and architectures.*

COHRA's synthesis algorithm resembles COSYN's algorithm: clustering, then allocation, then scheduling. COHRA also uses association tables to keep track of multiple copies of tasks.

*co-synthesizing fault tolerant systems*

Dave and Jha [Dav99b] developed the COFTA system to co-synthesize fault-tolerant systems. They used two types of checks at the task level.

- **Assertion tasks**—They compute assertion operations, such as checking an address against a valid range, and issue an error when the asserted condition is false.

- **Compare tasks**—They compare the results of duplicate copies of tasks and issue an error when the results do not agree.

The system designer specifies the assertions to be used; duplicate copies of tasks and the associated compare task are generated for tasks that do not have any assertions. The authors argue that assertion tasks are much more efficient than running duplicate copies of all tasks. An assertion task can catch many errors in a task without requiring that the entire computation of the task be repeated.

COFTA uses the clustering phase to enforce a fault-tolerant task allocation. It assigns an **assertion overhead** and **fault tolerant level** to each task. The assertion overhead of a task is the computation and communication times for all the processes in the transitive fanin of the process with an assertion. The fault tolerance level of a task is the assertion overhead of the task plus the maximum fault tolerance level of all processes in its fanout. These levels must

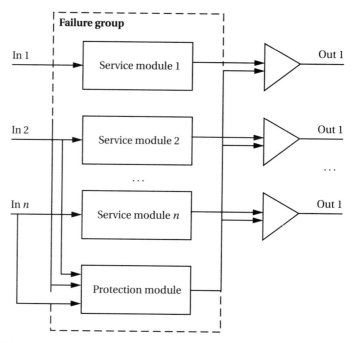

**Figure 7-18**  *Simple 1-by-n protection in a failure group [Dav99b].*

be recomputed as the clustering changes. During clustering, the fault tolerance level is used to select new tasks for the cluster—the fanout task with the highest fault tolerance level is chosen as the next addition to the cluster.

COFTA tries to share assertion tasks whenever possible. If several tasks use the same assertion but at nonoverlapping times, then one assertion task can be used to compute the assertion for all those tasks, saving hardware resources.

COFTA also generates a fault-tolerant hardware architecture. Figure 7-18 shows a simple 1-by-*n* **failure group** that consists of *n* service modules that perform the actual work of the system and one protection module. The protection module checks the service modules and substitutes results for bad service modules. In general, a failure group may use *m*-by-*n* protection with *m* protection modules. COFTA uses a restricted form of subgraph isomorphism to build failure groups into the architecture.

## 7.4.5  Multi-objective Optimization

*Pareto optimality*

Embedded system designs must meet several different design criteria. The traditional operations research approach of defining a single objective function and perhaps some minor objective functions, along with design constraints, may not adequately describe the system requirements. Economist Vilfredo Pareto (*http://www.en.wikipedia.org—Pareto efficiency*) developed a theory for multi-objective analysis known as **Pareto optimality**. An important concept provided by this theory is the way in which optimal solutions are judged: an optimal solution cannot be improved without making some other part of the solution worse.

*GOPS*

D'Ambrosio and Hu [D'Am94] developed the GOPS system to co-synthesize real-time embedded systems; they called this level of design **configuration synthesis** because it does not use detailed models of the processing elements.

*bounds on throughput*

GOPS uses a **feasibility factor** to estimate the schedulability of a set of tasks. Feasibility is determined relative to the speed of the PE and is defined in terms of several **throughput factors**. The **upper-bound throughput** $TR_U$ is an upper bound on the throughput required for the PE to finish the task. If rate-monotonic scheduling is used, then $TR_U$ for a set of $N$ tasks is

$$TR_U = \frac{1}{[N(2^{1/N} - 1)]} \sum_{1 \leq i \leq N} \frac{c_i}{d_i - a_i}, \qquad \text{(EQ 7-7)}$$

where $c_i$ is the computation time, $d_i$ is the deadline, and $a_i$ is the activation time, respectively, for task $i$. If earliest-deadline-first scheduling is used, then

$$TR_U = \sum_{1 \leq i \leq N} \frac{c_i}{d_i - a_i}. \qquad \text{(EQ 7-8)}$$

However, because these bounds are loose, D'Ambrosio and Hu provided some tighter bounds. They first showed that a set of $n$ tasks arranged in ascending order of deadlines cannot be feasibly scheduled if

$$\sum_{1 \leq i \leq n} \frac{k_i c_i}{d_n - a_i} > TR_P, \qquad \text{(EQ 7-9)}$$

where

$$k_i = \begin{cases} \lceil (d_n - a_i)/p_i \rceil & \text{if } \lfloor (d_n - a_i)/p_i \rfloor p_i + d_i \leq d_n \\ \lfloor (d_n - a_i)/p_i \rfloor & \text{otherwise.} \end{cases} \qquad \text{(EQ 7-10)}$$

They also showed that

$$\sum_{1 \leq i \leq n} \frac{h_i c_i}{d_n - a_i} > TR_P, \qquad \text{(EQ 7-11)}$$

where

$$k_i = \begin{cases} k_i - \lceil a_n - a_i/p_i \rceil & \text{if } a_i < a_n \\ k_i & \text{otherwise.} \end{cases} \qquad \text{(EQ 7-12)}$$

Based on these results, they showed that $TR_L$ can be computed as

$$TR_L = \max_{1 \le n \le N} \left\langle \frac{k_i c_i}{d_n - a_i}, \frac{h_i c_i}{d_n - a_i} \right\rangle. \qquad \text{(EQ 7-13)}$$

The actual throughput required to finish all tasks on time is $TR_P$, which lies between $TR_L$ and $TR_U$. They define the feasibility factor $\lambda_P$ in terms of these throughput estimates:

$$\lambda_P = \begin{cases} \dfrac{TR_P - TR_L}{TR_U - TR_L} & \text{if } (TR_P - TR_L) < (TR_U - TR_L) \\ 1 & \text{otherwise.} \end{cases} \qquad \text{(EQ 7-14)}$$

*feasibility factor as a constraint*

During optimization, the feasibility factor can be used to prune the search space. Candidate architectures with negative feasibility factors can be eliminated as infeasible.

*feasibility factor as an objective*

The feasibility factor is also used as an optimization objective. The two criteria of GOPS are cost and feasibility factor.

*genetic algorithms*

**Genetic algorithms** have been used for co-synthesis. This class of algorithms is modeled on genes and mutations. A solution to the problem is represented by a string of symbols. Strings can be modified and combined in various ways to create new designs. There are three basic types of moves in genetic algorithms:

1. A reproduction step makes a copy of a string.

2. A mutation step randomly changes a string.

3. A crossover step interchanges parts of two strings.

The new designs are then evaluated for quality and possibly reused to create still further mutations. One advantage of genetic algorithms is that they can easily handle complex objective functions.

*genetic algorithms for co-synthesis*

Dick and Jha [Dic97; Dic98] developed a genetic algorithm for hardware/software co-synthesis. Their algorithm can generate architectures with multiple processors and communication links; the architecture is optimized for both performance and power consumption. The synthesis procedure characterizes PEs as either independent or grouped. A *processor* can perform only one task at a time; an *IC* can have multiple *cores* on one chip so that a chip can simultaneously run several tasks.

*MOGAC components*

The tasks are characterized by technology tables that give the worst-case execution time and power consumption of each task on each feasible processor. It also keeps arrays that map given the worst-case performance, average power consumption, and peak power consumption for each task on each feasible core.

A *communication link* has several attributes: packet size, average power consumption per packet, worst-case communication time per packet, cost, number of contacts (the number of points connected by the link), number of pins, and idle power consumption. Busses are modeled as communication links with more than two contacts.

*MOGAC genetic model*

MOGAC keeps track of multiple objective functions and ranks designs on each objective function. The designer also specifies hard constraints on design characteristics. The genetic model for the design has several elements.

■ The processing element allocation string lists all the PEs and their types that are allocated in the architecture. The grouped processing element allocation string records the allocation of grouped PEs.

■ The task allocation string shows which processing element has been assigned to each task.

■ The link allocation string shows how communication within the tasks is mapped to communication links. The link connectivity string records how chips and independent PEs are connected to communication links.

■ The IC allocation string records how tasks are assigned to chips.

■ The IC allocation string shows how PEs are allocated to chips; in general, the architecture can include multiple chips with different numbers of PEs on each chip.

*MOGAC genetic algorithm*

The MOGAC optimization procedure is summarized in Figure 7-19. MOGAC constructs an initial solution and then repeatedly performs the evolve–evaluate cycle. The evaluation phase, consisting of evaluation and ranking, determines which solutions are noninferior—that is, which solutions are as good as any other for some design objective. Noninferior solutions are more likely to be selected for evolution, but some inferior solutions will be selected as well. If the optimization procedure is not done, some low-rank solutions are terminated while other high-rank solutions are replicated. This pool of solutions is modified using crossover and mutation.

To reduce the time required to search the design space, MOGAC organizes possible solutions into clusters. Each member of a cluster has the same allocation

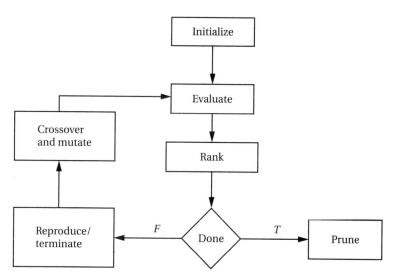

**Figure 7-19** *The MOGAC optimization procedure [Dic98] © 1998 IEEE.*

*MOGAC constraints*

string but different link allocations and assignments. Some operations are applied to the cluster and affect every member of the cluster. Other operations are applied only to a single solution within the cluster.

Real-time performance constraints are treated as hard constraints. The system's real-time constraint violation is the sum of all the violations of all nodes in the system's task graphs. Price and average power consumption are treated as soft constraints. Solutions are ranked by their Pareto-rank, which is the number of other current solutions that do not dominate it in the multi-objective space. The rank of a cluster is defined by

$$clust\_domination(x, y) = \max[a \in nis(x)] \sum_{b \in nis(y)} dom(a, b) \quad \text{(EQ 7-15)}$$

$$rank[x] = \sum_{y \in set\ of\ clusters\ \land\ y \neq x} clust\_domination(x, y), \quad \text{(EQ 7-16)}$$

where *nis(x)* is the set of noninferior solutions in *x* and *dom(a,b)* is 1 if *a* is not dominated by *b* and 0 if *a* is dominated by *b*.

A variable called *solution_selection_elitism* is used to weight the probability that a solution is selected for reproduction; its value monotonically increases during the optimization procedure. Near the end of its run, MOGAC uses greedy procedures to help it converge on local minima. The number of crossovers and mutations per generation are specified by the user.

*energy-aware*
*scheduling*

Yang et al. [Yan01] developed an energy-aware task scheduling algorithm for multiprocessors. Their method combines design-time and runtime scheduling methods. At design time, a scheduler evaluates different scheduling and allocation choices for the set of threads to run on the multiprocessor. The cost function is described as a Pareto curve over the performance–energy space. They use a genetic algorithm to find a schedule and assignment for the tasks. Yang et al. generate a table that is used at runtime to select the best schedule. They use heuristic algorithms to select which of the available scheduling/allocation patterns should be used.

*wireless system*
*co-synthesis*

Dick and Jha [Dic04] developed the COWLS system to co-synthesize client-server systems that used low-power clients communicating over wireless links to servers. Allocation of wireless links and scheduling of data transfers over those links is an important part of this problem, since wireless links are both relatively expensive and consume large amounts of energy.

COWLS uses a parallel recombinative simulated annealing approach similar to that used in MOGAC. Clusters of candidate solutions are analyzed, mutated, and recombined to search a large solution space. It Pareto-ranks candidate solutions by finding whether one cluster of candidates is better than or equal in all solution dimensions to all the members of another cluster. It uses three costs to guide mutation of solutions: communication time, computation time, and utilization. COWLS ranks candidate PEs during mutation by these costs; the candidate processing elements are sorted by their ranks and mutation favors highly ranked PEs.

Scheduling helps determine both the power consumption and timing of the solution. COWLS uses slack to assign task priorities, with tasks that have little slack assigned to high priorities. Inter-task communication on the same PE is considered to be free, while communication between PEs uses the wireless links. The scheduler allocates communications to wireless links. The scheduler models bus contention.

## 7.4.6   Control and I/O Synthesis

Control is often central to communication between processes. Control operations also dominate most I/O routines. Control-dominated systems pose different challenges for co-synthesis.

*CFSMs*

The **control finite-state machine (CFSM)** model [Chi94] was developed to model control-dominated systems. In contrast to traditional FSMs, which operate synchronously, CFSMs have finite, non-zero, unbounded reaction times. The inputs and outputs of CFSMs are events. CFSMs are used as an intermediate form for languages such as Esterel, hardware description languages, and so on. This results in a network of communicating CFSMs.

Design partitioning assigns each component machine to either hardware or software implementation. A hardware implementation of a CFSM uses combinational logic guarded by latches to implement the next-state and output functions. A software implementation is created by generating another intermediate form known as an **s-graph**, then translating that model into C code. An s-graph is a DAG that is a reduced form of a control-flow graph.

*modal processes*    Chou et al. [Cho98] developed a **modal process** model as a framework for the description and implementation of distributed control. A modal process can be in one of several modes; its I/O behavior depends on its current mode as well as the input events presented to it. **Abstract control types (ACTs)** define control operations with known properties. Examples of abstract control types include unify, which keeps the modes in several processes the same; mutual exclusion; and preemption. The mode manager interprets the constraints on process modes and implements ACT call requests. A mode manager can be implemented in either centralized or distributed form.

*interface co-synthesis*    Chou et al. [Cho95b] developed a methodology to synthesize interfaces for embedded controllers. The I/O behavior is represented as control flow graphs. The designer manually selects which input/output tasks are to be implemented in hardware or software. They first generate hardware or software implementations of the I/O tasks. Next, they allocate I/O ports to the processes, which may require adding multiplexers to share ports. The algorithm can split an operation into several steps if the device data is wider than the bit width of the I/O device. If not enough I/O ports are available, they implement some devices using memory-mapped input/output. They then generate an I/O sequencer that ensures devices meet their response time and rate requirements.

Daveau et al. [Dav97] took an allocation-oriented approach to communication synthesis. A library describes the properties of the available communication units: the cost of a component, the protocol it implements, the maximum bus rate at which data can be transferred, a set of services it provides, and the maximum number of parallel communication operations it can perform simultaneously. These authors model the system behavior as a process graph. Each abstract channel has several constraints: the protocol it wants to use, the services it provides to the processes, and its average and peak transfer rates.

A communication unit can implement an abstract channel if it provides the required services, uses the right protocol, and has a large enough maximum data rate to satisfy at least the channel's average communication rate. Synthesis builds a tree of all possible implementations, then performs a depth-first search of the tree. An operation allocates several abstract channels to the same communication unit.

## 7.4.7 Memory Systems

Memory accesses dominate many embedded applications. Several co-synthesis techniques have been developed to optimize the memory system.

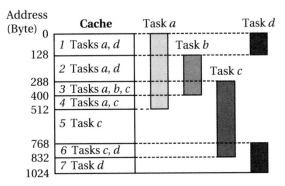

Addresses of tasks in the main memory (byte)
        Task *a*: 2048–2560    Task *b*: 3200–3472    Task *c*: 4384–4928    Task *d*: 6912–7296
                    **1 KB direct-mapped cache**

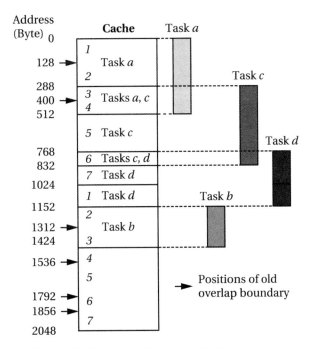

Addresses of tasks in the main memory (byte)
        Task *a*: 2048–2560    Task *b*: 3200–3472    Task *c*: 4384–4928    Task *d*: 6912–7296
                    **2 KB direct-mapped cache**

**Figure 7-20**  *How code placement changes with cache size. From Li and Wolf [Li99] © 1999 IEEE. Reprinted with permission.*

*co-synthesizing cache sizes and code placement*

Li and Wolf [Li99] developed a co-synthesis algorithm that determines the proper cache size to tune the performance of the memory system. Their target architecture was a bus-based multiprocessor. As described in Section 4.2.4, they used a simple model for processes in the instruction cache. A process occupied a contiguous range of addresses in the cache; this assumes that the program has a small kernel that is responsible for most of the execution cycles. They used a binary variable $\kappa_i$ to represent the presence or absence of a process in the cache: $\kappa_i = 1$ if process $i$ is in the cache and 0 otherwise.

Their algorithm uses simulation data to estimate the execution times of programs. Co-synthesis would be infeasible if a new simulation had to be run for every new cache configuration. However, when direct-mapped caches change in size by powers of two, the new placement of programs in the cache is easy to determine. The example in Figure 7-20 shows several processes originally placed in a 1 KB direct-mapped cache. If we double the cache size to 2 KB, then some overlaps disappear but new overlaps cannot be created. As a result, we can easily predict cache conflicts for larger caches based on the simulation results from a smaller cache.

During co-synthesis, they compute the total system cost as

$$C(system) = \sum_{i \in CPUs} C(CPU_i) + C(icache_i) + C(dcache_i) + \quad \text{(EQ 7-17)}$$

$$\sum_{j \in ASICs} [C(ASIC_j) + C(dcache_j)] +$$

$$\sum_{k \in links} C(commlink_k),$$

where $C(x)$ is the cost of component $x$.

The authors use a hierarchical scheduling algorithm that builds the full hyperperiod schedule using tasks, then individually moves processes to refine the schedule. Co-synthesis first finds an allocation that results in a feasible schedule, then reduces the cost of the hardware. To reduce system cost, it tries to move processes from lightly loaded PEs to other processing elements; once all the processes have been removed from a PE, that processing element can be eliminated from the system. It also tries to reduce the cost of a PE by reducing its cache size. However, when processes are moved onto a PE, the size of that processing element's cache may have to grow to maintain the schedule's feasibility.

Because the execution time of a process is not constant, we must find a measure other than simple CPU time to guide allocation decisions. **Dynamic urgency** describes how likely a process is to reuse the cache state to reduce misses:

$$DU(task_i, PE_i) = SU(task_i) -$$
$$\max(ready(task_i) - available(task_i)) + \qquad \text{(EQ 7-18)}$$
$$[medianWCETbase(task_i) - WCET(task_i, PE_i)]$$

In this formula, $SU$ is the static urgency of a task, or the difference between the execution time and its deadline; the worst-case execution times are measured relative to the current cache configuration.

*memory*
*management*

Wuytack et al. [Wuy99] developed a methodology for the design of memory management for applications, such as networking, that require dynamic memory management. Their methodology refined the memory system design through the following several steps.

1. The application is defined in terms of abstract data types (ADTs).

2. The ADTs are fined into concrete data structures. The proper data structures are chosen based on size, power consumption, and so on.

3. The virtual memory is divided among one or more virtual memory managers. Data structures can be grouped or separated based on usage. For example, some data structures that are lined to each other may be put together.

4. The virtual memory segments are split into basic groups. The groups are organized to allow parallel access to data structures that require high memory performance.

5. Background memory accesses are ordered to optimize memory bandwidth; this step looks at scheduling conflicts.

6. The physical memories are allocated. Multiport memories can be used to improve memory bandwidth.

### 7.4.8  Co-synthesis for Reconfigurable Systems

FPGAs are widely used as implementation vehicles for digital logic. One use of SRAM-based FPGAs is **reconfigurable systems**—machines whose logic is reconfigured on-the-fly during execution. As shown in Figure 7-21, an FPGA may be able to hold several accelerators; the logic for these accelerators is embedded in the two-dimensional FPGA fabric. The configuration can be changed during execution to remove some accelerators and add others.

Reconfiguration during execution imposes new costs on the system.

■ It takes time to reconfigure the FPGA. Reconfiguration times may be in the milliseconds for commercial FPGAs. Some experimental FPGA architectures can be reconfigured in a small number of clock cycles.

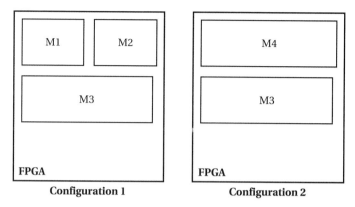

**Figure 7-21** *Successive configurations of an FPGA.*

- Reconfiguration consumes energy.

- Not all combinations of accelerators can be accommodated in the FPGA simultaneously. Scheduling is influenced by which combinations of accelerators can fit at any given time.

Determining the feasibility of a schedule is much more difficult for a reconfigurable system than for a traditional digital system. If we want to schedule a task at a given time, we have to first determine whether its accelerator is already resident in the FPGA. If not, we have to determine what combination of accelerators must be removed to make room for the new one (a task known in IC design as **floorplanning** [Wol02]). Reconfiguration time must be added to the schedule's execution time and reconfiguration energy must be added to the cost of the schedule.

*CORDS*  CORDS [Dic98b], uses an evolutionary algorithm to synthesize programs onto reconfigurable platforms. Its basic algorithms are similar to those used by MOGAC. CORDS adds reconfiguration delay to the costs evaluated during optimization; reconfiguration delay must be adjusted as the state of the schedule changes. The dynamic priority of a task is equal to the negation of the sum of its slack and its reconfiguration delay. CORDS increases the dynamic priority of tasks with low reconfiguration times to encourage several similar tasks to be scheduled together, reducing total reconfiguration time.

*Nimble*  The Nimble system [Li00] performs fine-grained partitioning that exploits instruction-level parallelism to map an algorithm onto a reconfigurable platform, which consists of an embedded CPU coupled to a reconfigurable data path. The details of the platform are configurable and are described in an architecture description language. The program to be implemented is represented as a control flow graph. Loops in the program may contain multiple kernels; profiling information is attached to the basic blocks and loop kernels.

The execution time of a loop that is implemented in whole or in part in hardware depends on several factors: execution time of the hardware loop, execution time of any software portion of the loop, communication time between hardware and software, and the time required to configure the hardware unit on the FPGA. Configuration time depends on program state—if the hardware unit had been previously instantiated and not removed by subsequent activity, then no configuration time is required.

Synthesis concentrates on interesting loops that consume most of the execution time. Given an interesting loop, the portions of that loop selected as hardware candidates are determined by the execution and communication time, but not the configuration time, since the order of hardware loop body invocations is not yet known. Inter-loop selection determines the overall hardware/software allocation based on global costs. The synthesis algorithm walks through a graph of the loops and procedures; this graph is similar to the control dependence graph of Ferrante et al. [Fer87]. An example is shown in Figure 7-22.

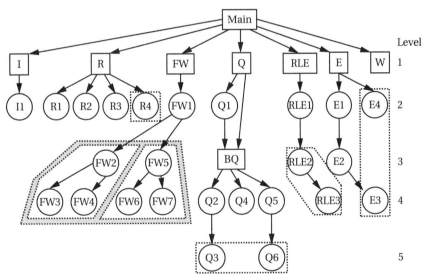

I Initialization    R Read image    FW Forward wavelet    Q Quantization    BQ Block quantization
RLE Run-length encoding    E Entropy encoding    W Write compressed file    (ⓛ) Loop    ⬜R Procedure
⬜ Loop cluster

**Figure 7-22**  *An example loop-procedure hierarchy graph. From Li et al. [Li00]*
*© 2000 IEEE.*

This graph helps identify loops that compete. Two loops that have different first-level predecessors do not conflict in the trace and could be put into different clusters. Loops that share a common predecessor may compete with each other and are preferentially placed in the same cluster. Loops are clustered based on a bottom-up walkthrough of the loop-procedure hierarchy graph, with the size of each cluster limited by a parameter based on the size of the FPGA.

## 7.5 Hardware/Software Co-simulation

Even after we verify the hardware and components of a system independently, we need to make sure that the components work together properly. Because hardware/software systems are both large and operate at many different time scales, powerful verification tools are needed to identify improper behavior and help the designer determine the origin of a bug. Designers should run the hardware against the software to find bugs on both sides of the interface. Hardware/software co-simulation gives the designer traditional debugging tools; co-simulators also run fast enough to give satisfactory turnaround times for design experiments.

*co-simulation backplanes*

Co-simulators provide mechanisms that allow different types of simulators to communicate. A brute force approach to simulating software that talks to hardware would be to simulate a register–transfer implementation of the CPU along with the custom hardware, setting the software bits as state in the CPU simulation and running the software by exercising the RTL model. Even if we have a register–transfer model of the processor, which is not always the case, this approach would be unreasonably slow. Because we have cycle-accurate simulators that run considerably faster than RTL models of processors, we can use them to execute software and simulate only the custom hardware using traditional event-driven hardware simulation.

As shown in Figure 7-23, a **simulation backplane** is the mechanism that allows different simulators to communicate and synchronize. Each simulator uses a bus interface module to connect to the backplane. The backplane uses concurrent programming techniques to pass data between the simulators. The backplane must also ensure that the simulators receive the data at the proper time. The bus interface includes controls that allow the backplane to pause a simulator. The backplane controls the temporal progress of the simulators so that they see data arriving at the correct times.

*co-simulators*

Becker et al. [Bec92] built an early co-simulator to simulate a large network system. They used the programming language interface (PLI) of the Cadence Verilog-XL simulator to add C code that could communicate with software simulation modules. They used UNIX networking operations to connect the hardware simulator to the other elements of the system being simulated, the

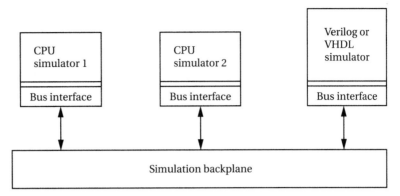

**Figure 7-23**  *Hardware/software co-simulation using a simulation backplane.*

firmware, and a monitor program. They did not simulate a processor at the cycle level.

Ghosh et al. [Gho95] later built a more general simulation environment that also used the Verilog-XL PLI to coordinate the hardware and software simulators over a backplane. Their simulator included a CPU simulator. Zivojnovic and Meyr [Ziv96] compiled software instructions to be simulated into native instructions on the host simulation processor; they attached these models to a hardware simulator for co-simulation.

The next example describes a commercial co-verification tool.

## Example 7-4

*Seamless Co-verification*

> The Mentor Graphics Seamless system (*http://www.mentor.com/seamless*) simulates heterogeneous hardware/software systems. Hardware modules can be described using standard hardware description languages; software can be loaded into the simulator as binary code or as C language models. A bus interface model connects the designer's hardware modules with the processor's instruction set simulator. A coherent memory server allows some parts of the memory to be shared between hardware and software models while isolating other parts of memory; only shared memory segments need to be mediated by the co-simulation framework. A graphic profiler allows the designer to visualize system behavior.

## 7.6 Summary

Hardware/software co-design's goal is to search a very large design space to find reasonable system architectures for application-specific systems. To plausibly formulate this design space, let alone efficiently search it, we typically make some assumptions about the design. We may work from a template, use a library of predesigned components, or use particular objective functions to drive a search. Even a few assumptions make the design problem much more tractable.

Hardware/software co-design is not a push-button solution to embedded system design. We still need the techniques described in earlier chapters to implement many of the components of the embedded system identified by co-synthesis. Co-synthesis, however, can help organize the search for reasonable architectures.

### What We Have Learned

- A variety of platforms can be used as the target for co-design, ranging from systems-on-chips to FPGAs.

- Hardware/software co-synthesis can start either from programs or task graphs.

- Platform-driven co-synthesis allocates processes onto a predefined hardware architecture, tuning the parameters of that architecture during synthesis.

- Co-synthesis algorithms that do not rely on platforms often must make other assumptions, such as fixed component libraries, to make their search spaces more reasonable.

- Reconfigurable systems complicate co-synthesis because scheduling and floorplanning interact.

- Hardware/software co-simulation links heterogeneous simulators together through a simulation bus to provide a uniform view of time across hardware and software execution.

### Further Reading

Staunstrup and Wolf's edited volume [Sta97b] surveys hardware/software co-design, including techniques for accelerated systems like those described in this chapter. Gupta and De Micheli [Gup93] and Ernst et al. [Ern93] describe early techniques for co-synthesis of accelerated systems. Callahan et al. [Cal00] describe an on-chip reconfigurable co-processor connected to a CPU.

## Questions

**Q7-1**  Compare and contrast a co-processor and an accelerator.

**Q7-2**  What factors determine the time required for two processes to communicate? Does your analysis depend on whether the processes are implemented in hardware or software?

**Q7-3**  Which is better suited to implementation in an accelerator: Viterbi decoding or discrete cosine transform? Explain.

**Q7-4**  Estimate the execution time and required hardware units for each data flow graph. Assume that one operator executes in one clock cycle and that each operator type is implemented in a distinct module (no ALUs).

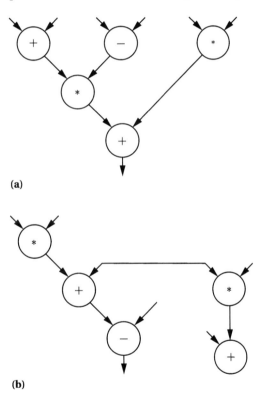

(a)

(b)

**Q7-5**  Show how to calculate the parameters of (EQ 7-2) using the information in the table of Figure 7-7.

**Q7-6**  How might task partitioning affect the results of scheduling and allocation?

**Q7-7** Compare and contrast the CDFG and the task graph as a representation of system function for co-synthesis.

**Q7-8** How could you use an execution-time technology table to capture the characteristics of configurable processors with custom instruction sets?

**Q7-9** Explain the characteristics of (EQ 7-3) that allow it to be used in a binary search algorithm.

**Q7-10** Compare and contrast the objective functions of (EQ 7-3) and (EQ 7-4).

**Q7-11** Explain the physical motivation behind the terms of the speedup formula (EQ 7-5).

**Q7-12** Explain how global slack and local slack can be used to reduce the cost of an accelerator.

**Q7-13** How do scheduling and allocation interact when co-synthesizing systems with arbitrary architectures?

**Q7-14** Give examples of control-related refinement, data-related refinement, and architecture-related refinement.

**Q7-15** How can we take advantage of multiple copies of a task graph during scheduling and allocation?

**Q7-16** Explain why making multiple copies of a task for fault tolerance may not require much additional hardware.

**Q7-17** Show how to model the co-synthesis of a video motion-estimation engine using genetic algorithms, assuming that all functions will be implemented on a single chip. Show the form of the PE allocation string, task allocation string, and link allocation string.

## Lab Exercises

**L7-1** Develop a simple hardware/software partitioning tool that accepts as input a task graph and the execution times of the software implementations of the tasks. Allocate processes to hardware or software and generate a feasible system schedule.

**L7-2** Develop a tool that allows you to quickly estimate the performance and area of an accelerator, given a hardware description.

**L7-3** Develop a simple hardware/software partitioning tool that uses genetic algorithms to search the design space.

**L7-4** Develop a simple co-simulation system that allows one CPU model to talk to one accelerator model.

# Glossary

**1% rule**   A rule used in instruction set design requiring that an instruction improve performance by at least 1% for it to be included in the architecture.

**[1, ∞] class**   A class of CPU architectures in which either one or an unbounded number of locations is available. (Section 3.2.3)

**α**   In scheduling for dynamic voltage scheduling, a symbol used for slowdown factor. (Section 4.2.3)

**η**   In scheduling for dynamic voltage scheduling, a symbol used for slowdown factor. (Section 4.2.3)

**abstract analysis**   A general technique in computer science, used in WCET analysis, that models variables as sets of values. (Section 3.4.3)

**access density**   A metric used for scratch pad optimization that relates the total conflict factor to the maximum number of variables in use. (Section 3.3.4)

**ACPI**   Advanced Configuration and Power Interface, an industry standard for power management interfaces. (Section 1.1)

**action automaton**   In Metropolis, a model for a thread. (Section 3.5.5)

**action point**   The boundary between macroticks in FlexRay. (Section 5.8.2)

**active star**   A FlexRay term for a star network with an active star hub. (Section 5.8.2)

**actor**   A process in a dataflow language. (Section 3.5.5)

**actuator port**   A Giotto construct for connecting to primary outputs. (Section 4.3)

**ad hoc network**   A network that is not explicitly managed but organizes itself. (Section 1.2.4)

**adaptive routing**   Packet routing that changes with network state. (Section 5.6.3)

**address generation**   In code generation, a step that determines what operations and instructions to use to generate addresses needed by the program. (Section 3.2)

**AFAP scheduling**   See *as-fast-as-possible*.

**AHB**   AMBA high-speed bus.

**allocation**   The assignment of responsibility for a computation to a processing element.

**application**   Any algorithm or other use to which an embedded computer is put. (Section 1.1)

**application-specific instruction processor**   A CPU whose instruction set is designed to support a particular application. (Section 2.9) See also *configurable processor*.

**application layer**   In the OSI model, the end-user interface. (Section 1.2.1)

**architectural template**   A model for a family of architectures that may be generated during co-synthesis. (Section 7.4.3)

**architecture**   The structure of a system; may refer to hardware or software. (Section 1.1)

**ALAP**   See *as-late-as-possible*.

**AMBA**   An open bus standard promulgated by ARM.

**AND-activation**   An AND-like combination of events. (Section 6.3.2)

**APB**   AMBA peripherals bus.

**arbitration grid**   The relationships between messages within a static or dynamic segment in FlexRay. (Section 5.8.2)

**architecture-related refinements**   A refinement that adds behaviors to resolve conflicts in a hardware system. (Section 7.4.4)

**ASAP**   See *as-soon-as-possible*.

**as-fast-as-possible**   A scheduling algorithm that uses clique covering to determine schedules along paths. (Section 7.3.1)

**ASIC**   Application-specific integrated circuit.

**as-late-as-possible**    A schedule in which every operation is performed at the latest possible time. (Section 4.2.2)

**as-soon-as-possible**    A schedule in which every operation is performed at the earliest possible time. (Section 4.2.2)

**ASIP**    See *application-specific instruction processor.*

**aspect ratio**    In a memory, the ratio of the number of addressable units to the number of bits read per request.

**assertion overhead**    The added cost of computing assertions for fault tolerance. (Section 7.4.4)

**assertion task**    A task that computes assertions used in fault tolerance. (Section 7.4.4)

**association graph**    A graph that describes how tasks are repeated in a system. (Section 7.4.4)

**attack**    An attempt to disrupt the operation to a computer system. (Section 1.6.3)

**average-case execution time**    A typical execution time for typical inputs. (Section 3.4)

**average performance**    The average performance (typically measured by throughput) of a computer system. (Section 2.2.1)

**average power vector**    A vector that describes the average power consumed by a process on different types of processing elements. (Section 7.4.4)

**average rate heuristic**    In scheduling for dynamic voltage scheduling, a schedule that sets the processor speed based on the average CPU load. (Section 4.2.3)

**banked memory**    A memory system that allows multiple parallel accesses. (Section 3.3.5)

**basic priority inheritance protocol**    A priority inheritance avoidance mechanism that keeps processes from interrupting critical sections. (Section 1.6.2)

**basic scheduling block**    A unit of computation in LYCOS. (Section 7.4.3)

**bathtub function**    A function of time with high values at small and large values of time; typically describes the failure rate of components. (Section 1.6.2)

**battery attack**    An attack on an embedded system that tries to make the system fail or misbehave by draining its internal battery. (Section 1.6.3)

**BCET** See *best-case execution time*.

**behavior adapter** A software component used in Metropolis to connect components with different models of computation or protocols.

**best-case execution time** The shortest execution time for any possible set of inputs. (Section 3.4)

**best-effort routing** The Internet routing methodology, which does not guarantee completion. (Section 1.2.1)

**better-than-worst-case design** A microarchitectural design style that adapts to the internal delays of the logic, taking advantage of the early arrival of signals. (Section 2.5.2)

**black-box testing** Testing a program without knowledge of its implementation.

**block** In code compression, the unit of instructions that is compressed together. (Section 2.7.1)

**blocking communication** Communication that requires a process to wait after sending a message.

**bottom-up design** Using information from lower levels of abstraction to modify the design at higher levels of abstraction.

**branch patching** A technique for code compression that replaces branch addresses with the addresses of the compressed versions of their targets. (Section 2.7.1)

**branch table** A data structure used in code decompression to identify the location of the compressed version of a branch. (Section 2.7.1)

**branching-time temporal logic** A temporal logic that models several alternative timelines. (Section 4.5)

**BSB** See *basic scheduling block*.

**BSS** See *byte start sequence*.

**buddy list** Data structure used for load balancing during dynamic task scheduling on multiprocessors. (Section 6.3.3)

**burst access mode** See *burst transfer*.

**burst transfer** A bus transfer that transfers several contiguous locations without separate addresses for each. (Section 3.3.5)

**bus encoding** A technique for reducing the power consumption of busses by recoding bus traffic to reduce the number of transitions. (Section 2.7.3)

**bus-invert coding**   A bus coding algorithm that selectively inverts the polarity of signals on the bus to reduce toggles. (Section 2.7.3)

**bus guardian**   In FlexRay, a node that observes network behavior and takes action when it observes an error. (Section 5.8.2)

**bus transaction model**   A system model that captures the bus protocol but is not cycle-accurate. (Section 5.3.2)

**byte start sequence**   The start of a byte sequence in FlexRay. (Section 5.8.2)

**bytecode**   An instruction in the Java Virtual Machine. (Section 3.5.4)

**cache**   A small memory that holds copies of certain main memory locations for fast access. (Section 2.6.3)

**cache conflict graph**   A graph that models access conflicts within the cache. (Section 3.4.2)

**CAN bus**   A serial bus for networked embedded systems, widely used in automobiles.

**candidate architecture**   A multiprocessor architecture used to evaluate a design. (Section 5.3.1)

**candidate schedule time**   An initial schedule time in force-directed synthesis. (Section 7.3.1)

**capacity miss**   A cache miss that occurs because the program's working set is too large for the cache. (Section 2.6.3)

**CCFG**   See *concurrent control flow graph*.

**CDFG**   See *control/data flow graph*.

**CDG**   See *control dependence graph*.

**CFSM**   See *co-design finite state machine*.

**channel adapter**   A software component used in Metropolis to adapt for discrepancies between the desired and actual characteristics of a channel. (Section 6.4.2)

**class**   A type description in an object-oriented language.

**client**   In a multiprocessor network, a sender or receiver. (Section 5.6)

**clip**   An object in ARMADA that guarantees to deliver a certain number of packets in a given interval. (Section 6.4.1)

**clique**   A set of nodes in a graph such that every pair of vertices in the clique is connected by an edge. (Section 3.2.2)

**clique avoidance algorithm** An algorithm that resolves inconsistencies due to node failures in the time-triggered architecture. (Section 5.8.1)

**clock synchronization process** The process of generating a global clock in FlexRay. (Section 5.8.2)

**Clos network** A communication network that uses interconnected crossbars to provide non-blocking point-to-point communication but not nonblocking multicast. (Section 5.6.2)

**cluster** In VLIW architecture, a set of function units and a register file that operate as a unit. Operations on data held in another cluster requries an inter-cluster transfer. (Section 2.4.1)

**code compression** Compressing instructions so that they can be dynamically decompressed during execution. (Section 2.7.1)

**code and data compression** A technique for storing compressed versions of both code and data in main memory; requires recompressing data writes as well as decompressing data and instruction reads. (Section 2.7.2)

**code generation** The process of generating assembly language or machine instructions from an intermediate representation of a program. (Section 3.2)

**code motion** A technique for moving operations in a program without affecting its behavior.

**code placement** The placement of object code and data in memory to achieve certain criteria, such as cache behavior. (Section 3.2.4)

**co-design finite state machine** A control-oriented model for embedded systems that can be used to describe combinations of hardware and software. (Section 4.3)

**coding tree** A tree used to develop Huffman codes whose leaves are symbols to be coded and whose branches are code bits. (Section 2.7.1)

**cold miss** See *compulsory miss.*

**coldstart** Initiation of the TDMA process in FlexRay. (Section 5.8.2)

**coloring** Assigning labels to nodes in a graph, such as in register allocation. (Section 3.2.2)

**common code space set** A set of operations of a related iteration in a synchronous dataflow graph. (Section 3.5.2)

**common code space set graph** A graph that describes the ordering of iterations in a synchronous dataflow graph schedule. (Section 3.5.2)

**Common Object Request Broker Architecture**™ A software architecture for middleware services. (Section 6.4.1)

**communication link**    A connection between processing elements.

**communications network architecture**    A component of the time-triggered architecture that helps to maintain a consistent view of time across the network. (Section 5.8.1)

**communication vector**    A description of a task graph for genetic algorithm-based search. (Section 7.4.4)

**communications controller**    The low-level network interface in a communications network interface in the time-triggered architecture. (Section 5.8.1)

**communications cycle**    The sequence of communication modes in FlexRay, including a static segment, a dynamic segment, a symbol window, and network idle time. (Section 5.8.2)

**compare task**    A task that compares the results of duplicate copies of a task for fault tolerance. (Section 7.4.4)

**compression ratio**    The ratio of the sizes of the compressed and uncompressed versions of a program. (Section 2.7.1)

**completion time**    The time at which a process finishes its work. (Section 4.2.1)

**compulsory miss**    A cache miss that occurs the first time a location is used. (Section 2.6.3)

**computational kernel**    A small portion of an algorithm that performs a long function.

**computing platform**    A hardware system used for embedded computing.

**concurrent control flow graph**    A control flow graph with concurrency constructs. (Section 3.5.3)

**configurable cache**    A cache whose set associativity, line size, etc. can be changed on-the-fly. (Section 2.6.3)

**configurable processor**    A CPU that has been designed for a particular application; does not mean reconfigurable at run time. (Section 2.9) See also *application-specific instruction processor.*

**configuration synthesis**    Co-synthesis using simplified models of components. (Section 7.4.5)

**conflict graph**    A graph that represents incompatibilities between entities; used in register allocation. (Section 3.2.2)

**conflict miss**    A cache miss caused by two locations in use mapping to the same cache location. (Section 2.6.3)

**conjunction node**    A node in a conditional task graph that is the sink of a conditional edge. (Section 7.4.1)

**constellation**    A set of symbols in a digital communications system in a space defined by the modulation parameters. (Section 1.2.1)

**constructive scheduling**    Scheduling without iterative improvement. (Section 4.2.1)

**context-dependent behavior**    System behavior that changes based upon some part of the system state. (Section 6.3.2)

**context switch**    The process by which a CPU transfers control from one process to another. (Section 4.2.1)

**contract**    A state in a quality-of-service system that denotes agreement between a client and a server as to the characteristics of a communications channel provided by the system. (Section 6.4.3)

**contract object**    A software object that embodies the state of a QoS contract. (Section 6.4.3)

**control dependence graph**    A data structure that shows the depth of conditionals in a program. (Section 4.3)

**control flow graph**    A simple, non-Turing complete model of computation. (Section 1.5.3)

**control/data flow graph**    A graph that models both the data and control operations in a program. (Section 1.5.3)

**control-related refinement**    A refinement that preserves execution order when a behavior is split. (Section 7.4.4)

**control step**    A single clock cycle in a schedule, such as in high-level synthesis. (Section 7.3.1) See also *time step*.

**convolutional coder**    An error correction coder that convolves the data to produce the encoded form. (Section 1.2.1)

**coordination language**    A language designed to act as an interface between different programming models. (Section 3.5.5)

**co-processor**    An optional unit added to a CPU that is responsible for executing some of the CPU's instructions. (Section 2.3.2)

**CORBA**    See *Common Object Request Broker Architecture.*

**co-simulation**    See *hardware/software co-simulation.*

**CNI**    See *communications network architecture.*

**critical**    In scheduling, an operation on the critical path. (Section 4.2.2)

**critical cycle**   In multiprocessor scheduling, a cycle through the process graph whose cycle limits the cycle for the entire graph. (Section 6.3.2)

**critical group**   In scheduling for dynamic voltage scheduling, the set of processes that run in the critical interval. (Section 4.2.3)

**critical interval**   In scheduling for dynamic voltage scheduling, the interval that maximizes the intensity. (Section 4.2.3)

**critical path**   In scheduling, the set of constraint that determines the minimum schedule length. A scheduling algorithm which schedules operations on the critical path first. (Section 7.3.1)

**critical instant**   In RMA, the worst-case combination of process activations. (Section 4.2.2)

**crossbar**   A network that fully connects a set of inputs and outputs. (Section 5.6.2)

**CSP**   See *clock synchronization process.*

**cycle-accurate communication model**   A system model that accurately captures communication times but not computation times. (Section 5.3.2)

**cycle-accurate computation model**   A system model that accurately captures computation times but not communication times. (Section 5.3.2)

**cycle mean**   The asymptotic iteration period for an IPC graph. (Section 6.3.2)

**cycle timer**   A CPU simulation technique that uses a detailed microarchitectural model that is clock-cycle accurate. (Section 2.8.3)

**data flow graph**   A model of computation that exists in many variants. (Section 1.5.3)

**data level parallelism**   Parallelism in a program that can be found by looking at operators and data flow. (Section 1.5.5)

**data link layer**   In the OSI model, the layer responsible for reliable data transport. (Section 1.2.1)

**data-related refinement**   A refinement that updates the values of variables that are shared by several behaviors. (Section 7.4.4)

**DCT**   See *discrete cosine transform.*

**deadline**   The time at which a process must finish. (Section 4.2.1)

**deadlock**   A system state from which there is no exit. (Section 4.5)

**definition**   In compilers, an assignment of a value to a variable. (Section 3.2.2)

**delegate object**   A proxy for a remote object. (Section 6.4.3)

**denial-of-service attack**    An attack that tries to overwhelm a computer system, causing it to drop service to legitimate users. (Section 1.6.3)

**design diversity**    A design methodology that uses components from different sources, methodologies, etc. to avoid systematic errors among multiple components. (Section 1.6.2)

**design flow**    A series of steps used to implement a system. (Section 1.4)

**design productivity gap**    Designer productivity is growing more slowly than the size of the largest manufacturable chip. (Section 1.4)

**design methodology**    A method of proceeding through levels of abstraction to complete a design. (Section 1.4)

**destination process identifier**    A packet address in Nostrum. (Section 6.4.2)

**deterministic routing**    Packet routing that does not change with network state. (Section 5.6.3)

**differential power analysis**    A technique for power attacks that compares multiple traces. (Section 2.7.4)

**digital signal processor**    A microprocessor whose architecture is optimized for digital signal processing applications. (Section 2.3.2)

**direct execution**    Performance analysis of a program by executing instructions in the host's native instruction set, not through an interpretive simulator. (Section 2.8.3)

**direct-mapped cache**    A cache with a single set.

**direct memory access**    A bus transfer performed by a device without executing instructions on the CPU.

**digital rights management**    The process of ensuring that a user and computer have permission to access copyrighted or otherwise protected material. (Section 1.7.4)

**discrete cosine transform**    A frequency transform that is used to guide lossy coding of images. (Section 1.2.2)

**disjunction node**    A node in a conditional task graph that is the source of a conditional edge. (Section 7.4.1)

**distributed embedded system**    An embedded system built around a network.

**distributed system object component**    An object-oriented model of middleware services. (Section 6.4.2)

**DMA**    See *direct memory access*.

**DMSL**    See *domain-specific modeling language*.

**domain-specific modeling language**    A language that is designed for a specific application. (Section 3.5.5)

**DRM**    See *digital rights management*.

**DSOC**    See *distributed system object component*.

**DSP**    See *digital signal processor*. May also stand for *digital signal processing*.

**dynamic phase**    In FlexRay, the phase of the schedule in which operations are scheduled dynamically. (Section 5.8.2)

**dynamic power management**    A power management technique that looks at the CPU activity.

**dynamic priority**    A process priority that may change during execution. (Section 4.2.2)

**dynamic scheduling**    Determination of a schedule at run time. (Section 4.2.1)

**dynamic trailing sequence field**    A field in a dynamically-scheduled transmission in FlexRay. (Section 5.8.2)

**dynamic voltage scaling**    See *dynamic voltage and frequency scaling*.

**dynamic voltage and frequency scaling**    An architectural technique for power saving that reduces the CPU's power supply voltage and operating frequency when the CPU does not need to run at full speed. (Section 2.5.1)

**earliest deadline first**    A variable priority scheduling scheme. (Section 4.2.2)

**EDF**    See *earliest deadline first*.

**embedded computer system**    A computer used to implement some of the functionality of something other than a general-purpose computer.

**embedded file system**    A file system designed for use on embedded systems. (Section 4.4.7)

**enable**    In Petri nets, a transition is enabled when each place incoming to that transition is marked with at least as many tokens as is specified by the weight of the edge from the place to the transition. (Section 1.5.4)

**energy**    The ability to do work.

**event-driven state machine**    A state machine that responds to changes at its inputs. (Section 3.5.3)

**event function model**    A model of events that allows the number of events in an interval to vary. (Section 6.3.2)

**execution time**   In real-time scheduling, the run time of a process in isolation. (Section 4.2.1)

**exception**   Any unusual condition in the CPU that is recognized during execution.

**exclusion vector**   A descripiton of processes that cannot share a processing element. (Section 7.4.4)

**expansion**   An acyclic Petri net in which every transition has at least one input or output place but at least one place that has no input transitions and one place that has no output transitions. (Section 4.3)

**extremity measures**   A measure that helps determine whether to allocate a function to hardware or software. (Section 7.4.4)

**fault tolerance**   A specificaiton of the required fault tolerance. (Section 7.4.4)

**feasibility factor**   A metric that evaluates the schedulability of a set of tasks. (Section 7.4.5)

**FES**   See *frame end sequence.*

**finishing phase**   The smallest inteval between the finishing time of one process and the first request time of the next iteration of the next data-dependent process. (Section 6.3.2)

**finite-state machine**   A model of computation. (Section 1.5)

**firing rule**   A rule that determines when a data flow graph node performs a computation; a rule that determines how tokens move from state to state in Petri nets. (Section 1.5.3; Section 3.5.5)

**first-come-first-served**   A scheduling policy for hardware that schedules operators as early as possible given resource constraints. (Section 7.3.1)

**first-level cache**   The cache closest to the CPU. (Section 2.6.3)

**first-reaches table**   A table used in the analysis of synchronous dataflow graph schedules that shows whether paths with certain properties exist in the graph. (Section 3.5.2)

**flash file system**   A file system designed for use with flash memory, particularly block writes and wear mechanisms. (Section 4.4.7)

**FlexRay**   An automotive networking standard. (Section 5.8.2)

**flit**   A packet is broken up into several flits for transmission in a multiprocessor network. (Section 5.6.2)

**floorplanning**   Abstract design of a large chip layout. (Section 7.4.5)

**flow control**   A method of allocation of resources for data transmission. (Section 5.6.2)

**flow fact**   A constraint on the value of a variable in a scope of a program used for program path timing. (Section 3.4.3)

**fluff**   Basic blocks that are never executed. (Section 3.4.2)

**fly-by-wire**   Direct control of aircraft control surfaces by computers. (Section 1.2.3)

**force-directed synthesis**   A hardware scheduling algorithm that uses a spring model. (Section 7.3.1)

**FPGA**   See *field-programmable gate array.*

**frame end sequence**   The end of a frame in FlexRay. (Section 5.8.2)

**frame start sequence**   The start of a frame in FlexRay. (Section 5.8.2)

**FSS**   See *frame start sequence.*

**full-duplex**   Two-way communication. (Section 5.6)

**functional requirements**   Requirements that describe the logical behavior of the system. (Section 1.3)

**genetic algorithm**   A family of optimization algorithms that uses strings to model optimization state and transformations on those strings to search the design space. (Section 7.4.5)

**global slack**   Slack between the completion of a task and its deadline. (Section 7.4.3)

**global time service**   A synchronization service in Dynamic Real-Time CORBA. (Section 6.4.1)

**group-spatial reference**   Reuse of the same cache line by different parts of the program. (Section 2.6.3)

**group-temporal reference**   Data reuse of the same array element by different parts of the program. (Section 2.6.3)

**guard**   A Boolean condition on an edge in a conditional task graph. (Section 7.4.1)

**H.26x**   A family of standards for video compression. (Section 1.2.2)

**HAL**   See *hardware abstraction layer.*

**half-duplex**   One-way communication. (Section 5.6)

**hard real time**   A system in which failure to meet a deadline causes an unsafe situation. (Section 4.2.1)

**hardware abstraction layer**    A software layer that hides details of the hardware platform. (Section 6.4.2)

**hardware/software co-design**    The simultaneous design of hardware and software components to meet system requirements. (Chapter 7)

**hardware/software co-simulation**    Simultaneous simulation of hardware and software at different time granularities. (Section 5.3.2; Section 7.5)

**hardware/software partitioning**    Co-synthesis into an architectural template built around a CPU and a bus. (Section 7.4.3)

**harness**    A set of wires used for point-to-point wiring. (Section 1.2.3)

**hazard function**    A function that describes the failure rate of components. (Section 1.6.2)

**heterogeneous multiprocessor**    A multiprocessor that uses some combination of different types of processing elements, a nonuniform interconnection network, or a nonuniform memory structure. (Section 5.2.3)

**hierarchy tree**    A data structure used to represent set inclusion in a Statechart program. (Section 3.5.3)

**high-level synthesis**    A family of techniques used to schedule and allocate hardware from an abstract representation such as a dataflow graph. (Section 7.3.1)

**hit rate**    The probability of a memory access being a cache hit.

**host**    The processor that talks to special-purpose processing elements. (Section 7.2)

**host node**    A processing element in the time-triggered architecture. (Section 5.8.1)

**hot swapping**    A scheduling algorithm that accounts for transient effects when switching between implementations of a process. (Section 4.2.2)

**Huffman coding**    An algorithm for lossless encoding. (Section 1.2.2; Section 2.7.1)

**IDL**    See *interactive data language.*

**implementation model**    A system model that corresponds directly to hardware and provides a cycle-accurate description of both computation and communication. (Section 5.3.2)

**index rewriting**    Changing the representation of loop indexes. (Section 3.3.1)

**initiation time**    The time at which a process becomes ready to execute. (Section 4.2.1)

**instruction-level parallelism**   Parallelism in a program that can only be identified by examining the instructions in the program. (Section 1.5.5)

**instruction-level simulator**   A CPU simulator that is accurate to the level of the programming model but not to timing. (Section 2.8.3)

**instruction scheduler**   A computer simulation technique that uses an approximate microarchitectural model that is not cycle-accurate. (Section 2.8.3)

**instruction selection**   A step in code generation that determines the opcodes and modes used to implement operations. (Section 3.2)

**integer linear programming**   A form of optimization problem with an objective function and constraints whose variables have integer values. (Section 3.4.2)

**intensity**   In scheduling for dynamic voltage scheduling, a lower bound on the average processing speed required to create a feasible schedule. (Section 4.2.3)

**interactive data language**   A language used to describe interfaces in CORBA. (Section 6.4.1)

**interference access count**   A metric used for scratch pad optimization that counts the number of times that other variables are accessed during the lifetime of a given variable. (Section 3.3.4)

**interference factor**   A metric used for scratch pad optimization that is the sum of variable and interference access counts. (Section 3.3.4)

**intermodule connection graph**   An undirected graph that describes the communication between processes for Stone's multiprocessor scheduling algorithm. (Section 6.3.2)

**Internet**   A network of networks; the global internetwork. (Section 1.2.1)

**internetworking**   A network protocol that links two networks. (Section 1.2.1)

**interprocess communication**   A mechanism for communication between processes. (Section 4.4.5)

**interprocessor communication modeling graph**   An abstraction of a synchronous dataflow graph used for multiprocessor scheduling. (Section 6.3.2)

**interrupt service routine**   A low-level interrupt handler, usually kernel mode. (Section 4.4.2)

**interrupt service thread**   A high-level interrupt handler, usually user-mode. (Section 4.4.2)

**interval scheduling**   An algorithm for static scheduling. (Section 4.4.2)

**inter-event stream context**   Correlations between streams. (Section 6.3.2)

**intra-event stream context** Correlations within a single stream. (Section 6.3.2)

**IPC graph** See *interprocessor communication modeling graph.*

**iterative improvement scheduling** Scheduling by refinement over several stages. (Section 4.2.1)

**Java virtual machine** The abstract machine on which Java is defined. (Section 3.5.4)

**JIT compiler** See *just-in-time compiler.*

**jitter event model** A model of an event including period and jitter. (Section 6.3.2)

**journaling** See *log-structured file system.*

**JPEG** A family of standards for still image encoding. (Section 1.2.2)

**just-in-time compiler** A compiler that compiles program sections on demand during execution. (Section 3.5.4)

**Kahn process** A model of computation in which operators are guarded by queues. (Section 1.5.3; Section 3.5.5)

**Kahn process network** A network of Kahn processes. (Section 3.5.5)

**L1 cache** See *first-level cache.*

**L2 cache** See *second-level cache.*

**L2CAP** See *logical link control and adaptation protocol.*

**latency** The time from the start to the completion of an operation or task. (Section 2.2.1)

**latency service** A service in Dynamic Real-Time CORBA that allows components to determine the latency of services in the system. (Section 6.4.1)

**least-laxity first** A dynamic scheduling policy that determines priorities by the slack remaining to the deadline. (Section 4.2.2)

**Lempel-Ziv coding** A family of dictionary-based lossless coders. (Section 2.7.2)

**Lempel-Ziv-Welch coding** A dictionary-based coder that uses a fixed-size dictionary. (Section 2.7.2)

**lightweight process** A process that shares its memory spaces with other processes.

**line** The transmission medium of a communications link. (Section 5.6)

**line size** The number of bits/bytes/words in a single line (location in one set) in a cache. (Section 2.6.3)

**linear-time temporal logic** A logic of time in which time evolves over a single thread. (Section 3.5.5; Section 4.5)

**link** A communcations channel in a network. (Section 5.6.1)

**list scheduler** A scheduler that sorts operations onto a list that is used to determine the order of operations. (Section 4.2.2)

**live** In register allocation, a variable that is currently in use. (Section 3.2.2) In protocols, a system that is not trapped in a subset of its states. (Section 4.5)

**LLF** See *least-laxity first*.

**load balancing** Adjusting scheduling and allocation to even out system load in a network. (Section 6.3.3)

**load threshold estimator** A tool that schedules multiprocessor processes using a statistical load model. (Section 6.3.2)

**local slack** The slack between the completion time of an accelerator and the start of its successor tasks. (Section 7.4.3)

**log-structured file system** A file system that stores changes to a file from which the current state of the file can be reconstructed. (Section 4.4.7)

**logical link control and adaptation protocol** A mid-level protocol layer in Bluetooth. (Section 1.7.1)

**long-term memory** A data structure used in tabu search that holds information on search moves over a long interval. (Section 7.4.3)

**loop-carried dependency** A data dependency that stretches from one iteration of a loop to another. (Section 3.3.1)

**loop conflict factor** A metric used for scratch pad optimization that counts the accesses for a variable and other variables in a set of loops. (Section 3.3.4)

**loop fusion** Merging the bodies of several loops into a single loop. (Section 3.3.1)

**loop nest** A set of loops, one inside the other. (Section 3.3.1)

**loop padding** Adding elements to an array to change the memory behavior of the array. (Section 3.3.1)

**loop permutation** Changing the order of loops in a loop nest. (Section 3.3.1)

**loop preparation** A general term for loop transformations that enable other code optimizations. (Section 3.3.2)

**loop reordering**   A general term for any loop transformation that changes the order of operations performed by a loop. (Section 3.3.2)

**loop splitting**   Splitting the operations in the body of a loop across multiple loops. (Section 3.3.1)

**loop unrolling**   Rewriting a loop so that several instances of the loop body are included in a single iteration of the modified loop. (Section 3.3.1)

**looped containers**   A method for reserving bandwidth in a network-on-chip. (Section 6.4.3)

**loosely independent**   A synchronous dataflow graph that can be partitioned into two subgraphs that are subindependent of each other. (Section 3.5.2)

**low-density parity check**   An error correction coding method that performs a sparse set of parity checks. (Section 1.2.1)

**macrotick**   The global clock in FlexRay. (Section 5.8.2)

**macrotick generation process**   The generation of macroticks in FlexRay, including updates. (Section 5.8.2)

**mailbox**   A form of interprocess communication that is usually implemented as a set of hardware registers. (Section 4.4.5)

**marking**   In Petri nets, a mapping of tokens to places. (Section 1.5.4)

**master PE**   A processor that determines the schedules for processes on other slave PEs in a multiprocessor. (Section 6.3.1)

**maximum utilization**   See *utilization*.

**may analysis**   Analysis that determines when a variable may be in the cache. (Section 3.4.3)

**Markov model**   A probabilistic state machine whose edges are assigned transition probabilities; widely used, including in code compression. (Section 2.7.1)

**maximal expansion**   A transitively closed expansion of a Petri net. (Section 4.3)

**maximum distance function**   The maximum allowed distance between two or more events. (Section 6.3.2)

**mean time to failure**   The mean time from initiation of operation to first failure of a system. (Section 1.6.2)

**memory cell**   The basic circuit of a memory array, which typically holds one bit of memory. (Section 2.6.1)

**memory hierarchy**   The system of memories of various sizes and speeds used in a computer system.

**memory vector**   A vector that describes the storage requirement of processes. (Section 7.4.4)

**message passing**   A style of interprocess communication.

**metagenerator**   A generator for metamodels. (Section 3.5.5)

**metamodel**   A model used to describe other models. (Section 3.5.5)

**methodology**   Used to describe an overall design process. (Section 1.1; Section 1.4)

**microtick**   The local clock in FlexRay. (Section 5.8.2)

**middleware**   Software that provides services on multiprocessors. (Section 6.4)

**MIMD**   Multiple-instruction, multiple-data execution, one of the categories in Flynn's taxonomy of computation. (Section 2.2.2)

**minimum distance function**   The minimum allowed distance between two or more events. (Section 6.3.2)

**MISD**   Multiple-instruction, single-data execution, one of the categories in Flynn's taxonomy of computation. (Section 2.2.2)

**miss rate**   The probability that a memory access will be a cache miss.

**mode**   In general, a category of behavior induced by a particular state. In Giotto, a configuration of tasks, etc. (Section 4.3)

**mode switch**   In Giotto, a specification of the parameters that govern the transfer of execution from one mode to another. (Section 4.3)

**model extraction**   Analysis of the memory requirements of the phases of a program. (Section 3.3.2)

**motion estimation**   A method for predicting a video frame from a previous frame by measuring the motion of portions of the frame. (Section 1.2.2)

**model-integrated computing**   A design methodology that uses metamodels to describe domains. (Section 3.5.5)

**motion vector**   A vector describing the displacement between two units of an image. (Section 1.2.2)

**MP3**   MPEG-1 Layer 3 audio coding, a widely-used standard for audio compression. (Section 1.2.2)

**MPEG**   A family of standards for video encoding.

**MPSoC**   See *multiprocessor system-on-chip.*

**MTTF**   See *mean time to failure.*

**multihop network**   A network in which messages may go through an intermediate PE when traveling from source to destination. (Section 1.2.4)

**multiport memory**   A memory with multiple address and data ports that can be accessed simultaneously. (Section 2.6.1)

**multiprocessor system-on-chip**   A multiprocessor integrated onto an integrated circuit along with other support components such as I/O and memory. (Section 5.4)

**multirate**   Operations that have different deadlines, causing the operations to be performed at different rates.

**multithreading**   A fine-grained concurrency technique that interleaves execution of several instruction streams. (Section 2.2.2)

**must analysis**   Analysis that determines if a variable is guaranteed to be in the cache. (Section 3.4.3)

**mutator**   In garbage collection, the application program whose garbage is being collected. (Section 3.5.4)

**myopic algorithm**   An algorithm for dynamically scheduling real-time tasks. (Section 6.3.3)

**network layer**   In the OSI model, the layer responsible for basic end-to-end service. (Section 1.2.1)

**network-on-chip**   A multiprocessor network designed for implementation on a single chip. (Section 5.6.2)

**never set**   A set of tasks that cannot execute at the same time. (Section 7.4.3)

**nonblocking communication**   Interprocess communication that allows the sender to continue execution after sending a message.

**nondeterministic finite-state machine**   A variant of the FSM model of computation. (Section 1.5)

**nonfunctional requirements**   Requirements that do not describe the logical behavior of the system; examples include size, weight, and power consumption. (Section 1.3)

**notification service**   A publish/subscribe system. (Section 6.4.3)

**object**   A program unit that includes both internal data and methods that provide an interface to the data.

**object-oriented**   Any use of objects and classes in design; can be applied at many different levels of abstraction.

**object reference**   An object identifier in CORBA. (Section 6.4.1)

**object request broker**   A CORBA component that manages the communication between clients and objects. (Section 6.4.1)

**operator fusion**   A technique for instruction set design by combining smaller operations into a single instruction. (Section 2.9.2)

**OR-activation**   An OR-like combination of events. (Section 6.3.2)

**ORB**   See *object request broker.*

**OSI model**   A model for levels of abstraction in networks. (Section 1.2.1)

**overhead**   In operating systems, the CPU time required for the operating system to switch contexts. (Section 4.2.2)

**P()**   Traditional name for the procedure that takes a semaphore.

**packet**   In VLIW processors, a set of instructions that can be executed together. (Section 2.4.1) In networks, a unit of data transfer. (Section 1.2.1)

**page description language**   A language used as input to printers. (Section 5.7.3)

**paged memory**   A memory whose access properties are determined by the sequence of internal pages referred to by the accesses. (Section 3.3.5)

**Pareto optimality**   A theory of multi-objective optimization. (Section 7.4.5)

**partial evaluation**   Compile-time evaluation of expressions. (Section 3.3.2)

**PASS**   See *periodic admissible sequential schedule.*

**path-based estimation**   A co-synthesis estimation method that uses path-based scheduling. (Section 7.3.2)

**path-based scheduling**   A hardware scheduling algorithm that uses as-fast-as-possible scheduling to balance schedules along multiple scheduling paths. (Section 7.3.2)

**path ratio**   In a loop, the ratio of instructions executed per iteration to the total number of instructions in the loop. (Section 2.4.5)

**path analysis**   In software performance analysis, the determination of a worst-case execution path through the program. (Section 3.4)

**path timing**   In software performance analysis, the determination of the execution time along a path. (Section 3.4)

**PC sampling**   Generating a program trace by periodically sampling the PC during execution. (Section 2.8.1)

**PE**   See *processing element.*

**PE-assembly model**    A system model built from processing elements communicating through channels, with untimed communication and approximately-timed computation. (Section 5.3.2)

**peak access rate**    Maximum access rate in a memory system. (Section 5.7.1)

**peak performance**    The maximum performance of a computer system. (Section 2.2.1)

**perceptual coding**    Lossy coding that takes into account the abilities of humans to perceive or not perceive certain phenomena. (Section 1.2.2)

**performance**    In computer architecture, the speed at which operations occur. May mean other metrics in different disciplines, such as image quality in image processing. (Section 2.2.1)

**performance index**    In Metropolis, a nonfunctional requirement such as throughput or enegy consumption. (Section 3.5.5)

**period**    In real-time scheduling, a periodic interval of execution. (Section 4.2.1)

**periodic admissible sequential schedule**    In synchronous dataflow, a finite, periodic schedule that performs operations sequentially. (Section 3.5.2)

**persistence analysis**    Analysis that determines whether accesses after the first one will be in the cache. (Section 3.4.3)

**personal area network**    A network formed around a person, such as Bluetooth. (Section 1.7.1)

**Petri net**    A Turing-complete model of computation. (Section 1.5.4)

**physical layer**    In the OSI model, the layer that defines electrical and mechanical properties. (Section 1.2.1)

**pipeline**    A logic structure that allows several operations of the same type to be performed simultaneously on multiple values, with each value having a different part of the operation performed at any one time. (Section 2.2.1)

**pipeline diagram**    A method for drawing the state of a pipeline in time and across functional units. (Section 2.2.1)

**place**    In Petri nets, a node that may hold tokens denoting state. (Section 1.5.4)

**plant**    In control systems, the system being controlled.

**platform-based design**    Design based on a hardware/software platform that can be used for several different products. (Section 1.4)

**platform-dependent characteristics**    A set of application characteristics that will influence the design or selection of the platform. (Section 5.3.1)

**platform-dependent optimizations**   Software optimizations that do not depend on the specifics of the platform. (Section 5.3.1)

**platform-independent optimizations**   Software optimizations that take advantage of the  platform, such as specialized instructions, memory system characteristics, or libraries. (Section 5.3.1)

**polyhedral reduced dependence graph**   A graph that relates the polytopes that represent parts of a program. (Section 3.5.2)

**polytope model**   A model for data dependencies in loops in which sets of dependencies are modeled as polytopes in a multi-dimensional space whose dimensions are the array indexes. (Section 3.3.1)

**port**   A connection to a component; a connection to a network. (Section 5.6)

**post-cache compression**   A microarchitectural technique that stores compressed code in the cache and decompresses upon fetching from the cache. (Section 2.7.1)

**power**   Energy per unit time.

**power attack**   An attack that tries to infer the internal activity of the computer by monitoring its power consumption. (Section 1.6.3)

**power-down mode**   A mode invoked in a CPU that causes the CPU to reduce its power consumption.

**power management policy**   A scheme for making power management decisions.

**power reduction ratio**   The ratio of power consumption for microarchitectures that execute compressed and uncompressed code. (Section 2.7.1)

**power simulator**   A CPU simulator that provides power estimates. (Section 2.8.3)

**power state machine**   A finite-state machine model for the behavior of a component under power management.

**PRDG**   See *polyhedral reduced dependence graph.*

**predecessor/successor forces**   Forces from one operator to nearby operators in force-directed scheduling. (Section 7.3.1)

**predictive shutdown**   A power management technique that predicts appropriate times for system shutdown.

**preemptive multitasking**   A scheme for sharing the CPU in which the operating system can interrupt the execution of processes.

**preference vector**    A vector that shows what processes can be mapped to what processing elements. (Section 7.4.4)

**prefetch**    Fetching a value before it is needed. In caches, a long cache line is used to prefetch the values in that line. (Section 2.6.3)

**presentation layer**    In the OSI model, the layer responsible for data formats. (Section 1.2.1)

**priority**    A value that is used during scheduling to rank processes. (Section 4.2.1)

**priority ceiling protocol**    A priority inheritance protocol. (Section 4.2.2)

**priority-driven scheduling**    Any scheduling technique that uses priorities of processes to determine the running process. (Section 4.2.1)

**priority inheritance protocol**    A family of algorithms for avoiding priority inversion. (Section 4.2.2)

**priority inversion**    A situation in which a lower-priority process prevents a higher-priority process from executing. (Section 4.2.2)

**priority service**    A service in Dynamic Real-Time CORBA that records the priorities for system objects. (Section 6.4.1)

**procedure cache**    A mechanism for software-controlled code compression. (Section 2.7.1)

**procedure restructuring**    A general term for transformations on procedures such as inlining, tail recursion elimination, etc. (Section 3.3.2)

**procedure splitting**    Splitting the object code for a procedure using branches to change the code placement and/or cache behavior. (Section 3.2.4)

**process**    A unique execution of a program. (Section 4.2.1)

**processing element**    A component that performs a computation under the coordination of the system. (Section 5.1)

**procrastination scheduling**    A family of scheduling algorithms for dynamic voltage scaling that maximizes the lengths of idle periods. (Section 4.2.3)

**programming environment**    A suite of tools used to generate code for a processor. (Section 3.2.5)

**property manager**    An object that handles QoS implementation. (Section 6.4.3)

**protocol data unit**    A minimum messaging unit. (Section 5.6.4)

**quality description language**    A language used to describe quality-of-service contracts. (Section 6.4.3)

**quality of service**   A communication service that provides a certain amount of bandwidth for a given period. (Section 5.6; Section 6.4.3)

**quality-of-service attack**   An attack that tries to cause an embedded system to fail by disrupting its timing. (Section 1.6.3)

**QoS**   See *quality of service.*

**rate**   Inverse of period. (Section 4.2.1)

**rate-monotonic scheduling**   A fixed-priority scheduling scheme. (Section 4.2.2)

**razor**   A microarchitectural method for better-than-worst-case design that uses latches that can detect late-arriving signals. (Section 2.5.2)

**reactive system**   A system designed to react to external events. (Section 3.5)

**real time**   A system that must perform operations by a certain time. (Section 4.2.1)

**Real-Time Connection Ordination Protocol**   A service in ARMADA that manages requests to create and destroy connections. (Section 6.4.1)

**real-time daemon**   A component that implements the dynamic aspects of real-time services in Dynamic Real-Time CORBA. (Section 6.4.1)

**real-time event service**   A service in Dynamic Real-Time CORBA that exchanges named events. (Section 6.4.1)

**real-time operating system**   An operating system designed to be able to satisfy real-time constraints. (Section 4.2)

**real-time primary-backup service**   An ARMADA service that allows state to be replicated to provide fault tolerance. (Section 6.4.1)

**reconfigurable system**   A hardware platform whose logic functions can be reconfigured on-the-fly during execution. (Section 7.4.8)

**reference implementation**   An implementation of a standard that is made available for use by design teams. (Section 1.4)

**register allocation**   In code generation, a step that assigns variables to registers. (Section 3.2)

**relative computational load**   A measure of the load induced by a part of a program relative to the load presented by the entire program. (Section 7.4.3)

**release time**   The time at which a process becomes ready to run. (Section 4.2.1)

**reliable system**   A system that works even in the face of internal or external errors. (Section 1.6)

**reliability function** A function that describes the probability that a system will work properly in the time interval $[0,t]$. (Section 1.6.2)

**request phase** The smallest interval between the execution of one process on one iteration and the start of a the next data-dependent process on the succeeding iteration. (Section 6.3.2)

**requirements** An informal description of what a system should do. A precursor to a specification.

**resource dependency** In scheduling, a scheduling constraint that comes from the use of an external resource. (Section 4.2.2)

**response time** The difference between completion and release time of a process. (Section 4.2.1)

**ripple scheduling** A method for scheduling and allocating quality-of-service requests in a distributed system. (Section 6.4.3)

**RISC** A reduced instruction set processor, a fairly general term for modern processors with general-purpose register files, fairly orthogonal instruction sets, and largely completing one instruction per cycle. (Section 2.3.1)

**RMA** Rate-monotonic analysis, another term for *rate-monotonic scheduling*.

**RMS** See *rate-monotonic scheduling*.

**round** In Giotto, a single invocation of a mode.

**routing** The selection of a path for a packet. (Section 5.6.2)

**RT-CORBA** A specification for real-time CORBA. (Section 6.4.1)

**RTOS** See *real-time operating system*.

**s-graph** A model of the transition function of a co-design finite state machine. (Section 4.3)

**safety-critical system** A system whose failure can cause the injury or death of people. (Section 1.6)

**secure system** A system that resists malicious (or sometimes inadvertent) attacks. (Section 1.6)

**schedule** A mapping of operations to time. (Section 4.2.1)

**scheduling** Determining the time at which an operation will occur. (Section 4.2.1)

**scheduling overhead** The execution time required to make a scheduling decision. (Section 4.2.1)

**scheduling policy**  A methodology for making scheduling decisions. (Section 4.2.1)

**scratch pad**  A small memory at the same level in the memory hierarchy as a level 1 cache but managed by software. (Section 2.6.4; Section 3.3.4)

**second-level cache**  A cache after the first-level cache but before main memory. (Section 2.6.3)

**self-spatial reference**  Reuse of the same cache line in a different loop iteration. (Section 2.6.3)

**self-temporal reference**  Data reuse of the same array element in a different loop iteration. (Section 2.6.3)

**SDF**  See *synchronous data flow graph*.

**self forces**  Forces from an operator to itself that influence its schedule in force-directed scheduling. (Section 7.3.1)

**self-programmable one-chip microcomputer**  A secure CPU/memory architecture used in smart cards. (Section 2.7.4)

**semaphore**  A mechanism for coordinating communicating processes. (Section 3.5)

**sensor port**  A Giotto construct for communication with primary inputs. (Section 4.3)

**service discovery**  The act of finding services available on a network, such as file access, printing, etc. (Section 1.7.4)

**service record**  A record of a Bluetooth service in the form of *<ID,value>* attributes. (Section 1.7.1)

**session layer**  In the OSI model, the network layer responsible for session-oriented actions such as checkpointing. (Section 1.2.1)

**set-associative cache**  A cache with multiple sets. (Section 2.6.3)

**shared memory**  A communication style that allows multiple processes to access the same memory locations.

**short-term memory**  A data structure used in tabu search that holds information on recent search moves. (Section 7.4.3)

**side channel attack**  An attack that makes use of information not directly related to the attack, such as power consumption. (Section 2.7.4)

**side information**  In bus encoding, information transmitted about the encoding of information on the bus. (Section 2.7.3)

**signal**   In the SIGNAL programming language, a sequence of data values with an implicit time sequence. (Section 3.5.2)

**SIMD**   Single-instruction, multiple-data execution, one of the categories in Flynn's taxonomy of computation. (Section 2.2.2)

**simple event model**   A basic event in SymTA/S. (Section 6.3.2)

**simulation**   In computer architecture, execution of a program though a software model. (Section 2.8.1)

**simulation backplane**   A protocol for connecting different types of simulators in a co-simulator. (Section 7.5)

**simultaneous multithreading**   A multithreading technique that fetches instructions from multiple threads on each cycle. (Section 2.4.4)

**signal flow graph**   A stateful model of dataflow widely used to describe digital filters. (Section 1.5.3)

**single-appearance schedule**   A synchronous dataflow graph schedule in which each node appears only once. (Section 3.5.2)

**single-hop network**   A network in which messages can travel from one PE to any other PE without going through a third PE.

**sink SCC**   A strongly connected component of an IPC graph such that any edge with a source in the SCC also has its sink in the SCC. (Section 6.3.2)

**SISD**   Single-instruction, single-data execution, one of the categories in Flynn's taxonomy of computation. (Section 2.2.2)

**slave PE**   A processor that takes the schedules for its processes from a master PE in a multiprocessor. (Section 6.3.1)

**slave thread**   A thread in CoWare that is associated with a slave port. (Section 7.4.3)

**slowdown factor**   In scheduling for dynamic voltage scheduling, the factor by which the processor clock speed is reduced. (Section 4.2.3)

**smart card**   A credit card, identification card, etc. that uses a microprocessor and memory to store, retrieve, and protect data. (Section 2.7.4)

**snooping cache**   A multiprocessor cache that monitors memory activity from other processors to keep its contents up to date. (Section 5.7.4)

**SoC**   See *system-on-chip*.

**soft real time**   An application for which missing a deadline does not create a safety problem. (Section 4.2.1)

**software-defined radio**   May be synonymous with *software radio*; may also be a radio whose functions are controlled by software but not entirely implemented with stored programs. (Section 1.2.1)

**software pipelining**   A technique for scheduling instructions in loops.

**software radio**   A radio whose main functions are implemented in software. (Section 1.2.1)

**software thread integration**   A method for synthesizing a statically scheduled implementation of a set of processes. (Section 4.3)

**source**   The unit that transmits data on a communications link. (Section 5.6.1)

**source SCC**   A strongly-connected component of an IPC graph such that an edge whose sink is in the SCC also has its source in the SCC. (Section 6.3.2)

**specification**   A formal description of what a system should do. More precise than a requirements document.

**specification model**   A system model that is primarily functional without implementation details. (Section 5.3.2)

**speedup**   The ratio of system performance before and after a design modification.

**spill**   The act of copying a register to memory to make room for another variable in the register, with the original value being retrieved later for further processing. (Section 2.6.2)

**spin lock**   An atomic test-and-set operator. (Section 5.7.4)

**spiral model**   A design methodology in which the design iterates through specification, design, and test at increasingly detailed levels of abstraction. (Section 1.4)

**SPOM**   See *self-programmable one-chip microcomputer*.

**Statecharts**   A specification technique that uses compound states. (Section 3.5.3)

**static power management**   A power management technique that does not consider the current CPU behavior.

**static phase**   In FlexRay, the phase of the schedule in which operations are scheduled statically. (Section 5.8.2)

**static priority**   A process priority that does not change during execution. (Section 4.2.2)

**static random-access memory**   A RAM that consumes power to continuously maintain its stored values.

**static scheduling**   A schedule that is determined off-line. (Section 4.2.1)

**store-and-forward routing**   A routing algorithm that stores the packet at intermediate points along the route. (Section 5.6.3)

**stream**   A model of data as a partially or fully ordered sequence of symbols. (Section 1.5.2; Section 3.5.5)

**subindependent**   In synchronous data flow graphs, a subgraph that does not consume samples from another subsset in the same schedule period in which they are produced. (Section 3.5.2)

**subword parallelism**   A technique in computer architecture that divides data words into subwords that can be operated on independently for example, a 32-bit word that can be divided into four eight-bit subwords. (Section 2.4.3)

**successive refinement**   A design methodology in which the design goes through the levels of abstraction several times, adding detail in each refinement phase.

**superscalar**   An execution method that can perform several different instructions simultaneously. (Section 2.2.2)

**switch frequency**   In Giotto, the frequency at which mode switches are evaluated. (Section 4.3)

**symmetric multiprocessing**   In hardware, a multiprocessor with uniform processing elements and memory. In software, a middleware services model. (Section 6.4.2)

**synchronous language**   A class of programming languages in which communication occurs simultaneously and synchronously. (Section 3.5)

**SystemC**   A language and simulation system for systems-on-chips and heterogeneous multiprocessors. (Section 5.3.2)

**system-on-chip**   A single-chip system that includes computation, memory, and I/O. (Section 5.4)

**synchronous data flow graph**   A data flow model for which certain properties can be verified and implementations can be synthesized. (Section 1.5.3; Section 3.5.2)

**target mode**   In Giotto, the mode that constitutes the end result of a mode switch. (Section 4.3)

**task-level parallelism**   Parallelism in a program that is found among the coarse-grained tasks. (Section 1.5.5)

**task**   Sometimes used as synonymous with *process*, sometimes used as synonymous with *task graph*. (Section 4.2.1)

**task graph**   A graph that shows processes and data dependencies among them. (Section 1.5.4)

**TDMI**   See *timed distributed method invocation.*

**technology library**   A set of components used in high-level synthesis, logic synthesis, etc. (Section 7.3.1)

**technology table**   A table that gives the characteristics of a process on different platform elements, such as performance or power consumption. (Section 7.4.2)

**temporal firewall**   A FlexRay term for the division between statically- and dynamically-scheduled activities. (Section 5.8.2)

**temporal logic**   A logic that quantifies over time. (Section 4.5)

**termination**   The unit that receives data on a communications link. (Section 5.6.1)

**thread**   A process that shares its memory space with other threads. (Section 4.2.1)

**thread pool**   A set of threads used to satisfy requests in CORBA. (Section 6.4.1)

**throughput**   The rate at which data is produced by a system. (Section 2.2.1)

**throughput factor**   A measure of feasibility based on throughput. (Section 7.4.5)

**time-loop thread**   A thread in CoWare that is not associated with a port and that is repeatedly executed. (Section 7.4.3)

**time step**   A single clock cycle in a schedule, such as in high-level synthesis. See also *control step.* (Section 7.3.1)

**time-triggered architecture**   A real-time network architecture that alternates between active and idle intervals. (Section 5.8.1)

**timed distributed method invocation**   A method used to specify timing constraints in Dynamic Real-Time CORBA. (Section 6.4.1)

**timing accident**   An event in the processor that causes an increase in execution time for an instruction. (Section 3.4.1)

**timing attack**   See *quality-of-service attack.*

**timing penalty**   The increased execution time attributable to a timing accident. (Section 3.4.1)

**top-down design**   Designing from higher levels of abstraction to lower levels of abstraction.

**topology** The structure of links that connect nodes in a communication system. (Section 5.6)

**toggle count** The number of transitions on a signal or a bus.(Section 2.7.3)

**total conflict factor** A metric used for scratch pad optimization equal to the sum of the loop conflict factor and interference factor. (Section 3.3.4)

**trace** A record of the execution path of a program. (Section 2.8.1)

**trace-driven analysis** Analyzing a trace of a program's execution. (Section 2.8.1)

**transition** In finite-state machines, an edge from one state to another; in Petri nets, a type of node that defines firing behavior. (Section 1.5.4)

**transition rule** In Petri nets, a rule that determines how tokens move from place to place, synonymous with *firing rule*. (Section 1.5.4)

**transmission start sequence** The start of a FlexRay transmission. (Section 5.8.2)

**transport layer** In the OSI model, the layer responsible for connections. (Section 1.2.1)

**triple modular redundancy** A reliability-oriented architecture that uses several function units who vote on the results of an operation. (Section 1.6.2)

**TSS** See *transmission start sequence.*

**TTA** See *time-triggered architecture.*

**turbo code** An error correction code that uses multiple coders. (Section 1.2.1)

**Tunstall code** A variable-to-fixed length coding algorithm. (Section 2.7.1)

**Turing machine** A model of computation. (Section 1.5.2)

**unified cache** A cache that holds both instructions and data.

**upper-bound throughput** An upper bound on the throughput required for a processing element to finish a task. (Section 7.4.5)

**use** In compilers, access to a variable. (Section 3.2.2)

**utilization** In real-time scheduling, the percentage of time for which a CPU does useful work. (Section 4.2.1)

**V()** Traditional name for the procedure that releases a semaphore.

**variable access count** A metric used for scratch pad optimization that counts the number of accesses to a variable. (Section 3.3.4)

**variable lifetime chart**   A graph of variables vs. time that shows the lifetimes of the variables. (Section 3.2.2)

**vector processing**   A technique in computer architecture in programming that operates on single- or multi-dimensional arrays. (Section 2.4.3)

**Verilog**   A hardware description language.

**very long instruction word**   A style of computer architecture that issues multiple instructions or operations per clock cycle but relies on static scheduling to determine the set of operations that can be performed concurrently. (Section 2.4.1)

**virtual channel flow control**   A method for resource allocation in multiprocessor networks. (Section 5.6.2)

**virtual cutthrough routing**   A routing algorithm that ensures that adequate resources are available along the entire route before starting to transmit the packet. (Section 5.6.3)

**VHDL**   A hardware description language.

**VLIW**   See *very long instruction word.*

**von Neumann architecture**   A computer architecture that stores instructions and data in the same memory.

**watchdog timer**   A timer used to check the operation of a digital system. The system must reset the timer periodically. If the watchdog timer is not reset, it will send an error signal that resets the system. (Section 1.6.2)

**waterfall model**   A design methodology in which the design proceeds from higher to lower levels of abstraction. (Section 1.4)

**watermark**   A verifiable mark, used in software, hardware, and data. (Section 2.7.4)

**WCET**   See *worst-case execution time.*

**wear leveling**   A family of techniques that evens out writes, and therefore wear, to flash memory. (Section 4.4.7)

**working-zone encoding**   A bus coding method that takes advantage of locality. (Section 2.7.3)

**wormhole routing**   A routing method that blocks all the flits in a packet when the header becomes blocked. (Section 5.6.2)

**worst-case execution time**   The longest execution time for any possible set of inputs. Section 3.4)

**write-back**  Writing to main memory only when a line is removed from the cache. (Section 2.6.3)

**write-through**  Writing to main memory for every write into the cache. (Section 2.6.3)

**X-by-wire**  A generic term for computer control of critical vehicle functions (drive-by-wire, steer-by-wire, fly-by-wire, etc.). (Section 1.2.3)

# References

[Abd99] T. Abdelzaher, S. Dawson, W.-C. Feng, F. Jahanian, S. Johnson, A. Mehra, T. Mitton, A. Shaika, K. Shin, Z. Wang, H. Zou, M. Bjorkland, and P. Marron, "ARMADA middleware and communication services," *Journal of Real-Time Systems*, 16, 1999, pp. 127–153.

[Ack00] B. Ackland, A, Anesko, D. Brinthaupt, S.J. Daubert, A. Kalavade, J. Knobloch, E. Micca, M. Moturi, C.J. Nicol, J.H. O'Neill, J. Othmer, E. Sackinger, K.J. Singh, J. Sweet, C.J. Terman, and J. Williams, "A single-chip, 1.6 billion, 16-b MAC/s multiprocessor DSP," *IEEE Journal of Solid-State Circuits*, 35(3), March 2000, pp. 412–423.

[Ado96] Joakim Adomat, Johan Furunas, Lennart Lindh, and Johan Starner, "Real-time kernel in hardware RTU: a step towards deterministic and high performance real-time systems," *Proceedings of the 8th Euromicro Workshop on Real-Time Systems*, L'Aquila, Italy, June 1996.

[Ahl05] Jaswinder Ahluwalia, Ingolf H. Kruger, Walter Philips, and Michael Meisinger, "Model-based run-time monitoring of end-to-end systems," in *Proceedings of the Fifth ACM Conference on Embedded Software*, ACM Press, 2005, pp. 100–109.

[Aho86] Alfred V. Aho, Ravi Sethi, and Jeffrey D. Ullman, *Compilers: Principles, Techniques, and Tools*, Reading MA: Addison-Wesley, 1986.

[Aho89] Alfred V. Aho, Mahadevan Ganpathi, and Steven W. K. Tjiang, "Code generation using tree matching and dynamic programming," *ACM Transactions on Programming Languages and Systems*, 11(4), October 1989, pp. 491–516.

[Air04] Airlines Electronic Engineering Committee, Aircraft Radio, Inc., "ARINC Specification 664: Aircraft Data Network," available in multiple parts from *http://www.arinc.com*.

[Akg02] Bilge E.S. Akgul and Vincent J. Mooney III, "The system-on-a-chip lock cache," *Design Automation for Embedded Systems*, 7, 2002, pp. 139–174.

[Alb05] Karsten Albers and Frank Slomka, "Efficient feasibility analysis for real-time systems with EDF scheduling," in *Proceedings of the Conference on Design Automation and Test in Europe*, IEEE Computer Society Press, 2005, pp. 492–497.

[Ale05] Aleph One, *http://www.aleph1.co.uk/yaffs*.

[Alu01] Rajeev Alur and Mihalis Yannakakis, "Model checking of hierarchical finite state machines," *ACM Transactions on Programming Languages and Systems*, 23(3), May 2001, pp. 273–303.

[Ara95] Guido Araujo and Sharad Malik, "Optimal code generation for embedded memory non-homogeneous register architectures," in *Proceedings of the 8th International Symposium on System Synthesis*, ACM Press, 1995, p. 36–41.

[ARM00] ARM Limited, Integrator/LM-XCV400+ Logic Module, ARM DUI 0130A, February 2000. Available at *www.arm.com*.

[ARM05a] ARM, *ARM1136JF-S and ARM1136J-S Technical Reference Manual*, revision r1p1, 2005, *http://www.arm.com*.

[ARM05b] ARM, "ARM SecurCore Family Flyer," 2005, *http://www.arm.com*.

[ARM05c] ARM, "SafeNet EIP-25 Datasheet," 2005, *http://www.arm.com*.

[Ata03] Kubilay Atasu, Laura Pozzi, and Paolo Ienne, "Automatic Application-Specific Instruction-Set Extensions under Microarchitectural Constraints," *Proceedings of the 40th Design Automation Conference*, ACM Press, 2003.

[Aus04] Todd Austin, David Blaauw, Scott Mahlke, Trevor Mudge, Chaitali Chakrabarti, and Wayne Wolf, "Mobile Supercomputers," *IEEE Computer*, 37(5), May 2004, pp. 81–83.

[Avi04] Algridas Avizienis, Jean-Claude Laprie, Brian Randell, and Carl Landewehr, "Basic concepts and taxonomy of dependable and secure computing," *IEEE Transactions on Dependable and Secure Computing*, 1(1), January–March 2004, pp. 11–33.

[Axi05] Axis Communications AB, *http://developer.axis.com/software/jffs/doc/jffs.shtml*.

[Aze02] Ana Azevedo, Ilya Issenin, Radu Cornea, Rajesh Gupta, Nikil Dutt, Alex Viedenbaum, and Alex Nicolau, "Profile-based dynamic voltage scheduling using program checkpoints," *Proceedings of the Conference on Design Automation and Test in Europe*, IEEE Computer Society Press, 2002, pp. 168–176.

[Bac94] David F. Bacon, Susan L. Graham, and Oliver J. Sharp, "Compiler transformations for high-performance computing," *ACM Computing Surveys*, 26(4), December 1994, pp. 345–420.

[Bac03a] David F. Bacon, Perry Cheng, and V. T. Rajan, "Controlling fragmentation and space consumption in the Metronome, a real-time garbage collector for Java," in *Proceedings of the 2003 ACM SIGPLAN Conference on Languages, Compilers, and Tools for Embedded Systems*, ACM Press, 2003, pp. 81–92.

[Bac03b] David F. Bacon, Perry Cheng, and V. T. Rajan, "A real-time garbage collector with low overhead and consistent utilization," in *Proceedings of the 30th ACM SIGPLAN-SIGACT Symposium on Principles of Programming Languages*, ACM Press, 2003, pp. 285–298.

[Bal96] Felice Balarin, Harry Hsieh, Atilla Jurecska, Luciano Lavagno, and Alberto Sangiovanni-Vincentelli, "Formal verification of embedded systems based on CFSM networks," in *Proceedings, 33rd Design Automation Conference*, ACM Press, 1996, pp. 568–571.

[Bal02] Felice Balarin, Luciano Lavagno, Claudio Passerone, Alberto Sangiovanni-Vincentelli, Yosinori Watanabe, and Guang Yang, "Concurrent execution semantics and sequential simulation algorithms for the Metropolis meta-model," in *Proceedings of the 10th International Symposium on Hardware/Software Codesign*, IEEE Computer Society Press, 2002, pp. 13–18.

[Bal03] Rajeev Balasubramonian, David Albonesi, Alper Buyuktosunoglu, and Sandhya Dworkadas, "A dynamically tunable memory hierarchy," *IEEE Transactions on Computers*, 52(10), October 2003, pp. 1243–1258.

[Bal04] Felice Balarin, Harry Hsieh, Luciano Lavagno, Claudio Passerone, Allesandro Pinto, Alberto Sangiovanni-Vincentelli, Yosinori Watanabe, and Guang Yang, "Metropolis: a design environment for heterogeneous systems," Chapter 16 in Ahmed A. Jerraya and Wayne Wolf, eds., *Multiprocessor Systems-on-Chips*, Morgan Kaufmann, 2004.

[Ban93] Uptal Banerjee, *Loop Transformations for Restructuring Compilers: The Foundations*, Boston: Kluwer Academic Publishers, 1993.

[Ban94] Uptal Banerjee, *Loop Parallelization*, Boston: Kluwer Academic Publishers, 1994.

[Ban95] Amir Ban, "Flash file system," U.S. patent 5,404,485, April 4, 1995.

[Bar94] Edna Barros, Xun Xiong, and Wolfgang Rosenstiel, "A method for partitioning UNITY language in hardware and software," in *Proceedings of the Conference on European Design Automation*, IEEE Computer Society Press, 1994, pp. 220–225.

[Bec92] David Becker, Raj K. Singh, and Stephen G. Tell, "An engineering environment for hardware/software co-simulation," in *Proceedings, 29th ACM/ IEEE Design Automation Conference*, Los Alamitos CA: IEEE Computer Society Press, 1992, pp. 129–134.

[Ben91] Albert Benveniste and Gerard Berry, "The synchronous approach to reactive and real-time systems," *Proceedings of the IEEE*, 79(9), pp. 1270–1282.

[Ben98] Luca Benini, Giovanni De Micheli, Enrico Macii, Massimo Poncino, and Stefano Quer, "Power optimization of core-based systems by address bus coding," *IEEE Transactions on VLSI Systems*, 6(4), December 1998, pp. 554–562.

[Ben99] L. Benini, A. Bogliolo, G.A. Paleologo, and G. De Micheli, "Policy optimization for dynamic power management," *IEEE Transactions on Computer-Aided Design*, 18(6), September 1991, June 1999, pp. 742–760.

[Ben00] L. Benini, A. Bogliolo, and G. De Micheli, "A survey of design techniques for system-level dynamic power management," *IEEE Transactions on VLSI Systems*, 8(3), June 2000, pp. 299–316.

[Ben01a] Luca Benini, Alberto Macii, and Alberto Nannarelli, "Cached-code compression for energy minimization in embedded processors," in *Proceedings of the 2001 International Symposium on Low Power Electronics and Design*, ACM Press, 2001, pp. 322–327.

[Ben01b] Luca Benini and Giovanni De Micheli, "Powering networks on chips," in *Proceedings of the 14th International Symposium on System Synthesis*, IEEE, 2001, pp. 33–38.

[Ben02] Luca Benini, Davide Bruni, Alberto Macii, and Enrico Macii, "Hardware-assisted data compression for energy minimization in systems with embedded processors," in *Proceedings of the Conference on Design Automation and Test in Europe*, ACM Press, 2002, pp. 449–454.

[Ber01] Reinaldo Bergamaschi, Subhrajit Bhattacharya, Ronaldo Wagner, Colleen Fellenz, Michael Muhlada, Foster White, William R. Lee, and Jean-Marc Daveau, "Automating the design of SOCs using cores," *IEEE Design & Test of Computers*, 18(5), September–October 2001, pp. 32–45.

[Bha94a] Shuvra S. Bhattacharyya, "Compiling Dataflow Programs for Digital Signal Processing," Ph.D. diss., University of California at Berkeley, July 1994.

[Bha94b] Shuvra S. Bhattacharyya and Edward A. Lee, "Memory management for dataflow programming of multirate signal processing algorithms," *IEEE Transactions on Signal Processing*, 42(5), pp. 1190–1201.

[Bha95] Shuvra S. Bhattacharyya, Joseph T. Buck, Soonhoi Ha, and Edward A. Lee, "Generating compact code from dataflow specificaitons of multirate signal processing algorithms," *IEEE Transactions on Circuits and Systems I—Fundamental Theory and Applications*, 42(3), March 1995, pp. 138–150.

[Bha97] Shuvra S. Bhattacharyya, Sundararajan Sriram, and Edward A. Lee, "Optimizing synchronization in multiprocessor DSP systems," *IEEE Transactions on Signal Processing*, 45(6), June 1997, pp. 1605–1618.

[Bir96] P. Bird and T. Mudge, "An instruction stream compression technique," Electrical Engineering and Computer Science Department, University of Michigan, Tech. Rep. CSE-TR-319-96, November 1996.

[Bis05] Partha Biswas, Sudarshan Banerjee, Nikil Dutt, Laura Pozzi, and Paolo Ienne, "ISGEN: Generation of high-quality instruction-set extensions by iterative improvement," *Proceedings of the Design Automation and Test Conference and Exhibition*, IEEE Computer Society Press, 2005.

[Bje06] Tobias Bjerregaard and Shankhar Mahadevan, "A survey of research and practices of network-on-chip," *ACM Computing Surveys*, to appear in 2006.

[Boe92] Robert A. Boeller, Samuel A. Stodder, John F. Meyer, and Victor T. Escobedo, "A large-format thermal inkjet drafting plotter," *Hewlett-Packard Journal*, 43(6), December 1992, pp. 6–15.

[Bol00] Greg Bollella and James Gosling, "The real-time specification for Java," *IEEE Computer*, 33(6), June 2000, pp. 47–54.

[Bol03] Douglas Boling, *Programming Microsoft Windows CE .NET*, Microsoft Press, 2003.

[Bol04] E. Bolotin, I. Cidon, R. Ginosar, and A. Kolodny, "QNoC: QoS architecture and design process for network on chip," *The Journal of Systems Architecture*, 50(2-3), February 2004, pp. 105–128.

[Bou91] Frederic Boussinot and Robert De Simone "The Esterel language," *Proceedings of the IEEE*, 79(9), September 1991, pp. 1293–1304.

[Bro00] David Brooks, Vivek Tiwari, and Margaret Martonosi. "Wattch: A Framework for Architectural-Level Power Analysis and Optimizations," *Twenty-seventh International Symposium on Computer Architecture*, IEEE, 2000, pp. 83–94.

[Bry86] Randal E. Bryant, "Graph-based algorithms for Boolean function manipulation," *IEEE Transactions on Computers*, 35(8), 1986, pp. 677–691.

[Bur99] Wayne Burleson, Jason Ko, Douglas Niehaus, Krithi Ramamrithan, John A. Stankovic, Gary Wallace, and Charles Weems, "The Spring Scheduling Coprocessor: a scheduling accelerator," *IEEE Transactions on VLSI Systems*, 7(1), March 1999, pp. 38–47.

[But02] B.K. Butler, King-Chung Lai, K. Saints, and B. Meagher, "The MSM5100™ cdma2000 + AMPS + gpsOne™ + Bluetooth multimode ASIC for 3G handsets," *Proceedings, Radio Frequency Integrated Circuits (RFIC) Symposium*, IEEE June 2002, pp. 186_A–186_F.

[Cad01] Sidney Cadot, Frits Kuijlman, Koen Langendoen, Kees van Reeuwijk, and Henk Sips, "ENSEMBLE: a communication layer for embedded multi-processor systems," in *Proceedings of the ACM SIGPLAN Workshop on Languages, Compilers, and Tools for Embedded Systems*, ACM Press, 2001, pp. 56–63.

[Cai03] Lukai Cai and Daniel Gajski, "Transaction level modeling in system level design," CECS Technical Report 03-10, Center for Embedded Computing Systems, University of California, Irvine, March 28, 2003.

[Cal00] Timothy J. Callahan, John R. Hauser, and John Wawrzynek, "The Garp architecture and C compiler," *IEEE Computer*, 33(4), April 2000, pp. 62–69.

[Cam91] Raul Camposano, "Path-based scheduling for synthesis," *IEEE Transactions on CAD/ICAS*, 10(1), January 1991, pp. 85–93.

[Cas99] Paul Caspi, Alkain Girault, and Daniel Pilaud, "Automatic distribution of reactive systems for asynchronous networks of processors," *IEEE Transactions on Software Engineering*, 25(3), pp. 416–427.

[Cat98] Francky Catthoor, Sven Wuytack, Eddy De Greef, Florin Balasa, Lode Nachtergaele, and Arnout Vandecappelle, *Custom Memory Management Methodology: Exploration of Memory Organization for Embedded Multimedia System Design*, Kluwer Academic Publishers, 1998).

[Ces05] Wander O. Cesario and Ahmed Amine Jerraya, "Component-Based Design for Multiprocessor Systems-on-Chips," in *Multiprocessor Systems-on-Chips*, Ahmed Amine Jerraya and Wayne Wolf, eds., Morgan Kaufmann, May/ June 1999, 2005.

[Cha88] K. Mani Chandy and Jayadev Misra, *Parallel Program Design: A Foundation*, Addison-Wesley, 1988.

[Cha92] Anantha P. Chandrakasan, Samuel Sheng, and Robert W. Brodersen, "Low-power CMOS digital design," *IEEE Journal of Solid-State Circuits*, 27(4), April 1992, pp. 473–484.

[Che02] G. Chen, M. Kandemir, N. Vijaykrishnan, M.J. Irwin, and W. Wolf, "Energy savings through compression in embedded Java environments," *Proceedings of the 10th International Symposium on Hardware/Software Codesign*, IEEE Computer Society Press, 2002, pp. 163–168.

[Chi94] Massimiliano Chiodo, Paolo Giusto, Atilla Jurecska, Harry C. Hsieh, Alberto Sangiovanni-Vincentelli, and Luciano Lavagno, "Hardware-software codesign of embedded systems," *IEEE Micro*, 14(4), August 1994, pp. 26–36.

[Chi95] Massimiliano Chiodo, Paolo Giusto, Atilla Jurecska, Luciano Lavagno, Ellen Sentovich, Harry Hsieh, Kei Suzuki, and Alberto Sangiovanni-Vincentelli, "Synthesis of software programs for embedded control application," *Proceedings of the 32nd ACM/IEEE Conference on Design Automation*, ACM Press, 1995, pp. 587–592.

[Cho95a] Pai Chou and Gaetano Borriello, "Interval scheduling: fine-grained code scheduling for embedded systems," in *Proceedings of the 32nd ACM/IEEE Conference on Design Automation*, ACM Press, 1995, pp. 462–467.

[Cho95b] Pai Chou, Ross B. Ortega, and Gaetano Borriello, "Interface co-synthesis techniques for embedded systems," in *Proceedings, ICCAD 95*, IEEE Computer Society Press, 1995, pp. 280–87.

[Cho98] Pai Chou, Ken Hines, Kurt Partridge, and Gateano Borriello, "Control generation for embedded systems based on composition of modal processes," in *Proceedings, ICCAD 98*, ACM Press, 1998, pp. 46–53.

[Clo53] C. Clos, "A study of non-blocking switching networks," *Bell System Technical Journal*, 32(2), March 1953, pp. 406–424.

[Com05] Jacques Combaz, Jean-Claude Fernandez, Thierry Lepley, and Joseph Sifakis, "QoS control for optimality and safety," in *Proceedings of the Fifth ACM Conference on Embedded Software*, ACM Press, 2005, pp. 90–99.

[Con92] Thomas M. Conte, *Systematic Computer Architecture Prototyping*, Ph.D. diss., University of Illinois at Urbana-Champaign, 1992.

[Con04] Christopher L. Conway and Stephen A. Edwards, "NDL: a domain-specific language for device driers," *Proceedings of the 2004 ACM SIGPLAN/SIGBED Conference on Languages, Compilers, and Tools for Embedded Systems*, ACM Press, 2004, pp. 30–36.

[Cop04] Marcello Coppola, Stephane Curaba, Miltos D. Grammatikakis, Giuseppe Maruccia, and Francesco Papariello, "OCCN: a network-on-chip modeling and simulation framework," *Proceedings of the Conference on Design Automation and Test in Europe*, vol. 3, IEEE Computer Society Press, 2004, p. 30174.

[Cor05] Marc L. Corliss, E. Christopher Lewis, and Amir Roth, "The implementation and evaluation of dynamic code decompression using DISE," *ACM Transactions on Embedded Computing Systems*, 4(1), February 2005, pp. 38–72.

[Dal90] William J. Dally, "Performance analysis of $k$-ary $n$-cube interconnection networks," *IEEE Transactions on Computers*, 39(6), June 1990, pp. 775–785.

[Dal92] William J. Dally, "Virtual-channel flow control," *IEEE Transactions on Parallel and Distributed Systems*, 3(2), March 1992, pp. 194–205.

[Dal04] William Dally and Brian Towles, *Principles and Practices of Interconnection Networks*, Morgan Kaufmann, 2004.

[D'Am94] Joseph G. D'Ambrosio and Xiaobo Sharon Hu, "Configuration-level hardware/software partitioning for real-time embedded systems," in *Proceedings of the 3rd International Workshop on Hardware-Software Co-Design*, IEEE, 1994, pp. 34–41.

[Dar98] Alain Darte, Pierre Boulet, George-Andre Silber, and Frederic Vivien, "Loop parallelization algorithms: from parallelism extraction to code generation," *Parallel Computing*, 24(3), 1998, pp. 421–444.

[Dav81] Scott Davidson, David Landskov, Bruce D. Shriver, and Patrick W. Malletet, "Some experiments in local microcode compaction for horizontal machines," *IEEE Transactions on Computers*, C-30(7), July 1981, pp. 460–477.

[Dav97] Jean-Marc Daveau, Gilberto Fernandes Marchioro, Tarek Ben-Ismail, and Ahmed A. Jerraya, "Protocol selection and interface generation for HW-SW codesign," *IEEE Transactions on VLSI Systems*, 5(1), March 1997, pp. 136–144.

[Dav98] Bharat P. Dave and Niraj K. Jha, "COHRA: hardware-software cosynthesis of hierarchical heterogeneous distributed embedded systems," *IEEE Transactions on CAD/ICAS*, 17(10), October 1998, pp. 900–919.

[Dav99a] Bharat P. Dave, Ganesh Lakshminarayana, and Niraj K. Jha, "COSYN: hardware-software co-synthesis of heterogeneous distributed embedded systems," *IEEE Transactions on VLSI Systems*, 7(1), March 1999, pp. 92–104.

[Dav99b] Bharat P. Dave and Niraj K. Jha, "COFTA: hardware-software co-synthesis of heterogeneous distributed embedded systems for low overhead fault tolerance," *IEEE Transactions on Computers*, 48(4), April 1999, pp. 417–441.

[Dea04] Alexander G. Dean, "Efficient real-time concurrency on low-cost microcontrollers," *IEEE Micro*, 24(4), July/August 2004, pp. 10–22.

[DeG95] E. De Greef, F. Catthoor, and H. De Man, "Memory organization for video algorithms on programmable system processors," *Proceedings of ICCD '95*, IEEE Computer Society Press, 1995, pp. 552–557.

[DeM01] Giovanni De Micheli, Rolf Ernst, and Wayne Wolf, eds., *Readings in Hardware/Software Co-Design*, Morgan Kaufmann, 2001.

[Dic97] Robert P. Dick and Niraj K. Jha, "MOGAC: a multiobjective genetic algorithm for the co-synthesis of hardware-software embedded systems," in *Proceedings, ICCAD-97*, IEEE, 1997, pp. 522–529.

[Dic98a] Robert P. Dick and Niraj K. Jha, "MOGAC: A multiobjective genetic algorithm for hardware-software cosynthesis of distributed embedded systems," *IEEE Transactions on CAD/ICAS*, 17(10), October 1998, pp. 920–935.

[Dic98b] Robert P. Dick and Niraj K. Jha, "CORDS: hardware-software co-synthesis of reconfigurable real-time distributed embedded systems," in *Digest of Technical Papers, 1988 IEEE/ACM International Conference on Computer-Aided Design*, IEEE, 1998, pp. 62–68.

[Dic98c] Robert P. Dick, David L. Rhodes, and Wayne Wolf, "TGFF: task graphs for free," in Proceedings of the Sixth International Workshop on Hardware/Software Codesign, IEEE Computer Society Press, 1998, pp. 97–101.

[Dic04] Robert P. Dick and Niraj K. Jha, "COWLS: hardware-software cosynthesis of wireless low-power distributed embedded clent-server systems," *IEEE Transactions on CAD/ICAS*, 23(1), January 2004, pp. 2–16.

[Dog99] Peter Dogan, *Instrument Flight Training Manual*, Aviation Book Co., 1999.

[Dou98] Bruce Powel Douglass, *Real-Time UML: Developing Efficient Objects for Embedded Systems*, Reading MA: Addison-Wesley Longman, 1998.

[Dou99] Bruce Powel Douglass, *Doing Hard Time: Developing Real-Time Systems with UML, Objects, Frameworks, and Patterns*, Reading MA: Addison-Wesley Longman, 1999.

[Dua02] Jose Duato, Sudkahar Yalamanchili, and Lionel Ni, *Interconnection Networks*, Morgan Kaufmann, 2002.

[Dua02] Jose Duato, Sudhakar Yalamanchili, and Lionel Ni, *Interconnection Networks,* Morgan Kaufmann, 2002.

[Dut96] Santanu Dutta and Wayne Wolf, "A flexible parallel architecture adapted to block-matching motion-estimation algorithms," *IEEE Transactions on Circuits and Systems for Video Technology*, 6(1), February 1996, pp. 74–86.

[Dut98] Santanu Dutta, Wayne Wolf, and Andrew Wolfe, "A methodology to evaluate memory architecture design tradeoffs for video signal processors," *IEEE Transactions on Circuits and Systems for Video Technology*, 8(1), February 1998, pp. 36–53.

[Dut01] Santanu Dutta, Rune Jensen, and Alf Rieckmann, "Viper: a multiprocessor SOC for advanced set-top box and digital TV systems," *IEEE Design & Test of Computers*, 18(5), September–October 2001, pp. 21–31.

[Eck03] Johan Ecker, Joern W. Janneck, Edward A. Lee, Jie Liu, Xiaojun Liu, Jozsef Ludvig, Stephen Neuendorffer, Sonia Sachs, and Yuhong Xiong, "Taming heterogeneity—the Ptolemy Approach," *Proceedings of the IEEE*, 91(1), January 2003, pp. 127–144.

[Edl03] Jan Edler and Mark D. Hill, "Dinero IV Trace-Driven Uniprocessor Cache Simulator," 2003, *http://www.cs.wisc.edu/~markhill/DineroIV/*.

[Edw97] Stephen Edwards, Luciano Lavagno, Edward A. Lee, and Alberto San-giovanni-Vincentelli, "Design of embedded systems: formal models, validation, and synthesis," *Proceedings of the IEEE*, 85(3), March 1997, pp. 773–99.

[Edw00] Stephen A. Edwards, "Compiling Esterel into sequential code," in *Proceedings of the 37th ACM/IEEE Conference on Design Automation*, ACM Press, 2000, pp. 322–327.

[Edw05] Stephen A. Edwards and Olivier Tardieu, "SHIM: a deterministic model for heterogeneous embedded systems," *Proceedings of the 5th International Conference on Embedded Software*, ACM Press, 2005, pp. 264–272.

[Ele96] Petru Eles, Zebo Peng, Krzysztof Kuchcinski, and Alexa Doboli, "System level hardware/software partitioning based on simulated annealing and tabu search," *Design Automation for Embedded Systems*, 2, 1996, pp. 5–32.

[Ele98] Petru Eles, Krzysztof Kuchcinski, Zebo Peng, Alexa Doboli, and Paul Pop, "Scheduling of conditional process graphs for the synthesis of embedded systems," in *Proceedings of the Conference on Design Automation and Test in Europe*, IEEE Press, 1998, pp. 132–139.

[Eng99a] Jakob Engblom and Andreas Ermedahl, "Pipeline timing analysis using a trace-driven simulator," in *Proceedings, Sixth International Conference on Real-Time Computing Systems and Applications (RTSCA '99)*, IEEE, 1999, pp. 88–95.

[Eng99b] Jakob Engblom, "Why SpecInt95 should not be used to benchmark embedded systems tools," in *Proceedings of the ACM SIGPLAN 1999 Workshop on Languages, Compilers, and Tools for Embedded Systems*, ACM Press, 1999, pp. 96–103.

[Eng02] Jakob Engblom and Bengt Jonsson, "Processor pipelines and their properties for static WCET analysis," *Proceedings of the Second Embedded Software Conference*, Lecture Notes in Computer Science, vol. 2491, 2002, Springer Verlag.

[Erm05] Andreas Ermedahl, Friedhelm Stappert, and Jakob Engblom, "Clustered worst-case execution-time calculation," *IEEE Transactions on Computers*, 54(9), pp. 1104–1122.

[Ern93] Rolf Ernst, Joerg Henkel, and Thomas Benner, "Hardware-software cosynthesis for microcontrollers," *IEEE Design and Test of Computers,* 10(4), December 1993, pp. 64–75.

[Ern03] Dan Ernst, Nam Sung Kim, Shidhartha Das, Sanjay Pant, Rajeev Rao, Toan Pham, Conrad Ziesler, David Blaauw, Todd Austin, Krisztian Flautner, and Trevor Mudge, "Razor: A low-power pipeline based on circuit-level timing speculation," *Proceedings of the 36th Annual Symposium on Microarchitecture, MICRO-36*, IEEE Computer Society Press, 2003.

[Ext05] Extension Media, "Embedded Resource Catalog," 2005, *http://www.extensionmedia.com/powerpc.*

[Fan03] Claire F. Fang, Rob A. Rutenbar, and Tsuhan Chen, "Fast, accurate analysis for fixed-point finite-precision effects in DSP designs," *Proceedings, ICCAD-03*, ACM Press, 2003, pp. 275–282.

[Fei92] Ephraim Feig and Shmuel Winograd, "Fast algorithms for the discrete conse transform," *IEEE Transactions on Signal Processing*, 40(9), September 1992, pp. 2174–2193.

[Fen98] Jay Fenlason and Richard Stallman, "GNU gprof, the GNU profiler," November 7, 1998, *http://www.gnu.org/software/binutils/manual/gprof-2.9.1/html_mono/gprof.html.*

[Fer87] Jeanne Ferrante, Karl J. Ottenstein, and Joe D. Warren, "The program dependence graph and its use in optimization," *ACM Transactions on Programming Languages and Systems*, 9(3), pp. 319–349.

[Fis05] Joseph A. Fisher, Paolo Faraboschi, and Cliff Young, *Embedded Computing: A VLIW Approach to Architecture, Compilers, and Tools*, Morgan Kaufmann, 2005.

[Fle05] FlexRay Consortium, FlexRay Communication System Protocol Specification, version 2.1 revision A, December 22, 2005.

[Fly72] Michael Flynn, "*Some Computer Organizations and Their Effectiveness,*" *IEEE Transactions on Computers*, C-21(9), 1972, pp. 948–960.

[Fra94] F. Franssen, I. Nachtergaele, H. Samsom, F. Catthoor, and H. De Man, "control flow optimization for fast system simulation and storage minimization," *Proceedings of the International Conference on Design and Test*, IEEE, 1994, pp. 20–24.

[Fri00] Jason Fritts, *Architecture and Compiler Design Issues in Programmable Media Processors*, Ph.D. diss., Princeton University, January 2000.

[Ful98] Sam Fuller, "Motorola's AltiVec™ Technology," document ALTIVE-CWP, Motorola, 1998, http://www.freescale.com/files/32bit/doc/fact_sheet/ALTIVECWP.pdf?srch=1.

[Gaj98] Daniel D. Gajski, Frank Vahid, Sanjiv Narayan, and Jie Gong, "System-level exploration with SpecSyn," *Proceedings of the 25th Annual Conference on Design Automation,* ACM Press, 1998, pp. 812–817.

[Gar79] M. R. Garey and D. S. Johnson, *Computers and Intractability: A Guide to the Theory of NP-Completeness*, W. H. Freeman, 1979.

[Gho95] A. Ghosh, M. Bershteyn, R. Casley, C. Chien, A. Jain, M. Lipsie, D. Tarrodaycik, and O. Yamamoto, "A hardware-software co-simulator for embedded system design and debugging," in *Proceedings, ASP-DAC 95*, ACM, 1995, paper A-3B.3.

[Gil03] Christopher D. Gill, Ron K. Cytron, and Douglas C. Schmidt, "Multiparadigm scheduling for distributed real-time embedded computing," *Proceedings of the IEEE*, 91(1), January 2003, pp. 183–197.

[Glo03] John Glossner, Daniel Iancu, Jin Lu, Erdem Hokenek, and Mayan Moudgill, "A software-defined communications baseband design," *IEEE Communications Magazine*, 41(1), January 2003, pp. 120–128.

[Glo05] John Glossner, Mayan Moudgill, Daniel Iancu, Gary Nacer, Sanjay Jinturkar, Stuart Stanley, Michael Samori, Tanuj Raja, and Michael Schulte, "The Sandbridge Sandblaster Convergence Platform," 2005, *http://www.sandbridgetech.com*.

[Gon97a] Jie Gong, Daniel D. Gajski, and Smita Bakshi, "Model refinement for hardware-software codesign," *ACM Transactions on Design Automation of Embedded Systems,* 2(1), January 1997, pp. 22–41.

[Gon97b] Ricardo Gonzales, Benjamin M. Gordon, and Mark A. Horowitz, "Supply and threshold voltage scaling for low power CMOS," *IEEE Journal of Solid-State Circuits*, 32(8), August 1997, pp. 1210–1216.

[Goo97] Gert Goossens, Johan van Praet, Dirk Lanneer, Werner Geurts, Augusli Kifli, Clifford Liem, and Pierre G. Paulin, "Embedded software in real-time signal processing systems: design technologies," *Proceedings of the IEEE*, 85(3), March 1997, pp. 436–454.

[Goo05] Kees Goossens, John Dielissen, Om Prakash Gangwal, Santiago Gonzales Pestana, Andrei Radulescu, and Edwin Rijpkema, "A design flow for application-specific networks on chip with guaranteed performance to accelerate SOC design and verification," in *Proceedings of the Conference on Design Automation and Test in Europe,* vol. 2, IEEE Computer Society Press, 2005, pp. 1182–1187.

[Gor01] Pradeep Gore, Ron Cytron, Douglas Schmidt, Carlos O'Ryan, "Designing and optimizing a scalable CORBA notification service," in *Proceedings of the ACM SIGPLAN Workshop on Languages, Compilers, and Tools for Embedded Systems*, ACM Press, 2001, pp. 196–204.

[Gor04] Ann Gordon-Ross, Frank Vahid, and Nikil Dutt, "Automatic tuning of two-level caches to embedded applications," in *Proceedings, DATE '04*, IEEE Computer Society Press, 2004.

[Gos00] Greg Bolella and James Gosling, "The real-time specification for Java," *IEEE Computer,* 39(6), June 2000, pp. 47–54.

[Gru00] Peter Grun, Nikil Dutt, and Alex Nicolau, "Memory aware compilation through accurate timing extraction," in *Proceedings, DAC 2000*, ACM Press, 2000, pp. 316–321.

[Gue00] Pierre Guerrier and Alain Grenier, "A generic architecture for on-chip packet-switched interconnections," in *Proceedings of the Conference on Design Automation and Test in Europe*, ACM Press, 2000, pp. 250–256.

[Gup93] Rajesh K. Gupta and Giovanni De Micheli, "Hardware-software cosynthesis for digital systems," *IEEE Design and Test of Computers*, 10(3), September 1993, pp. 29–40.

[Hal91] Nicholas Halbwachs, Paul Caspi, Pascal Raymond, and Daniel Pilaud, "The synchronous data flow programming language LUSTRE," *Proceedings of the IEEE*, 79(9), September 1991, pp. 1305–1320.

[Har87] David Harel, "Statecharts: a visual formalism for complex systems," *Science of Computer Programming,* 8, 1987, pp. 231–274.

[Har90] David Harel, Hagi Lachover, Amnon Naamad, Amir Pnueli, Michal Politi, Rivi Sherman, Aharon Shtull-Trauring, and Mark Trakthenbrot, "STATEMATE: a working environment for the development of complex reactive systems," *IEEE Transactions on Software Engineering*, 16(4), April 1990, pp. 403–414.

[Hea99a] Christopher Healy, Mikael Sjodin, Viresh Rustagi, David Whalley, and Robert van Englen, "Supporting timing analysis by automatic bounding of loop iterations," *Journal of Real-Time Systems*, 18(2–3), 1999, pp. 129–156.

[Hea99b] Christopher A. Healy, Robert D. Arnold, Frank Mueller, David B. Whalley, and Marion G. Harmon, "Bounding pipeline and instruction cache performance," *IEEE Transactions on Computers*, 48(1), January 1999, pp. 53–70.

[Hel99] Graham R. Hellestrand, "The revolution in systems engineering," *IEEE Specturm*, 36(9), September 1999, pp. 43–51.

[Hel04] Albert Helfrick, *Principles of Avionics*, Avionics Communications Inc., 2004.

[Hen94] J. Henkel, R. Ernst, U. Holtmann, and T. Benner, "Adaptation of partitioning and high-level synthesis in hardware/software co-synthesis," in *Proceedings, ICCAD-94*, Los Alamitos CA: IEEE Computer Society Press, 1994, pp. 96–100.

[Hen95] Joerg Henkel and Rolf Ernst, "A path-based technique for estimationg hardware runtime in HW/SW cosynthesis," in *Proceedings, Eighth IEEE International Symposium on System Synthesis*, IEEE, 1995, pp. 116–121.

[Hen01] Joerg Henkel and Rolf Ernst, "An approach to automated hardware/software partitioning using a flexible granularity that is driven by high-level estimation techniques," *IEEE Transactions on VLSI Systems*, 9(2), April 2001, pp. 273–289.

[Hen03] Thomas A. Henzinger, Benjamin Horowitz, and Christoph M. Kirsch, "Giotto: a time-triggered language for embedded programming," *Proceedings of the IEEE*, 91(1), January 2003, pp. 84-99.

[Hen05] Rafik Henia, Arne Hamann, Marek Jersak, Razvan Racu, Kai Richter, and Rolf Ernst, "System-level performance analysis—the SymTA/S approach," *IEE Proceedings Computers and Digital Techniques*, 2005.

[Her94] D. Herrmann, J. Henkel, and R. Ernst, "An approach to the adaptation of estimated cost parameters in the COSYMA system," in Proceedings, Third International Workshop on Hardware/Software Codesign, IEEE Computer Society Press, 1994, pp. 100–107.

[Hof01] Andreas Hoffman, Tim Kogel, Achim Nohl, Gunnar Braun, Oliver Schliebusch, Oliver Wahlen, Andreas Wieferink, and Heinrich Meyr, "A novel methodology for the design of application-specific instruction-set processors (ASIPs) using a machine description language," *IEEE Transactions on CAD/ICAS*, 20(11), November 2001, pp. 1138–1354.

[Hol91] Bruce K. Holmer and Alvin M. Despain, "Viewing instruction set design as an optimization problem," *Proceedings of the 24th International Symposium on Microarchitecture*, ACM Press, 1991, pp. 153–162.

[Hol97] Gerard J. Holzmann, "The model checker SPIN," *IEEE Transactions on Software Engineering*, 23(5), pp. 279–295.

[How92] P.G. Howard and J.S. Vitter, "Practical implementations of arithmetic coding," *Image and Data Compression*, Norwell MA: Kluwer Academic Publishers, 1992, pp. 85–112.

[Hua95] Ing-Jer Huang and Alvin M. Despain, "Synthesis of application specific instruction sets," *IEEE Transactions on CAD/ICAS*, 14(6), June 1995, pp. 663–675.

[Hua99] J. Huang, Y. Wang, and F. Cao, "On developing distributed middleware services for QoS- and criticality-based resource negotiation and adaptation," *Journal of Real-Time Systems*, 16, 1999, pp. 187–221.

[Huf52] D. A. Huffman, "A method for the construction of minimum-redundancy codes," *Proceedings of the IRE*, vol. 4D, September 1952, pp. 1098–1101.

[Hwu89] Wen-Mei W. Hwu and Pohua P. Chang, "Achieving high instruction cache performance with an optimizing compiler," in *Proceedings of the 16th*

*Annual International Symposium on Computer Architecture*, ACM Press, 1989, pp. 242–251.

[IBM05] IBM, "IBM PowerPC 970FX RISC Microprocessor Data Sheet," SA14-2760-05, version 2.1, October 14, 2005, *http://www.ibm.com*.

[Int96] Intel, Microsoft, and Toshiba, *Advanced Configuration and Power Interface Specification,* 1996, *http://www.teleport.com/~acpi*.

[Int98] Intel, *Flash File System Selector Guide*, Application note AP-686, December 1998.

[Int00] Intel, "Intel XScale™ Microarchitecture," 2000, *http://www.intel.com*.

[Int04] Intel Corporation, Intel Flash File System Core Reference Guide, version 1, October 2004, *http://www.intel.com*.

[Ish98a] Tohru Ishihara and Hiroto Yasuura, "Voltage scheduling problem for dynamically variable voltage processors," *Proceedings, 1998 International Symposium on Low Power Electronics and Design*, IEEE, 1998, pp. 197–202.

[Ish98b] N. Ishiura and M. Yamaguchi, "Instruction code compression for application specific VLIW processors based on automatic field partitioning," in *Proceedings of the 8th Workshop on Synthesis and System Integratin of Mixed Technologies (SASIMI '98)*, SASIMI, 1998, pp. 105–109.

[ISO93] ISO/IEC, *Information Technology—Coding of Moving Pictures and Associated Audio for Digital Storage Media At Up To About 1,5 Mbit/sec—Part 3: Audio,* ISO/IEC 11172-3:1993, 1993.

[Ito00] Makiko Itoh, Shigeaki Higaki, Jun Sato, Akichika Shiomi, Yoshinori Takuchi, Akira Kitajima, and Masaharu Imai, "PEAS-III: An ASIP design environment," *International Conference on Computer Design: VLSI in Computers and Processors*, IEEE Computer Society Press, 2000, pp. 430–436.

[ITU92] International Telecommunication Union, *Terminal Equipment and Protocols for Telematic Services: Information Technology—Digital Compression and Coding of Continuous-Tone Still Images—Requirements and Guidelines*, Recommendation T.81, September 1992.

[Jac99] M. F. Jacome and G. de Veciana, "Lower bound on latency for VLIW ASIP datapaths," *Proceedings, International Conference on Computer-Aided Design 1999*, IEEE Computer Society Press, 1999, pp. 261–268.

[Jal04] A. Jalabert, S. Murali, L. Benini, and G. De Micheli, "xpipesCompiler: a tool for instantiating application specific networks-on-chips," *Proceedings of Design Automation and Testing in Europe Conference*, IEEE, 2004, pp. 884–889.

[Jan03] A. Jantsch and Hannu Tenhunen, eds., *Networks on Chip,* Kluwer Academic Publishers, 2003.

[Jap05] "World's 1st cell phone virus confirmed in 12 countries; not Japan," February 19, 2005, *www.japantoday.com.*

[Jej04] Ravindra Jejurikar, Cristiano Pereira, and Rajesh Gupta, "Leakage aware dynamic voltage scaling for real-time embedded systems," *Proceedings, Design Automation Conference,* ACM Press, 2004, pp. 275–281.

[Jer05] Ahmed Amine Jerraya and Wayne Wolf, eds., *Multiprocessor Systems-on-Chips*, Morgan Kaufmann, 2005.

[JTR05] Joint Tactical Radio System web site, *http://jtrs.army.mil.*

[Jua02] Philo Juang, Hidekazu Oki, Yong Wang, Margaret Martonosi, Li-Shiuan Peh, and Daniel Rubenstein, "Energy-efficient computing for wildlife tracking: design tradeoffs and early experiences with ZebraNet," *Proceedings, ASPLOS-X,* ACM Press, 2002.

[Kal97] A. Kalavade and E.A. Lee, "The extended partitioning problem: hardware/software mapping, scheduling, and implementatin-bin selection," Design Automation for Embedded Systems, 2(3), March 1997, pp. 125–163.

[Kam97] M. B. Kamble and K. Ghose, "Analytical energy dissipation models for low power caches," *Proceedings, International Symposium on Low Power Electronics and Design*, IEEE, 1997.

[Kan99a] Mahmut Kandemir, J. Ramanujam, and Alok Choudhary, "Improving cache locality by a combination of loop and data transformations," *IEEE Transactions on Computers*, 48(2), February 1999, pp. 159–167.

[Kan99b] D.-I. Kang, R. Gerber, L. Golubchik, J.K. Hollingsworth, and M. Saksena, "A software synthesis tool for distributed embedded system design," in *Proceedings of the ACM SIGPLAN 1999 Workshop on Languages, Compilers, and Tools for Embedded Systems*, ACM Press, 1999, pp. 87–95.

[Kan00] M. Kandemir, N. Vijaykrishnan, M.J. Irwin, and W. Ye, "Influence of compiler optimizations on system power," in *Proceedings of the 37th Conference on Design Automation*, ACM Press, 2000, pp. 304–307.

[Kan05] Mahmut Kandemir and Nikil Dutt, "Memory systems and compiler support for MPSoC architectures," Chapter 9 in Ahmed Amine Jerraya and Wayne Wolf, eds., *Multiprocessor Systems-on-Chips*, Morgan Kaufmann, 2005.

[Kar03] Gabor Karsai, Janos Sztipanovits, Akos Ledeczi, and Ted Bapty, "Model-integrated development of embedded software," *Proceedings of the IEEE*, 91(1), January 2003, pp. 145–164.

[Kas98] Daniel Kastner and Stephan Thesing, "Cache sensitive pre-runtime scheduling," in *Proceedings of the CM SIGPLAN Workshop on Languages,*

*Compilers, and Tools for Embedded Systems*, Frank Mueller and Azer Bestavros, eds., Lecture Notes in Computer Science, vol. 1474, 1998, Springer, pp. 131–145.

[Kas02] R. Kastner, A. Kaplan, S. Ogrenci Memek, and E. Bozorgzadeh, "Instruction generation for hybrid reconfigurable systems," *ACM Transaction on Design Automation for Embedded Systems*, 7(4), October 2002, pp. 605–627.

[Kem98] T.M. Kemp, R.K. Montoye, J.D. Harper, J.D. Palmer, and D.J. Auerbach, "A decompression core for PowerPC," *IBM Journal of Research and Development*, 42(6), November 1998, pp. 807–812.

[Ker78] Brian W. Kernighan and Dennis M. Ritchie, *The C Programming Language*, Prentice-Hall, 1978.

[Kie02] Bart Kienhuis, Edwin Rijpkema, and Ed Deprettere, "Compaan: deriving process networks from Matlab for embedded signal processing architectures," *Proceedings of the 8th International Workshop on Hardware/Software Codesign*, IEEE Computer Society Press, 2002, pp. 13–17.

[Kim99] Taehyoun Kim, Naehyuck Chang, Namyun Kim, and Heonshik Shin, "Scheduling garbage collector for embedded real-time systems," *Proceedings of the ACM SIGPLAN 1999 Workshop on Languages, Compilers, and Tools for Embedded Systems*, ACM Press, 1999, pp. 55–64.

[Kim02] Woonseok Kim, Johong Kim, and Sang Lyul Min, "A dynamic voltage scaling algorithm for dynamic-priority hard real-time systems using slack time analysis," *Proceedings of the 2002 Design Automation and Test in Europe Conference*, IEEE Computer Society Press, 2002, pp. 788–794.

[Kir90] David B. Kirk and Jay K. Strosnider, "SMART (Strategic Memory Allocation for Real-Time) cache design using the MIPS R3000," *Proceedings, 11th Real-Time Systems Symposium*, IEEE, 1990, pp. 322–330.

[Kir97] Darko Kirovski, Johnson Kin, and William H. Mangione-Smith, "Procedure based program compression," *Proceedings, 13th Annual IEEE/ACM International Symposium on Microarchitecture*, IEEE, 1997, pp. 204–213.

[Kob02] Shinsuke Kobayashi, Kentaro Mita, Yoshinori Takeuchi, and Masaharu Imai, "A compiler generation method for HW/SW codesign based on configurable processors," *IEICE Transactions on Fundamentals*, E85-A(12), December 2002.

[Kob03] Shinsuke Kobayashi, Kentaro Mita, Yoshinori Takeuchi, and Masaharu Imai, "Rapid Prototyping of JPEG Encoder using the ASIP Development System: PEAS-III," *Proceedings of IEEE International Conference on Acoustics, Speech, and Signal Processing 2003*, vol. 2, IEEE, April 2003, pp. 485–488.

[Koc99] P. Kocher, J. Jaffe, and B. Jun, "Differential power analysis," *Proceedings, 19th International Advances in Cryptography Conference: CRYPTO '99*, IEEE, 1999, pp. 388–397.

[Koh03] Paul Kohout, Brinda Ganesh, and Bruce Jacob, "Hardware support for real-time operating systems," *Proceedings of the First IEEE/ACM/IFIP International Conference on Hardware/Software Codesign and System Synthesis*, IEEE, 2003, pp. 45–51.

[Kop97] Hermann Kopetz, *Real-Time Systems: Design Principles for Distributed Embedded Applications*, Boston: Kluwer Academic Publishers, 1997.

[Kop03] Hermann Kopetz and Gunther Bauer, "The time-triggered architecture," *Proceedings of the IEEE*, 91(1), January 2003, pp. 112–126.

[Kri01] Yamuna Krishnamurthy, Vishal Kachroo, David A. Carr, Craig Rodrigues, Joseph P. Loyall, Richard Schantz, and Douglas C. Schmidt, "Integration of QoS-enabled distributed object computing middleware for developing next-generation distributed application," in *Proceedings of the ACM SIGPLAN Workshop on Languages, Compilers, and Tools for Embedded Systems*, ACM Press, 2001, pp. 230–237.

[Kum02] Sashi Kumar, Axel Jantsch, Juha-Pekka Soininen, Martti Forsell, Mikael Millberg, Jonny Oberg, Kari Tiensyrja, and Ahmed Hemani, "A network on chip architecture and design methodology," *Proceedings of the IEEE Computer Society Annual Symposium on VLSI*, IEEE Computer Society Press, 2002.

[Lah88] S. Laha, J.A. Patel, and R.K. Iyer, "Accurate low-cost methods for performance evaluation of cache memory systems," *IEEE Transactions on Computers*, C-37(11), November 1988, pp. 1325–1336.

[Lam80] Butler W. Lampson and David D. Redell, "Experience with processes and monitors in Mesa," *Communications of the ACM*, 23(2), February 1980, pp. 105–117.

[Lan04] Joachim Langenwalter and Tom Erkkinen, "Embedded steer-by-wire system development," *Proceedings, Embedded World*, Germany, 2004, *http://www.mathworks.com*.

[Lar99] Sergei Y. Larin and Thomas M. Conte, "Compiler-driven cached code compression schemes for embedded ILP processors," in *Proceedings, 32nd Annual International Symposium on Microarchitecture*, IEEE, 1999, pp. 82–92.

[Lee87] Edward Ashford Lee and David G. Messerschmitt, "Static scheduling of synchronous data flow programs for signal processing," *IEEE Transactions on Computers*, C-36(1), January 1987, pp. 24–35.

[Lee94] Ruby Lee, "Multimedia enhancements for PA-RISC architectures," *Proceedings, Hot Chips VI*, IEEE, 1994, pp. 183–192.

[Lee95] Edward A. Lee and Thomas M. Parks, "Dataflow process networks," *Proceedings of the IEEE*, 85(3), May 1995, pp. 773–799.

[Lee97] Chunho Lee, Miodrag Potkonjak, and William H. Mangione-Smith, "MediaBench: a tool for evaluating and synthesizing multimedia and communications systems," *Proceedings, International Symposium on Microarchitecture*, IEEE, 1997, pp. 330–335.

[Lee01] Yann-Hang Lee, Yoonmee Doh, and C. M. Krishna, "EDF scheduling using two-mode voltage-clock-scaling for hard real-time systems," in *Proceedings, CASES '01*, ACM, 2001, pp. 221–229.

[Lee02a] Tin-Man Lee, Joerg Henkel, and Wayne Wolf, "Dynamic runtime rescheduling allowing multiple implementations of a task for platform-based designs," *Proceedings, IEEE Conference on Design Automation and Test in Europe*, IEEE Computer Society Press, 2002, pp. 296–302.

[Lee02b] Gabriel Leen and Daniel Heffernan, "Expanding automotive electronic systems," *IEEE Computer*, 35(1), January 2002, pp. 88–93.

[Lee05] Se-Joong Lee, Kangmin Lee, and Hoi-Jun Yoo, "Analysis and implementation of practical, cost-effective networks-on-chips," *IEEE Design & Test of Computers*, 22(5), September/October 2005, pp. 422–433.

[Lef97] Charles Lefurgy, Peter Bird, I-Cheng Chen, and Trevor Mudge, "Improving code density using compression techniques," in *Proceedings of the 13th Annual IEEE/ACM International Symposium on Microarchitecture*, IEEE, 1997, pp. 194–203.

[Lef00] Charles Lefurgy, Eva Piccininni, and Trevor Mudge, "Reducing code size with run-time decompression," *Proceedings, Sixth International Symposium on High-Performance Computer Architecture*, IEEE, 2000, pp. 18–220.

[LeG91] Paul Le Guernic, Thierry Gautier, Michel Le Borgne, and Claude Le Maire, "Programming real-time applications with SIGNAL," *Proceedings of the IEEE*, 79(9), September 1991, pp. 1321–1336.

[Leh89] J. Lehoczy, L. Sha, and Y. Ding, "The rate monotonic scheduling algorithm: exact characterization and average case behavior," in *Proceedings, IEEE Real-Time Systems Symposium*, IEEE, 1989.

[Lei85] C. Leiserson, "Fat-Trees: universal networks for hardware-efficient supercomputing," *IEEE Transactions on Computers*, C-34(10), October 1985, pp. 892–901.

[Lek98] H. Lekatsas and W. Wolf, "Code compression for embedded systems," in *Proceedings*, Design Automation Conference, IEEE, 1998, pp. 516–521.

[Lek99a] H. Lekatsas and W. Wolf, "Random access decompression using binary arithmetic coding," in *Proceedings, DCC '99*, Data Compression Conference, IEEE, 1999, pp. 306–315

[Lek99b] Haris Lekatsas and Wayne Wolf, "SAMC: a code compression algorithm for embedded processors," *IEEE Transactions on Computer-Aided Design of Integrated Circuits and Systems*, 18(12), December 1999, pp. 1689–1701.

[Lek99c] H. Lekatsas and W. Wolf, "SAMC: a code compression algorithm for embedded processors," *IEEE Transactions on Computer-Aided Design of Integrated Circuits and Systems*, 18(12), December 1999, pp. 1689–1701.

[Lek00a] Haris Lekatsas, Joerg Henkel, and W.ayne Wolf, "Code compression for low power embedded system design," in *Proceedings 2000. 37th Design Automation Conference*, IEEE, 2000, pp. 294–299.

[Lek00b] Haris Lekatsas, Joerg Henkel, and Wayne Wolf, "Arithmetic coding for low power embedded system design," in *Proceedings. DCC 2000 Data Compression Conference*, IEEE, 2000, pp. 430–439.

[Lek04] Haris Lekatsas, Joerg Henkel, Srimat T. Chakradhar, and Venkata Jakkula, "Cypress: Compression and encryption of data and code for embedded multimedia systems," *IEEE Design & Test of Computers*, 21(5), September/October 2004, pp. 406–415.

[Leu95] Rainer Leupers and Peter Marwedel, "Instruction-set modelling for ASIP code generation," in *Proceedings, 9th International Conference on VLSI Design*, IEEE, 1996, pp. 77–80.

[Lev94] Nancy G. Leveson, Mats Per Erik Heimdahl, Holly Hildreth, and Jon Damon Reese, "Requirements specification for process-control systems," *IEEE Transactions on Software Engineering*, 20(9), September 1994, pp. 684–707.

[Lev05] Markus Levy, "Evaluating digital entertainment system peformance," *IEEE Computer*, 38(7), July 2005, p. 72.

[Li95] Yau-Tsun Steven Li, Sharad Malik, and Andrew Wolfe, "Performance estimation of embedded software with instruction cache modeling," *Proceedings of the 1995 IEEE/ACM International Conference on Computer-Aided Design*, IEEE Computer Society Press, 1995, pp. 380–387.

[Li97a] Yanbing Li and Wayne Wolf, "Scheduling and allocation of multirate real-time embedded systems," *Proceedings, ED&TC '97* IEEE Computer Society Press, 1997), pp. 134–139.

[Li97b] Yanbing Li and Wayne Wolf, "A task-level hierarchical memory model for system synthesis of multiprocessors," *Proceedings, 34th Design Automation Conference*, ACM Press, 1997, pp. 153–156.

[Li97c] Yau-Tsun Steven Li and Sharad Malik, "Performance analysis of embedded software using implicit path enumeration," *IEEE Transactions on CAD/ICAS*, 16(12), December 1997, pp. 1477–1487.

[Li98a] Yanbing Li and Joerg Henkel, "A framework for estimating and minimizing energy dissipation of embedded HW/SW systems," *Proceedings, DAC '98* ACM Press: 1998, pp. 188–193.

[Li98b] Yanbing C. Li, *Hardware-Software Co-Synthesis of Embedded Real-Time Multiprocessors*, Ph.D. diss., Department of Electrical Engineering, Princeton University, November 1998.

[Li99] Yanbing Li and Wayne Wolf, "Hardware/software co-synthesis with memory hierarchies," *IEEE Transactions on CAD*, 18(10), October 1999, pp. 1405–1417.

[Li00] Yanbing Li, Tim Callahan, Ervan Darnell, Randolph Harr, Uday Kurkure, and Jon Stockwoodk, "Hardware-software co-design of embedded reoconfigurable architectures," in *Proceedings of the 37th Conference on Design Automation*, IEEE, 2000, pp. 507–512.

[Lia95] Stan Y. Liao, Srinivas Devadas, and Kurt Keutzer, "Code density optimization for embedded DSP processors using data compression techniques," *Proceedings, Sixteenth Conference on Advanced Research in VLSI*, IEEE, 1995, pp. 272–285.

[Lie94] Clifford Liem, Trevor May, and Pierre Paulin, "Instruction-set matching and selection for DSP and ASIP code generation," *Proceedings, European Design and Test Conference*, IEEE, 1994, pp. 31–37.

[Lie98] Clifford Liem and Pierre Paulin, "Compilation Techniques and Tools for Embedded Processor Architectures," Chapter 5 in J. Staunstrup and W. Wolf, eds., *Hardware/Software Co-Design: Principles and Practice*, Boston: Kluwer Academic Publishers, 1998.

[Lin98] Bill Lin, "Efficient compilation of process-based concurrent programs without run-time scheduling," *Proceedings of the Conference on Design Automation and Test in Europe*, IEEE Computer Society Press, 1998, pp. 211–217.

[Liu73] C.L. Liu and James W. Layland, "Scheduling algorithms for multiprogramming in a hard–real-time environment," *Journal of the ACM*, 20(1), January 1973, pp. 46–61.

[Liu00] Jane W.S. Liu, *Real-Time Systems*, Prentice Hall, 2000.

[Los97] Pete Loshin, *TCP/IP Clearly Explained*, second edition, Academic Press, 1997.

[Lv03] Tiehan Lv, J. Henkel, H. Lekatsas, and W. Wolf, "A dictionary-based en/decoding scheme for low-power data buses," *IEEE Transactions on VLSI Systems*, 11(5), October 2003, pp. 943–951.

[Mad97] J. Madsen, J. Grode, P. V. Knudsen, M. E. Petersen, and A. Haxthausen, "LYCOS: the Lyngby Co-Synthesis System," *Design Automation for Embedded Systems*, 2, 1997, pp. 195–235.

[Mah01] Scott Mahlke, Rajiv Ravindran, Michael Schlansker, Robert Schreiber, and Timothy Sherwood, "Bitwidth cognizant architecture synthesis of custom hardware accelerators," *IEEE Transactions on CAD/ICAS*, 20(11), November 2001, pp. 1355–1371.

[Mar84] Peter Marwedel, "The MIMOLA Design System: Tools for the design of digital processors," *Proceedings of the 21st Design Automation Conference*, IEEE Computer Society Press, 1984, pp. 587–593.

[Mas99] K. Masselos, F. Catthoor, C.E. Goutis, and H. De Man, "A performance oriented use methodology of power optimizing code transformations for multimedia applications realized on programmable multimedia processors," *Proceedings of the IEEE Workshop on Signal Processing Systems*, IEEE Computer Society Press, 1999, pp. 261–270.

[Mat98] Anmol Mathur, Ali Dasdan, and Rajesh K. Gupta, "Rate analysis for embedded systems," *ACM Transactions on Design Automation of Electronic Systems,* 3(3), July 1998, p. 408–436.

[McF89] Scott McFarling, "Program optimization for instruction caches," *Proceedings of the Third International Conference on Architectural Support for Programming Languages and Operating Systems*, ACM Press, 1989, pp. 183–191.

[McF91] Scott McFarling, "Procedure merging with instruction caches," *Proceedings of the ACM SIGPLAN 1991 Conference on Programming Language Design and Implementation*, ACM Press, 1991, pp. 71–79.

[McM92] K. McMillan and D. Dill, "Algorithms for interface timing verification," in *Proceedings, IEEE International Conference on Computer Design*, 1992.

[Meb92] Alfred Holt Mebane IV, James R. Schmedake, Iue-Shuenn Chen, and Anne P. Kadonaga, "Electronic and firmware design of the HP DesignJet Drafting Plotter," *Hewlett-Packard Journal*, 43(6), December 1992, pp. 16–23.

[Mes97] Bart Mesman, Marino T.J. Strik, Adwin H. Timmer, Jef L. van Meerbergen, and Jochen A.G. Jess, "Constraint analysis for DSP code generation," *Proceedings, International Symposium on System Synthesis*, IEEE, 1997, pp. 33–40.

[Mic04] Microsoft Corporation, "Architecture of Windows Media Rights Manager," May 2004, available at http://www.microsoft.com.

[Mil04a] Mikael Millberg, Erland Nilsson, Rikard Thid, Shasti Kumar, and Axel Jantsch, "The Nostrum backbone—a communication protocol stack for networks on chips," in *Proceedings of the VLSI Design Conference,* January 2004.

[Mil04b] Mikael Millberg, Erland Nilsson, Rikard Thid, and Axel Jantsch, "Guaranteed bandwidth using looped containers in temporally disjoint networks within the Nostrum network on chip," in *Proceedings of the Conference on Design Automation and Test in Europe,* IEEE Computer Society Press, 2004, p. 20890.

[MIP05] MIPS Technologies, "SmartMIPS architecture smart card extensions," 2005, *http://www.mips.com.*

[Moo00] Vincent John Mooney III and Giovanni De Micheli, "Hardware/software co-design of run-time schedulers for real-time systems," *Design Automation for Embedded Systems*, 6, 2000, pp. 89–144.

[Mos01] Andreas Moshovos, Gokhan Memik, Babak Falsafi, and Alok Choudhary, "JETTY: filtering snoops for reduced power consumption in SMP servers," *Proceedings of the ACM/IEEE International Symposium on High-Performance Computer Architecture*, IEEE, 2001, pp. 85–96.

[Mud04] Trevor Mudge, Scott Mahlke, Todd Austin, David Blaauw, Chaitali Chakrabarti, and Wayne Wolf, "Mobile Supercomputers," *IEEE Computer*, May 2004.

[Mue95] Frank Mueller, "Compiler support for software-based cache partitioning," *Proceedings of the ACM SIGPLAN 1995 Workshop on Languages, Compilers, and Tools for Real-Time Systems*, ACM Press, 1995, pp. 125–133.

[Mur89] Tadao Murata, "Petri nets: properties, analysis and applications," *Proceedings of the IEEE*, 77(4), April 1989, pp. 541–580.

[Mur04] S. Murali and G. De Micheli, "Bandwidth-constrained mapping of cores onto NoC architectures," *Proceedings of the Design Automation and Test Conference in Europe*, IEEE, 2004, pp. 20986–20902.

[Mus98] Enric Musoll, Tomas Lang, and Jordi Cortadella, "Working-zone encoding for reducing the energy in microprocessor address busses," *IEEE Transactions on VLSI Systems*, 6(4), December 1998, pp. 568–572.

[Ni93] Lionel M. Ni and Philip K. McKinley, "A survey of wormhole rouitng techniques in direct networks," *IEEE Computer*, 26(2), February 1993, pp. 62–76.

[Obj06] Object Management Group, CORBA Basics, 2006, http://www.omg.org/gettingstarted/corbafaq.htm.

[Oss03] M.D. Osso, G. Biccari, L. Giovanni, D. Bertozzi, and L. Benini, "xpipes: a latency insensitive parameterized network-on-chip architecture for multi-processor SoCs," *Proceedings of the 21st International Conference on Computer Design*, IEEE Computer Society Press, 2003, pp. 536–539.

[Pam03] D. Pamunuwa, J. Oberg, L.R. Zheng, M. Millberg, A. Jantsch, and H. Tenhunen, "Layout, performance and power trade-offs in mesh-based network-on-chip architectures," *IFIP International Conference on Very Large Scale Integration (VLSI-SOC)*, Darmstadt, Germany, December 2003.

[Pan97] Preeti Ranjan Panda, Nikil D. Dutt, and Alexandru Nicolau, "Memory data organization for improved cache performance in embedded processor applications," *ACM Transactions on Design Automation of Electronic Systems*, 2(4), October 1997, pp. 384–409.

[Pan99a] Preeti Ranjan Panda, Nikil Dutt, and Alexandru Nicolau, *Memory Issues in Embedded Systems-on-Chip: Optimizations and Exploration*, Norwell MA: Kluwer Academic Publishers, 1999.

[Pan99b] Preeti Ranjan Panda, Nikil D. Dutt, and Alexandru Nicolau, "Local memory optimization and in embedded systems," *IEEE Transactions on CAD/ICAS*, 18(1), January 1999, pp. 3–13.

[Pan99c] Preeti Ranjan Panda, "Memory bank customization and assignment in behavioral synthesis," *Proceedings of the 1999 IEEE/ACM International Conference on Computer-Aided Design*, IEEE, pp. 477–481.

[Pan00] Preeti Ranjan Panda, Nikil D. Dutt, and Alexandru Nicolau, "On-chip vs. off-chip memory: the data partitioning problem in embedded processor-based systems," *ACM Transactions on Design Automation of Embedded Systems*, 5(3), July 2000, pp. 682–704.

[Pan01] P.R. Panda, F. Catthoor, N.D. Dutt, K. Danckaert, E. Brockmeyer, C. Kulkarni, A. Vandercappelle, and P.G. Kjeldsberg, "Data and memory optimization techniques for embedded systems," *ACM Transactions on Design Automation of Electronic Systems*, 6(2), April 2001, pp. 149–206.

[Pan05] Partha Pratim Pande, Cristian Grecu, Andre Ivanov, Resve Saleh, and Giovanni De Micheli, "Design, synthesis and test of networks on chips," *IEEE Design & Test of Computers*, 22(5), September/October 2005, pp. 404–413.

[Par91] Chang Yun Park and Alan C. Shaw, "Experiments with a program timing tool based on source-level timing scheme," *IEEE Computer*, 24(5), May 1991, pp. 48–57.

[Pau89] Pierre G. Paulin and John P. Knight, "Force-directed scheduling for the behavioral synthesis of ASIC's," *IEEE Trans. CAD/ICAS*, 8(6), June 1989, pp. 661–679.

[Pau02a] Pierre G. Paulin and Miguel Santana, "FlexWare: a retargetable embedded-software development environment," *IEEE Design & Test of Computers*, 19(4), July/August 2002, pp. 59–69.

[Pau02b] JoAnn Paul and Donald Thomas, "A layered, codesign virtual machine approach to modeling computer systems," in *Proceedings of the Conference on Design Automation and Test in Europe*, IEEE Computer Society Press, 2002, pp. 522–529.

[Pau04] Pierre G. Paulin, Chuck Pilkington, Michel Langevin, Essaid Bensoudane, and Gabriela Nicolescu, "Parallel programming models for a multiprocessor SoC platform applied to high-speed traffic management," in *Proceedings of CODES+ISSS 2004*, IEEE, 2004, pp. 48–53.

[Pau06] Pierre G. Paulin, Chuck Pilkington, Michel Langevin, Essaid Bensoudane, Damien Lyonnard, Olivier Benny, Bruno Lavigeur, David Lo, Giovanni Beltrame, Vincent Gagne, and Gabriela Nicolescu, "Parallel programming models for a multi-processor SoC platform applied to networking and multimedia," *IEEE Transactions on VLSI Systems,* to appear in 2006.

[Pet90] Karl Pettis and Robert C. Hansen, "Profile guided code positioning," *Proceedings of the ACM SIGPLAN 1990 Conference on Programming Language Design and Implementation*, ACM Press, 1990, pp. 16–27.

[Pet03] Larry Peterson and Bruce Davie, *Computer Networks: A Systems Approach*, Morgan Kaufmann, 2003.

[Pil01] Padmanabhan Pillai and Kang G. Shin, "Real-time dynamic voltage scaling for low-power embedded operating systems," *Proceedings of the 18th ACM Symposium on Operating Systems Principles*, ACM Press, 2001, pp. 89–102.

[Poz05] Laura Pozzi and Paolo Ienne, "Exploiting pipelining to relax register-file port constraints of instruction-set extensions," *Proceedings, CASES '05*, ACM Press, 2005.

[Pto05] UC Berkeley, Ptolemy web site, *http://www.eecs.berkeley.edu*.

[Pus89] Peter Puschner and Christian Koza, "Calculating the maximum execution time of real-time programs," *Journal of Real-Time Systems*, 1(2), 1989, pp. 159–176.

[Pus93] Peter Puschner and Anton Schell, "A tool for the computation of worst case task execution times," *Proceedings, 5th Euromicro Workshop on Real-Time Systems*, 1993, pp. 224–229.

[Pus99] Peter Puschner and Alan Burns, "A review of worst-case execution time analysis," *Journal of Real-Time Systems*, 18(2/3), 1989, pp. 115–128.

[RTC92] RTCA, Inc., Software Considerations in Airborne Systems and Equipment Certification, DO-178B, RCTA, December 1, 1992.

[Ram90a] Krithi Ramaritham, John A. Stankovic, and Perng-Fei Shiah, "Efficient scheduling algorithms for real-time multiprocessor systems," *IEEE Transactions on Parallel and Distributed Systems*, 1(2), April 1990, pp. 184–194.

[Ram90b] Krithi Ramamritham, "Allocation and scheduling of complex periodic tasks," in *Proceedings, 10th International Conference on Distributed Computing Systems*, IEEE, 1990, pp. 108–115.

[Rav04] Srivaths Ravi, Anand Ragunathan, Paul Kocher, and Sunil Hattangady, "Security in embedded systems: design challenges," *ACM Transactions on Embedded Computing Systems*, 3(3), August 2004, pp. 461–491.

[Ree02] Jeffrey H. Reed, *Software Radio: A Modern Approach to Radio Engineering*, Prentice Hall PTR, 2002.

[Reg05] John Reghr, "Random testing of interrupt-driven software," in *Proceedings of the 5th ACM International Conference on Embedded Software*, ACM Press, 2005, pp. 290–298.

[Rho99] David Rhodes and Wayne Wolf, "Overhead effects in embedded real-time systems," Proceedings, *7th International Workshop on Hardware/Software Codesign*, IEEE Computer Society Press, 1999.

[Ros92] Mendel Rosenblum and John K. Osterhout, "The design and implementation of a log-structured file system," *ACM Transactions on Computer Systems*, 10(1), February 1992, pp. 26–52.

[Rot05] Eric Rotenberg and Aravindh Anantararaman, "Architecture of Embedded Processors," Chapter 4 in *Multiprocessor Systems-on-Chips*, Ahmed Amine Jerraya and Wayne Wolf, eds., Morgan Kaufmann, 2005.

[Row05] Chris Rowen, private communication, August 23, 2005.

[Sas01] Toshiyuki Sasaki, Shinsuke Kobayashi, Tomohide Maeda, Makkiko Itoh, Yoshinori Takeushi, and Masahiru Imai, "Rapid prototyping of complex instructions for embedded processors using PEAS-III," *Proceedings, SASIMI 2001*, pp. 61–66.

[Sch00] Douglas C. Schmidt and Fred Kuhns, "An overview of the real-time CORBA specification," *IEEE Computer*, 33(6), June 2000, pp. 56–63.

[SDR05] SDR Forum, "SDR Forum Bylaws," *http://www.sdrforum.org/tech_comm/definitions.html*.

[Sgr01] M. Sgroi, M. Sheets, A. Mihal, A., K. Keutzer, S. Malik, J. Rabaey, A. Sangiovanni-Vincentelli, "Addressing the system-on-a-chip interconnect woes through communication-based design," *Proceedings of the Design Automation Conference*, ACM Press, 2001, pp. 667–672.

[Sha89] Alan C. Shaw, "Reasoning about time in higher-level language software," *IEEE Transactions on Software Engineering*, 15(7), July 1989, pp. 875–889.

[Sha90] Lui Sha, Ragunathan Rajkumar, and John P. Lehoczky, "Priority inheritance protocols: an approach to real-time synchronization," *IEEE Transactions on Computers*, 39(9), September 1990, pp. 1175–1185.

[Sha02] Li Shang and Niraj K. Jha, "Hardware-software co-synthesis of low power real-time distributed embedded systems with dynamically reconfigurable FPGAs," *Proceedings of the IEEE International Conference on VLSI Design*, IEEE, 2002, pp. 345–352.

[Sha03] Nik Shaylor, Douglas N. Simon, and William R. Bush, "A Java virtual machine for very small devices," *Proceedings of the 2003 ACM SIGPLAN Conference on Languages, Compilers,and Tools for Embedded Systems*, ACM Press, 2003, pp. 34–41.

[Shi89a] Kang G. Shin and Yi-Chieh Chang, "Load-sharing in distributed real-time systems with state-change broadcasts," *IEEE Transactions on Computers*, 38(8), August 1989, pp. 1124–1141.

[Shi89b] Wen-Tsong Shiue, Sathishkumar Udayanarayanan, and Chaitali Chakrabarti, "Data memory design and exploration for low power embedded systems," in *ACM Transactions on Design Automation of Electronic Systems*, 6(4),October 2001, pp. 553-569.

[Shi05] Sang Shin, "Jini™ Network Technology Architecture," slide presentation, *http://www.javapassion.com/jini/architecture.pdf.*

[Sie98] Daniel P. Siewiorek and Robert S. Swarz, *Reliable Computer Systems: Design and Evaluation*, A K Peters, 1998.

[Sie04] Daniel P. Siewiorek, Ram Chillarege, and Zbigniew T. Kalbarczyk, "Reflections on industry trends and experimental research in dependability," *IEEE Transactions on Dependable and Secure Computing*, 1(2), April–June 2004, pp. 109–127.

[Slo04] Andrew N. Sloss, Dominic Symes, and Chris Wright, *ARM System Developer's Guide*, Morgan Kaufmann, 2004.

[Son02] Sonics, SiliconBackplane II Micronetwork IP, 2002, *http://www.sonics-inc.com.*

[Sta95] Mircea R. Stan and Wayne P. Burleson, "Bus-invert coding for low-power I/O," *IEEE Transactions on VLSI Systems*, 3(1), March 1995, pp. 49–58.

[Sta97a] William Stallings, *Data and Computer Communication*, fifth ed., Prentice Hall, 1997.

[Sta97b] Joergen Staunstrup and Wayne Wolf, eds., *Hardware/Software Co-Design: Principles and Practice*, Kluwer Academic Publishers, 1998.

[Sta04] William Stallings, *Data and Computer Communications*, seventh ed., Prentice Hall, 2004.

[Ste90] Per Stenstrom, "A survey of cache coherence schemes for multiprocessors," *IEEE Computer*, 23(6), June 1990, pp. 12–24.

[STM04] STMicroelectronics, "Nomadik—open multimedia platform for next generation mobile devices," technical article TA305.

[Sto77] Harold S. Stone, "Multiprocessor scheduling with the aid of network flow algorithms," *IEEE Transactions on Software Engineering*, SE-3(1), January 1977, pp. 85–93.

[Sto96] Neil Storey, *Safety-Critical Computer Systems*, Addison-Wesley Longman England, 1996.

[Sun04] Fei Sun, Srivath Ravi, Anand Rangunathan, and Niraj K. Jha, "Custom-instruction synthesis for extensible processor platforms," *IEEE Transactions on CAD/ICAS*, 23(2), February 2004, pp. 216–228.

[Sun05] Sun Developer Network, "Connected Limited Device Configuration (CLDC)," *http://java.sun.com/products/cldc*.

[Tal03] Deepu Tallua, Lizy Kurian John, and Doug Burger, "Bottlenecks in multimedia processing with SIMD style extensions and multimedia enhancements," *IEEE Transactions on Computers*, 52(8), August 2003, pp. 1015–1031.

[Tar97] Igor Tartalija and Veljko Milutinovic, "Classifying software-based cache coherence solutions," *IEEE Software*, 14(3), May-June 1997, pp. 90–101.

[Tay04] Michael Bedford Taylor, Walter Lee, Jason Miller, David Wentzlaff, Ian Bratt, Ben Greenwald, Henry Hoffmann, Paul Johnson, Jason Kim, James Psota, Arvind Saraf, Nathan Shnidman, Volker Strumpen, Matt Frank, Saman Amarasinghe, and Anant Agarwal, "Evaluation of the Raw Microprocessor: An Exposed-Wire-Delay Architecture for ILP and Streams," *Proceedings, International Conference on Computer Architecture*, IEEE, 2004.

[Ten04] Tensilica, "Xpres Product Brief," 2004, *http://www.tensilica.com*.

[Tex01a] Texas Instruments, *TMS320C54x DSP Reference Set, Volume 1: CPU and Peripherals*, literature number SPRU131G, March 2001.

[Tex01b] Texas Instruments, *TMS320C55x DSP Reference Guide*, literature number SPRU371D, March 2001.

[Tex05] Texas Instruments, *TMS320C6000 DSP Multichannel Buffered Serial Port (McBSP) Reference Guide*, literature number SPRU580E, December 2005.

[The99] Henrik Theiling, Christian Ferdinand, and Reinhard Wilhelm, "Fast and precise WCET prediction by separated cache and path analyses," *Real-Time Systems*, 5(1), 1999, pp. 1–22.

[Thi99] Scott A. Thibault, Renaud Marlet, and Charles Consel, "Domain-specific languages: from design to implementation applicatio nto video device drivers generation," *IEEE Transactions on Software Engineering*, 25(3), May-June 1999, pp. 363–377.

[Tiw94] Vivek Tiwari, Sharad Malik, and Andrew Wolfe, "Power analysis of embedded software: A first step toward software power minimization," *IEEE Transactions on VLSI Systems*, 2(4), December 1994, pp. 437–445.

[Tok90] Hideyuki Tokuda, Tatsuo Nakajima, and Prithvi Rao, "Real-time Mach: towards a predictable real-time system," *Proceedings of the USENIX Mach Workshop*, October 1990, pp. 73–82.

[Tom97] Hiroyuki Tomiyama and HIroto Yasuura, "Code placement techniques for cache miss rate reduction," *ACM Transactions on Design Automation of Embedded Systems*, 2(4), October 1997, pp. 410–429.

[Tos05] Toshiba, "Introduction to the MeP (Media embedded Processor)," *http://www.mepcore.com*.

[Tre01] R.B. Tremaine, P.A.Franaszek, J.T. Robinson, C.O. Schulz, T.B. Smith, M.E. Wazlowski, and P.M. Bland, "IBM Memory Expansion Technology (MXT)," *IBM Journal of Research and Development*, 45(2), March 2001, pp. 271–285.

[Tse86] C. J. Tseng and Daniel P. Siewiorek, "Automated synthesis of datapaths in digital systems," *IEEE Trans. CAD/ICAS*, CAD-5(3), July 1986, pp. 379–395.

[Tun67] B. Tunstall, *Synthesis of Noiseless Compression Codes*, Ph.D. diss., Georgia Institute of Technology, Atlanta GA, September 1967.

[Ugo83] Michel Ugon, "Single-chip microprocessor with on-board modifiable memory," U.S. Patent 4,382,279, May 3, 1983.

[Vah94] Frank Vahid. Jie Gong, Daniel D. Gajski, "A binary-constraint search algorithm for minimizing hardware during hardware/software partitioning," in *Proceedings of the Conference on European Design Automation*, IEEE Computer Society Press, 1994, pp. 214–219.

[Vah95] F. Vahid and D. D. Gajski, "Incremental hardware estimation during hardware/software functional partitioning," *IEEE Transactions on VLSI Systems*, 3(3), September 1995, pp. 459–64.

[Van04] Vieri Vanghi, Aleksandar Damnjanovic, and Branimir Vojcic, *The cdma2000 System for Mobile Communications*, Prentice Hall PTR, 2004.

[Ver96] S. Vercauteren, B. Lin, and H. De Man, "A strategy for real-time kernel support in application-specific HW/SW embedded architectures," in *Proceedings, 33rd Design Automation Conference*, ACM Press, 1996, pp. 678–683.

[Ver97] D. Verkest, K. Van Rompaey, I. Bolsens, and H. De Man, "CoWare—a design environment for heterogeneous hardware/software systems," *Deisgn Automation for Embedded Systems*, 1(4), October 1996, pp. 357–86.

[Viv01] Emilio Vivancos, Christopher Healy, Frank Mueller, and David Whalley, "Parametric timing analysis," *Proceedings of the ACM SIGPLAN Workshop on Languages, Compilers, and Tools for Embedded Systems*, ACM Press, 2001, pp. 88–93.

[Vos89] L. D. Vos and M. Stegherr, "Parameterizable VLSI architectures for the full-search block-matching algorithm," *IEEE Transactions on Circuits and Systems*, 36(10), October 1989, pp. 1309–1316.

[Was03] Andrzei Wasowski, "On efficient program synthesis from Statecharts," *Proceedings of the 2003 ACM SIGPLAN Conference on Languages, Compilers, and Tools for Embedded Systems*, ACM Press, 2003, pp. 163–170.

[Weh01] L. Wehmeyr, M.K. Jain, S. Steinke, P. Marwedel, and M. Balakrishnan, "Analysis of the influence of register file size on energy consumption, code size, and execution time," *IEEE Transactions on CAD/ICAS*, 20(11), November 2001, pp. 1329–1337.

[Wei94] M. Weiser, B. Welch, A. Demers, and S. Shenker, "Scheduling for reduced CPU energy," *Proceedings, First USENIX Symposium on Operating Systems Design and Implementation (OSDI '94)*, USENIX, 1994, pp. 13–23.

[Wel84] T.A. Welch, "A method for high-performance data compression," *IEEE Computer*, June 1984, pp. 8–19.

[Whi87] I. H. Whitten, R. M. Neal, and J. G. Cleary, "Arithmetic coding for data compression," *Communications of the ACM*, 30(6), June 1987, pp. 520–540.

[Wil04] Reinhard Wilhelm, "Why AI + ILP is good for WCET, but MC is not, nor ILP alone," *Proceedings, VMCAI 2004*, Laboratory Notes in Computer Science vol. 2937, Springer Verlag, 2004, pp. 309–322.

[Wol91a] Michael Wolf and Monica Lam, "A data locality optimizing algorithm," in *Proceedings, SIGPLAN '91 Conference on Programming Language Design and Implementation*, ACM, 1991, pp. 30–44.

[Wol91b] Michael E. Wolf and Monica Lam, "A loop transformation theory and an algorithm to maximize parallelism," *IEEE Transactions on Parallel and Distributed Systems*, 2(4), October 1991, pp. 452–471.

[Wol92] Andrew Wolfe and Alex Chanin, "Executing compressed programs on an embedded RISC architecture," in *Proceedings, 25th Annual International Symposium on Microarchitecture*, IEEE, 1992, pp. 81–91.

[Wol96a] Michael Wolfe, *High Performance Compilers for Parallel Computing*, Addison Wesley, 1996.

[Wol97b] Wayne Wolf, "An architectural co-synthesis algorithm for distributed embedded computing systems," *IEEE Transactions on VLSI Systems*, 5(2), June 1997, pp. 218–29.

[Wol99] Victor Fay Wolfe, Lisa Cingiser Dipippo, Roman Ginis, Michael Squadrito, Steven Wohlever, Igor Zykh, and Russell Johnston, "Expressing and enforcing timing constraints in a dynamic real-time CORBA environment," *Journal of Real-Time Systems*, 16, 1999, pp. 253–280.

[Wol02] Wayne Wolf, *Modern VLSI Design*, Upper Saddle River, New Jersey: Prentice Hall, 1998.

[Wol03] Wayne Wolf and Mahmut Kandemir, "Memory system optimization of embedded software," *Proceedings of the IEEE*, 91(1), January 2003, pp. 165–182.

[Wol04] Wayne Wolf, "Multimedia applications of systems-on-chips," *Proceedings, DATE '05 Designers' Forum*, ACM Press, 2005, pp. 86–89.

[Woo02] Anthony D. Wood and John A. Stankovic, "Denial of service in sensor networks," *IEEE Computer*, 35(10), October 2002, pp. 54–62.

[Wu06] Yiyan Wu, Shuji Hirakawa, Ulrich H. Reimers, and Jerry Whittaker, "Overview of digital television development worldwide," *Proceedings of the IEEE*, 94(1), January 2006, pp. 8–21.

[Wuy99] S. Wuytack, J. da Silva, F. Catthoor, G. de Jong, and F. Ykman-Couveur, "Memory management for embedded network applications," *IEEE Transactions on CAD*, 18(5), May 1999, pp. 533–544.

[Xie00] Yuan Xie and Wayne Wolf, "Hardware/software co-synthesis with custom ASICs," in *Proceedings, ASPDAC '00*, IEEE, 2000, pp. 129–133.

[Xie01] Yuan Xie and Wayne Wolf, "Allocation and scheduling of conditional task graph in hardware/software co-synthesis," in *Proceedings of the Conference on Design Automation and Test in Europe*, IEEE Press, 2001, pp. 620–625.

[Xie02] Yuan Xie, W. Wolf, and H. Lekatsas, "Code compression for VLIW processors using variable-to-fixed coding," *15th International Symposium on System Synthesis*, IEEE, 2002, pp. 138–143.

[Xil05] Xilinx, "Virtex-4 Family Overview," DS112 (v1.4), June 17, 2005. *http://www.xiilnx.com*.

[Xu06] Jiang Xu, Wayne Wolf, Joerg Henkel, and Srimat Chakradhar, "A design methodology for application-specific networks-on-chips," *ACM Transactions on Embedded Computing Systems*, to appear in the Special Issue on Multiprocessor Systems-on-Chips.

[Yan89] Kun-Min Yang, Ming-Ting Sun, and Lancelot Wu, "A family of VLSI designs for the motion compensation block-matching algorithm," *IEEE Transactions on Circuits and Systems*, 36(10), October 1989, pp. 1317–1325.

[Yan01] Peng Yang, Chun Wong, Paul Marchal, Francky Catthoor, Dirk Desmet, Diederik Verkest, and Rudy Lauwereins, "Energy-aware runtime scheduling for embedded multiprocessor SoCs," *IEEE Design & Test of Computers*, 18(5), September/October 2001, pp. 46–85.

[Yan05] Shengqi Yang, Wayne Wolf, Narayan Vijaykrishnan, Dimitrios Serpanos, and Yuan Xie, "Power attack resistant cryptosystem design: a dynamic voltage and frequency scalilng approach," in *Proceedings, DATE '05 Designers' Forum*, ACM Press, 2005, pp. 70–75.

[Yao95] Frances Yao, Alan Demers, and Scott Shenker, "A scheduling model for reduced CPU energy," *Proceedings, 36th Annual Symposium on Foundations of Computer Science*, IEEE Press, 1995, pp. 374–382.

[Ye00] W. Ye, N. Vijaykrishna, M. Kandemir, and M.J. Irwin, "The Design and Use of SimplePower: A Cycle-Accurate Energy Estimation Tool," *Proceedings of the Design Automation Conference*, ACM Press, 2000.

[Ye03] Terry Tao Ye, Luca Benini, and Giovanni De Micheli, "Packetized on-chip itnerconnect communication analysis for MPSoCs," *Proceedings of the Conference on Design Automation and Test in Europe*, vol. 1, IEEE Computer Society Press, 2003, p. 10344.

[Yen98] Ti-Yen Yen and Wayne Wolf, "Performance analysis of distributed embedded systems," *IEEE Transactions on Parallel and Distributed Systems*, 9(11), November 1998, pp. 1125–1136.

[Yos97] Yokihiro Yoshida, Bao-Yu Song, Hiroyuki Okuhata, Takao Onoye, and Isao Shirikawa, "An object code compression approach to embedded processors," in Proceedings of the 1997 International Symposium on Low Power Electronics and Design, IEEE, 1997, pp. 265–268.

[Zam05] Joseph Zambreno, Alok Choudhary, Rahul Simha, Bhagi Narahari, and Nasir Memon, "SAFE-OPS: an approach to embedded software security," *ACM Transactions on Embedded Software*, 4(1), February 2005, pp. 189–210.

[Zhu99] Xiaohan Zhu and Bill Lin, "Compositional software synthesis of communicating processes," *Proceedings of the International Conference on Computer Design*, IEEE Computer Society Press, 1999, pp. 646–651.

[Ziv77] J. Ziv and A. Lempel, "A universal algorithm for sequential data compression," *IEEE Transactions on Information Theory*, vol. IT-23(3), May 1977, pp. 337–343.

[Ziv96] V. Zivojnovic and H. Meyr, "Compiled HW/SW co-simulation," in *Proceedings, 33rd Design Automation Conference,* ACM, 1996, pp. 690–695.

# Index